Sociology of Sport

Sociology of Sport

John C. Phillips
University of the Pacific

Allyn and Bacon
Boston • London • Toronto • Sydney • Tokyo • Singapore

Series Editor: Karen Hanson
Senior Editorial Assistant: Marnie Greenhut
Production Editor: Deborah Brown
Editorial-Production Manager: Elaine Ober
Editorial-Production Service: P. M. Gordon Associates
Cover Administrator: Suzanne Harbison
Manufacturing Buyer: Megan Cochran
Composition Buyer: Linda Cox

A Division of Simon & Schuster, Inc.
160 Gould Street
Needham Heights, Massachusetts 02194

Library of Congress Cataloging-in-Publication Data

Phillips, John C., 1941–
Sociology of sport / John C. Phillips.
p. cm.
Includes bibliographical references and index.
ISBN 0–205–13983–3
1. Sports—Social aspects. I. Title.
GV706.5.P45 1993
306.483—dc20

92–22181
CIP

Printed in the United States of America

10 9 8 7 6 5 4 3 2 1 97 96 95 94 93 92

Contents

Preface

As of the 1992 season not one of the head coaches of the 106 National Collegiate Athletic Association Division IA football teams was black even though about 40 percent of the players are black. Why not? What does it take to be hired as an assistant coach and then rise through the ranks to be considered a candidate for a head coaching position? What happens to prevent African-American coaches from rising to top-level positions? Why are coaching opportunities at the professional level (two of the 26 National Football League head coaches are African-American) more open to African-American aspirants than at the best universities in the United States? The answer to these questions can teach us a great deal about sports, the coaching profession, and our universities. They can teach us much about American society as well. These and many other questions about sports are important. *Sociology of Sport* seeks to organize the existing knowledge about the myriad of questions that are suggested by the sociological study of sport.

One of the first questions asked by sport sociologists back in the middle 1960s, when the field was just becoming a "subject" in sociology, was why sociology paid so little attention to this obviously important subject. Without a sports page most newspapers would probably be bankrupted. Television rights to major-league baseball and football cost networks hundreds of millions of dollars each year. Well over a billion people watch the World Cup soccer final every four years. Countless people throughout the world invest time, money, and energy in playing and watching sports. Nonetheless, sport has been very much a "minor league" subject of study in the sociological hierarchy.

We sociologists are wrong to ignore sport as a topic of serious study. The sheer number of people involved suggest that sport deserves our attention, and there are at least two additional good reasons to study sports. First, sport sociologists have long believed that sport reflects the social conditions within which it exists. By studying a part of a social system, we might learn about the whole system. Studies of topics as diverse as magic in sports, racial and sexual discrimination in sports, and the nature of sport (or what passes for sport) in various cultures suggest that sport is indeed a "mirror of society."

Second, many people believe that a knowledge of how sports affect people might lead to reforms that could help enrich the lives of athletes, or at least reduce some of the harmful effects of sports. For example, there is a lot of evidence in the United States that the academic performance of high school students is improved by sports participation. There is no evidence to suggest that sports somehow harm academic performance. Perhaps the popular C-average rules that have limited participation in several states to students with a C average or better should be scrapped so that weak students can enjoy the benefits of sports. The importance of examining the effect of sports on people is also exemplified by steroid use. Harmful steroid use in sports does not just happen. There is evidence that economic incentives in many sports encourage steroid use. On the other hand, drug-free weight lifting and body building organizations have shown that steroid use can be controlled when sports leadership has the will to control it.

Among the many "subfields" of sociology, the sociology of sport stands alone in many ways. The field has a rather diverse following. Authors of articles in the most recent issues of the *International Review for the Sociology of Sport* and *Sport Sociology Journal* hail from Canada, the United States, Britain, Nigeria, Austria, and Poland. Not surprisingly, most of these authors are sociology and sports studies professors, but professors of psychology, anthropology, medicine, education, and women's studies are also represented as well as three sports administrators.

A second special aspect of sport sociology is the familiarity of the subject matter. Students know a lot about sports. Chances are you will be able to contribute an informed opinion about most of the issues covered in this book. Many sociology subjects are far less familiar and far less accessible to students than is the subject of sport. Most college students not only experience sport—playing, reading, observing—every day but also posses a store of experience from high school and youth sports. Students have participated in some very valuable research in sport sociology. Students currently playing football are best qualified to observe which positions call for leadership responsibility. Students have participated in the systematic observation of children at play, contributing to our understanding of differences between free play and play organized by adults.

As with any textbook, *Sociology of Sport* represents its subject not as it "is," but as it is seen through the eyes of the author. My biases and preferences are reflected in the book even though I have tried to provide a balanced, comprehensive review of the field. Let me express some of those biases. First, I give much more credence to work that involves systematic research than to work that is more speculative or philosophical, even if it is well-reasoned speculation or philosophy. Second, I believe that contemporary ideas and contemporary social conditions are best understood in terms of their historical roots. I pay a lot of attention to the history of sport in this book because the past allows us to understand the present. Third, I am far more convinced of the potential benefits of sports participation than I am of the potential harm sports can do. I favor expansion of opportunities for participation among all kinds of people. Whether you agree or disagree with these views, or other views of the author, I hope this book helps you develop a deeper and wider appreciation for the subject of sport.

The Plan of This Book

It should be clear by now that the world of sport provides some fascinating and important topics for investigation. The following chapters in this book attempt to outline the main issues and findings in the sociology of sport. Chapter 1 introduces several of the interesting topics currently being studied by sport sociologists. Chapter

2 introduces the meaning of sociology, especially the scientific discipline that separates sociology from sermonizing or editorializing. The meaning of the term "sport" is also examined in Chapter 2.

Chapters 3 and 4 examine sport from a societal point of view. Chapter 3 employs the concept of culture as it relates to sport. Can sport affect culture by bringing in new ideas about health or authority? Can sport be affected by existing cultures through such factors as witchcraft or the warrior ethic? Finally the interesting, albeit unanswerable, question, "Why do some countries do so well in international competition?" Chapter 4 traces how sport has changed (not necessarily for the better) in Western societies with special attention to the game of football (including soccer, rugby, and football). The idea that social institutions like football have changed from local, informal, and simple games to national or international, highly regularized, and complex events, is a dominating theme in sociology.

How sports participation affects individuals is an important issue for friends as well as critics of sport. Chapters 5 and 6 look at ways sport affects participants. Chapter 5 examines the evidence regarding the effects of youth sports and more advanced levels of sports on the personality or "character" of participants. Chapter 6 zeros in on school sports and their effects on student careers.

Chapters 7 and 8 take up the topic of race and sport. Here is an arena where clear racial differences prevail, and nobody seems to know why. Can black-white physical differences explain why African-Americans do poorly in tennis? Why does Nigeria produce so few world-class sprinters? Why do African-Americans do well in basketball? If physical theories are inadequate then what else can explain the black domination of so many sports? Evidence of racial discrimination in sport is presented in Chapter 8 along with theories of why and how this discrimination happens. Interestingly, a decline in discrimination is now evident, although it remains in some areas. On the subject of discrimination, women have been denied sporting opportunities too, although the process of discrimination is rather different than that faced by African-Americans. The case of women in sport is explored in Chapter 9.

Chapter 10 is about the business of sport. One could argue that the sports business is no more sports than the art business is art, but the business of sports clearly affects sports, so the subject rates some attention.

Sport affects our lives in ways that transcend sprained ankles and blisters. Just as sport can be exploited for harmful purposes, so can it serve as a force for good. For this reason alone sport deserves our serious attention.

Acknowledgments

The preparation of a textbook is a prodigious task. I would not have been able to complete this book without the able support of many people. I want to express my appreciation to some of them.

Walt Schafer taught me about the sociology of sport. I still benefit from his teaching. Several friends and colleagues took time to share their experiences and expertise to help me write this book. Wendy Jerome, Jane Swagerty, John Boelter, Peg Ciccolella, Chris Muok, Dennis Cusick, and Ray Purpur are all deserving of thanks along with the many students, coaches, and teammates I have known over the years.

Special thanks are due to Karen Hope and Sara Elliott who typed portions of the manuscript and Vi Le who helped prepare photographs. Joan Sykes and Pamela Altree performed a variety of tasks to prepare important portions of the manuscript. Angela White and Julie Turner reviewed the manuscript and offered a number of useful ideas.

My wife Kay was a reservoir of support and morale during the two years I have worked on this project.

Thanks to all!

Chapter 1

Introduction

On April 15, 1947, Jackie Robinson of the Brooklyn Dodgers became the first black player to appear in a modern Major League baseball game. Critics of this integration had predicted dire consequences ranging from riots in the stands to a change in the game caused by black speed. There were no riots. The game remained unchanged. Aside from problems forced by segregation policies in hotels and restaurants, especially in the South, the entry of black and Latin American players into professional baseball was remarkably trouble-free (see Broom & Selznick, 1963, pp. 528–532; Tygiel, 1983).

Robinson's hiring was a conspicuous violation of the color line that prevailed throughout most of the United States at that time. Virtually all industries were segregated. The *Brown* v. *the Board of Education* Supreme Court decision of 1954, which struck down the "separate but equal" doctrine, was still years away. President Harry Truman's order to integrate the armed forces of the United States was still more than a year away. Here was a very public event proving that blacks and whites could work together successfully—Brooklyn won the National League championship in 1947. Grapefruit League (spring exhibition) games in subsequent years between Brooklyn and other teams in Southern towns required at least the suspension of Jim Crow laws forbidding integrated competition between black and white players. The financial opportunity of a major league exhibition game, coupled with a gradual erosion of Southern segregation in the pre–civil-rights era South, led authorities in many cities to seek games involving integrated teams and to work to avoid ugly incidents that might be provoked by such groups as the Ku Klux Klan (Tygiel, 1983, pp. 265–269).

The success of the integrated Dodgers, and shortly thereafter the Cleveland Indians, could not be ignored by people who feared the consequences of an integrated workplace or by those who favored integration. The sports pages in newspapers throughout the United States blared day in and day out that *it could be done.* Robinson and other black players experienced many ugly incidents and major league baseball is still not free of discrimination, but baseball had, albeit reluctantly, demonstrated to the nation that integration in the workplace was feasible.

Historian Jules Tygiel concludes his book on the integration of baseball with a contention that many share. The Brooklyn Dodger organization created an impact that extended well beyond organized baseball:

> [Dodger president Branch] Rickey and Robinson, however, did not simply end baseball segregation. Their tours through the South, later emulated by other teams, challenged deeply entrenched Jim Crow traditions. Racial exclusion in most southern baseball leagues terminated before the onset of the major civil rights agitation. Furthermore, as Rickey noted, "Integration in baseball started public integration on trains, in Pullmans, in dining cars, in restaurants in the South, long before the issue of public accommodations became daily news." In 1952 a Boston University professor introduced Rickey as a man who "can take ball clubs with Negro players to a hotel where a Negro bishop can't stay." Within two decades, most barriers had fallen for ballplayer, bishop, or bellhop. Federal legislation, court actions, and moral pressures precipitated most of these advances. But throughout the nation, black athletes represented both the harbingers and the agents of change. "We were paying our dues long before the civil rights marches," states Don Newcombe proudly. "Martin Luther King told me, in my home one night, 'You'll never know what you and Jackie and Roy did to make it possible to do my job.'" (Tygiel, 1983, p. 343)

The integration of baseball was an important episode in American history. Not black history. Not baseball history. American history.

An event in the career of heavyweight boxer champion Joe Louis also rates as historically important. In 1936 Louis had been knocked out by German Max Schmeling. After going on to win the heavyweight championship, Louis agreed to a 1938 rematch. Before the 1936 fight the white press had been sympathetic to Schmeling on the basis of race (an attitude Schmeling did not share). But the increasing aggressiveness of the Nazi government (Austria had been occupied in March) and Hitler's plans to take over the Sudetenland region of Czechoslovakia (an effort that was soon to be recognized by the infamous Munich agreement)—produced a strong anti-German sentiment among Americans. This anti-German sentiment cast the black Louis as the representative of all Americans, white and black, in a contest against what was being recognized ever more clearly as an evil ideology.

> There was no question that the American public attached a strong symbolic importance to the second Louis-Schmeling fight and accepted Louis—a black man—as a representative of American strength and virtue. This was revolutionary—so much so that some writers felt obliged to downplay the significance of Louis's role. (Mead, 1985, p. 142)

FIGURE 1–1 The second fight between Joe Louis and Max Schmeling in 1938 marked the first time a black was seen by white Americans as a "national representative." Schmeling was seen as a representative of Nazi Germany while Louis was seen as a representative of American democracy. Louis won in a first-round knockout.

(AP Wide World Photos)

Reaction to his crushing one round knockout of Schmeling made Louis an "All American" hero who had struck down a despised Nazi ideology.

> In the eyes of most Americans, Joe Louis had exploded the [Nazi] myth of white supremacy. In the process he had won a measure of acceptance as America's national representative, something no black had ever enjoyed before. Louis was a revolutionary by coincidence. (Mead, 1985, p. 159)

While lacking the sustained, palpable impact of the integration of baseball, the Louis-Schmeling fight, or rather the press reaction to it, constitutes another important event in American history. A substantial proportion of the white public identified with a black boxer, viewing him as a symbol of American virtue doing battle against

Nazism. No black had ever approached the stature of Louis as a national hero to white and black alike.

We may disagree about the importance of Jackie Robinson or Joe Louis, but few would argue that their lives are so insignificant that their names should fade from memory. However, a reader of contemporary "Introduction to Sociology" or even "Race and Ethnic Relations" textbooks in sociology would find little or nothing about the contributions of Robinson and Louis. Their widely recognized contributions to history have nearly been lost to sociologists. Indeed, only a handful of sociology texts make reference to *any* aspect of sport (Charnofsky, 1988).

Even sociological work that uses sport as a "case study" for the development of a more general theory about the wider society seems to cause amnesia among subsequent writers in sociology. Hubert Blalock's respected book, *Toward a Theory of Minority Relations* (1967), in which racial discrimination in sport is carefully analyzed (pp. 92–100), seems to have been forgotten by authors of race/ethnic relations books, save one book by the same author (Blalock, 1982).

Some two decades ago Eric Dunning analyzed the 892 sociology of sport items that had been listed in a recent issue of *Current Sociology* (Lueschen, 1968). Nearly all items of this apparently impressive number were written by physical education specialists or by sociologists for journals devoted to sport sociology. Subtracting these left only a handful of articles in general sociology journals. "At a fairly generous estimate, this leaves only something like twenty to thirty articles . . . written by specialist sociologists and published in sociology journals" (Dunning, 1971, p. 35).

More recently Hal Charnofsky complained:

> Introductory sociology text books, with only a small number of notable exceptions, virtually ignore sports in American society. Considering the millions of dollars spent on sports yearly, the popularity on TV of events such as the Super Bowl, the World Series, and the NBA Championship Series, along with hundreds of other professional and college sports events, and considering the sheets of print devoted to the world of sports, not to mention conversation *ad nauseum* that goes on in offices, schools, bars, on playgrounds, and no doubt in households both in the breakfast room over the morning coffee and newspaper and in the bedroom during who knows what, isn't it a little surprising that the majority of introductory text books on the sociology of American life and behavior either do not or only nominally mention the word sport? (Charnofsky, 1988, p. 4)

Why Is Sport Ignored?

In short, general sociology has not and does not treat sport as a suitable topic for systematic sociological inquiry. In a sort of "sociology of sociology," sport sociologists have guessed at the reasons behind the sociological neglect of sport. There is little question that sports are important. Nearly 217 million Americans report some participation in sports! Swimming is the most popular, with 32.8 million, then fishing, with 24.3 million. Most of the swimming and some of the fishing may fit better under the term recreation than under sports, but activities so widely practiced ought not to be ignored. Neither should sociologists ignore the 10.7 million who play basketball at some level, the 6.2 million who play baseball/softball, the 17.5 million bowlers, or the 10.6 million runner/joggers! Substantial numbers watch sports as well. Roughly 54 million fans attended major league baseball games in 1988. How many more watched minor league, high school, collegiate baseball and softball games? The Toronto Blue Jays are said to have been sold out for all 81 games of the 1990 season! More than 52 million spectators attended college and professional football games in 1988 and almost 50 million witnessed NBA or collegiate (men's and women's) basketball, again not counting high school and other leagues. The National Hockey League attendance exceeded 13.7 million, with millions more attending collegiate and junior league games.[1]

No less than 13 Super Bowl contests rank among the 30 all-time most watched television programs (Hoffman, 1990, p. 318). Several sports magazines, especially those devoted to hunting and fishing and golf, rank among the best selling magazines in the United States. *Sports Illustrated* outsells such magazines as *Playboy, People,* and *Newsweek* (Hoffman, 1990, p. 312).

Harry Edwards describes an "experiment" he performed in New York City in September, 1969, during a heated mayoral campaign:

> Standing in front of my hotel . . . in the heart of downtown Manhattan, I asked one question without prompting or further explanation to 150 people . . . "Who is going to win?" The results were as follows: thirteen, no relevant response; twenty-seven, Lindsay (for mayor); six, Proccacino (for mayor); one Marchi (for mayor); 103 the Mets (for the world championship of professional baseball). (Edwards, 1973, p. 4)

Chances are you and I could perform a similar "survey" and obtain similar results. Why then don't sociologists seem to take sport seriously enough to study it? Nobody knows, but observers suggest several possible reasons.

The traditional mind-body dichotomy in Western thought is cited by some (see Edwards, 1973, pp. 6–7). Former Sunday school students are familiar with biblical injunctions like "The spirit indeed is willing, but the flesh is weak" (Matthew 26:41); or "Walk by the spirit and do not gratify the desires of the flesh. For the desires of the flesh are against the Spirit and the desires of the Spirit are against the flesh" (Galatians 5:16, 17). Sport would seem to belong to the "flesh." We play at sports for pleasure. There is little evidence that sport is spiritually uplifting, but the body (the flesh) is of central importance. No one denies that sport is physically pleasurable—ask a fit athlete how he or she feels after a good workout. Gerald Kenyon (1969) surveyed nearly 900 people to discover why they enjoyed participating. Many of the experiences they associated with sports fall under the general rubric of pleasure. Vertigo (". . . an element of thrill through the medium of speed . . .") and catharsis

("... release from tension ...") are especially "fleshy" among the six aspects of the sports experience Kenyon found. Asceticism—sacrifice and self-denial—was also part of the sport experience, so Kenyon's study cannot be seen as an unambiguous demonstration that sport is solely "of the flesh."

The distinction between mind and body leaves the body, especially *pleasure* associated with the body, morally inferior to pursuits that are intellectual and not physically pleasurable. How do you think the faculty senate at your college would react to a major designed to help those who have decided to "give all" in the pursuit of a performance career in music or drama? How do you think the same faculty senate might react to a proposal to establish a major to help those who have decided to "give all" in the pursuit of a career in baseball or football?

Eric Dunning cited the influence of a tradition related to the mind-body dichotomy, "a more or less secularized 'Protestant Ethic' according to which work ranks higher than leisure" (Dunning, 1971, p. 35) as another source of the antisport bias among intellectuals. The "Protestant Ethic" refers to the early Calvinist belief that all people have a "calling" that they ought to pursue to the exclusion of worldly pursuits. A good person would devote his or her time to work and not defy God's plan by neglecting the calling and indulging in "fleshy" pleasures such as drinking and playing games.

Sociologists are no less influenced by the "Protestant Ethic" than any other professional group. Sport, recreation, and play seem trivial compared to work. "Playful" activities such as sexual activity, drug use, and delinquency receive attention, but only as problems to be solved. Sport is not a problem, but it is trivial, so it does not merit serious attention, according to this bias.

Lyn Lofland in her 1990 presidential address to the Pacific Sociological Association suggests one additional reason for the neglect of sport and other "trivial" subjects:

> I am suggesting, that in choosing and evaluating research topics . . . many sociologists express a quite exaggerated "manliness." We like *big* topics, *important* issues. . . . We eschew the modest, the mundane, the homely, and, let me not forget: the frivolous aspects of human life and association. (Lofland, 1990, pp. 315–316)

Lofland reviewed the topics of articles in two major sociological journals (*The American Sociological Review* and *The American Journal of Sociology*) and found only *21* of 293 articles devoted to "modest" topics while the bulk of the articles were devoted to "big" topics involving political and economic issues of whole societies or problems such as crime, immigration or oppression. Sport, while important in many ways, is hardly the sort of thing that could produce a war, a recession, or a rise in the divorce rate. Sport is viewed as modest, mundane, and frivolous and, hence, is left out of "serious" sociological inquiry—even when it is genuinely "big" as with the integration of baseball or the "hero" image attributed to Joe Louis.

Is Sport Important?

Jackie Robinson and Joe Louis are clearly important, but the importance of two sportsmen does not demonstrate that sport in general merits more attention than it receives among sociologists. A few examples from the sport sociology literature show us that sociology's ignorance of sport constitutes an ignorance of information that could widen and strengthen our understanding of many important issues.

Racial Discrimination

Sport sociologists have long recognized the special utility of sport for the study of racial discrimination. A constant problem in studying this problem is the difficulty in ruling out nonracial, possibly legitimate, reasons for differential treatment of blacks and whites. The special character of sport makes the "ruling out" of alternative explanations rather easy:

> Suppose it were possible to find an occupation for which the quality of formal schooling and the general cultural background of an aspirant made relatively little difference in his ability to succeed, in which ability was clearly apparent to interested observers and in which the link between ability and reward could be observed. Then, differences in earnings for individuals of equal ability but different color would be a relatively unambiguous measure of discrimination in the labor market. The professional athlete follows such an occupation. (Pascal & Rapping, 1971)

Job performance, years of experience, team success, and salary are all easily available data in the case of professional baseball players. Players don't have to be graduates of the "right schools," be able to give a good dinner party, or know the subtleties of proper dress or other potentially important, but difficult to measure, nuances of conduct that may exert a legitimate influence on hiring practices, salaries, or promotions in other occupations. For example, a recent study of discrimination in the promotion of noncommissioned officers in the United States Army showed an apparent antiblack bias. Whites tended to leave the army sooner when not promoted, while blacks were willing to wait longer for promotions. This made it look as if black soldiers had to serve more time to be promoted over similarly qualified whites, when in fact they were treated fairly, at least insofar as promotion opportunities were concerned (David, Smith, & Nord, 1990).

An extensive literature on racial discrimination in sports has developed during the past quarter century. This literature is reviewed in Chapters 7 and 8 of this book. The study of racial discrimination in sport adds a lot to the study of racial discrimination in general. To ignore the literature on discrimination in sport is to ignore a "gold mine" of data and theory on racial discrimination. It is hard to imagine serious social scientists ignoring such useful information, but they do.

Some recent studies on discrimination in sports literature show substantial *change* in the severity of the problem. We have unambiguous evidence of changes toward fairness, so an examination of the sources of these changes is in order. Why are black quarterbacks finally appearing on NFL rosters? Why are there so few black coaches and administrators in NCAA institutions and in the NFL and Major League Baseball, but so many in the NBA? Why have NFL and professional baseball organizations started to hire "bad" black players (if there is such a thing as a bad player at the major-league level) when a decade or so ago weak black players were excluded (discriminated against) in favor of weak white players?

Much as the Brooklyn Dodgers' integration of baseball produced cracks in the edifice of racial segregation in the American South, New Zealand's insistence on fielding the All Black rugby team that included nonwhite Maori and other Polynesian players in international matches with South Africa produced "cracks" in the edifice of South African apartheid.[2] The consequences of these cracks, combined with a sustained international sports boycott of this sports-loving country (this includes all "racial groups" in South Africa), have contributed to the current process of the dismantling of apartheid there. One could argue that sports boycotts, especially by rugby powers such as New Zealand, were more significant than the international arms boycotts and disinvestment campaigns in recent years in that white South Africans probably *benefited* from these latter efforts, developing a world class arms industry with associated export opportunities and seizing the opportunity to purchase profitable enterprises at bargain basement prices. While not ignoring the importance of international pressure and pressure by such movements as the African National Congress and Inkatha, an analysis of the decline of apartheid is incomplete without an understanding of the role of sport (see Thompson, 1975).

Child's Play and Adult Careers

We all used to be children, but most of us have probably forgotten what we knew as children. One important way to learn about the process of growing up is to observe children at play.

Janet Lever (1976) observed fifth graders at play on school grounds and asked them (in class) to keep diaries of their daily activities. Lever was interested in different play patterns among boys and girls. She found plenty of differences. Boys played outdoors more, in larger groups and in groups with boys of different ages; girls usually played in small groups, even groups of two. A few girls with suitable skills got involved in boys games (e.g., baseball), but boys rarely joined in "girls' games" except to "goof off." Boys more often played at competitive games with some formal rules; girls more often were involved in informal, noncompetitive activities. Because of the size, formality and challenge, boys' games lasted longer than girls' play activities. The girls became bored after a time and switched to different activities. Finally boys argued more than girls over rules or interpretation of rules.

Look at the characteristics of boys' vs. girls' play again. It is clear that boys are much more involved in *sports,* while their female classmates are involved in relatively

TABLE 1–1 Some Differences Between Girls' and Boys' Play and Possible Skills Learned

Boys' Play	Girls' Play
Out of doors	More indoors
Larger groups	Smaller groups
Age heterogenous groups	Age homogenous groups
Rarely involved in "girls" games	A handful may play in "boys" games
Competitive games with some formal rules (e.g., baseball)	Cooperative play just for fun, no winners or losers (e.g., riding bikes, cooking)
Games last longer	Shorter duration
Disputes over rules frequent	Relatively few disputes partly due to informality and small group size
Boys	**Girls**
Possible Skills Learned	
Organization (e.g., choosing sides)	Interpersonal skills
Socialization, strategy (integrating younger, less skilled boys into teams)	Verbal skills (imaginative activities)
Coping with impersonal, competitive situations	Sensitivity to others
Negotiation (rules, teams)	Nurturance
Coordination of several specialized tasks (e.g., touch football, soccer)	
Sports skills (i.e., physical skills—catching, hitting, throwing, shooting, dribbling)	

From Lever (1976, 1978).

unstructured *play*. In a later article, Lever (1978) suggests that the sports-play distinction may have consequences for the future of the fifth graders she studied:

> Boys' games provide a valuable learning environment. It is reasonable to expect that the following social skills will be cultivated on the playground: the ability to deal with diversity in memberships where each person is performing a special task; the ability to coordinate actions and maintain cohesiveness among group members; the ability to cope with a set of impersonal rules, and the ability to work for collective as well as personal goals. (Lever, 1978, p. 480)

Moreover, "boys experience face-to-face confrontations—often opposing a close friend—and must learn to depersonalize the attack" (p. 481). All of these skills might serve as early training for effective organizational membership as a leader or a "follower." Contrast this to the skills cultivated in the play activities more typically joined by girls:

> Girls' play and games are very different. They are mostly spontaneous, imaginative and free of structure and rules. Turn taking activities like jump rope may be played without setting explicit goals. Girls have far less experience with interpersonal competition. The style of their competition is indirect, rather than face to face, individual, rather than team affiliated. Leadership roles are either missing or randomly filled. (Lever, 1978, p. 481)

Such activities probably serve to cultivate "affective and verbal development" (p. 481). They may improve the quality of future primary relationships, but not effectiveness in competitive, impersonal organizations. The sports activities in which preadolescent boys are involved may prepare them for life in an impersonal, competitive, bureaucratic setting, whereas girls' play may prepare them more for nurturing, caring relationships required for "female" occupations such as homemaker, teacher, or counselor. It could be that play preferences of (and opportunities available to) preadolescent boys and girls affect their fitness for certain future adult roles.

Academic Achievement in the Schools

The traditional mind-body dichotomy fits neatly with the "dumb jock" image that exists in the local culture of most high schools and universities. There is some justification for the "brains vs. brawn" image. From the beginning of intercollegiate sports competition in the United States, colleges recruited academically unqualified or underqualified students to play on varsity teams. Potential Canadian professional hockey players are often discouraged from pursuing academic goals because the demands of preprofessional junior league hockey interfere with their academic performance (King & Angi, 1968). That is, many school athletes do fit the "dumb jock" image. But does their participation in sports help or hinder their academic performance?

It is hard not to overemphasize the importance of this issue. Whole states, notably California and Texas, have passed laws requiring high school students to earn a C average before they can participate on school sports teams. A primary purpose of these laws is to improve the academic performance of athletes and nonathletes alike (AB 2613, 1986), presumably by requiring would-be athletes to work hard in the classroom to retain eligibility. These laws clearly keep below-average students from participating, but do they enhance students' academic performance?

A recent study by Jean Fitzgibbons (1988) suggests that excluding poor students from sports teams has no impact on the overall academic performance of students in a school or of individual athletes. That is, the C average rule does *not* appear to improve academic achievement. What it does do is affect the attendance of excluded students (see Fitzgibbons, 1988, Ch. 4). Athletes rejected from school teams do not work harder in the classroom to improve their grades. Rather they tend to retreat from school, miss classes, and eventually drop out. "One might conclude that the rule has had effects opposite those intended by policy makers" (Fitzgibbons, 1988, p. 58).

The past decade is not the first time sports has been blamed for the academic shortcomings of American schools. After a rash of American failures to orbit a satellite after the Soviet Union's successful Sputnik launch, James Coleman (1961) suggested that the status (respect and recognition) accorded athletes in American high schools encouraged students to devote time and energy to athletic pursuits while the relative lack of status accorded top scholars discouraged potentially brilliant students from concentrating on academic pursuits. The net effect was to optimize the production of good athletes but limit the development of potentially outstanding scholars (see Coleman, 1961, Ch. 5). Coleman's thinking deserved to be taken seriously. It was based on a thorough study of students at nine high schools, and Coleman was one of the most respected sociologists in the United States.[3]

For all that, it took another study (which led to a series of similar studies) to test Coleman's theory about athletics inhibiting academic success. A study of male athletes at two Michigan high schools provided a direct test of the notion that rewards provided for athletic success led to decreased academic achievement. Schafer and Armer (1968) reasoned that if Coleman was correct, then the following should be true:

1. Athletes should not perform as well as nonathletes.
2. The greater the student's participation in sports, the greater the detriment to his studies.
3. Sports that are given the greatest recognition [i.e. football and basketball] should harm . . . academic performance more than the minor sports. . . . (Schafer & Armer, 1968, p. 23)

Comparing 152 athletes with 152 nonathletes who matched on IQ, father's occupation, curriculum track, and ninth grade GPA, Schafer and Armer found that

1. Athletes performed *better*, not worse, than their nonathlete counterparts.
2. The more a student participated in sports, the greater his advantage over the nonathlete.
3. Athletes in the "high reward" sports did best of all when compared to the nonathletes.

In other words Coleman was dead wrong! Athletic participation *helps* academic performance. It's too bad that proponents of the C average rule hadn't read this and several other studies that came to similar conclusions about athletics and academics.

Studies of the academic effects of scholastic sports programs have provided one of the most fertile themes in the sociology of sport. *Why* and *how* might athletics enhance academic performance? Along with this interesting theoretical problem, the athletics-academics issue has a substantial policy importance. If sports do indeed help students to perform better in school (and it looks like they do), what are schools accomplishing when they deny a sub–C-average student the opportunity to participate?

International Relations

President Jimmy Carter had a problem. How was he to retaliate against the former Soviet Union's 1979 military invasion of Afghanistan? A military action was out of the question. A military confrontation had the potential of leading to a disastrous war at worst or to a costly Soviet retaliation in another part of the world at best. Economic action would also have been risky. Refusing to sell certain products to the Soviet Union could have cost the economy of the United States and the other participating Western countries more than it would have cost the Soviet Union. Whatever the United States and its supporters refused to sell, such as wheat or high technology, could have been purchased from other countries.

After some internal debate, Carter's advisors agreed that the United States should announce that the United States Olympic team would not participate in the 1980 Moscow Olympic Games. These games were seen by the Soviet government as a very important opportunity to obtain good will from other governments of the world. A well-organized, well-staged games in a "happy" Moscow would go a long way to restore the good name of the Soviet Union after the criticism of their invasion of Afghanistan. Carter wanted to prevent this result (Brzezinski, 1983, p. 433).

The 1980 games turned out to be an athletic success but a political and propaganda failure. Several, although not all, major sports powers stayed out. China, Canada, Germany, Japan, and Kenya joined with the United States in the boycott. The boycott made manifest the fact that everything was not all right. The invasion of Afghanistan and the denial of human rights to Soviet dissidents in the Soviet Union was not acceptable.

Even the partly successful boycott of the Moscow Games hurt Soviet prestige. It added to the price Carter wanted them to pay for their invasion of Afghanistan. Importantly, the Olympic boycott cost the boycotting countries almost nothing. A handful of deserving athletes were denied the opportunity to participate in the Olympics, but this very real human cost paled in comparison to the potential costs to the people out of work because of an economic embargo or to people killed or injured in some form of military action.

Sport has been used as a political tool in a number of situations. The sports boycott of South Africa comes to mind, as does the 1971 "ping pong diplomacy" between the United States and China. In the latter case, both sides were ready to establish friendly diplomatic relations after a quarter century of hostility. Neither side knew how such an initiative would be received by their respective publics. In April of 1971, China invited a United States table tennis team to tour China. After it was apparent that United States–Chinese sports relations were approved by the public in both countries, the two sides proceeded to initiate official diplomatic contact. Had the table tennis tour met with disfavor, the two countries would have known that more ground work would be required before "going public." The table tennis failure would have been of little consequence to either country.

The 1980 and 1971 incidents illustrate one value of sports in international politics. Their symbolic importance, coupled with their practical unimportance, allows nations to approach one another or punish one another in a very public way, but with little real harm to either side. Here, the very unimportance of sport makes sport important!

Summary

Sociology has not accorded sport the serious study it deserves. Many people are involved in sports in one role or another, and most people care about sports. Several episodes illustrate the practical importance of sports in our lives. The integration of Major League Baseball facilitated the subsequent integration of the military and of schools. Sports have been used as an effective tool in international politics. Sport may also affect us in more personal ways. It is possible that sports experiences help prepare young people for future adult roles through socialization and enhancement of educational achievement.

Notes

1. These figures are from the U.S. Bureau of the Census, *Statistical Abstract of the United States* (1990), Table 392. Spectator numbers are from Table 390 of the Abstract.

2. The popular name of the New Zealand national rugby team is the All Blacks. In earlier tours of South Africa, Maori and other Polynesian players were excluded in deference to South African apartheid laws prompting the ironic term "all white All Blacks" (see Thompson, 1975, Ch. 3).

3. There is evidence that systems that do reward scholarship produce good scholars. Carl Sagan (1990) reports that "25 percent of Canadian 18 year olds knew just as much chemistry as a select 1 percent of American high school seniors . . ." (p. 265). Sagan blames the failure of American education on bad teaching, not sports. Student culture in Canadian schools rewards good scholarship much more than it does in American schools (Jerome & Phillips, 1971). This school reward structure may encourage athletic excellence in American schools and academic excellence in Canadian schools. Coleman's claim, though, was that rewarding athletics somehow inhibits academic pursuits.

References

AB 2613 (1986). Section 35160.5, Chapter 422, *California Education Code.*

Blalock, H. M. (1967). *Toward a Theory of Minority Relations.* New York: Wiley.

Blalock, H. M. (1982). *Race and Ethnic Relations.* Englewood Cliffs, NJ: Prentice Hall.

Broom, L., and Selznick, P. (1963). *Sociology.* New York: Harper & Row.

Brzezinski, Z. (1983). *Power and Principle.* New York: Farrar, Straus, Giroux.

Bureau of the Census (1990). *Statistical Abstract of the United States 1990.* Washington DC: U.S. Government Printing Office.

Charnofsky, H. (1988). Sport sociology and race relations: Where have you gone Jackie Robinson? Paper presented at the meetings of the Pacific Sociological Association.

Coleman, J. C. (1961). *The Adolescent Society.* New York: Free Press.

David, T., Smith, D. A., and Nord, R. (1990). Inequality in the military: Fact or fiction? *American Sociological Review, 55,* 714–718.

Dunning, E. (1971). Some conceptual dilemmas in the sociology of sport. In R. Albonico and K. Pfister-Binz, Eds., *Sociology of Sport: Theoretical Foundations and Research Methods.* Basel: Birkhauser, pp. 34–47.

Edwards, H. (1973). *The Sociology of Sport.* Homewood, IL: Dorsey.

Fitzgibbons, J. K. (1988). The impact of the "C" Average policy . . . Unpublished doctoral dissertation, University of the Pacific, Stockton, CA.

Hoffman, M. S., Ed. (1990). *World Almanac and Book of Facts 1991.* New York: World Almanac.

Jerome, W. C., and Phillips, J. C. (1971). The relationship between academic achievement and interscholastic participation: A comparison of Canadian and American high schools. *CAHPER Journal, 37* (3), 18–21.

Kenyon, G. S. (1969). A conceptual model for characterizing physical activity. In J. W. Loy and G. S. Kenyon, Eds., *Sport Culture and Society.* Toronto: Collier-MacMillan, pp. 71–81.

King, A. J. C., and Angi, C. E. (1968). The hockey playing student. *CAHPER Journal, 35* (1), 25–28.

Lever, J. (1976). Sex differences in the games children play. *Social Problems, 23,* 478–487.

Lever, J. (1978). Sex differences in the complexity of children's games. *American Sociological Review, 43,* 471–483.

Lofland, L. (1990). Is peace possible? *Sociological Perspectives, 33,* 313–325.

Lueschen, G., Ed. (1968). The sociology of sport. *Current Sociology, 15* (3) (entire issue).

Mead, C. (1985). *Champion Joe Louis: Black Hero in White America.* New York: Charles Scribner's Sons.

Pascal, A. M., and Rapping, L. A. (1970). *Racial Discrimination in Organized Baseball.* Santa Monica, CA: Rand.

Sagan, C. (1990). Why we need to understand science. *Skeptical Inquirer, 14,* 263–269.

Schafer, W. E., and Armer, J. M. (1968). Athletes are not inferior students. *Trans-action, 5,* 21–26, 61–62.

Thompson, R. (1975). *Retreat from Apartheid.* London: Oxford University.

Tygiel, J. (1983). *Baseball's Great Experiment.* New York: Oxford.

Chapter 2

Sport, Social Science, and Pseudoscience

What Is Sociology?

Few people have difficulty thinking about the main subject matter of such fields as astronomy, genetics, or biochemistry. Sociology is different. Many new college students have a vague idea of what sociology is about—something to do with societies—but little more. Sociology is about societies and, more generally, groups. Arising in the middle and late 19th century, sociology concerned itself with the problems associated with the rapid and profound changes taking place in Europe at that time. France had only recently experienced a wrenching revolution followed by nearly two decades of military dictatorship; Germany and Italy were just becoming unified nations. Britain was experiencing unprecedented economic, military, and diplomatic expansion accompanied by economic disasters at home. The United States, European in culture if not in geography, had experienced a bloody and in some ways revolutionary civil war. Many thinkers asked questions relating to the upheaval. What produced the changes? What new sources of authority would replace the obsolete triad of family, church, and royalty? Could the common people rule themselves? Could capitalism, the new form of economic organization, survive or would it collapse under the weight of its own success? Could civilization itself survive in the fast growing industrial cities of Europe and North America?

Many social thinkers believed that these sorts of social questions could be addressed through scientific study, just as natural phenomena were being understood in the natural sciences. But the subject matter would be different from that of any other science. In 1895, Emile Durkheim attempted to explain the subject matter of this "new science":

> There is in every society a certain group of phenomena which may be differentiated from those studied by the other natural sciences. When I fulfill my obligations as brother, husband, or citizen . . . I perform duties which are defined, externally to myself and my acts, in law and custom. Even if they conform to my own sentiments and I feel their reality subjectively, such reality is still objective, for I did not create them; I merely inherited them through my education. . . .
>
> Similarly, the church-member finds the beliefs and practices of his religious life ready-made at birth; their existence prior to his own implies their existence outside of himself. The system of signs I use to express my thought, the system of currency I employ to pay my debts . . . the practices followed in my profession, etc., function independently of my own use of them. And these statements can be repeated for each member of society. Here, then, are ways of acting, thinking, and feeling that present the noteworthy property of existing outside the individual consciousness. (Durkheim, 1938, pp. 1–2)

That is, there are "social forces" or "social facts" that exist in society as a whole and affect individuals. The English speaking population of 1860 is now dead, yet the English language remains alive and well. We could quit playing baseball for a year and yet "baseball" as a social reality would remain in the form of oral and written tradition, rules, equipment, and physical facilities (fields). (See Loy, 1969, pp. 62–67, for a similar argument about sport as a social fact.)

The causes and consequences of various kinds of behavior—crime, divorce, technical innovation, religious experiences—are also studied by the sociologist. Sometimes behaviors are seen as symptoms of social forces or conditions, sometimes as consequences of individual experiences. The study of the intersection between group and individual is called social psychology. An example of sociology's interest in both social facts and individual experiences may be seen in the Marxian theory of revolution. Karl Marx believed that the capitalist economic system (a social fact) would self destruct when enough members of the working class (a social fact) developed *class consciousness* (an individual experience), an understanding of their role in the economy as producers of wealth that unjustly went to land and factory owners (another social fact).

One of the best ways to introduce the meaning of sociology is to review classic studies in the field. We will review two such studies, Emile Durkheim's study of suicide and Richard LaPiere's study of racial prejudice and racial discrimination.

Durkheim on Suicide

Emile Durkheim's book *Suicide* provides an example of a sociological study that emphasizes social facts rather than individual experiences. The book first appeared in 1897 and was translated into English in 1951.

On first sight suicide would appear to be a "natural" for a social psychological approach. One could follow up a number of suicide cases by reading suicide notes, interviewing friends and family of the deceased, and looking for any personal or career crises in each victim's recent past. This information could be synthesized to discover any commonalities between the suicide victims. This indeed is a good social psychological approach to the subject, but Durkheim observed that this approach would miss one very important fact about suicide:

> Not merely are there suicides every year, but there are as a general rule as many each year as in the year preceding. The state of mind which causes men to kill themselves is not purely and simply transmitted, but—something much more remarkable—transmitted to an equal number of persons. . . . How can this be if only individuals are concerned? The number as such cannot be directly transmitted. Today's population has not learned from yesterday's the size of the contribution it must make to suicide; nevertheless, it will make one of identical size with that of the past, unless circumstances change. (Durkheim, 1951, p. 308)

However many separate cases of suicide one might examine, the cause of the *rate* of suicide in a given society cannot be discovered. Only an examination of the society as a whole can reveal the causes of things that characterize the society as a whole.

Durkheim showed that the year-to-year variation in the number of suicides in France was more stable than the year-to-year variation in the overall number of deaths. Now the general mortality rate was, and still is, produced by certain factors that characterize a society—the fraction of the population over age 65, health conditions, accident hazards, degree of poverty. Still, suicide rates were stable, although the reasons for suicide were unknown. Such stability had to be the consequence of factors that, like the causes of general mortality, characterized French society as a whole. Thus, Durkheim set out to discover what social conditions could explain suicide rates in France and other European countries. Suicide rates varied sharply from country to country and between regions within countries.

Durkheim recognized that social factors were by no means the only possible causes of suicide rates. Such things as climate, prevalence of mental illness or racial tendencies (remember Durkheim was writing in 1897) might affect whole nations just as much as sociological factors.

Some investigators had argued that the high rate of suicide in Denmark and Sweden might be caused by the long, cold winters that residents of these countries had to endure. Durkheim rejected this view on the ground that suicide tended to occur mostly in the spring and summer seasons, not during the winter months. Others believed that the heat of the summer caused irritability, which in turn produced an elevated incidence of suicide, but Durkheim rejected this thesis on the ground that European countries with the hottest summer weather (Italy, Greece) had very low suicide rates, while countries with cool summers (Denmark, Prussia) usually had high suicide rates. The facts about suicide just did not coincide with the theories linking suicide to weather (see Durkheim, 1951, Book I, Ch. 3).

What about mental illness? Is not suicide a consequence of this *by definition?* This would mean that all suicides result from mental illness. If this were so, then

Durkheim would simply have changed the name "suicide" to "the mental illness underlying suicide" and proceeded as before. Excluding the "suicide equals mental illness (or a special form of mental illness)" position Durkheim was able to examine the general hypothesis: If mental illness in general increases suicide rates, then suicide should vary with insanity rates. That is, if women are more prone to mental illness, then women should be more prone to commit suicide; if Jews are more prone to mental illness, then Jews should be more prone to commit suicide than people of other faiths; and countries with high rates of mental illness should also have high rates of suicide. Durkheim found no evidence of a correlation between sex, religion, or national mental illness rate and rate of suicide. Rather, women, who were more likely than men to suffer from mental illness, and Jews, who were more likely than Catholics or Protestants to suffer from mental illness, had lower rates of suicide than other groups. Countries with high mental illness rates were no more likely to be high in suicide than were countries with low mental illness rates. As with weather and climate, mental illness rates did not equate to suicide rates as they would have to if mental illness caused suicide (see Durkheim, 1951, Book I, Ch. 1).

Durkheim also examined whether excessive alcohol consumption increased suicide rates. A comparison of alcohol consumption, drunkenness arrests, and admissions to hospitals for alcoholism in dozens of French departments (counties) to suicide rates showed no indication that high rates of alcohol use (or abuse) were associated with high suicide rates. The "alcohol abuse causes suicide" hypothesis predicted a strong association, but Durkheim found none (see Durkheim, 1951, Book I, Ch. 1).

Climate is clearly not a sociological factor, but Durkheim thought it might affect suicide rates. He found no connection. Rates of alcoholism or mental illness are social facts, but Durkheim found no association between either of these factors and suicide rate. Durkheim then looked at one more possible cause of variations in national suicide rates—racial variations.

In the 1890s race was a respectable explanation for many phenomena. Such explanations enjoyed undeserved credibility because of the general esteem granted to anything coming out of the science of biology at that time. Biology was finding cures to diseases that had scourged humankind. Every few years would yield cures or vaccines for such dread diseases as cholera, typhoid, small pox, and syphilis. Just imagine the public esteem that would be accorded the scientist who found a cure for AIDS. AIDS is a minor threat compared to the deadly diseases conquered by 19th century biology. Along with the spectacular successes of germ theorists, biology had "solved" the old intellectual problem of the source of evolution and biological diversity with Charles Darwin's theory of natural selection.

No serious effort to explain national variations in suicide could ignore the possibility that some innate tendency toward self-destruction varied between the races of people constituting the several nations of Europe. Durkheim's discussion of race as a cause of suicide provides a model for the examination of race as an explanation for any behavior (race is frequently used today in man-on-the-street explanations of athletic success). Durkheim begins his discussion of race and suicide with a warning:

> The sociologist must be very careful in searching for the influences of races on any social phenomenon. For to solve such problems the different races and their distinctions from each other must be known. This caution is the more essential because this anthropological uncertainty might well be due to the fact that the word "race" no longer corresponds to anything definite . . . [races] today seem to be only peoples or societies of peoples, brothers by civilization rather than by blood. Thus conceived, race becomes almost identical with nationality. (Durkheim, 1951, p. 85)

Assuming that there is such a thing as race, can it influence suicide? If so, certain things must hold true. Durkheim should have found that suicide was fairly constant among members of the same race, and that it varied consistently between races. Danes (Scandinavians) had very high suicide rates; Norwegians (also Scandinavians) had low suicide rates. German Catholics had low suicide rates, whereas German Protestants had high rates. The same was true among the French Catholics and Protestants. Suicide varied between men and women of the same races and between old and young of the same races. Further, suicide rates had shown a gradual rise in French society throughout the previous century. In short, suicide rates were quite variable between persons of the same race even though race, the supposed cause of suicide, was constant. Durkheim reasoned that a "cause" that remains constant cannot produce variable effects, hence race cannot be a cause of suicide (see Book I, Ch. 2).

Durkheim's rejection of "extra-social factors" as forces in the production of suicide provided clues to factors that might explain it. Suicide did vary systematically by age, sex, and religion. What social conditions might explain these variations? Durkheim pointed to two, "egoism" and "anomie."

Catholics were less prone than Protestants to commit suicide because the Catholic Church required a degree of participation by communicants, whereas Protestants were under much less pressure to be personally involved in church. Married people were less likely than the unmarried to commit suicide, especially when children were present. One reason for the low suicide rate among women was that unmarried women remained with their parents, while bachelors most often lived alone. Suicide rates were shown to decline during times of war, when citizens presumably felt a greater sense of "belonging" to their country. All of these facts about suicide rates (examined, of course, in great detail by Durkheim) pointed to ***social integration*** or a general feeling of belonging and of being needed as a preventative to suicide. Absence of social integration, *egoism,* elevated suicide rates (see Book II, Ch. 2 and 3).

Anomie was seen as less important than egoism in the production of suicide. Nonetheless it was important. Anomie may best be conceived as a gap between what people have and what they collectively believe they should have. Durkheim observed that suicide rose in times of economic crisis, when the well-to-do suddenly found themselves less wealthy (even though they still had a comfortable income). This desire-means gap could explain the long-term rise in suicide in European countries during the 19th century. The Industrial Revolution had increased wealth beyond the point that most ordinary people dreamed. The culture, which told people when to be satisfied, became irrelevant when the general standard of living rapidly rose. Durkheim believed, probably correctly, that without social (cultural) regulation we would never be satisfied with our material wealth:

> It is not human nature which can assign the variable limits necessary to our needs. They are thus unlimited so far as they depend on the individual alone. Irrespective of any external regulatory force our capacity for feeling is in itself an insatiable and bottomless abyss. (Durkheim, 1951, p. 247)

Until culture "caught up" with advances in the standard of living, people would never know when to be satisfied, and thus never achieve success because there would be no "success" to achieve. This idea of anomie seems rather apropos now at the close of the so-called "me" generation, when multimillionaires on Wall Street and in savings-and-loan institutions set out to acquire even more millions by dishonest means. Suicide, as well as economic crime, accompanies this state of dissatisfaction with material wealth (see Book II of Durkheim, 1951, Ch. 5).

Durkheim had much more to say about the social causes of suicide, but this synopsis suffices to show how the sociological approach emphasizes social conditions as causes of other social phenomena. Many phenomena are not easily explained by social factors. Indeed, some kinds of behaviors have little to do with general social conditions but may be best understood through a focus on the individual and how he or she experiences his or her world. Richard LaPiere's study of racial prejudice and racial discrimination illustrates this focus.

LaPiere on Prejudice

Richard LaPiere (1934) questioned the truth of something everybody knew was true—attitudes predispose people to behave in ways consistent with the attitudes. In the early 1930s the western regions of the United States were characterized by considerable anti-Asian racial prejudice. What would happen to a Chinese couple touring the Western United States when they approached restaurants and motels?

LaPiere had an obvious way to answer this question. He toured with a Chinese couple during three summers. Staying in the background as much as possible, LaPiere kept track of the treatment accorded his Chinese friends. Rather surprisingly the Chinese couple was received courteously:

> In something like ten thousand miles of motor travel . . . we met definite rejection from those asked to serve us just once. We were received at 66 hotels . . . refused at one. We were served in 184 restaurants and cafes . . . and treated with what I judged to be more than ordinary consideration in 72 of them. (LaPiere, 1934, p. 16)

But wait a minute! Wasn't there a climate of racial prejudice at the time? LaPiere assessed the level of racial prejudice by sending a questionnaire to the motels, hotels, and restaurants six months after he and his friends had visited them. One of the questions was a straightforward, "Will you accept members of the Chinese race as guests in your establishment?" (p. 18). Responses were unambiguous. Of the 128 establishments who returned the questionnaire 118 said "no," they would not serve Chinese patrons. Nine said "maybe," and only one said "yes" (p. 18). Had LaPiere sent his questionnaire *before* taking the tour, he probably would have advised his Chinese friends to stay home!

LaPiere cautioned sociologists to distinguish between *attitudes,* which after all are only symbolic reactions to hypothetical situations, and *behavior,* which involves real reactions with real consequences. A person's response to a paper-and-pencil questionnaire does not necessarily indicate how that person will behave in a real-world situation.

This study has clear implications for people concerned with racism. Can education to reduce prejudice be trusted to result in less discrimination? Or might a direct attack on discrimination be more productive? Is it not likely that motel and restaurant keepers wanted to avoid a possible "scene" that rejection of the Chinese couple might create? Is it not likely that proprietors in the 1930s were unwilling to forgo any business even if it meant "violating" their anti-Asian prejudices? These issues relate to discrimination in sport. They will be explored later in this book.

Social Science and Pseudoscience

Durkheim's study of suicide statistics in 19th century Europe and LaPiere's careful observation of the treatment his Chinese friends received at 251 motels and restaurants, which seem so different, have much in common. Both are excellent examples of *social science.* Good sociology tries to conform to the rigors of science. Not all sociology is good, though, often because of a disinterest in scientific rigor on the part of some sociologists.

When we think of science certain images come to mind—people with white coats, test tubes, oscilloscopes, maybe mice being injected—but a little reflection reveals that science is not people or mice or measurement instruments. Contrast a chemistry lab with the "lab" of a geologist or the "tools" of an astronomer with those of an archaeologist. Science does not consist in things. Rather it is an approach to find "truth."

The various instruments we associate with science reveal an important concern of the field, *systematic observation.* Microscopes, telescopes, spectroscopes, and the like are devices to aid observation. Scientists are continually collecting dinosaur fossils, samples of pollens, or whatever natural phenomena seem relevant. Durkheim and LaPiere, of course, collected information (usually called "data") that they deemed relevant to the scientific problems they were studying.

How did Durkheim or LaPiere know what was and was not worth studying? What was worth investigating and what was trivial? This is one function of *theory.* A theory in science attempts to explain the facts. What happens? How does it happen? Why does it happen? In answering these questions scientists conduct systematic observation to test whether the theory is true. Some theories are almost certainly true and may even be used as the basis for behavior—many diseases are caused by germs, so to cure the disease, attack the germ. Positive thinking or spinal adjustments are useless as they have no effect on germs. Other scientific theories may well be untrue, even though they are at least partially supported by evidence. Walter Alvarez and Frank Asaro (1990) theorize that dinosaurs disappeared some 65 million years ago (systematic observation in the form of the fossil records tells us this) because an extraterrestrial object, perhaps a huge meteor, struck the earth and caused a global disaster. There is some evidence consistent with this theory. Many species became extinct at about the same time, and a thin layer of iridium, a metal not found in high concentrations on earth, has been found in widely dispersed sites in geological strata corresponding at least approximately to the time dinosaurs disappeared. This theory, right or wrong, could hardly guide behavior, but it provides an illustration of a scientific theory based on systematic observation that may very well prove to be wrong when more evidence becomes available. Courtillot (1990) contends that it is more likely that a series of massive volcanic eruptions, not an extraterrestrial impact, produced an atmospheric catastrophe that led to the extinction of dinosaurs. The Deccan Plateau in India was produced by this volcanic activity.

However right or wrong one or the other theories proves to be, both do what a theory is supposed to do—provide a guide for further research. If a meteor struck the earth and produced a sort of "nuclear winter" that killed the dinosaurs (and many other species), then a thin layer of "fallout" with a high concentration of iridium might have dusted the entire surface of the earth in a short time. Likewise the extinction should have taken place in a very short time. The volcanic explanation would suggest that the extinction happened over tens of thousands of years and not one or two years. Is there a fossil bed from that era that will show how long it took for the extinction to take place? Could volcanic activity produce the layer of iridium that appears to exist? Was that layer deposited in a few years or over thousands of years? Research questions seem to roll off of these theories!

The same goes for Durkheim's work on suicide and LaPiere's work on prejudice and discrimination. Would an unpopular war (e.g., Vietnam or, for the Soviet Union, Afghanistan) affect suicide rates like a popular war? Can egoism or anomie be measured in individuals (recall that these ideas were supposed to describe societies and not individual people)? For LaPiere, would the motels have accepted black people under the same circumstances? If economic conditions had been better would they have discriminated? In what other areas of life do we say one thing and do another? In what areas are we most likely to say and do the same thing?

The interplay between theory and the search for facts suggests a second facet of science, *organized skepticism*. Good science does not tolerate dogma. No theory, no assumption is above question. In this respect science differs from everyday intellectual activity—and from bad science. Research in science is directed at *disproving* theories or assumptions. "True" theories will not be overturned. False ones may survive for a while, but will sooner or later have to be abandoned or revised.

Morris Cohen and Ernest Nagel (1934, pp. 193–196) in their classic book on the philosophy of science identify three everyday "methods" we all use to determine truth. The method of *tenacity* involves the loyal clinging to one's beliefs, rejecting contrary ideas and data. Try to change the views of a racially prejudiced person with facts. The facts will be rejected and you may well be invited to shut up! That is tenacity. Of course many innocuous beliefs are sustained this way. What is the best toothpaste? Are Republicans or Democrats "better"? What should one serve at Thanksgiving dinner? The method of *authority* involves using some highly respected source to determine what is true. We all must rely on textbooks, almanacs, and experts to get along in everyday life, but a little reflection shows why reliance on knowledgeable authority is unlike science. What happens when authorities disagree? Clearly the best authorities, especially in social science, are fallible. Are junior high baseball players significantly affected by the conduct of famous major leaguers? Knowledgeable authorities take positions on all sides of this issue. We have to believe something (tenacity); we have to trust someone (authority); and we ought to be able to trust in the obvious (intuition). Nonetheless, even the obvious may prove to be wrong. The sun does not revolve around the earth. Colds are not caused by cold weather. Sports probably do not build character, good or bad.

Science differs from the above methods in that it is *skeptical.*

> What is called *scientific method* differs radically from these by encouraging and developing the utmost possible doubt, so that what is left after such doubt is always supported by the best available evidence. As new evidence or new doubts arise it is the essence of scientific method to incorporate them. . . . Its method, then, makes science progressive because it is never too certain about its results. (Cohen & Nagel, 1934, p. 195, emphasis in original)

Perhaps you recall the recent furor over cold fusion. The creation of energy from nuclear fusion could provide an unlimited supply of cheap energy throughout the world. Two Utah scientists, Stanley Pons and Martin Fleishmann, reported that they "had achieved nuclear fusion by running electricity through a coil of palladium immersed in a beaker of heavy water" (Horgan, 1990, p. 22). Needless to say this announcement produced a flurry of activity inside and outside of the scientific community.

The activity inside the scientific community illustrates the "utmost possible doubt" aspect of the scientific method. Upon learning how Pons and Fleishmann conducted their experiment (Pons and Fleishmann were at first a little vague about this) scientists at labs all around the world set out to replicate the experiment, to see if the Pons-Fleishmann discovery was real or illusory. This is what scientific skepticism is about. New findings are tested again and again to minimize the possibility that they resulted from some kind of error. This skepticism, it would appear, has served us well in the case of cold fusion. "Although a few investigators have reported observing fleeting excesses of heat or radiation the vast majority have found nothing to support the cold fusion claim" (Horgan, 1990, p. 22).

The skepticism was not limited to replication of the original experiments. Scientists calculated the amount and effect of radiation that *should have* been produced if fusion occurred for possible sources of erroneous findings. These theoretical and methodological studies, along with the experimental replications, have virtually disproved the original findings of the Utah scientists.

Science, then, is built upon observation and explanation. The skepticism inherent in science compels scientists to test the accuracy of observations and explanations. A final characteristic of science, ***value neutrality,*** poses problems in social science. Social science is not about bacteria or molecules, it is about issues that may affect people's lives, including the life of the social scientist. Almost everyone believes that it is good to improve public health by reducing exposure to disease-bearing vectors such as rats, mosquitos, or flies, but when social policy rather than nature must be modified few can really remain "value neutral." Should condoms be distributed to high school students to reduce the incidence of sexually transmitted diseases? Should cities provide clean needles to drug addicts? Should students with less than a C average be allowed to participate in sports? One may easily stake out a position on one or another of these issues, but it is not at all easy to adopt a value-neutral stance.

Traditional thinking suggests that the scientist should set his/her values aside. Diverse critics of this position argue that:

1. No one can "set aside" his/her values for the purpose of scientific work, and failure to recognize this may lead to biased work—to social science, which pretends to be objective but selects and twists evidence to conform to consciously or unconsciously preordained values. The recent report of the Attorney-General's Commission on Pornography (1986) is an example of this.

2. The values themselves may provide a guide to important research topics. The scientific emphasis on discovering pathogens, germs that caused diseases, was guided not by value-neutral curiosity, but by an earnest desire to cure diseases.

3. Especially in social science, knowledge is power (sometimes at least), so the social scientist has an obligation to support right over wrong. A value-neutral approach to issues of injustice or exploitation amounts to acceptance of the abuses:

> It is the academic establishment . . . that has betrayed its intellectual mission by acquiescing in . . . the open transformation of the university into an elaborate service station for the dominant forces of wealth and power in society. (Horowitz, 1971, p. 3)

Supporters of the value-neutral position remind us that clearly biased research will not and should not be given the respect due to genuinely scientific, value-neutral, research, and that biased work will do little to provide information on which to base strategies for the realization of one's biases.

> A radical rhetoric or ideological posture does not inevitably result in politically useful sociological work. Ideologically "correct" analyses cannot substitute for cogent, empirically verified knowledge of the world as a basis for effective action. Ideological radicalism cannot provide a workable understanding of the relative roles of China and India in the developmental process of Asia. Ideological radicalism cannot prove the merits or demerits of one or another form of economic investment. When radicalism without sociology is employed as a surrogate for truth, it becomes fanaticism—a foolish effort to replace substance with style. (Becker & Horowitz, 1972, pp. 64–65)

But is it possible to set our values aside? Aren't so-called value-neutral sociologists deluding themselves about the ideal of being unbiased?

> Such criticism is quite true and equally irrelevant: although the ideal is indeed not fully attainable, there are radically different degrees of approximation to it that are attainable, and these quantitative differences add up to a significant difference in quality; which is to say that if we try like hell we can come very close to the ideal and enormously improve the state of our science thereby. But the critics . . . aren't interested in trying. They apparently believe that because we cannot be virgin pure with respect to value-neutral social science we might as well be whores. (Polsky, 1967, pp. 144–145)

There is a wide separation of opinions among sport sociologists about the issue of value neutrality. I tend to agree with author Ned Polsky. Polsky complained that by always trying to reduce crime (a value), criminologists failed to get a "true" picture of crime. Polsky studied the lives and careers of pool hustlers—sociology of sport as well as criminology—but set aside any concern for reforming the hustlers. He tried to see hustling from the point of view of the hustler. No one would accuse Polsky of having no morals, or of not caring about injustices in our society, but he could not learn about pool hustling if he simultaneously tried to prevent hustlers from taking advantage of the fish who came into the pool hall, or from burglarizing local stores. Was Polsky able to set aside his biases completely? I do not think so. Was he able to recognize his biases and values in order to minimize their effect on him? I think so. I think this enhanced the quality of his observations.

Pseudoscience

I have tried to describe science as intellectual activity based on an interaction between observation and explanation. The quality of value neutrality allows a search for truth even when the truth may be unpalatable, and skepticism always encourages more observation to determine whether the "truth" is really true. Along with science one may find a lot of activity that looks like science but is only science-like—pseudoscience. Pseudoscience may be fake—characterized by dishonesty or self delusion; pseudoscience may be false—activity that honestly tries to discover truth but that neglects (or rejects) one or more of the aspects of science discussed above: explanation, observation, skepticism, value neutrality.

Any student of the sociology of sport encounters a considerable amount of pseudoscience. Sport sociologists, being human beings, are inclined to hold certain values dear and to make some questionable assumptions about the nature of sport in society. That is, they may employ intuition, authority, or tenacity rather than science to determine truth. Before reviewing two examples of pseudoscience in sport sociology, I want to emphasize that in sport sociology the term pseudoscience should be thought of as *false* science, intellectual activity that seeks the truth but fails to rigorously follow the discipline required by science.

Fake science is not hard to find. Creationism is fake science. The book of Genesis is not scientific evidence. "Creation science" wants no part of the mountain of evidence that is explained by the theory of natural selection. Martin Gardner (1957) in his now classic book on (fake) pseudoscience reviews a variety of ideas that are clearly based on outright dishonesty or self-delusion. The planet Venus did not enter the inner solar system and pass by earth, temporarily slowing the earth's rotation and, among other natural cataclysms, causing the Red Sea to part just as the Israelites crossed it on their escape from bondage in Egypt. Nonetheless many loyalists closed their eyes to obvious refutations of Immanuel Velikovsky's *Worlds in Collision* (see Gardner, 1957, Ch. 3). Many people believe in mind reading, and reputable scientists have attempted to discover evidence of extrasensory perception. None have, although many retain a faith in ESP by interpreting any finding, positive or negative, as positive evidence of ESP. ESP theorists have learned that ESP does not work when skeptical people are present, but works well when subjects receive a reward for successfully reading minds and when subjects can participate in the experimental design. Could it be that amateur magicians help design conditions that allow them to use a trick to "read" the ESP cards and collect extra rewards when repeated trials are made to verify original results (see Gardner, 1957, Ch. 25)?

There is nothing in sport sociology to compare to the sorts of crackpot science reviewed above, but we often fall far short of ideal science, and much that passes for sociology might better be considered "false" pseudoscience. Any student of sport sociology should try to discriminate between pseudoscientific thinking and social scientific thinking. Perhaps a critique of two recent articles which, in my opinion, exemplify pseudoscience will help clarify the distinction.

Sports Violence and Male Domination

Michael Messner (1990) sought to connect two meanings of sports violence: "its broader social, cultural and ideological meanings" and "the meanings which athletes construct as participants" (p. 204). Messner sees sports violence as a source of "hegemonic masculinity" (p. 204). Presumably this means that cultural beliefs about men's domination over women in modern societies are sustained partly by sport.

Interviews with a handful of former athletes illustrate the commonplace observation that athletes may demonstrate manly virtues in competition—delivering and taking, violence. This may be easily confirmed in interviews with athletes or in watching how much crowds applaud "big hits" or courageous plays. That is, "meanings which athletes construct" may be understood through social science. "Broader social, cultural, and ideological meanings" appear to be more in the realm of pseudoscience. What sort of evidence would a skeptical scientist require before he or she believed the following statement by Messner?

> It has been suggested here that as cultural symbols, these men serve to stabilize a structure of domination and oppression in the gender order. The media's framing of violent sports as public spectacle serves . . . to unite men in the domination of women. (Messner, 1990, p. 215)

At a minimum a serious scientist would need to know in what ways men dominate women and try to see if communities (or eras) with relatively less violent sports are characterized by less domination of women. Are there communities where boxing, football, and hockey are or were not especially popular? Are women less dominated in these communities? This approach has been used by criminologists to determine the impact of access to guns on violent crime or of the death penalty on homicide.

Messner makes no effort to do this. Rather he seems to "know" that violent sports function to reinforce male domination of women. This sort of science-like activity is not new in sociology. (Messner did good research. Messner had a plausible theory. But he didn't connect the research to the theory!) Fully a half century ago R. M. MacIver, in his classic book *Social Causation* (1942), complained about this sort of thinking in sociology under the aptly named heading "facile imputation":

> Cases or examples [are] offered showing the presence of the alleged cause, as though that were sufficient to establish its causal relation to the social phenomenon. (MacIver, 1942, p. 74)

Improving the Study of Racial Relations in Sport

In a recent article in the *Sociology of Sport Journal,* Susan Birrell (1989) proposes improvements in theoretical approaches to the study of racial relations in sport. Birrell contends that two old approaches are inadequate because of their lack of theoretical sophistication, and two new ones offer promise. It is my view that the two inadequate (in Birrell's view) models are rejected because they stem from social science and her promising ones are attractive because they are pseudoscientific.

The first inadequate approach, *bias,* emphasizes prejudice and discrimination in sport. This approach is chastised for being "atheoretical" or merely descriptive (p. 216). The work, which is thoroughly reviewed in Chapters 7 and 8 in this book, consists of an extensive examination of black-white performance differences in a variety of sports, but mainly major league baseball and NFL and NCAA football. For example, there are few black catchers in baseball, black quarterbacks in football, or black head coaches in either sport. In baseball black batters have historically outhit their white teammates (but in recent years this black superiority has virtually disappeared).

It is fair to say that the absence of black catchers, quarterbacks, or coaches constitutes no more than a collection of facts, but the researchers who uncovered the facts were quick to develop explanations for the facts. Loy and McElvogue (1970) developed one of the most important theories in sport sociology out of these facts (after first satisfying themselves that they were indeed facts). Their *centrality theory* states that the more a playing position requires interaction, leadership, and judgment, the greater the resistance (by white management) to black occupancy of the position. Quarterbacks, catchers, and coaches must interact with others, lead, and exercise judgment. Hence, blacks who might want to occupy these positions face barriers (discrimination).

Loy and McElvogue examined other possible explanations of the facts, such as physical or mental differences between the races or some form of self-selection by young black athletes. These explanations were found wanting by the authors and by many subsequent researchers (see Chapters 7 and 8) because the theories did not fit the facts. The Loy and McElvogue article developed a plausible theory about racial discrimination in sports and examined two other theories that suggested that black-white performance differences might not reflect racial discrimination. Three theories hardly deserve to be called "merely descriptions" or "atheoretical" (Birrell, 1989, p. 216). Indeed the interplay between facts and explanation in the Loy and McElvogue article constitutes one of the best available examples of good social science theory.

The second "inadequate" theoretical perspective is "assimilation theories" (Birrell, 1989, p. 216). This perspective is based on an old idea that immigrant groups pass through a certain sequence of stages—contact, conflict, accommodation, and assimilation (see Park, 1950). Several researchers in sport sociology have looked to see whether sports served to integrate ethnic groups into the mainstream culture or, perhaps, to accentuate cultural identity. For example, Pooley (1981) studied several ethnic soccer clubs in Milwaukee, Wisconsin. He found that these clubs did little to encourage integration among the various European ethnic groups comprising the clubs. Indeed, some clubs had policies aimed at preventing such integration. Hare (1971) studied 58 boxers. Boxing did little to assist the poor black boxer's access to middle-class opportunities. If anything, boxing served to inhibit any educational or occupational mobility by boxers.

Are these kinds of studies a waste of time or, as Birrell implies (see p. 217), somehow bad? The several studies of cultural assimilation ask a question, "Does sport encourage assimilation and, if so, how?" These studies gather facts to provide answers. Like studies of racial discrimination, these studies represent an interplay between ideas (theory) and observations (research). They constitute good social science.

If Birrell dislikes good social science what does she like? Using the previous discussion of science and pseudoscience as a guide, it seems she prefers pseudoscience or what she calls materialist (Marxist) or "cultural" theories, because:

> The culturalist approach focuses upon cultural suppression and cultural hegemony on the one hand (the colonial models applied to the Black experience; the internal colony model applied to Chicanos) and cultural regeneration, cultural survival, or cultural nationalism on the other. (Birrell, 1989, p. 219)

There is a debate between Marxists, who choose to explain everything in terms of the suppression and control of the working class by the bourgeoisie, and the culturalists, who are concerned about ethnic identity and solidarity as well as class conflict.

Contrast the material examined by the "bias" and "assimilation" models—batting averages, playing positions, who one's friends are, off-field occupational and educational opportunities—with the material Birrell says cultural studies theory is supposed to deal with: "cultural hegemony" (see quotation above) "cultural genocide" (p. 219),[1] "contours of the particular relations of dominance and subordination among groups . . ." (p. 220). What do these words mean? What are we supposed to look for to see if these terms are "out there"? How can we tell if statements containing terms like these are true or false?

Theory in science is about observable events that are happening in the world. Birrell's "cultural studies" article argues that wordy statements about the world are preferable even though the words cannot be related to events in the world (show me some cultural hegemony). This sort of thing is pseudoscience in the literal sense of the word. It is like science in many ways. There are theories that say things are related to each other in certain ways. It represents serious thinking and scholarship. *But, it is not open to tests of truth or falsehood.*

There is an old word, *logomachy,* that describes cultural studies as well. One meaning of logomachy is arguing about issues that are irrelevant to the real world, and that can never be settled. Birrell's article represents a part of sport sociology that devotes itself to this type of research rather than to the rigorous search for "truth." This work has produced some good ideas and some lively debate, but it should be seen as something other than social science.

Let us close this section with a look at a review of Gary Fine's *With the Boys* (1987), a highly regarded "participant observation" study of boys in little league baseball. Reviewer Alan Klein (1988), although not a part of the cultural studies/critical theory branch of sport sociology, appears to be influenced by it in his review. I offer two final quotations, the first to illustrate Klein's preference for arguments that cannot be related to real world observation, the second to illustrate his hostility toward those who can.

> The possibility for interesting insights certainly exists. Looking at the coach-spectator-player interaction in Brechtian theatrical sense might have been inter-

> esting. Instead, we are treated to lengthy interviews that reveal to us that coaches "like working with the boys." (Klein, 1988, p. 292)
>
> Fine feels moved to create propositions: "Knowledge and acceptance of a group's idioculture is a necessary and sufficient condition for distinguishing members of a group from nonmembers." And further, "A group becomes significantly less open when a nonmember is present. Groups attempt to hide their idioculture until it is believed that the newcomer can be trusted not to reveal the secrets of the group." . . . The only thing worse than the callow nature of these statements is his presumption that they constitute social scientific propositions. (Klein, 1988, p. 292)

Social science is often "callow" when compared to pseudoscience. Rigorous social science should be separated from work that relies more on intuition, tenacity, and authority.

The Meaning of Sport

So far this chapter has discussed the meaning of sociology in terms of the sorts of things it studies and the scientific approach by which sociology is (or should be) disciplined. Let us devote some attention to the second term in *The Sociology of Sport.*

In one sense the word *sport* need not be analyzed. Anyone who speaks English knows what sport is and is not. No special definition of sport is used in this or any other book about sport. Nonetheless, students of sport sociology find it useful to think seriously about what is and is not sport. Visitors at Yosemite National Park agree that climbing to the top of Half Dome (a 16-mile round trip with a climb of some 4,600 feet) is sport. Walking through the Yosemite valley to see the wonderful sights it offers is not sport. The two activities differ in many ways. Climbing to Half Dome requires a lot of effort, some planning, and even some danger. Although no special talent or skill is required, many fail to make it to the top. Anyone can walk around the valley. No one "fails" at this effort. There is no challenge, no special skill, and no special effort required.

A rock climber is clearly engaged in sport. Should the climber get hurt, rescuers would not be engaging in sport even if they climb the same rock face. The climber is testing his or her skill and determination against a standard of excellence. The climber is acting freely and voluntarily, seeking enjoyment. Rescuers would appear to be doing much the same thing as the climber, but they would have no sense of "fair play." Rather, rescuers would use any means to get up the rock, including dangling a rope from the top. Rescuers would be at work. Failure would probably mean death or serious injury for someone, not simply having to retreat down the rock. The rescue would not be fun. Rather it would be hard, dangerous work.

In what ways do the climbers (sport) differ from walkers and rescuers (nonsport)? Table 2–1 provides a list of differences. The reader may want to add to this list after

TABLE 2–1 Some Distinguishing Characteristics of Sport

Sport	Nonsport
Voluntary participation (fun)	More obligatory (job)
Intrinsic reward important	Extrinsic reward more important
Physical skill and exertion	May or may not require these (e.g., chess, moving furniture)
Competition against an opponent or standard of achievement (e.g., par in golf)	Usually routine work, no competition
Some doubt as to outcome	Uncertainty minimized
Consequences (win or lose) limited	Failure could mean financial ruin (e.g., business competition) or injury (e.g., war, fire fighting)
Time bound (beginning, end clearly defined)	Not bound by time

NOTE: Training for sports which is routine and rarely intrinsically rewarding is like "work" but is clearly "sport." Professional positions—coaching, professional play—mix sport and nonsport. World series winners don't *pretend* to be excited, and the excitement isn't over the winner's share of the money.

reflecting on other examples of activities that are sports (e.g., football, white-water rafting, gymnastics) and activities that are like sport but are not (e.g., aerial combat in war, commercial fishing, playing bridge).

The Development of Sport

Trying to draw a line between activities that are and are not sport is one way to define sport. Another way to "define" sport is to trace the development of sport through Western history and across a variety of civilizations. Norbert Elias (1971) contends that sport as we know it did not exist until the early 19th century, and that sport was "invented" in England and then diffused throughout Europe and the rest of the world. The so-called "sports" of medieval Europe and ancient Greece and Rome (e.g., the Ancient Olympic Games) were not sport in the modern sense. Medieval jousting not sport? Ancient Greek racing, wrestling, or throwing contests not sport? A claim like this deserves some attention!

Elias supports his claim with a description of some ancient Greek contests which, when observed closely, indeed do not fit our modern understanding of sport. Let us start with a description of modern professional boxing, a sport that is not really a sport in the eyes of many people. Boxers are almost sure to suffer brain damage from the force of the blows they suffer. Blows to the head move the skull but not the brain, just as the yolk of a raw egg remains stationary when you spin the shell. Capillaries are broken and brain damage ensues. Less severe but more apparent damage to eyes and skin (scars), as well as the economic exploitation of boxers by the industry, adds to the ugly image of boxing.

However crude or brutal modern boxing is, it does not compare to ancient boxing.

Modern boxers are protected by a matching system, which reduces mismatches somewhat, by gloves, by required medical clearances, by a three knockdown or ten-second knockout rule, by a technical knockout rule in the case of injuries, by three-minute rounds, and by a limit on the number of rounds. Compare ancient boxing:

> One did not distinguish between different classes of boxers. One did not try, therefore, to match people according to their weight either in this or in any other contests. The only distinction made was that between boys and men. Boxers did not only fight with their fists. As in almost all older forms of boxing, the legs played a part in the struggle. Kicking the shins of an opponent was a normal part of the boxing tradition. . . . Only the hand and the upper parts of four fingers were bound with leather thongs fastened to the forearm. Fists could be clenched or fingers stretched and, with hard nails, rammed into the opponent's body and face. As time went on, soft leather thongs gave way to harder thongs specially made from tanned ox-hide. These were then fitted with several strips of hard thick leather with sharp projecting edges. (Elias, 1971, p. 100)

Ancient boxers stood toe-to-toe. As with the warrior ethic of the time retreat was unthinkable. Better to be crushed by one's opponent than to back away. This spirit served well in warfare, where a break in formation would expose all to the swords and spears of the enemy, but a tight formation would enhance the safety of all. This "no retreat" practice, coupled with almost no limits on the level of violence, frequently led to death or serious injury:

> We hear of two boxers who agreed to exchange blow for blow. The first struck a blow to the head which his opponent survived. When he lowered his guard, the other man struck him under the ribs with his outstretched fingers, burst through his side with his hard nails, seized his bowels and killed him. (Elias, 1971, p. 102)

Elias also mentions *pancration,* a contest which we might recognize as "catch as catch can" professional wrestling, except that pancration was not staged, but real. Kicking, breaking of fingers, arms and legs, or choking the opponent were all lawful. This level of violence, along with an absence of strict rules to regulate it, separates these contests from "the type of contest we nowadays characterize as 'sport'" (Elias, 1971, p. 99).

Not all of the traditional Greek "sports" were as violent as boxing and pancration. Wrestling (Greco-Roman), running, jumping, and throwing also were contested—and still are in modern track-and-field sports. Even these might best be seen as separate from our present understanding of sport. Athletics was highly professionalized. The very word *athletics* refers to competing for a prize (Huizinga, 1950, p. 51). All of the classical events (e.g., javelin, discus, long jumping, sprinting, shot put) had clear military applications in ancient times. The only sports today that have a clear military

FIGURE 2–1 A close look at this third century B.C. bronze statute of an ancient Greek boxer reveals the brutality of boxing at that time. This boxer, presumably a victor, has a broken nose, a cauliflower ear, and missing teeth, probably from previous bouts. The boxer has several recent injuries—lacerations on his nose, his cheekbone, over his eye, below the hairline, and on his already scarred ear. As brutal as modern boxing may be, one or two of these injuries would have ended the fight with a technical knockout. Given the condition of this boxer's nose and ear, he would probably be barred from the sport today.

(Photograph from Hyde, 1921, p. 146)

application are orienteering (running and map reading) and biathlon (cross-country skiing combined with marksmanship) (see Figure 2–2). Neither is a "big time" sport, even though biathlon is contested in the modern Winter Olympic Games. Ancient Greek sports also had a religious link. Book 23 of the Iliad relates the funeral of Patroclus and the games contested in his honor. This account provides a good description of the kinds of contests that Greeks competed in. The famous "games"

FIGURE 2–2 In contrast to classical Greek game contests, few modern sports have a practical connection to "real life" skills. Biathlon (skiing and shooting) has a military application, and police dog trials have a clear connection to police work. Other sports are practiced for their own sake, not for their relevance to role skills.

(Courtesy Manteca Police Department, Manteca, CA)

of ancient Greece "at Olympia, on the Isthmus, at Delphi and Nemea" (Huizinga, 1950, p. 73) were contested in honor of the gods. These links to war and to religion separate even the noncombative ancient Greek "sports" from sport as we know it.

So ancient Greco-Roman contests do not fit our conception of sport. But the claim that it is a 19th century English cultural "invention" that diffused to Europe and the world requires a lot more examination. Eric Dunning (1971) provides it in a discussion of the development of modern football from the wild folk contests of the past to the well-ordered games of rugby and soccer.

Rules, even those defining winning and losing, were rather vague in folk football. Games were not played between matched teams but between members of natural social units—married men vs. bachelors, students vs. townies, guild vs. guild, village vs. village. Team size was not defined, so the number of players on each side could be different. With goals sometimes miles apart, and with dozens of players for close-in defense, outscoring an opponent or scoring at all was unlikely. Rather, the tough, somewhat unorganized game offered members of rival groups a convenient way to join the fray and probably to settle a score or two.

> In the year 1579, for example, a group of Cambridge students went, as was customary, to the village of Chesterton to play "at foteball." They went there, so we are told, peacefully and without any weapons but the townsmen of Chesterton had secretly hidden a number of sticks in the porch of their church. After the match had started, they picked quarrels with the students, brought out their sticks, broke them over the heads of the students and gave them such a severe beating that they had to run through the river in order to escape. Some of them asked the Constable of Chesterton to keep the "Queene's peace" but he was among those playing against them and, in fact, accused the students of being first to break the peace. (Elias & Dunning, 1971, p. 123)

This amorphous, sometimes violent game-contest did not really become a sport until it was "civilized" in the English public (i.e., private) schools. These schools, officially accessible to all boys but in practice available only to the wealthy elite, were located in the countryside. School boys had the opportunity to observe the local folk football games of the time, and to adapt them to school conditions. Games came to be played on a regular basis (Dunning, 1971, p. 135). The older boys or "prefects" ran the games, which, while they varied from school to school, generally could be described as mass pushing and shoving contests.

This wild game, now confined to school grounds, was limited by the peculiarities of each school. Hence "football in the cloisters" at Charterhouse School was played in an area "seventy yards long by twelve feet wide, paved with smooth flagstones" (Dunning, 1971, p. 137) and surrounded by stone walls with buttresses protruding into the area. Goals were rare. Rather it was the struggle that counted. Even at this early stage, Dunning says, significant "civilization" had taken place. There was *some* authority (older boys); the game was played in a regular season, and the contest was constrained in space (school facilities) and time (had to fit with the school schedule).

The real "civilization" of the game occurred during the 1830s at Rugby School under the headmastership of Thomas Arnold. Arnold saw games as a tool for the building of character. To achieve this, Arnold made the older boys (the prefects) his lieutenants, with the duty of serving as exemplars of Rugby School's "Christian gentleman" ideal. Football, with its hard knocks, became a situation in which courage and character could be developed, with the older boys enforcing the rules and proper conduct. Soon school rules were committed to writing. *The game and its administration had been removed from the control of immediate players. Rules were no longer traditional, but written. The game was constrained to "fit in" to the needs of the school*—gentlemanly conduct, the need to return to class, restraint (especially self-restraint) in the heat of competition, the size of the playing field (see Dunning, 1971, pp. 136–145).

Once rules were committed to paper by senior people in a position to enforce them, and once these rules included self-restraint (unsportsmanlike conduct is a major

EXHIBIT 2–1 Hurlinge to the Countrie

Richard Carew's delightful description of the wild contest from which the relatively civilized sport of rugby originated (Carew, 1602; quoted in Elias and Dunning, 1971, pp. 127–129) illustrates how hurlinge was and was not like sport. Note especially the absence of rules, rule enforcement, and the potential for the contest to resemble a moving brawl more than a sporting event.

Hurlinge to the Countrie

The hurlinge to the Countrie, is more diffuse and confuse, as bound to few of these orders: Some two or more Gentlemen doe commonly make this match, appointing that on such a holyday, they will bring to such an indifferent place, two, three, or more parishes of the East or South quarter, to hurle against so many other, of the West or North. Their goales are either those Gentlemens houses, or some townes or villages, three or four miles asunder, of which either side maketh choice after the neernesse to their dwellings. When they meet, there is neyther comparing of numbers, nor matching of men: but a silver ball is cast up, and that company, which can catch, and cary it by force, or sleight, to their place assigned, gaineth the ball and victory. Whosoever getteth seizure of this ball, findeth himself generally pursued by the adverse party; neither will they leave, till (without all respects) he be layd flat on Gods deare earth: which fall once received, disableth him from any longer detayning the ball: hee therefore throweth the same . . . to some one of his fellowes, fardest before him, who maketh away withall in like maner. Such as see where the ball is played, give notice thereof to their mates, crying, Ware East, Ware West, etc. as the same is carried.

The Hurlers take their next way over hilles, dales, hedges, ditches; yea, and thorow bushes, briers, mires, plashes and rivers whatsoever; so as you shall sometimes see 20, or 30 lie tugging together in the water, scrambling and scratching for the ball. A play (verily) both rude and rough, and yet such, as is not destitute of policies, in some sort resembling the feats of warre: for you shall have companies layd out before, on the one side, to encounter them that come with the ball, and of the other party to succor them, in the maner of a foreward. Againe, other troups lye hovering on the sides, like wings, to helpe or stop their escape: and where the ball it selfe goeth, it resembleth the joyning of the two mayne battles: the slowest footed who come lagge, supply the showe of a rere-ward: yea, there are horsemen placed also on either party (as it were in ambush) and ready to ride away with the ball, if they can catch it at advantage. But they must not so steale the palme: for gallop any one of them never so fast, yet he shall be surely met at some hedge corner, crosse-lane, bridge, or deep water, which (by casting the Countrie) they know he must needs touch at: and if his good fortune gard him not the better, hee is likely to pay the price of his theft, with his owne and his horses overthrowe to the ground. Sometimes, the whole company runneth with the ball, seven or eight miles out of the direct way, which they should keepe. Sometimes a foote-man getting it by stealth, the better to scape unespied, will carry the same quite backwards, and so, at last, get to the goale by a windlace: which once knowne to be wonne, all that side flocke thither with great jolity: and if the same bee a Gentlemans house, they give him the ball for a Trophee, and the drinking out of his Beere to boote.

The ball in this play may bee compared to an infernall spirit: for whosoever catcheth it, fareth straightwayes like a madde man, strugling and fighting with those that goe

EXHIBIT 2–1 *Continued*

about to holde him: and no sooner is the ball gone from him, but he resigneth this fury to the next receyver, and himselfe becommeth peaceable as before. I cannot well resolve, whether I should more commend this game, for the manhood and exercise, or condemne it for the boysterousnes and harmes which it begetteth: for as on the one side it makes their bodies strong, hard, and nimble, and puts a courage into their hearts, to meete an enemie in the face: so on the other part, it is accompanied with many dangers, some of which so ever fall to the players share. For proofe whereof, when the hurling is ended, you shall see them retyring home, as from a pitched battaile, with bloody pates, bones broken, and out of joynt, and such bruses as serve to shorten their daies; yet al is good play, and never Attourney nor Crowner troubled for the matter.

violation in virtually all modern sports) and limited violent behavior (so that hopefully no one would be too injured to return to class), the game of football had become, in the modern sense, a "sport." If Dunning is correct, this did not happen until the middle of the 19th century.

The contention that the term "sport" is an English cultural form is buttressed somewhat by a look at European languages. The German word for "sport" is *sport*. The French word for "sport" is *sport*. The same in Russian. The Spanish *deporte* took on a new meaning in the 19th century to accommodate the English word *sport*. The English game of football, or as we know it, soccer, was adopted throughout Europe during the 19th century, and the term "football" was absorbed more or less unchanged along with the game (Elias, 1971, pp. 88–90). According to a standard etymological dictionary of the German language, "the word 'sport' was first used in German . . . in 1828, and the first sports club in Germany was founded in Hamburg in 1830—a rowing club established, significantly, by the British community there" (Mornin, 1976, p. 279).

The variety of human cultures almost guarantees that there are local contests and activities in non-European cultures that qualify as sport. Still many of the more famous—judo (before it was Westernized), sumo, Native American lacrosse, Polynesian fighting sports—all have economic, religious, military, or even political meanings that are not associated with modern sport (see Frederickson, 1960; Damm, 1970; and Dunlap, 1951, for discussions of non-Western "sports").

Inside Sport: The Play Element

Whatever the importance of modern sporting events (playoff games, big money bowls, international contests), however seriously participants may prepare, and whatever divine help they pray for, sport involves a strong element of *play*. The Minnesota Twins, jumping and cheering after their victory in the 1991 World Series, were not celebrating the money they had earned. These professionals, at least for the moment, were celebrating victory in a game. Other issues were, for the time, not relevant. The same goes for members of a national soccer team celebrating a goal in World Cup competition.

Sport must be playful or it becomes work, as in the case of the rock climbers and rescuers. Roger Caillois (1969) provides a good discussion of playfulness as a part of the meaning of sport. Caillois begins by discussing Huizinga's (1950) discussion of play. Play may be seen as:

> A free activity standing quite consciously outside "ordinary" life. . . . It is an activity connected with no material interest and no profit can be gained from it. It proceeds within its own proper boundaries of time and space according to fixed rules. (Huizinga, 1950, p. 13)

Huizinga, by the way, doubts that modern sport, with its professionalism and serious, systematic training and organization, qualifies as play (pp. 197–198). However, a look at victors and losers in even the most serious of sporting events, such as world championship baseball or soccer, shows a clear element of playfulness as Huizinga discussed it.

Caillois contends that play takes many forms but may be described in terms of four motives for play. He restricted his discussion to play, but these motives seem to fit more serious sports as well.

Âgon, a Greek word, relates to struggle or contest. The meaning of âgon may be found in English words in which it appears (e.g., agony, antagonism). Activities such as racing or lifting weights are sporting activities that reflect the motive of âgon. *Alea,* a Latin word meaning dice, refers to chance. No sports are purely controlled by chance, but none are free of the element of chance. The uncertainty associated with sports—a bad day for the opposing pitcher, a lucky rebound of a hockey puck—makes sports more exciting for spectators and more demanding for players, who must be able to cope with the unexpected. *Mimicry,* based on a Greek word meaning imitation or pretense, refers to pretending. The role of pretending in play is obvious, but it plays a role in sport as well. The uniforms, pomp and circumstance, and team spirit involved in sport all seem to fit under mimicry. The bluffs, fakes, threats, and psych jobs that appear in competition also are mimicry. Professional wrestling, which is not a sport because there is no competition involved, is all mimicry—and so good that many fans half believe that it is real. Finally, *ilinx,* a Greek word for whirlpool, describes the pursuit of vertigo, the disorientation that comes from spinning, somersaulting, or falling. This motive is clear in play activities ranging from swinging on a rope and dropping into a swimming hole to some kinds of drug use (e.g., the "rush" from cocaine), but this, like the other three motives, plays some role in sports too. Vertigo, under control, is an important part of such activities as skiing, surfing, river rafting, and high-speed driving, but activities such as running at top speed or falling or seeing one's opponents rapidly approaching can induce a feeling of vertigo. The feeling is at least briefly pleasurable, although it must be controlled if the athlete is to remain successful and safe.

Along with the four motives of play, Caillois introduces a dimension of organization or rationality. *Paidia* refers to childlike, frivolous, impulsive, and unorganized playfulness. ***Ludus*** refers to serious, ordered play. Activities under ***âgon, alea, mimicry,*** or ***ilinx*** may be placed on a continuum ranging from the frivolous ***paidia*** to the more ordered ***ludus***. How would such sports as golf, boxing, basketball, or figure skating be described? To what extent is golf characterized by âgon? alea? mimicry? ilinx? Where does golf fall on the continuum between frivolous ***paidia*** and orderly *ludus?* What about the experience of casual touch-football players, or the rock climbers and rescuers mentioned at the beginning of this chapter? Sports may be described in terms of Caillois' scheme, and sports may be separated from similar, but nonsport activities via this scheme. In this respect Caillois' scheme provides another way to define sport.

The Sociology of Sport

Given a knowledge of what sport is and what sociology is, the meaning of sociology of sport should be obvious. In fact it is not. Subsequent chapters will provide a "definition" of the sociology of sport, but textbooks make the field seem more well defined than it really is.

A recent review of the contents of a major sociology of sport journal, the *International Review for the Sociology of Sport* (Heinemann & Preuss, 1990), suggests that the field, in practice, defies any facile definition. After reviewing the contents of a quarter century's worth of articles in the *IRSS* the authors conclude:

> In spite of our careful multiple collection of data as well as our efforts to construct a typology, hardly any systematically definable focal issues could be ascertained. The sociology of sport presents itself as an extremely diffuse subject which cannot be described by determining a limited set of focal issues. (Heinemann & Preuss, 1990, p. 8)

Articles from a variety of theoretical and philosophical viewpoints appear. Many different countries are represented. Indeed, in no other field of sociology can students be so exposed to scholarship from such a variety of countries (a recent issue had authors from Holland, Finland, Belgium, the United States, Korea, Germany, Hungary, and New Zealand). While most modern sports appear at one time or another in the articles, the emphasis is on organized sports. Unorganized "sandlot" sports and traditional ethnic sports played around the world do not receive a lot of attention (see Heinemann & Preuss, 1990, pp. 5–6).

The Heinemann and Preuss review provides a good picture of the sociology of sport. The field is still developing. Many research issues have yet to be tackled. Different perspectives are welcome. Newcomers, including students, who are willing to engage in the sometimes tedious work of research, can produce useful ideas and information in the sociology of sport. The field offers some good sociology and, through this, a deeper understanding of sport.

Summary

Sociology grew out of the social disruptions of the 18th and 19th centuries. Scholars wanted to discover what produced such cataclysms as wars and revolutions. Emile Durkheim was among the first to apply the scientific method to discover the causes of social phenomena, most notably the suicide rate. Likewise, the work of Richard LaPiere sought to understand the nature of racial prejudice through this method.

Not all of sociology adheres to the discipline required by science. A lot of the sociology of sport literature might be better characterized as philosophy or moralization than as social science. Social science is distinguished by statements and ideas that are carefully crafted to allow empirical testing to determine their truth or falsehood. Social science is also characterized by skepticism, a readiness to disprove ideas, rather than by tenacity, a desire to retain one's beliefs even in the face of contrary evidence.

Some of the work in sport sociology can be characterized as pseudoscience, resembling science in some ways but rejecting it in others. This work is often interesting, even exciting, but it should not be confused with social science.

The idea of sport as we know it has existed only since the early 19th century. Many people have tried to define the meaning of sport. Sport involves competition, rules, and playfulness. Consequences of winning or losing are limited; thus, professional sports are more like work than sport. Elias and Dunning have shown how wild, often violent games of ancient and medieval times were "domesticated" to become rule bound, nonviolent, and "just for fun."

Sport sociology studies the phenomenon of sport from a variety of perspectives. This young field has yet to develop a shared understanding of what its boundaries and central concerns should be.

Note

1. The term genocide is especially offensive to me. I have several friends from Cambodia. The use of "genocide" in the way Birrell speaks of it trivializes a word that represents the monstrous cruelty many of my friends experienced.

References

Alvarez, W., and Asaro, F. (1990). Extraterrestrial impact. *Scientific American, 263* (4), 78–84.

Attorney-General's Commission on Pornography. (1986). *Report to the Attorney General.* Washington, DC: Government Printing Office.

Becker, H. S., and Horowitz, I. L. (1972). Radical politics and sociological research: Observations on methodology and ideology. *American Journal of Sociology, 78,* 48–66.

Birrell, S. (1989). Racial relations theories and sport: Suggestions for a more critical analysis. *Sociology of Sport Journal, 6,* 212–227.

Caillois, R. (1969). The structure and classification of games. In J. W. and G. S. Kenyon, Eds., *Sport*

Culture and Society. Toronto: MacMillan, pp. 44–55.

Cohen, M. R., and Nagel, E. (1934). *An Introduction to Logic and Scientific Method.* London: Routledge and Kegan Paul.

Courtillot, V. E. (1990). A volcanic eruption. *Scientific American, 263* (4), 85–92.

Damm, H. (1970). The so-called sport activities of primitive people: A contribution toward the genesis of sport, trans. G. Luschen and R. Keenan. In G. Luschen, Ed., *The Cross-Cultural Analysis of Sport and Games.* Champaign, IL: Stipes, pp. 52–69.

Dempsey, J., and Dempsey, B. P. (1977). The destruction of a giant: How I beat Jess Willard. *American Heritage, 28* (3), 72–83.

Dunlap, H. (1951). Games, sport, dancing, and other recreational activities and their function in Somoan culture. *The Research Quarterly, 22,* 298–311.

Dunning, E. (1971). The development of modern football. In E. Dunning, Ed., *Sport: Readings from a Sociological Perspective.* Toronto: University of Toronto, pp. 133–151.

Durkheim, E. (1938). *The Rules of Sociological Method,* trans. S. A. Soloray and J. H. Mueller. Edited by G. E. G. Catlin. New York: The Free Press. (Original work published 1895.)

Durkheim, E. (1951). *Suicide,* trans. J. A. Spaulding and G. Simpson. New York: The Free Press. (Original work published in 1897.)

Elias, N. (1971). The genesis of sport as a sociological problem. In E. Dunning, Ed., *Sport: Readings from a Sociological Perspective.* Toronto: University of Toronto, pp. 88–115.

Elias, N., and Dunning, E. (1971). Folk football in medieval and early modern Britain. In E. Dunning, Ed., *Sport: Readings from a Sociological Perspective.* Toronto: University of Toronto, pp. 116–132.

Fine, G. A. (1987). *With the Boys.* Chicago: University of Chicago.

Frederickson, F. S. (1960). Sports and the Cultures of Man. In W. R. Johnson, Ed., *Science, and Medicine of Exercise and Sports.* New York: Harper, pp. 643–646.

Gardner, M. (1957). *Fads and Fallacies in the Name of Science.* New York: Dover.

Hare, N. (1971). A study of the black fighter. *The Black Scholar, 3* (November), 2–8.

Heinemann, K., and Preuss, W. (1990). 25 years of the *International Review for the Sociology of Sport*—a content analysis. *International Review for the Sociology of Sport, 23,* 3–18.

Horgan, J. (1990). Death watch. *Scientific American, 262* (6), 22–25.

Horowitz, D. (1971). *Radical Sociology.* San Francisco: Canfield Press.

Huizinga, J. (1950). *Homo Ludens: A Study of the Play Element in Culture.* Boston: Beacon Press.

Hyde, W. W. (1921). *Olympic Victor Monuments and Greek Athletic Art.* Washington, DC: Carnegie Institution.

Klein, A. M. (1988). Review of *With the Boys,* by G. A. Fine. *Sociology of Sport Journal, 5,* 290–293.

LaPiere, R. T. (1934). Attitudes vs. actions. In I. Deutscher, Ed. (1973). *What we say/what we do.* Glenview, IL: Scott, Foresman, pp. 14–21.

Loy, J. W. (1969). The nature of sport: A definitional effort. In J. W. Loy and G. S. Kenyon, Eds., *Sport, Culture and Society.* New York: MacMillan, pp. 56–71.

Loy, J. W., and McElvogue, J. F. (1970). Racial segregation in American sport. *International Review of Sport Sociology, 5,* 5–23.

MacIver, R. M. (1942). *Social causation.* Boston: Ginn.

Messner, M. A. (1990). When bodies are weapons: Masculinity and violence in sport. *International Review for the Sociology of Sport, 25,* 203–220.

Mornin, E. (1976). Taking games seriously: Observations on the German sports novel. *The Germanic Review, 51,* 278–295.

Park, R. (1950). *Race and Culture.* New York: The Free Press.

Polsky, N. (1967). *Hustlers, Beats, and Others.* Chicago: Aldine.

Pooley, J. (1981). Ethnic soccer clubs in Milwaukee: A study of assimilation. In M. Hart and S. Birrell, Eds., *Sport in the Sociocultural Process,* 3rd ed. Dubuque, IA: Wm. C. Brown, pp. 430–477.

Chapter 3

Sport and Culture

The concept of culture plays an important role in many of the main theoretical orientations in sociology. Criminologists suspect that criminal behavior may reflect the values of a society or a part of a society. Robert Merton (1938) argued that the cultural value placed on material wealth in Western societies may encourage crime (some form of stealing or illegal business) among those who do not have access to lawful means of pursuing material wealth but still are driven to pursue it. That certain forms of criminal behavior might be encouraged by class of ethnic subcultures is suggested by several sociologists, most notably Cohen (1955). If the volume and kinds of criminal behavior can be influenced by cultural factors, is it not probable that the volume and kinds of sports behavior may also be influenced by culture?

Let us look at a recent study that shows that sport is indeed affected by culture. Any sport such as soccer or basketball is standard throughout the world insofar as rules, equipment, and technique are concerned. But styles of play and off-field practices may vary dramatically from society to society.

A study by Maria Allison and Guenther Lueschen (1979) provides an illustration of this. Allison and Lueschen observed the basketball play of Navaho and white high school players in the Southwestern United States. The Navaho culture retains its vitality in Arizona, thanks to the existence of a substantial Navaho community on a large reservation. While formal rules and coaching practices made competitive basketball largely the same for both groups, less formal "pick-up" games appeared to be substantially influenced by the cultures of the participants. In contrast to the white players, whose informal play closely approximated official basketball—fouls and violations were called and evenly matched teams played to win—Navaho pick-up games involved individuals taking shots more than matched teams competing. Given this lack of competition, rules such as traveling and out of bounds were not enforced. That is to say, the Navaho players avoided contest (*âgon, ludus*) in their informal play in favor of play (*paidia*).[1]

Navaho culture even influenced play in competitive interscholastic contests. Navaho players, according to Allison and Lueschen, avoided the physical aspects of the game (setting screens, blocking out on rebounds) in favor of a "finesse" game (p. 81), and although this occurred on and off the court, boys who became recognized as stars were put back in their place (equal to one's peers) through a variety of social devices, including rumors of witchcraft (p. 78). The Navaho norms that discourage openly excelling over one's peers and openly competing in activity that leaves a "victor and vanquished" do not fit well with competitive "Anglo" sports like basketball.

Culture

Before we move to some more specific studies of sport and culture, we should define the meaning of culture. Lower animals rely on instinct, biologically programmed behavior patterns, to provide for their survival. How to get food, provide shelter, find a mate, nurture their young, and keep safe from predators is preprogrammed. Anyone who has tried to teach tricks to a duck must be amazed at a duck's ability to migrate thousands of miles, build nests, and care for newly hatched ducklings. Higher animals rely less on instinct and more on learning acquired during a relatively lengthy period of youth and dependency. Hence a bear cub remains under the protection of its mother for about two years before it strikes out on its own. Human beings, like other primates, are virtually helpless at birth and remain highly dependent for many years. Among humans the learning that takes place constitutes everything a child knows and does. Humans have no instincts to guide behavior. Left alone save for a minimum of physical care and feeding, a human child will not become "human." Rather, he or she will have no adaptive skills at all, as the few tragic cases of isolated children show (Davis, 1940, 1947).

Human beings rely completely on culture to guide the ways of acting, thinking and feeling that allow them to survive. Culture may be defined as:

> . . . the sum total of integrated learned behavior patterns which are characteristic of members of a society. (Hoebel, 1958, p. 7)

This definition points out several important aspects of culture: 1) culture is shared among members of a society and, therefore, characterizes it; 2) culture is a global concept, a "sum total"; 3) culture is integrative—the "parts" of culture make sense in terms of one another; and 4) culture is learned. No part of culture is inherited or natural, even though it may seem that way. As much as this definition does say about culture, it does not say much about the *content* of culture. For this we turn to another discussion of the idea.

James Vander Zanden (1965) adds some content to Hoebel's rather vague definition (see pp. 50–63). For Vander Zanden, culture consists of values, norms, symbols, and beliefs. These four concepts are relatively easy to "pin down" and to measure with some precision, thereby allowing the concept of culture to be discussed in a systematic way.

Values are what we consider to be good or important in life. Americans are said to value, among other things, material wealth, achievement, rationality, work and activity, democracy, and humanitarianism (Vander Zanden, 1965, pp. 57–59). It takes little imagination to see how North American sports "fit" into this set of values. *Norms* may best be considered "rules" or guidelines for appropriate behavior. Norms, like values, may be measured via interviews with people about correct conduct in different settings, but they really exist outside the individual in the form of social pressure exerted against a person who publicly violates norms. To see these pressures in action, try eating your next meal with your fingers. *Symbols* refer to things that stand for other things. I make some marks on this page, "apple," and these marks, while inedible, bring to mind something that is good to eat. Words are symbols—sounds or markings that stand for something else. Groups of words organized according to certain patterns constitute language, one of the central (and most easily studied) aspects of any culture. *Beliefs* might better be termed knowledge, things everybody involved in a given culture knows. Breaking the idea of culture into values, norms, symbols, and beliefs sacrifices some of the holistic meaning of the concept, but it does make the term a lot easier to use in research. Many sociologists would add *material culture* to the definition of culture. The things people create are seen equally as important as values, norms, symbols, and beliefs. Others contend that it is nonmaterial culture in the form of norms and knowledge that gives meaning to things and their proper use.

Does Culture Influence Sport? Magic

The previous chapter reviewed the argument that sport is an English cultural form that arose in the English public school system, and then was diffused throughout British society and into other European societies. Sport became known worldwide through contacts between European colonial residents and local people. However, remember that culture is integrative. One "part" of culture only makes sense in the context of other parts. Sport sociology (and anthropology) provides some fascinating examples of European sports being adapted to "fit" the values, norms, symbols, and beliefs of other cultural traditions.

Zulu Football

Put aside for the moment the belief that "you make your own luck" and the notion that random breaks in life, good or bad, even out in the long run. Assume instead a belief that *nothing* happens by chance. Random or unpredictable events, like bad hops in baseball, an ill-timed injury to a star player, or a lucky goal in soccer, are not random at all. They are all *caused* by supernatural forces.[2] Assume also a belief that there are professionals who possess the talent and training to affect, maybe even control, these events. How might a person who *believes* these two assumptions explain the "breaks" that so often influence the outcome of sports such as soccer and baseball, especially if the games are hotly contested?

In an observational study of Zulu soccer teams in Durban, South Africa, Scotch (1961) found a widespread employment of sorcery by team officials. Sorcery was a regular part of traditional Zulu culture, much as religion is a regular part of Western culture. The individualism, competition, and material wealth associated with city life is not regulated by traditional Zulu culture. Thus a lot of interpersonal conflicts and resentments break out. One means of "getting back" at offending parties is employment of a sorcerer, or *inyanga,* who will help his client and/or harm his client's enemy.

Enter soccer, a sport passionately followed by the Zulu of South Africa. The league Scotch studied would be recognizable to us as semiprofessional. Talented players were scouted and induced to join clubs. Trainers (coaches) were hired to acquire and develop good players to win games rather than "to have fun playing." Soccer players recognize that an inferior team may, with good luck, beat or at least tie a better team. Good shots may go over the bar or just miss the goal for one team, while a lucky bounce may allow a goal for the other. A star player may sustain an injury in practice or just have a "bad day" in an important match. Luck is a part of soccer.

If luck is a part of soccer, then it would be prudent to employ a professional who can control luck. In Zulu culture this is the role of the inyanga. A Zulu informant explained part of the job of the inyanga:

> All the football teams have their own *inyanga* who doctors them all for each match. The night before a match they must "camp" together around a fire. They all sleep there together, they must stay naked and they are given umuthi and other medicines by the *inyanga*. Incisions are made on their knees, elbows, and joints. In the morning they are made to vomit. They must all go together on the same bus to the match, and they must enter the playing grounds together. Almost every team I know has an inyanga and does this—it is necessary to win. Even though players are Christians and have lived in towns for a long time, they do it, and believe in it. (Scotch, 1961, p. 23. Italics in original.)

Along with pregame protective magic a team's inyanga is expected to determine whether a player has been bewitched because, whatever his skill, a player's luck may go bad at critical moments. Finally, the inyanga is expected, unofficially, to bewitch opposing teams. The need for protective magic demonstrates the fact that inyangas from opposing teams can and will influence the luck of the opposition. A losing team will fire its inyanga, not its coach. Teams in a league are fairly evenly matched, so it is reasonable to suspect that consistent winners and losers were probably influenced for good or ill by sorcery.

Scotch contends that the pregame ritual reflects the traditional ceremonies among Zulu soldiers on the eve of battle (p. 73). This, along with other evidence (e.g., Elias and Dunning's description of folk football and Ancient Greek "sports"), suggests that ritual surrounding some sports may be rooted in archaic warfare practices. We will return to this issue later.

Hopi Baseball

The Hopi are a Native American people who live in Arizona and New Mexico. Traditional Hopi life concentrates the entire community in a small pueblo. Hopi culture forbids the open expression of anger or hostility, leading outsiders to view them as an extraordinarily peaceful, affable people. J. R. Fox (1961) begins by observing that the absence of publicly expressed hostility does not mean there is no hostility. Most Hopi, like most Zulu, are concerned with witchcraft, and open expression of anger is a good way to get bewitched or be accused of practicing witchcraft. The apparent placidity of Hopi pueblo life is the result of several overlapping social institutions that suppress the expression of hostility. The witchcraft institution itself helps, but families (thanks to a rule requiring marriage out of one's clan), clans, *Kivas* (religious societies), and church groups have members from all factions and serve to suppress any continuing cleavages by "cooling out" disputes before they grow.

A single baseball team, the Redskins, had long represented the pueblo and, in typical fashion, contained players representing all groups in the pueblo. The introduction of a second team, the Braves, created a potentially dangerous situation—the two pueblo teams would meet a number of times each season in open competition, which, of course, Hopi institutions avoid in favor of intergroup cooperation. Baseball, however, was not a Hopi institution. It reflected the Western (European) comfort with open competition. To further complicate matters, baseball is as well suited as any sport for eliciting accusations of witchcraft. The bad hop, the good pitcher with "bad stuff" on a given day, the timely hit or untimely pop out, and the critical error are bound to happen during a season. Recall, though, that *nothing happens by chance,* and *"luck" results from human agency* in the form of sorcery.

Not only did baseball require the Hopi to meet in a competitive situation, but the teams had formed along lines of half-forgotten family rivalries:

> The Braves when they broke away from the Redskins, broke away by family groups. . . . It seems . . . that there have always been, within living memory, two ill-defined groups of extended families which formed opposing "blocks" on the basis of quarrels now forgotten. Previously the two blocks had never had occasion or excuse to come out in opposition to each other . . . but in the baseball split there was a unique opportunity for the old latent hostilities to come to the surface. (Fox, 1961, p. 139)

The older women who lived in the pueblo (most men and many younger women worked or attended school away from the pueblo) harbored resentments, but were forbidden by Hopi norms to express them.

> These women who would formerly have had little chance to attack other women they disliked without invoking the frightening subject of witchcraft, now have excuse and opportunity to [do so]. The epithet *cheater* has become a virtual synonym for witch. (Fox, 1961, p. 140. Italics in original.)

Fox reported that the first contest between the Braves and the Redskins went well on the field, but mothers of the players ended up in a verbal and physical brawl (p. 139). Subsequent games between the two teams saw increasing expressions of hostility and thinly concealed accusations of witchcraft. "There's going to be a lot of accidents . . . cause them Braves is sure mad they lost last Sunday" (p. 142), said one Redskins mother. This final game between the teams turned out to be a disaster of sorts. The game was close. A dry thunderstorm (a bad portent to the Hopi) with attendant wind and thunder disturbed the game. A disputed call by the umpire (a nearly inevitable event in a baseball game) added to the suspicion that Someone was "influencing events" (pp. 142–143). Eventual victory by one team confirmed the suspicions of the losing faction. The game of baseball disrupted the traditional Hopi concord largely because it could not be made to fit into the Hopi system of cross-cutting memberships, and the open competition in combination with the chance element of baseball led to apparent witchcraft.

Magic in Modern Sport

The Zulu, Navaho, and Hopi groups discussed above are "modern" in that they live in the latter half of the twentieth century. However, they are influenced by cultural traditions that are centuries old—i.e., premodern. For all our science and rational education, magical thinking still provides an undercurrent to the approach to life we modern, urban, Western, sophisticated rationalists believe we adhere to.[2] Nancy Reagan's reliance on an astrologer can be seen as deviant only in terms of our "official" beliefs. Unofficially, many Americans express a belief in one paranormal force or another (Gallup & Newport, 1991). This "magical thinking" in the absence of formal cultural support for magic is understandable, if not commendable. Vogt and Hyman (1959) studied the practice of water witching among American farmers. They observed that rational behavior was often *impossible* because "rational behavior" is based on *long-term odds* calculated from data known to be correlated with a desired outcome (finding water). This requires a *series* of trials, but few farmers can afford a series of trials (e.g., pay for several wells). They must find water the first time. Water witching provides assurance that the one well drilled on a designated spot will provide water. Additionally, it is cheap. Why not spend a few extra dollars for a diviner "just in case" water witching works (see Vogt & Hyman, 1959, Ch. 9)? Like the farmer in need of a well, the athlete often faces important, one-time situations (a critical at bat, a last minute field goal, a big race), and there is ample evidence that they invoke magic.

George Gmelch (1972) found that the baseball players he studied practiced a variety of idiosyncratic magical techniques (in contrast to Hopi or Zulu culture, where magic is well established and hence standardized) ranging from wearing the same shirt or eating the same food that one wore or ate on a "good day," to tagging a certain base on the way in from the field to the dugout (pp. 131–134). Taboos prevent actions that may bring bad luck. The most well known (and standardized) baseball taboo forbids speaking about a no hitter in progress. Less known is the taboo against the crossing of bats (p. 134). A lucky coin, crucifix or pair of shoes may be "used" by a ballplayer to enhance his performance (p. 136).

The study by Gmelch was conducted via participant observation. Gmelch was able to see and understand a variety of behaviors performed by baseball players he played with. He was able to learn a lot of baseball folklore. A weakness of his study, and any other "participant observation" study, is its lack of breadth. Gmelch observed only a handful of the thousands of people who play baseball. He had no way to demonstrate that other players were like the players he studied, or that players in other sports engage in similar magical practices.

A survey of athletes at the University of Western Ontario found magical beliefs and practices among male and female athletes in a variety of sports. This survey, while providing less "depth" than a participant observation study like the Gmelch baseball study, allows an examination of a large number of individuals in a variety of sports. The athletes reported a variety of "lucky" practices, including ways of donning one's equipment, preferred uniform numbers, ritualized pregame routines, and the use of lucky charms (Gregory & Petrie, 1975). Taken together, the Gmelch and the Ontario studies show that "magic" is widespread among urban, modern Americans and Canadians.

The Hopi or Zulu concern for supernatural powers is understandable. Magic and witchcraft are an everyday part of their experience. Why, however, do American and Canadian athletes, who are raised in a culture whose beliefs reject magic, develop a widely shared set of magical beliefs? Sports, at least highly competitive sports, fit the profile of activities that encourage magical thinking. To repeat some of the ideas in the previous sections, magic or prayers for divine assistance do not hurt and might help, so it would be foolish not to employ them. Second, sports involve a lot of chance factors that are uncontrollable:

> A Melanesian knows that magic cannot dig the soil in which he must plant his yams, so he does his own digging. He knows that he must hoe to keep down weeds, so he hoes. But he also knows that, no matter how great his skill, pests, foraging animals, and climate are beyond his technological ability to control. Yet these and unknown factors affect his crop for better or worse. He desperately needs a good crop. It is the object of his most ardent wish, so he endeavors to control the unknown element by magic or religion. (Hoebel, 1958, p. 532. Hoebel is discussing the work of Malinowski, 1935.)

Athletes do not invoke supernatural assistance while practicing their skills or lifting weights. These things are controllable. Rather, religion or magic may be used to influence those uncontrollable forces that affect victory and defeat. Finally, the use of magic satisfies the need for a sense of control in an important, but uncontrollable, situation. The Melanesian farmer must have a successful crop. The American farmer must find water (Vogt & Hyman, 1959). Here magic can soothe anxiety by allowing the farmer (or batter or goalie) to feel he or she has done all that can be done to create a favorable outcome. Vogt and Hyman illustrate this in the case of people who hire water witchers:

> The action of the [divining] rod also provides reassurance at a time when the anxious seeker for water most needs it. The scientist, ever honest and aware of the fallibility of his method, qualifies his judgment and does not guarantee success. The water diviner goes about his business with the certitude that comes from blind faith. The scientist's cues may ultimately have a more valid connection with the presence of underground water, but at the moment of decision the decisiveness of the rod's action supplies the greater emotional relief. (Vogt & Hyman, 1959, pp. 199–200)

What about failures? When magical practices fail to deliver on their promises, do they fall into disrepute? First, magic has built-in explanations for failure. Many anthropologists use the term *pseudoscience* to describe the careful procedures required of a sorcerer who seeks to influence events (see Malinowski, 1954, pp. 85–87; Hoebel, 1958, p. 533). Magic is about cause and effect just as science is; but, unlike science, and very like the sociological pseudoscience discussed in Chapter 2 of this book, magic is "designed" to resist any fair test of its efficacy:

> The failures of magic can always be accounted for by the slip of memory, by slovenliness in performance or in observance of a taboo, and, not least, by the fact that someone else has performed some counter-magic. (Malinowski, 1954, p. 86)

Therefore, a failed water witcher may blame improper drilling, the effects of on-site heavy equipment, or unanticipated geological features for the failure of his or her wand to "read" water locations (see Vogt & Hyman, 1959, p. 201).

A rather common psychological phenomenon may also help explain why people who have "used" magic do not easily reject magical beliefs. Festinger, Riecken, and Schacter (1956) studied a small group of people who had publicly predicted the end of the world and spent the "final" night communicating with flying saucers who were going to pick the faithful up just prior to the flood that would destroy the world. When no flying saucers and no flood appeared on the designated day, the group felt no sense of defeat. Their faithfulness had rescued the world from destruction! They were excited at the prospect of bringing this message to the world. How could such an abject failure of a belief create a deeper faith in the belief? Very simply, we do not like to harbor conflicting cognitions. The cognitions "I am a decent, admirable person" and "I believe in a stupid idea" conflict, or, to use the term of Festinger and his colleagues, create *cognitive dissonance*.

Ordinary people who "try" magic are not anxious to think they have done something foolish or irrational. On the contrary, we are motivated to find reasons why what we did is not stupid, but sensible. That we select information that reinforces our self-image as sensible has been demonstrated in a variety of experiments. Bettors at the racetrack have more faith in their horse's chances of winning *after* they place their bets than immediately before they lay their money down (Knox & Inkster, 1968); observers of a football game tend to see fouls by the opposing team but not those by their own team (Hastorf & Cantril, 1954); people living close to the Three Mile Island nuclear power facility during the 1979 accident (which could have exposed them to dangerous levels of radiation) were quick to believe reassurances by plant officials that there was no threat, while people who lived farther away were much more skeptical of such reassurances (Mountain West Research, 1979). In all of these cases, people were motivated through cognitive dissonance to "see" facts that supported their self-image as "normal," "sensible," or "fair." (See Aronson, 1988, Ch. 4, for a good discussion of this phenomenon.)

It seems likely that whatever the reason to "try" magic in the first place—to follow cultural tradition, to hedge one's bet "just in case" it makes a difference, to do *something* to reduce anxiety—the phenomenon of cognitive dissonance, or, more correctly, the reduction of cognitive dissonance, motivates us all to seek out and cling to information that justifies our actions and overlook information that makes us look bad. We remember when magical practices "work" but ignore the times they fail. The tension and anxiety associated with close competition in sports encourages magical thinking. The pseudoscientific defenses against facts inherent in magic, along with the everyday effects of cognitive dissonance, combine to reaffirm the utility of magical practices.

Can Sport Influence Culture? Warfare

How a society undertakes warfare is largely determined by culture. In some instances war resembles sport. The first warfare among human beings was undoubtedly accomplished with the same tactics, weapons, and organization used in the hunting of large mammals. A small hunting party would stalk the enemy, set up an ambush, and attack with spears and clubs. It is unlikely that prior warning or any form of fairness was accorded the victim. Rather, the enemy was attacked as a boar or deer would be attacked. In this respect the most "primitive" of wars was similar to modern warfare—the enemy is to be destroyed with minimum risk to one's own forces. The enemy gets no fair fighting chance if such a chance can be denied. There is no fairness, no honor (although such values as courage, loyalty, and magnanimity may be shown) in modern war. To allow either would cost lives.

While much of what may be called primitive warfare was prosecuted on a rational basis, designed to inflict maximum damage on the enemy at minimum cost, cases in which the achievement of personal honor take precedence over maximizing enemy casualties (i.e., in which war resembles sport) are frequent. A few examples illustrate this point.

Goliath, a giant Philistine warrior, ambles out in front of the Philistine forces arrayed against King Saul's Israelites and shouts out to them:

> Do you need a whole army to settle this? I will represent the Philistines, and you choose someone to represent you, and we will settle this in a single combat! If your man is able to kill me, then we will be your slaves. But if I kill him, then you must be our slaves! I defy the armies of Israel! Send me a man who will fight with me! (I Samuel 17:8–10)

Goliath was killed by David, who bashed his head in with a large stone propelled by a sling. (For the record, David did not resort to any special prayer [magic] prior to his fight with Goliath. Rather he went to the river and found five smooth stones, which he knew would be sufficient to defeat his adversary. Contrast David's reliance on prayer to that of a big time football team.) The defeat of Goliath demoralized the Philistine army and they retreated in disorder from the field.

In the middle of the Battle of the Little Bighorn (Custer's Last Stand), a few Sioux and Cheyenne (called *Shahiyelas* by the Sioux) warriors sacrificed military considerations and their own safety to perform individual acts of reckless bravery. Joseph White Cow Bull, who was in this fight, describes two such acts:

> The soldiers' horses were so frightened by all the noise we made that they began to bolt in all directions. The soldiers held their fire while they tried to catch their horses. Just then Yellow Nose rushed in again and grabbed a small flag [guidon] from where the soldiers had stuck it in the ground. He carried it off and counted coup [struck blows] on a soldier with its sharp end. He was proving his courage more by counting that coup than if he had killed the soldier. . . .
>
> Once in a while some warrior showed his courage by making a charge all by himself. I saw one *Shahiyela,* wearing a spotted war bonnet and a spotted robe of mountain-lion skins, ride out alone.
>
> "He's charging!" someone shouted. He raced up to the long ridge where the soldiers of one band were making a defense—standing there holding their horses and keeping up a steady fire. This *Shahiyela* charged in almost close enough to touch some of the soldiers and rode around in circles in front of them with bullets kicking up dust all around him. He came galloping back, and we all cheered him.
>
> *"Ah! Ah!"* he said, meaning "yes" in *Shahiyela.*
>
> Then he unfastened his belt and opened his robe and shook many spent bullets out on the ground. (Miller, 1971, p. 34. Italics in original.)

Neither of these actions contributed to the defeat of Custer. Rather, they were aimed at earning individual acclaim for courage. One can imagine that against a troop of soldiers armed with rifles, counting coup or riding up to the enemy and racing away led to the death of more than a few Sioux and Cheyenne warriors.

The thin line between "sport," broadly defined, and war may have been best straddled by the feuding tradition of many Polynesian societies, such as the Maori of New Zealand.

> Intertribal feuding was a traditional pastime, and it was carried out almost like a rivalry in sports, with a season of fighting and a season for recouping, and punctilios were observed even toward the bitterest enemies. So prevalent was fighting that most villages were located with a view to defense and were skillfully fortified. Quarrels over land and women along with revenge for real or imagined wrongs kept the tribes continually alerted and their people fierce and fit. (Oliver, 1961, p. 168)

Like the American Indians, the several Maori tribes were dispossessed of their land partly through battle with the British, partly through commercial exploitation of intertribal wars, and partly through political-economic chicanery (Oliver, 1961, pp. 168–173). Also like the American Indians, the Maori "sporting" attitude toward war put them at a disadvantage in combat with Europeans:

> Maori tribesmen once surrounded a group of Britishers and kept them pinned down for days until their ammunition ran out. While the "thin red line of heroes" was making ready to "put up a good show at the end," the Maori, who had realized the situation, sent an envoy to the British position. He suggested that the British accept some Maori ammunition so that the highly entertaining fight might continue on a more equal basis! (Suggs, 1960, p. 203)

Johan Huizinga (1950) provides many further illustrations of a "sporting" attitude in ancient warfare in his famous book about the play element in culture. There can be little doubt that warfare can be prosecuted with a modicum of restraint on lethality of weapons and brutality towards the enemy. Unfortunately, practical considerations and the psychological impact fighting has on the individual soldier have too often led to virtually unlimited killing (see Elias, 1972, pp. 106–109; Nef, 1958, pp. 68–80). Sadly, there is little in modern industrial values or norms to restrain mass killing in warfare. Given the available technology (not even counting nuclear weapons) and the rational approach required in modern warfare (maximizing damage to the enemy's capacity to fight at minimum risk to one's own forces), "sporting" motives such as "showing up" an opponent or gentlemanly restraint appear to be a relic of the past.

Sport as a Substitute for War?

Few seriously believe that international conflicts can be settled by sporting competition. The war between the Israelites and the Philistines continued long after David killed Goliath. While the *Iliad* is replete with stories of sportlike individual contests between heros (Menelaus and Paris, Aias and Hector, Hector and Achilles), the war continued unabated. The Schmeling-Louis fight did nothing to improve U.S.-German relations. The famous USSR-Hungary water polo match during the 1956 Olympic Games, after the Soviet invasion of Hungary, did not improve relations between the two nations. A 1969 soccer match between Honduras and El Salvador actually touched off a brief border war between the two countries!

In spite of the dismal evidence, a starry-eyed dream that sport might "substitute" for war is reborn from time to time. The hope is that sport might somehow be able to serve a cultural function similar to that served by warfare. Much of the warfare of hunter-gatherer societies satisfies honor with a minimum of killing. That is, it is like sport. The combat may involve a ritual that allows the offended side to cast spears and wound (but not kill) a few transgressors, or a battle fought out of effective arrow range in which all have the opportunity to demonstrate personal courage, but neither side actually tries to "close with and destroy the enemy" as do modern armies (Hoebel, 1959, pp. 509–511).

The "substitute for war" belief is predicated on the idea that human beings have a "need" (either inborn or acquired) to express aggression (war) and sports competitions might somehow satisfy this need, much as keeping a pet might satisfy a "need" to nurture children. Not even those who are identified with the "innate pugnacity" school of thought really think that sports serve to sublimate aggressive tendencies.[3] Desmond Morris, in his book *The Naked Ape* (1967), contended that "no amount of boisterous international football" (p. 176) could relieve the pressure of competition between groups (nations) for territory given increasing world population pressures.

Konrad Lorenz, in his famous book *On Aggression* (1966), argued that human beings possess a biological instinct toward group defense. Stimuli that elicit this "warrior" instinct include perception of an outside threat, an identifiable enemy group, an acknowledged in-group leader, and the presence of other group members similarly stimulated (spoiling for a fight). This instinctual aggressive spirit is thought to be biologically functional for prehistoric societies but potentially disastrous for modern societies (pp. 271–274). The stimuli sound awfully familiar to anyone who has lived in a community, perhaps a campus, prior to a big game. The opposing team, the home coach and the enthusiastic crowd correspond rather closely to the stimuli thought by Lorenz to arouse our "warrior instinct."

Whether or not some innate pugnacious instinct is aroused by sport competition, the notion that it provides a catharsis for aggressive impulses is probably wrong (Berkowitz, 1969; Montague, 1976). Sport does not provide a cultural "substitute" for a need to engage in combat with a rival band of warriors. Lorenz himself saw the "safety valve" function of sporting competition as less significant than the role of sport in promoting intergroup understanding:

> [Sports] promote personal acquaintance between people of different nations or parties and they unite . . . people who otherwise would have little in common. (Lorenz, 1966, p. 282)

Friendship and understanding, far more than catharsis, were the ways sport could prevent intergroup conflict, according to Lorenz.

Let us restate the catharsis theory. We all have a "need" to express aggression. This need is useful to people who must hunt and defend their territory. Modern civilization forbids the expression of aggression, so cultures of modern civilizations must provide acceptable outlets or "safety valves" for the discharge of aggressive feelings. Sport is one such outlet. Two different surveys demonstrate that this catharsis theory is wrong.

Anthropologist Richard Sipes (1973) studied the correlation between combative sports and frequency of warlike activity in a sample of 130 different societies. Sipes reasoned that if sport serves as a "safety valve" to discharge aggressive feelings among members of a society, then societies with a lot of aggressive sports would be less involved in real war than societies practicing few aggressive sports. This proved to be wrong. Sipes found a *positive* correlation between the presence of violent sports and warfare. The more a society engaged in violent sports, the more likely that society would also be involved in warfare. The Sipes study provided no support for the "safety valve" theory. Indeed, since violent sports and warfare seem to happen together, it might be concluded that the presence of violent sports *increases* aggression or that frequent fighting requires the practice of fighting skills.

A study of changes in homicide rates following several heavyweight championship boxing matches also casts doubt on the "safety valve" theory. David Phillips (1983) reasoned that if viewing a violent sports contest like boxing reduced aggressive impulses, then the number of homicides in the United States should decline for a time after the matches. The more highly publicized a fight, the more people would experience it, so the greater the expected decline in homicides. Like Sipes, Phillips found the opposite to be true. Homicides *increased* after fights, especially highly publicized fights. Phillips attempted to control for many associated factors that could have affected homicide rates, such as day of week or season (homicide goes up on weekends and in the summer), so it is likely that it really was the fights themselves that produced the increase in homicides.

Both Sipes and Phillips suggest that violent sports and violent behavior increase each other rather than substitute for one another. The thesis that viewing sports *increases* aggressive tendencies may be subjected to sharp criticism, just as the catharsis theory has been. However, the relevant issue is that there is no evidence that violent sports somehow reduce violent urges and violent behavior. Survey studies of the effects of sporting events other than boxing (Lester, 1988) and experimental studies (e.g., Arms, Russell, & Sandilands, 1987) involving hockey and professional wrestling show no drop in violent tendencies by spectators following aggressive sports events. Since there is no drop, the thesis that sport serves as a cultural device to vent aggressive tendencies cannot be true.

The Function of Sport in Modern Cultures

While sport does not affect (at least to reduce it) interpersonal or intergroup aggression, it may serve many cultural functions. A standard axiom of the functionalist view of culture is that culture, like all human behavior, may be understood as solutions to collective problems (Cohen, 1955, Ch. 3). That these common problems may be "solved" in a variety of ways is reflected in the variability of cultures throughout the world. There are many ideas about cultural problems "solved" by sports. Here we review a handful of interesting ideas. The first recalls the idea that, for the Zulu, soccer provides a chance to reenact old warrior traditions.

Sport as a Modern Survival of Prowess

Thorsten Veblen, the turn of the century observer of American economic behavior, had a curious theory about the place of sport in modern industrial societies. Veblen (1899/1953) believed that the earliest basis on which men (not women, because women were not allowed to compete for status) gained status in the eyes of others was *exploit,* namely hunting and war (in the form of raids on neighboring bands). Routine work such as gathering roots or growing a garden contributed more to community welfare than big-game hunting or warfare, but these latter activities provided status, whereas the more routine activities did not (see Chs. 1 & 2).

Veblen believed that granting status to men who show evidence of successful exploit, while discounting the worth of routine labor, has persisted through all stages of social development—from its savage origins, through barbarism, right to modern civilized cultures. (Recall that Veblen wrote prior to World Wars I and II, which cast some discredit on the use of the word "civilized" in conjunction with "modern.") Veblen's *The Theory of the Leisure Class* focused on the importance of "showing" one's wealth in contemporary social status systems, and the relative lack of esteem granted to everyday things and activities that actually contributed to societal welfare. While predatory exploit no longer serves the purpose it did in primitive societies, the *spirit* of exploit still serves the would-be entrepreneur who must defeat his or her competition. In modern parlance both the primitive hunter/warrior and the modern business tycoon must be something of a ripoff artist.

Enter modern sports. Veblen, in the colorful English he used, argued that sports provided a modern arena for the survival of the primitive exploitive spirit:

> Sports of all kinds are of the same general character, including prize-fights, bull-fights, athletics, shooting, angling, yachting, and games of skill, even where the element of destructive physical efficiency is not an obtrusive feature. Sports shade off from the basis of hostile combat, through skill, to cunning and chicanery, without its being possible to draw a line at any point. The ground of an addiction to sports is an archaic spiritual constitution—the possession of the predatory emulative propensity in a relatively high potency. A strong proclivity of adventuresome exploit and to the infliction of damage is especially pronounced in those employments which are in colloquial usage specifically called sportsmanship. (Veblen, 1899/1953, p. 170)
>
> Strategy or cunning is an element invariably present in games, as also in warlike pursuits and in the chase. In all of these employments strategy tends to develop into finesse and chicanery. Chicanery, falsehood, browbeating, hold a well-secured place in the method of procedure of any athletic contest and in games generally. The habitual employment of an umpire, and the minute

> technical regulations governing the limits and details of permissible fraud and strategic advantage, sufficiently attest the fact that fraudulent practices and attempts to overreach one's opponents are not adventitious features of the game. In the nature of the case habituation to sports should conduce to a fuller development of the aptitude for fraud; and the prevalence in the community of that predatory temperament which inclines men to sports connotes a prevalence of sharp practice and callous disregard of the interests of others, individually and collectively. (Veblen, 1899/1953, p. 181)

One could argue with justice against Veblen's contention that modern sport represents the survival of a primitive spirit that still drives business competition. Veblen enjoyed the irony of discussing "savages" and "the modern upper class" in the same sentence, so one cannot be sure how much of his criticism of sport was serious theory and how much was intended as a put-down of the rich. It would seem unlikely that a particular spirit of exploit survived from savage origins of European society up to the present. If modern ethnography is any guide, status in "savage" (primitive) societies is accorded as much on the basis of age and descent as on individual accomplishment in hunting or war (Hoebel, 1958, Ch. 22). As for modern business competition, the fate of "junk bond" tycoons and leveraged buyout artists illustrate the value of the exploitative spirit (a fast road to financial ruin). The success of companies practicing what is loosely called "Japanese management" methods, based on principles of cooperation and community responsibility, also sheds light on the import of "modern survivals of prowess" in contemporary business.

Nonetheless, Veblen's less-than-complimentary description of the role of sport merits attention—partly because any of Veblen's ideas deserve serious consideration and partly because Veblen's views constitute another argument that sport and aggression are somehow culturally intertwined.

Sport as a Cause of Excitement

Whereas the catharsis or safety valve theory of sport argues that sport provides a release of tension, the opposite might be more correct. Perhaps we use sport as a *source* of tension. Modern societies are dull. Few of us need to worry about the vicissitudes of weather or the chance that we will not have food tomorrow. In the absence of warfare or political turbulence, which occasionally beset many modern societies, modern urban life is rather predictable. Dobriner (1969) has argued that modern life is more than dull; it is oppressively dull. The obligations associated with the many roles we play limit our freedom.

> To be joined with others in a permanent relationship—the family, the job, the community, the fraternity, the college, the church, the boy friend or girl friend—is to expose oneself to a constant condition of obligation. As son, father, employee, friend, neighbor, student, Methodist, "steady"—no matter what role or combination of roles we occupy—the essence of the role is defined by the prescriptive

> and proscriptive norms which give it its distinctive character. . . . [I]n all cultures and social systems, social life is an inevitable sequence of obligation. Through mutual obligatory relationships, through the principle of reciprocity, through specialization, through division of labor, through interrelationships and interdependence, the very essence of social life is distilled. To enter into social relationships with others (as we must), we submit to the inevitable obligations not only of the formal role structure, but also to the informal demands of interrelated human beings in other roles as well. (Dobriner, 1969, p. 135)

Dobriner thought the Western (cowboy) movie, to which we might add the contemporary police or monster movie, offered a vicarious release from the demands of modern society. After all, the Western hero was usually free of such demands—marginally employed, unmarried, a temporary resident of town (pp. 139–141). The same goes for the kung fu fighter, the rogue police officer, and adversaries of supernatural creatures in more recent examples of cinematic art. Movies provide "role release" opportunities, to relieve the psychological pressure of overbearing obligations (see Goffman, 1961, pp. 94–112).

Norbert Elias and Eric Dunning (1986) argue that sport provides another such "release" from the humdrum of modern life. Just as we might seek tension in the theater, so may we find it in sport. No one likes to play or watch a dull game. The excitement of a close contest can be rather pleasurable in that, unlike excitement produced by real danger (e.g., driving on icy roads or interviewing for a job), the outcome of a sporting contest really does not matter (Elias & Dunning, 1970, p. 40). We can get "all worked up" about a game of football without any real consequences from winning or losing save a temporary elation or disappointment (Figure 3–1).

Perhaps the extreme of this pleasurable excitement comes from good theater or, to meld sport with theater, good professional wrestling. My observation and that of several of my students indicates that professional wrestling fans do not "really" believe the wrestlers are hurting each other but, by pretending it really is real, fans can love the heros, detest the villains, and thrill to the ebb and flow of each match. In much the same way, horror movie fans can experience thrills and chills, even though they know those zombies or disembodied spirits are just actors or special film effects.

A final word on possible cultural functions of sport. Several sport sociologists have observed some relatively simple or obvious cultural effects (functions) of sport. Wohl (1966) studied the influence of several sport clubs in rural Poland. He argued that sport clubs contributed to cultural change (modernization) in several ways. The introduction of sport clubs in tradition-oriented Polish villages served to break up old cultural traditions, like fights with neighboring villages and the very strong constraints on the behavior of women. By participating in sports, young people formed positive ties with "outside" communities and practiced behaviors (e.g., women wearing sport clothing such as shorts) that were not condoned by traditional norms (Wohl, 1966, 1969).

Many have observed that sports may serve as a device for "smuggling" Western norms and values into the area. We may approve of some of these—good diet, quality

FIGURE 3–1 One of the appeals of sports competition is the tension or "pleasurable excitement" it creates in the lives of participants and spectators alike. People may experience elation or depression with relatively few "real life" consequences.

(Courtesy of the University of the Pacific)

medical care, cosmopolitan outlook—but we may not be so happy with others, such as the idea that indigenous sports are inferior or that indigenous culture is inferior. Maguire (1990) has remarked that the rise of American sports such as basketball and football in Britain may reflect a general importation of American commercial culture—TV, movies, and commercial sport. Imagine the capacity of a major economic power to influence the popular culture of a small, economically dependent third-world nation if American economic power can influence European culture!

If foreign games can smuggle foreign culture into a society, indigenous games can serve to affirm indigenous culture. Hence, the warlike "sports" of the Ancient Greeks supported the norms and values of that culture. Likewise, the traditional "sports" of Eskimos serve as a means of economic redistribution (gambling) and the inculcation of cooperative behavior required in hunting whales (Glassford, 1970).

International Sporting Success

Is success in international sporting competition affected by cultural differences between different countries? Sport sociologists have long been interested in this question.

Some three decades ago, John Roberts and Brian Sutton-Smith (1962) examined the connection between child-rearing practices and children's game preferences in some 111 widely disparate societies. Anthropologist Roberts and psychologist Sutton-Smith found that where child rearing emphasized *obedience,* games tended to emphasize *strategy* (perhaps to allow a sense of dominance in otherwise obedient children); where child rearing emphasized *routine responsibility,* games tended to involve *chance* (the reason for this was not clear). Child training that emphasized *achievement* was associated with games of skill (perhaps to achieve as one has been trained to do). This thesis has been criticized on statistical grounds (Phillips, 1977), but it remains interesting in that one part of a culture (child rearing) is seen to influence another part (games), because the child-rearing practices produce certain psychological needs and the games help to satisfy those needs (Sutton-Smith, 1971). Thus, the role of games in culture is to ease psychological tension. This recalls the notion that sport provides either excitement in unexciting societies or a catharsis for aggressive tendencies.

Another early contribution to sport sociology linked sporting success to religious orientation (Lueschen, 1967). Lueschen was not concerned with such things as team chaplains or pregame prayers, which are probably either nonreligious (good PR to have a chaplain; prayer aimed at "focusing" the team on a game) or magical (trying to induce God to help one's side to win or, at least, prevent injuries). Rather, Lueschen found that Protestants in Germany were far more involved in sports, especially individual sports, than Catholics. Lueschen suggested that the traditional Protestant emphasis on individualism and achievement (not some specific religious practice or belief) may explain this Protestant-Catholic difference (1967, pp. 132–134). A recent study of French- and English-speaking Canadians found a similar tendency. The English-speaking Canadians, of whom a higher percentage are Protestant, were more involved in competitive sports and more likely to value competition and challenge as a reason for participation. This difference, when applied both to males and females, remained even after statistical controls for differences in education, urban-rural residence, and income were applied (White & Curtis, 1990). This difference may reflect the same achievement orientation among Protestants that Lueschen found.

The "Protestant Ethic" and cross-cultural child-rearing studies provide at least weak evidence that the kinds of things we associate with culture can affect the sporting achievement of different societies or, in the case of Protestant-Catholic differences, groups within a society. What about success, or lack of it, in international competition? Medals won in the Olympic Games provides an easy way to compare the sporting achievement of different societies. Strictly speaking "culture" has not proven to explain differences in achievement, but this is a good place to examine the lively literature that has developed around the topic.

Two reasons for national Olympic success or a lack of it come to mind. First, small countries have a disadvantage in team events (e.g., soccer, hockey, relay events), so team medals should tend to go to countries with big populations. Second, and this is a cultural factor, the favorite sport of a country may draw a lot of that country's athletic talent, and, if the sport is not contested in the Olympics, the country will not have some of its best athletes in Olympic competition. Over the years such sports as baseball and football (United States), rugby (New Zealand), tennis (Australia) and soccer (many countries) have drawn potential talent away from Olympic sports, thereby reducing the "production" of Olympic victories in those nations.

Given such problems, researchers still have been able to identify differences between Olympic "winners" and "losers." The basic approach is to compare as many countries on as many variables that would seem to possibly have an impact on sports success as is reasonable to see which variables are associated with Olympic victories by different countries. Novikov and Maximenko (1972) conducted such an analysis on countries involved in the 1964 Olympic Summer Games in Tokyo. They found, not surprisingly, that those countries with a high degree of economic development (high per capita income, high number of calories consumed per capita, high average life expectancy, low illiteracy rates, and high percentage of residents living in cities) tended to win more than their "fair share" of Olympic medals. The two Soviet sociologists also found that Communist (i.e., Eastern Bloc) countries did much better than capitalist countries with comparable levels of economic development. The authors argued that development in Communist countries helped the whole population, while development in capitalist countries helped only the "rich minority" (p. 39), leaving the majority no better off.

A similar study was conducted on the 1972 Olympic Games by Levine (1979). Like Novikov and Maximenko, Levine found that economic development, as indicated by gross domestic product and newspaper circulation, could explain most of the variations in national success at winning Olympic medals. Levine also found that a Socialist (Communist would be a preferable word, as such Socialist countries as Denmark and Sweden were not counted as Socialist) economy was strongly associated with success in winning medals. Unlike his Soviet predecessors, Levine interpreted the success of Communist countries as the result of a deliberate sports policy in these countries. The policy tried to seek out and train athletic talent for Olympic competition. The work of Seppanen (1988) supports Levine's argument. Although he did not perform an analysis of data, Seppanen observed that Communist countries could and did focus resources on the achievement of certain goals, including sports—especially Olympic sports.

Overall then, success in the Olympic Games goes to countries with the economic development to support general health, widespread access to facilities, and, especially, the political will to focus resources (training centers) on the development of talent for Olympic sports, and/or provide economic incentives for success in Olympic sports (see Gaertner, 1989).

An interesting part of this line of research is the examination of countries that should do very poorly, but instead do well (e.g., Kenya, Cuba), and countries that should do well but do not (e.g., Nigeria, Saudi Arabia). This is called ***deviant case analysis***. It involves close examination of instances in which a general pattern does not hold true. Until this is done our understanding of "who wins Olympic medals" will be incomplete.

Summary

Although the term culture is difficult to define with precision, the concept has been useful in the understanding of sport. Cultural differences can clearly affect the way a given sport is played in different societies. Magic is a well-established belief in many cultures. Sports participants in these cultures may be motivated to employ magic to control chance elements that might control the outcome of an important contest. This can change the way sports such as soccer or baseball are played by peoples who share an institutionalized belief in the effectiveness of magic. Athletes in modern industrial societies lack a well-defined store of magical knowledge, but efforts to use magic are widespread. The seeming importance of sports, coupled with the uncertainty of the outcome of close contests, creates a tension that magic can help relieve.

If culture (magical beliefs) can influence sport, so can sport influence culture. Some have argued that modern warfare (a part of culture) may be influenced by sport. Warfare in many so-called primitive cultures resembles sport in several respects, but modern warfare appears to be unaffected by modern sport. There is no evidence that sports somehow reduce pugnacious instincts that might lead to war. Gentlemanly restraint and fair play (supposedly important values in sport) have no part in modern warfare, which is based on a purely rational effort to destroy the enemy at minimum cost to one's own forces.

Culture may be seen as so many collective "solutions" to collective "problems." As a part of modern culture, sport may be seen as a solution to problems of modern society. If the day-to-day predictability of modern, urban life may be seen as a problem, then the artificial excitement associated with sports may be seen as a solution to this problem. Sport may also be seen as a mechanism for inducing cultural change. Village girls in Poland were helped to break out of traditional sex role limitations by participating in a government-sponsored sports club; American culture may be smuggled into a society that adapts an American sport like football or basketball.

Culture may affect sporting success in modern societies. That Protestants appear to do better in sports than Catholics in Germany and Canada suggests the possible influence of culture in the form of the Protestant ethic. On the other hand, systematic cross-national studies of Olympic success suggest that structural factors such as per capita income, urbanization, and the availability of coaching, facilities and competition are far more important than any cultural factors in the production of Olympic medalists.

Notes

1. See Chapter 2 for a definition of these terms.

2. The reader may not find it hard to assume this. Nancy Reagan, the wife of the President, reported to have retained a San Francisco astrologer at $3,000 per month to provide information on "good" and "bad" days for important presidential events (Frazier, 1990). Many Americans entertain some faith that supernatural phenomena can influence events (Gallup & Newport, 1991).

3. Some sport sociologists think they do (see

Coakley, 1990, p. 142; Eitzen & Sage, 1989, p. 326). Lorenz appears to be used in sport sociology as a "straw man" whose ideas are first oversimplified and then attacked. There is no doubt that Lorenz believed in "aggressive instinct" and in the idea of catharsis, but he clearly saw the educational and social (friendship) values of sport as the main source of any antiwar benefits sport may provide (see Lorenz, 1966, Ch. 14).

References

Allison, M. T., and Lueschen, G. (1979). A comparative analysis of Navaho Indian and Anglo basketball sport systems. *International Review of Sport Sociology, 14* (3–4), 75–85.

Arms, R. L., Russell, G. W., and Sandilands, M. L. (1987). Effects on the hostility of spectators of viewing aggressive sports. In A. Yiannakis, T. D. McIntyre, M. J. Melnick, and D. P. Hart, Eds., *Sport Sociology: Contemporary Themes.* 3rd ed. Dubuque, IA: Kendell/Hunt, pp. 259–262.

Aronson, E. (1988). *The Social Animal,* 5th ed. New York: Freeman.

Berkowitz, L. (1969). Simple Views of Aggression. *American Scientist, 57,* 372–383.

Coakley, J. J. (1990). *Sport in Society: Issues and Controversies,* 4th ed. St. Louis: Times Mirror/Mosby.

Cohen, A. (1955). *Delinquent Boys.* New York: Free Press.

Davis, K. (1940). Extreme social isolation of a child. *American Journal of Sociology, 45,* 554–564.

Davis, K. (1947). Final note on a case of extreme isolation. *American Journal of Sociology, 50,* 432–437.

Dobriner, W. M. (1969). *Social Structures and Systems.* Pacific Palisades, CA: Goodyear.

Eitzen, D. S., and Sage, G. H. (1989). *Sociology of North American Sport,* 4th ed. Dubuque, IA: Brown.

Elias, N. (1972). The genesis of sport as a sociological problem. In E. Dunning, Ed. *Sport: Readings from a Sociological Perspective.* Toronto: University of Toronto, pp. 88–115.

Elias, M., and Dunning, E. (1970). The quest for excitement in unexciting societies. In G. Lueschen, Ed. *The Cross-Cultural Analysis of Sport and Games.* Champaign, IL: Stipes, pp. 31–51.

Elias, M., and Dunning, E. (1986). *Quest for Excitement: Sport and Leisure in the Civilising Process.* Blackwell: Oxford.

Festinger, L., Riecken, H. W., and Schacter, S. (1956). *When Prophecy Fails.* Minneapolis: University of Minnesota.

Fox, J. R. (1961). Pueblo baseball: A new use for old witchcraft. Reprinted in J. W. Loy and G. S. Kenyon (1969). *Sport, Culture and Society.* Toronto: Collier-Macmillan, pp. 136–144.

Frazier, K. (1990). Astrology in the White House: Nancy Reagan's view. *Skeptical Inquirer, 14,* 228–230.

Gaertner, M. (1989). Socialist countries' sporting success before peristroika—and after? *International Review for the Sociology of Sport, 24,* 283–296.

Gallup, G. H., and Newport, F. (1991). Belief in paranormal phenomena among adult Americans. *Skeptical Inquirer, 15,* 137–146.

Glassford, R. G. (1970). Organization of games and adaptive strategies of the Canadian Eskimo. In G. Lueschen, Ed. *The Cross-Cultural Analysis of Sport and Games.* Champaign, IL: Stipes, pp. 70–84.

Gmelch, G. (1972). Magic in professional baseball. In G. P. Stone, Ed. *Games Sport and Power.* New Brunswick, NJ: Transaction Books, pp. 128–137.

Goffman, E. (1975). *Asylums.* Garden City, NY: Anchor.

Gregory, C. J., and Petrie, B. M. (1975). Superstitions of Canadian intercollegiate athletes: An intersport comparison. *International Review of Sport Sociology, 10* (2), 59–66.

Hastorf, A., and Cantril, H. (1954). They saw a game: A case study. *Journal of Abnormal and Social Psychology, 49,* 129–134.

Hoebel, E. A. (1958). *Man in the Primitive World.* New York: McGraw-Hill.

Huizinga, J. (1950). *Homo ludens: A Study of the Play Element in Culture.* Boston: Beacon.

Knox, R., and Inkster, J. (1968). Post decision dissonance at past time. *Journal of Personality and Social Psychology, 8,* 319–323.

Lester, D. (1988). Suicide and homicide during major sports events 1972–1984. *Sociology of Sport Journal, 5,* 285.

Levine, N. (1979). Why do countries win Olympic medals? Some structural correlates of Olympic Games success: 1972. *Sociology and Social Research, 58,* 353–360.

Lorenz, K. (1966). *On Aggression,* trans. M. K. Wilson. New York: Harcourt, Brace & World (Original work published 1963).

Lueschen, G. (1967). The interdependence of sport and culture. *International Review of Sport Sociology, 2,* 127–139.

Maguire, J. (1990). More than a sporting touchdown: The making of American football in England 1982–1990. *Sociology of Sport Journal, 7,* 213–237.

Malinowski, B. (1935). *Coral Gardens and Their Magic.* New York: American.

Malinowski, B. (1954). *Magic, Science and Religion and Other Essays.* Garden City, NY: Doubleday Anchor.

Merton, R. (1938). Social structure and anomie. *American Sociological Review, 3,* 672–682.

Miller, D. H. (1971). Echoes of the Little Bighorn. *American Heritage, 22* (4), 28–39.

Montague, A. (1976). *The Nature of Human Aggression.* New York: Oxford.

Morris, D. (1967). *The Naked Ape.* New York: McGraw-Hill.

Mountain West Research Inc. (1979). Three Mile Island telephone survey. Cited in Aronson, E. (1988). *The Social Animal* (5th ed). New York: W. H. Freeman.

Nef, J. V. (1958). *Cultural Foundations of Industrial Civilization.* New York: Harper.

Novikov, A. D., and Maximenko, A. M. (1972). The influence of selected socio-economic factors on the level of sports achievements in the various countries. *International Review of Sport Sociology, 7,* 27–40.

Oliver, D. L. (1961). *The Pacific Islands.* Garden City, NY: Doubleday Anchor.

Phillips, David P. (1983). The impact of mass media violence on U.S. homicides. *American Sociological Review, 48,* 560–568.

Phillips, J. C. (1977). Some methodological problems in sport sociology literature. *International Review of Sport Sociology, 12* (1), 91–99.

Roberts, J. M., and Sutton-Smith, B. (1962). Child training and game involvement. *Ethnology, 1,* 166–185.

I Samuel 17. *The Living Bible* (Paraphrased) Wheaton, IL: Tyndale.

Scotch, N. A. (1961). Magic, sorcery and football among the urban Zulu. *Journal of Conflict Resolution, 5,* 70–74.

Seppanen, P. (1988). A revisit to social and cultural preconditions of top level sport. *International Review for the Sociology of Sport, 23,* 3–13.

Sipes, R. D. (1973). War, sports and aggression: An empirical test of two rival theories. *American Anthropologist, 75,* 64–86.

Suggs, R. C. (1960). *The Island Civilization of Polynesia.* New York: Mentor.

Sutton-Smith, Brian (1971). The sporting balance. In R. Albonico and K. Pfister-Binz, Eds., *Sociology of Sport: Theoretical Foundations and Research Methods.* Basel: Birkhauser.

Vander Zanden, J. W. (1965). *Sociology: A Systematic Approach.* New York: Ronald.

Veblen, T. (1899/1953). *The Theory of the Leisure Class.* New York: Mentor.

Vogt, E. Z., and Hyman, R. (1959). *Water Witching U.S.A.* Chicago: University of Chicago.

White, P. G., and Curtis, J. E. (1990). Participation in competitive sport among anglophones and francophones in Canada: Testing competing hypotheses. *International Review for the Sociology of Sport, 25,* 125–138.

Wohl, A. (1966). Social aspects of the development of rural sport in Poland, according to research. *International Review of Sport Sociology, 1,* 109–130.

Wohl, A. (1969). *Integrational Functions of Sport.* Warsaw, Poland: Akademia Wychowania Fizycznego.

Chapter 4

The Rise and Rationalization of Sport

Bureaucratization, rationalization, or formalization of social organization is considered a master trend in social development throughout the past few centuries (Durkheim, 1947). Government, military, religion, community, and economy have changed dramatically. The change has been *from* social life based on tradition, family background, long-term personal ties, and limited specialization *toward* social life characterized by efficiency, formal rules, short-lived and impersonal relationships, and highly specialized organizations that select personnel on the basis of merit. There was a time when separation from kith and kin was considered almost as bad as death. There was a time when most people lived their entire lives among fellow villagers, when a person's work and marriage options were determined at birth. This is no longer the case in industrial societies, and it is becoming less common in agricultural societies (see Hodges, 1974, pp. 147–155).

Modern life is characterized by a *lack* of traditional guidance, by merit (not family background) as the basis for selection and promotion in business and government, and by very highly specialized work in planned organizations that are designed to achieve certain goals, not in small, family-owned businesses. We tend to move often. We have relatively weak ties to neighborhood and community. Even marriage seems to be a temporary situation, with approximately 50 percent of them likely to end in divorce (Vander Zanden, 1988, p. 355).

Sport has for the most part followed this pattern. From tradition-oriented contests played among local folk, modern sport has become a highly regulated competition between rivals who may never have met. Former University of Oregon (and later of Yale University) basketball coach Howard Hobson (1984) provides many illustrations of this development. As far as *organization* is concerned, Hobson reports he never had one at the University of Oregon. He was the coach. He set up schedules, recruited, scouted opponents (mainly with the help of alumni), and assigned jobs (no scholarships as such were available) to players (p. xx).

In the early days of the game baskets were fastened to the walls of the playing court with virtually no out-of-bounds area. Courts varied widely in size. A player from the 1906 era reports that Oregon players were befuddled by the Willamette University team's "tactic of throwing the ball against the wall to make a bounce pass to a teammate, which they were allowed because there was no out of bounds. . . ." (Hobson, 1984, p. 22). Early on, coaching was usually done by recent players, not by professionally trained coaches. Timers and score keepers were often students at the host school, not professionals. Hobson points to a game that Oregon lost because a timekeeper was unable to fire the gun to end the game owing to damp ammunition (p. 43).

Rule changes in basketball reflect the gradual rationalization and bureaucratization of the sport—changes aimed at achieving certain goals. At first, these goals involved the enjoyment and physical exercise of players and were the aims of the "inventor" of basketball, James Naismith. Many early rule changes served to accommodate these goals. Moving backboards two feet in from the end of the court, requiring one hand dribbling, and removing the bottom from the basket all served to speed up the game, to make it more strenuous and more enjoyable.[1] Later rule changes may be seen as a gradual move from providing a good game for players to providing a good game for spectators and increasing game control by coaches.

In 1918 a player was allowed to reenter the game once, rather than having to stay out once he leaves. In 1935 a player was allowed to reenter twice, and in 1944 free substitution became the rule. This allowed increasing tactical control by coaches, who could make adjustments in personnel throughout the game. It was not until 1948 that collegiate players were allowed to speak to their coach during timeouts! This, too, added to the coach's control and reduced the tactical control by players on the floor. In 1929 the double-referee (and in recent years the three-referee) system was introduced, allowing more exact enforcement of the rules. In a highly rationalized social system rules, more than personal restraint, become the means of regulating behavior. Several rule changes were designed to enhance the spectator appeal of the game. In 1937 the center jump after each basket was eliminated, and the ball was inbounded by the team scored upon. More recently, jump balls were completely eliminated in the college game save for the start of the game. These changes made the game faster—and more strenuous—but also increased spectator appeal. The legalization of transparent backboards in 1946 clearly was aimed at spectator appeal, as were more recent rules allowing dunking, especially hanging on the rim after a dunk. Likewise, increasing the penalty for fouling—deliberate foul, 7 foul, and 10 foul "bonus" rules—serves to reduce or at least penalize "boring" halts in the flow of the game. Rules such as the ten-second rule (1932) and antistalling rules of recent years (closely guarding the basketball for five seconds constitutes a turnover), and especially the rule requiring the offensive team to shoot within 45 seconds, reduce slowdowns designed by the winning team to use up time. Such stalling makes great sense in terms of game tactics, but it does not appeal to spectators.

Nobody who has played basketball would say that the game is not fun to play. Dr. Naismith's game is a lot of fun and very demanding physically, but it seems clear that control of the game has shifted from players to coaches, and rule changes (about which players are never consulted) aim at pleasing spectators, not players.

A Short History of Football

A picture of "folk football" (Elias & Dunning, 1971) was presented in Chapter 2 of this book. Eric Dunning and Kenneth Sheard (1979) have continued this history through modern times. It is a history of movement from social organization based on local tradition to the highly organized, bureaucratized games of rugby and soccer. American football, originally a variation of rugby, may be seen as a continuation of the process of formalization.

The key factor in the modernization of football was its incorporation into the programs of English public schools during the middle of the 19th century. The traditional folk games were, by the 19th century, beginning to die out because of the decline of village life, a result of rapid industrialization in England. Adapted forms of "folk football," originally played against the wishes of school faculty, came to be a part of the program of several schools.

The leader in the movement to "use" sports as a part of the school program was Thomas Arnold, headmaster of Rugby School from 1828 to 1842. Arnold sought to include games such as football to build character. The aim of Arnold's program was to build *Christian gentlemen* who would be well educated in useful arts and sciences, considerate of others (including those of lesser rank), and able to take and deliver physical violence. Arnold attempted to make the older boys at Rugby exemplars of the Christian gentleman ideal by giving them responsibility for supervision of the younger boys. In doing so, he began to take control of the Rugby game from the boys who played it. Whereas the game had always been controlled by the older, dominant boys, these boys were now representatives of the school and its ideals (Dunning & Sheard, 1979, pp. 71–78).

Insofar as the leading players were also exemplars of school values, the game was at least partly removed from the control of the players and placed under the influence of an "outside" agency (the school). Arnold's success at incorporating football into the school program was soon emulated by other headmasters, requiring some formalization of the game at several schools.

> The wild forms of football inherited from the past . . . were ill-suited to the performance of the educational functions masters now expected of them. They needed to be "domesticated," to become far more orderly and controlled. Therefore, the masters encouraged the leading boys to regularize their football, to commit the rules to writing and to develop more regular procedures for settling disputes. (Dunning, 1971, p. 143)

The importance of this process should be apparent. What had been a folk game was becoming a more formalized activity with set rules, goals (character building) external to the game itself, and control was removed from the players on the field.

The next step in the formalization of football occurred when graduates of the several English schools, each with its own version of football, came together to play in the university or in city sports clubs. "Old boys" from the several schools were forced to work out a unified game if they were to play together. The Rugby game was sufficiently different from the soccer-like games of most other schools (especially Eton and Harrow) that two, rather than one, "standard" games emerged—rugby and soccer (see Dunning & Sheard, 1979, pp. 100–113). This "bifurcation" led to the formation of the Football Association (soccer) in 1863 and the Rugby Football Union in 1871 (Dunning & Sheard, 1979, pp. 109–110).

One of the first problems facing the Rugby Football Union was safety. Some 30 or 40 years later, American football faced similar problems. One way to take an opposing ball carrier down was to "hack," to kick him in the shins. Even before hacking was outlawed completely, injurious practices such as wearing iron-toed shoes and hacking with the heel had been outlawed in most rugby playing circles. Lawyers, businessmen, and government officials playing rugby on weekends could not be expected to return to work on Monday after they sustained painful kicks to the shin during a Saturday game, and critics of the game were not reluctant to point this out. The RFU outlawed hacking in 1871, preserving the shins of players and the reputation of the game. This was another step in modernization. A formal rule-making body also enacted new rules to achieve goals unrelated to play itself, such as who can play. In serving to issue rules and coordinate the scheduling of matches, the RFU came to be "the rugby bureaucracy," ultimately defining who may play, coordinating national as well as international matches, managing funds, setting standards for officials, and performing the multitude of functions that bureaucracies perform (see Dunning & Sheard, 1979, especially Ch. 5).

The first football game between two colleges in the United States took place in 1869. Rutgers defeated Princeton six goals to four. The game in one version or another had been played in America since the earliest British settlement (Danzig, 1956, pp. 6–7), appearing at the secondary school level long before being contested between college teams.

The Rutgers-Princeton game was played under rules adapted from the rules of both colleges (which were undoubtedly adapted versions of games played at different secondary schools). Teams had 25 players each; the free kick, in which a player who caught a ball kicked by the opposing side could kick it away unhindered, was eliminated at the request of the Rutgers captain; and the ball could not be handled, it could only be kicked or butted by the head (Danzig, 1956, p. 7). In other words, the first American intercollegiate football game was soccer, or a close version of it.

At about the same time students of Harvard University were playing a Rugby-like game they called the "Boston Game" (Danzig, 1956, p. 8). Unwilling to convert their version of football to the soccer-like game played at Yale, Rutgers, Princeton, and Columbia, Harvard footballers arranged a three-game series with McGill University in 1874. The first two matches were played in Cambridge, Massachusetts. The third was played in Montreal, Quebec, the home of McGill University. These games were a variation of rugby under McGill rules and a more soccer-like game, with some running and tackling, at Harvard. For the record, Harvard won the series with two wins and a tie (Danzig, 1956, p. 9).

This series of matches might better be seen as the origin of intercollegiate football in America. Yale, Princeton, and Columbia, undoubtedly at the urging of club members familiar with the Rugby rules, soon agreed to join with Harvard

> for the purpose of adopting a uniform system of rules and considering the advisability of forming an Intercollegiate Football Association. (Danzig, 1956, p. 10. Danzig is quoting from the invitation sent by Princeton representatives.)

The new association, with a slightly altered version of Rugby Football Union rules (e.g., the Yale football association constantly lobbied for 11- rather than 15-man teams), agreed on a set of rules from which American football evolved. One suspects that an American chapter of the Rugby Football Union or the Football Association might have kept American students playing rugby and soccer, rather than the modified game that would come to be praised as "a highly skilled game of a sweep, imagination, technique, and strategy far surpassing the elementary pastime of Rugby" (Danzig, 1956, p. 5) and damned as "Rugby's American pervert" (Stanford president David Starr Jordon, 1909, quoted in Watterson, 1988, p. 110).

The absence of regulation by the RFU or FA made it possible for American football to take its own course and change into a game quite distinct from its British "ancestors." David Riesman and Revel Denney (1954) suggest that certain aspects of the American game of rugby, and the context in which it was played, made it unsuitable in American colleges. While some American students were familiar with rugby, most were not. Rugby rules assumed a certain knowledge of the game. Riesman and Denney cite the rule for a touchdown, which required the ball to be "dead, or fairly so" (p. 246) for a touchdown to count. Such ambiguity didn't work well with American players unschooled in the nuances of the game. English players also had a need to show "good form" because matches were viewed by spectators from lower social strata, and players were judged as "gentlemen in action" (or at least they felt so). American college players felt no such need to show "good form" while playing (p. 249).

An alternate interpretation is that the game of football was still in its formative stages in the 1870s and 1880s. Different high schools and colleges played different versions of the game, and the compromise version reached by the Intercollegiate Football Association simply represented a separate version of the game, not an American modification of rugby.

One American difference was clear. Americans had little tradition (recall that the Rugby game was at least 50 years old by the time it "diffused" into English society), so Americans were more willing to innovate. Early on (1880) the American collegians modified the scrummage rule, which was used to put a downed ball into play, and adopted a scrimmage rule, in which the team in possession placed the ball in play via a snap kick to a back behind the snapper. Opposing players had to be behind their own scrimmage line prior to the snap. This practice allowed the offensive team to simply hold the ball without advancing it (whereas in a rugby scrummage either team has a chance to gain possession), so a rule requiring the offensive team to gain five yards or lose ten yards in three downs, or surrender the ball to the opposition, was quickly adopted in 1882 (Danzig, 1956, p. 16). Amos Alonzo Stagg explained the reason for this rule—Princeton, needing only a tie with Yale to win the 1880 championship, simply but lawfully refused to advance the ball.

> Safeties counted nothing, and once a side got the ball, there was nothing but a fumble to prevent their keeping it indefinitely. If pressed back upon their own goal line, they had only to touch the ball down behind their goal, bring it out without penalty to the twenty-five-yard line and resume play. The Princeton goal being endangered early in the first half by a long run by Walter Camp, the Tigers at once adopted this block defense. Eleven times in the game Princeton touched the ball down for safety, six times in fifteen minutes while Yale was on top of her goal, and the Tigers retained the ball throughout most of the second half, the game ending 0 to 0 as they had hoped. (Stagg & Stout, 1927, p. 64)

Perhaps the chief difference between the American and the Rugby versions of football is the practice of blocking. Obstruction was, and is, illegal in rugby and soccer, but from the beginning American players violated at least the spirit of the obstruction rule by running "interference," much as basketball players today provide moving screens (also illegal) for teammates. Stagg describes the early use of this tactic:

> [Blocking] grew out of Princeton's use in 1879 of two players to convoy the ballcarrier, one on each side but never in advance. It was introduced in the Harvard game, and Walter Camp, who refereed, warned the Princeton captain it was illegal. He seems not to have been sure of himself, however, for Yale was using the same play later in the season. (Stagg & Stout, 1927, p. 62)

Soon this marginally legal practice of running interference developed into the clearly illegal practice of leading the ball carrier. Stagg said that this development took place between 1880 and 1884, when blocking was becoming the "keystone" of offensive tactics. Rather than outlawing the new tactic college teams first exploited it and, in 1888, regulated it by forbidding extending one's arms while blocking (Danzig, 1956, p. 19).

Football's Violence Crisis

With blocking allowed, every player stood in jeopardy of contact during every play. Recall that safety equipment and pads were at best rudimentary, including helmets, which often were not worn anyway. Amazingly, helmets were not required until 1943 (Watterson, 1988, p. 111)! Football had been criticized from its earliest days for its violence and its inherent hazards. Rules were occasionally changed to reduce injuries. For example, wedge tactics, in which offensive players arranged themselves in a V-shaped formation and drove forward toward the apex of the V, were widely adopted as an effective way to advance the ball (three downs for five yards).

As can be imagined, the offensive and defensive players who met at the apex of the V were at risk of severe injury. When this formation was outlawed in 1894, innovative coaches simply developed new tactics to concentrate several blockers with a running start at a single point in the defense, which had to be somewhat spread out against the possibility of an end run. Exhibits 4–1 and 4–2 describe the famous "flying wedge" used on kickoffs and a wedge play from the "ends back" (six men in the backfield) formation, popular during the 1890s. In this formation the two ends were placed in the backfield, leaving a five-man line. A look at this formation reveals the powerful mass blocking it could generate on running plays. Of course a variety of end runs and reverses could also be run from this formation, so the defense, dispersed against these possibilities, could be driven back by linemen and two or three blockers coming hard out of the backfield.

But the hard collisions between blockers and defenders led to numerous injuries. Efforts to modify rules to reduce mass blocking tactics continued throughout the 1880s, at one point creating a rift between schools that favored such tactics (Penn and Harvard) and those that opposed them (Princeton and Yale). This rift among the "big four" led other colleges to join together to regulate football in the absence of leadership by the "big four." In 1896 the forerunner of the "Big Ten" conference was established, led by officials from Purdue and Minnesota, forcing the Eastern big four either to reform the game or to yield leadership in regulation of the game to Midwestern schools (Danzig, 1956, p. 28).

The fact that the Midwestern conference was led by college administrators and not by student leaders represents an important change that developed during the 1890s. Control of collegiate football, with its income potential, its effects on players and spectators, and its demand for facilities had begun to shift from student associations into the hands of administrators (Figure 4–1). Coaching was more and more being done by well-seasoned volunteers or professionals rather than by the players themselves. Playing conferences and rule-making bodies were developing into formal, rational organizations. Specialists began accomplishing tasks such as scheduling, finance, training, and rule making, whereas these tasks had been accomplished by player clubs in the past.

Perhaps the greatest single impetus to the formalization of American football was the threat by President Theodore Roosevelt to ban the game (Danzig, 1956; Watterson, 1988). Like many other observers of football, Roosevelt objected to its "extracurricular" violence, as well as the danger inherent in the game. No less than 23 players died from injuries sustained in high school and college football in 1905.[2] Some universities dropped football (Columbia being the most notable), and California and Stanford reverted to rugby rules for a few years (Danzig, 1956, p. 29). Other officials threatened to ban the game if reforms were not forthcoming. At a December 5, 1905, meeting of presidents of 13 Eastern colleges a proposal to abolish football failed by one vote. Instead, the presidents agreed to call a general convention of colleges to reform the

EXHIBIT 4–1 Running Mass Wedge between Guard and Center

To send the running mass wedge through the line between LG and C, the halfbacks draw back slightly before the ball is snapped to LH^2 and RH^2, in a line with FB, in order to give the ends more time to reach the opening ahead of them, and also to enable themselves to gain greater headway before striking the line.

RE also works over slightly to the left to RE^2.

At the instant the ball is snapped, all the men behind the line dash straight for the opening in the lines indicated.

C lifts his man back and to the *right*, and LG forces his man back and to the *left*.

LE passes through the opening ahead,* at an angle, and strikes the opposing C with his full force, while the RE, crossing directly behind him strikes the opposing guard in a similar manner.

At the same moment, FB with his head down and the ball held as before, strikes the opening so made, immediately behind the ends, with the greatest possible force, the halfbacks firmly attaching themselves to his flanks, as he receives the ball at x, and forcing him through. RT leaves the line as the ball is snapped, as shown for LT in diagram thirteen, and together with QB, closes in behind FB. All mass firmly together as before and drive directly through the line.

LT and RG hold their men and force them *out.*

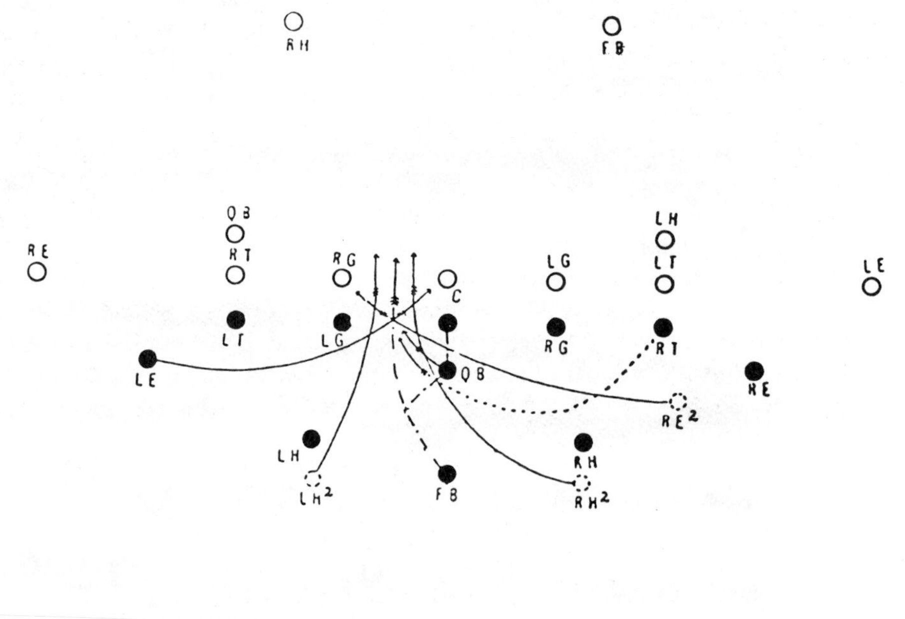

*When the ends find difficulty in reaching the opening ahead, they may follow the half-backs as in the preceding play.

From the 1983 *Scientific and Practical Treatise on American Football* by Amos Alonzo Stagg and Henry L. Williams, p. 173.

EXHIBIT 4–2 The Harvard Flying Wedge

QB stands with the ball in the center of the field. FB stands from 5 to 10 yards behind QB and a little to the right. The remainder of the team is divided in two sections.

Section No. 1 is composed of the heaviest men in the line and is drawn up from twenty to thirty yards from the center, back and to the right, facing QB. Section No. 2 is composed of the lighter and swifter men, drawn up five or ten yards back and to the left of the QB. Section No. 1 has the "right of way," the others regulating their play to its speed.

At a signal from QB, section No. 1 dashes forward at *utmost speed* passing close in front of QB.

At the same moment FB and section No. 2 advance, timing their speed to No. 1.

Just before the sections reach the line, QB puts the ball in play, and as they come together in a flying wedge and aim at the opposing RT, or straight down the field, passes to the RH and dashes forward with the wedge.

A slight opening is left in front of QB to draw in the opposing RT. (See small cut.)

As opposing RT dives into the wedge, LH and QB take him. RE and LE swing out to the left to block opposing RE. At the same moment RH puts on utmost speed and darts through the opening between the LH and the RE.

NOTE. The arrangement of the men is arbitrary. The wedge may be directed against any point desired. Its strength lies in the fact that the men are under full headway before the ball is put in play.

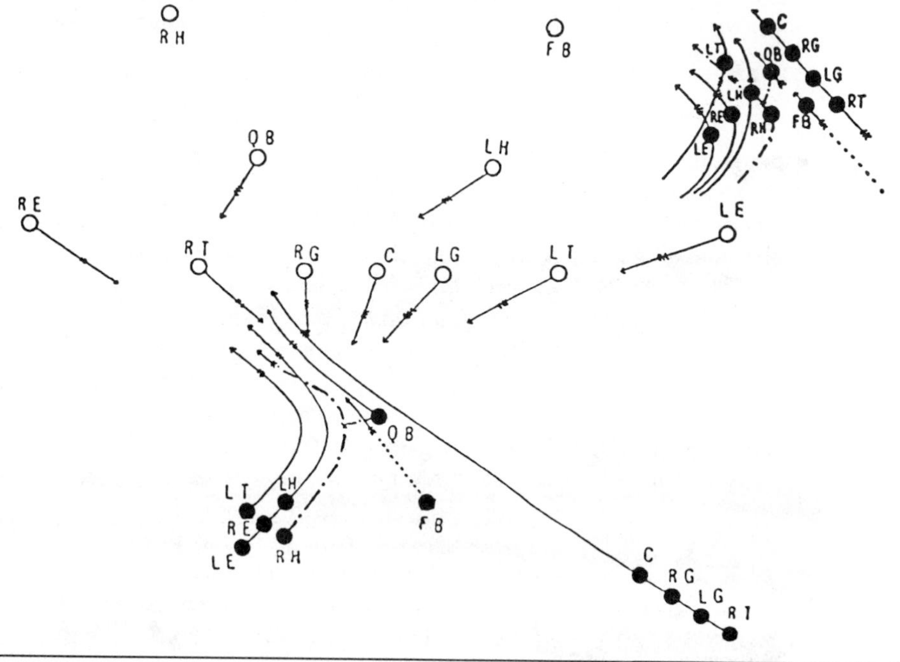

From the 1893 *Scientific and Practical Treatise on American Football* by Amos Alonzo Stagg and Henry L. Williams, p. 97.

FIGURE 4–1 This 1900 match between Michigan and Northwestern illustrates the less formal nature of the earlier game. Note that there are but two officials to enforce the rules. With the forward pass illegal, play consisted mainly in wedging the ball into the opposing line. The defense has two cornerbacks to defend against an end run, but otherwise everyone is aligned to join a shoving match between the opposing lines.

(Holt-Atherton Department of Special Collections; University of the Pacific libraries)

game. Sixty-two institutions were represented at this conference. A rules committee was appointed to propose reforms and to work with the Intercollegiate Football Rules Committee (Harvard, Yale, Princeton, Pennsylvania). By the spring of 1906, the old rules committee had amalgamated with the newer association to form the *Intercollegiate Athletic Association of the United States*. This organization, which in 1910 changed its name to the *National Collegiate Athletic Association* (NCAA), set out to change the rules of football (Danzig, 1956, pp. 29–38; Watterson, 1988, pp. 109–110).

E. K. Hall (quoted in Danzig, 1956, p. 31), a member of the 1906 rules committee, reports that the committee had several objectives besides making the game safer. The committee sought to open the game up (i.e., reduce mass plays), provide more strategic options to teams, and tilt the advantage from big players to smaller, more agile players. The committee also wanted to improve standards of sportsmanship and improve the quality of officials. Better trained officials would reduce the borderline rule violations so common to the game at that time.

One aspect of the sociological concept of *rationalization* involves creating organizational structures with attendant rules and regulations designed to accomplish certain overt goals (see Exhibit 4–3). By 1906, American football had an organization whose purpose was to change the rules and officiating standards of the game in order to achieve certain goals. Football, achieving increasing popularity in American high

EXHIBIT 4–3 Formalization of the NCAA

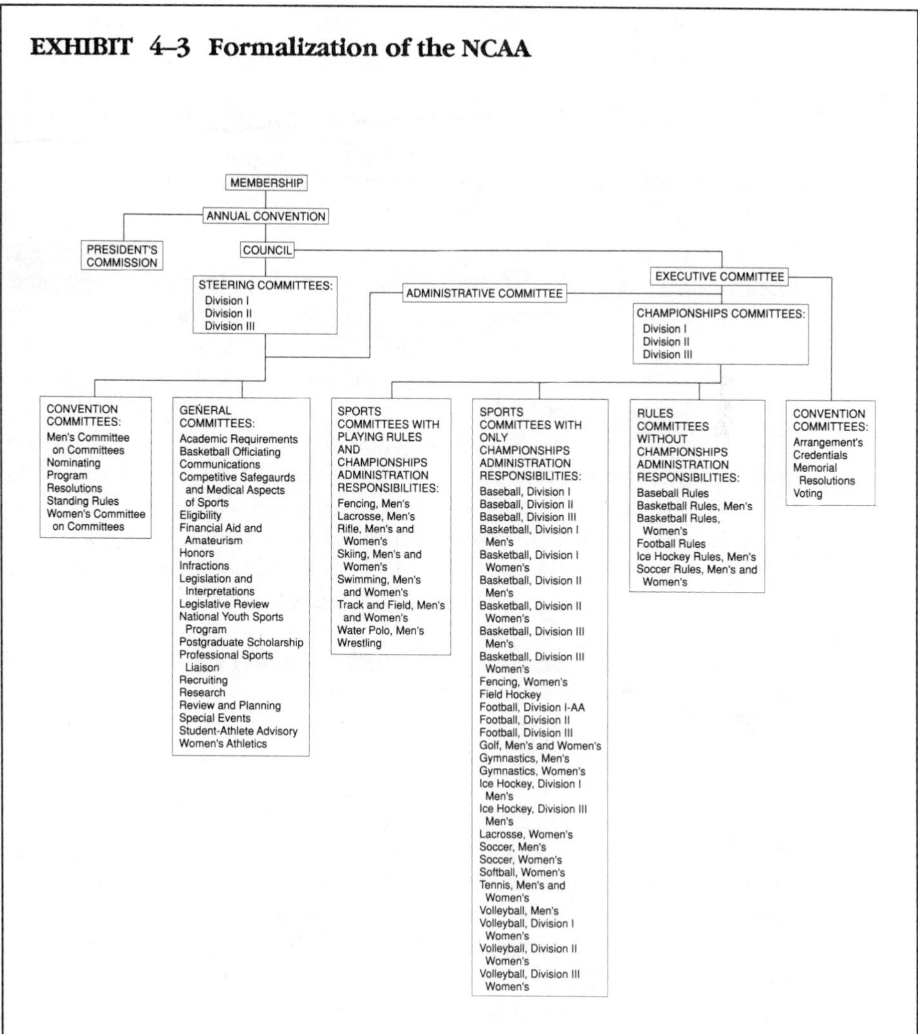

The NCAA began as a convention of representatives of 62 collegiate institutions who had met to reform the game of football. A rules committee was charged to change the rules of the game mainly to reduce rough play and injuries. The process of rationalization and formalization may be illustrated by a comparison of this committee to a contemporary NCAA committee organization chart. What would happen to intercollegiate sports if there were no national regulatory organization like the NCAA? The committee structure does not reflect the complex executive organization which provides for administrations, enforcement, tournaments, legislation, public relations, publishing and the like.

schools and colleges, was well along the road from local, informal, tradition-oriented social organization toward rational, formal, goal-oriented organization (see Furst, 1971).

The 1906 committee installed a number of new rules. The forward pass, long a topic of debate, was legalized. A neutral zone in front of the line of scrimmage was created to eliminate "sparring" between opposing linemen. This practice was not unlike the arm bar technique used by basketball rebounders today, but it occasionally escalated to slugging contests once the play began. The length of the game was reduced to 60 minutes—fatigue was thought to lead to injuries. Hurdling by runners was forbidden. Three downs and ten yards replaced three downs and five yards for a first down. Other rules tried to reduce mass blocking by forbidding linemen to drop back unless they fell a full five yards behind the line of scrimmage. A third official was added to watch for fouls (Danzig, 1956, p. 31; Stagg & Stout, 1927, pp. 253–257).

Like many reforms, the introduction of the forward pass may have produced unanticipated consequences. By forcing the defense to disperse against the possibility of a pass, the new rule made mass-blocking plays all the more attractive, especially to tradition-oriented teams who considered the forward pass not "real" football. In 1910, with the game still on "probation" for its frequent injuries, mass play was finally minimized with the rule of seven men on the line and by the elimination of many restrictions on forward passes (Danzig, 1956, p. 39; Watterson, 1988, p. 110).

By 1912 a fourth down for ten yards was added and a restriction on long passes was eliminated, leading to the rise in the modern passing game. This was heralded by the famous Dorais to Rockne combination in the 1913 Notre Dame–Army game (Danzig, 1956, pp. 39–41; Watterson, 1988, p. 110).

Subsequent years have seen numerous, but minor relative to the 1906–1912 rule changes, modifications of the game. Once the NCAA began to oversee the game, rule changes could be connected to the goals of safety and spectator appeal rather than tradition or improvement of the game for players as in the pre-1906 days. Of course safety and spectator appeal may go hand-in-hand with player enjoyment, but often fun for the players suffers in the interest of safety and spectator enjoyment. An early example of this is the rule that only backs and ends may receive a pass. Guards and tackles must stay on the line. This virtually eliminates their opportunity to carry the ball, and it is a lot of fun to carry the ball and receive a pass on occasion.

Several rule changes and aims of the changes are listed below.[3]

Coaching. NCAA rules restrict the number of coaches to nine as of 1991. Exhibit 4–4 illustrates one aspect of the formalization of the coaching profession. Before 1940 no incoming player could communicate with his teammates until a play had been run. Today, of course, most coaches call plays through hand signals or incoming players. Early on, a player who left the field could not return in the same half. Later he could not return the same quarter. Still later, free substitution was allowed, bringing on two-platoon football. During the 1950s substitution was restricted, restoring one-platoon football, and, in the 1960s, free substitution was restored. Free substitution allows coaches to recruit much bigger squads and makes specialization by players attractive. One-platoon football reduces options for coaches and requires players to

EXHIBIT 4–4 What Is a Coach?

One way to distinguish between formal and informal organization is to compare formal and informal meanings of words. Compare your everyday use of the term "coach" to the definition found in the NCAA Manual.

11.02.2 Coach, Head or Assistant. A head or assistant coach is any coach who receives compensation or remuneration from the institution's athletic department that exceeds the amount of a full grant-in-aid at the institution or any coach, regardless of compensation, who is designated by the institution as a head or assistant coach. (See 15.02.4 for the definition of "full grant-in-aid.") This definition applies only to those sports that have limitations on the numbers of coaches that may be employed.

11.02.3 Coach, Part-Time Assistant. A part-time assistant coach is any coach who receives compensation or remuneration from the institution's athletics department that is not in excess of the amount of a full grant-in-aid at that institution, based on nonresident tuition and fees. (See 15.02.4 for the definition of "full grant-in-aid.") This definition applies only to those sports that have limitations for the numbers of coaches that may be employed (see 11.6). See 11.3.4 for additional restrictions on compensation, benefits and expenses to part-time coaches.

11.02.4 Coach, Graduate Assistant. A graduate assistant coach is any coach who has received a baccalaureate degree and is a graduate student enrolled in at least 50 percent of the institution's minimum regular graduate program of studies. The following provisions shall apply.

(a) The individual may not receive compensation or remuneration in excess of the value of a full grant-in-aid for a full-time student, based on the resident status of that individual, and the receipt of four complimentary tickets to the institution's intercollegiate football and basketball games.

(b) Graduate and postgraduate financial assistance administered outside the institution (e.g., NCAA postgraduate scholarship) shall be excluded from the individual's limit on remuneration, provided that such assistance is awarded through an established and continuing program to aid graduate students and that the donor of the assistance does not restrict the recipient's choice of institutions; (Adopted: 1/11/89).

(c) The individual may not serve as a graduate assistant coach for a period of more than two years unless the council, by a two-thirds majority of its members present and voting, approves a waiver of this two-year limitation based on bona fide academic reasons, and such a waiver may not be granted solely to permit the completion of a graduate program.

(d) The member institution may not arrange additional employment opportunities except for summer employment, regardless of whether the student remains enrolled in the graduate program over the summer.

(e) The individual may receive only those expenses incurred on road trips that are received by individual team members, and only those expenses incurred in scouting opponents that are received by individual coaches. However, a graduate student coach may accept employment benefits available to all institutional employees (e.g., life

Continued

EXHIBIT 4–4 *Continued*

insurance, health insurance, disability insurance), as well as expenses to attend the conventions of the national coaches associations in basketball and football, without the value of those benefits being computed; and CB 391.

(f) The institution may provide actual and necessary expenses for the individual's spouse and children to attend a certified postseason football game or an NCAA championship in the sport of football.

(g) The individual may not evaluate or contact prospective student-athletes off campus, regardless of whether compensation is received for such activities.

11.02.5 Coach, Undergraduate Assistant. An undergraduate student-coach is any coach who is an undergraduate student-athlete who has exhausted his or her eligibility in the sport or has become injured to the point that he or she is unable to practice or compete ever again, and who meets the following additional criteria:

(a) Is enrolled at the institution at which he or she participated in intercollegiate athletics.
(b) Is participating as a student-coach within the five-year/ten-semester eligibility period.
(c) Is completing the requirements for his or her baccalaureate degree.
(d) Is a full-time student.
(e) Is receiving no compensation or remuneration from the institution other than the financial aid received as a student-athlete and expenses incurred on road trips that are received by individual team members.
(f) Is not involved in contacting and evaluating prospective student-athletes off campus or scouting opponents off campus.

11.02.5.1 This definition applies only to those sports that have limitations on the numbers of coaches that may be employed.

11.02.6 Coach, Volunteer. A volunteer coach is a coach who is prohibited from contacting and evaluating prospective student-athletes off campus or from scouting opponents off campus and who does not receive compensation or remuneration from the institution's athletics department except for the following:

(a) Those expenses directly related to the individual's coaching duties.
(b) Training-table meals.
(c) Transportation to and from and room and board at away games.
(d) Actual and necessary expenses for the individual's spouse and children to attend a certified postseason football game or an NCAA championship in the sport of football.
(e) A maximum of four complimentary tickets.

From the *1989–1990 NCAA Manual* (1989). Mission, KS: NCAA, pp. 45–46.

have both offensive and defensive skills. A return to one-platoon football would allow a dramatic reduction in football scholarships, while leaving the level of competition unchanged. Teams would be less skilled due to less specialization, but the competition would still be roughly equal. The number of allowable time-outs has grown from zero to three in a half (12 in a game counting both teams), allowing more control by coaches.

Roughness. Slugging opponents was as much a part of early football as forearm shivers are today. Unnecessary roughness has been reduced by the addition of officials, restrictions against piling on and roughing kickers or passers, and the stoppage of play when a runner's forward progress is stopped. Recent restrictions on crack-back blocks and on downfield blocking require blockers to hit opponents above the waist. Likewise, head tackling (clotheslining) is forbidden to protect ball carriers.

Safety. Dangerous blocking tactics such as leg whipping and clipping (blocking from behind, especially below the waist) have been progressively restricted. Likewise, tackling practices such as spearing and grabbing the face mask have been outlawed. The use of helmets, face masks, proper padding, and mouth pieces, and the availability of emergency medical personnel, have gradually been added to the game. Helmets were not required until 1943, although an examination of photographs from the 1920s and '30s indicates that almost everyone wore the felt-lined leather helmets of the day.

Spectator Appeal. Jersey numerals appeared as early as 1908, when Pittsburgh University publicity man Karl Davis used them to stimulate program sales, changing the numbers each week to prevent reuse of a program. By 1946 the *size* of the numerals was legislated. Many teams now place player names on jerseys. Commercial time-outs are now allowed in televised games. The role of the passing game is affected by legislation—allowing defensive backs latitude in controlling receivers and restricting blocking tactics, mainly use of hands, by offensive players, or encouraging it by restricting the defense and tolerating use of hands by blockers. Recent NCAA legislation eliminated the use of the kicking tee for place-kicking to reduce the dominance of place kickers using "soccer style" kicking. The kickoff line, formerly the 40 yard line, has been moved to the 35 to reduce long kickoffs, which end in touchbacks rather than exciting runbacks. Side zones (hash marks), where an out-of-bounds ball is put into play, have varied from one yard inside the side line to the present 18 yards inside the line. This allows room for play to go left or right, helping the offense.

Sources of Formalization

Social scientists interested in sports have paid some attention to the process by which sports have become formalized. Historian John R. Betts documented many 19th century changes that facilitated the movement of sports from local, traditional games to the highly organized activities they are today (1974, pp. 69–85). Along with continuing urbanization, which required people from different regions to come together and standardize their local games, several technological innovations contributed to this process. Transportation, especially the expansion of railroad lines and urban trolley lines, allowed players to compete with teams from more distant areas. This required increasing standardization of rules, and it allowed a growth in spectator involvement not previously possible. Supporting the effects of transportation was the rise of the telegraph and the "penny press." Now fans could follow their home team, and a national audience could enjoy a nearly simultaneous description of important events like a championship boxing match (by standing outside a telegraph office) or read about it the next day. Cheap printing methods also facilitated the promulgation of rules and "how to" books.

Mass production techniques of the late 19th century allowed the production of inexpensive, standardized equipment. By 1887 the Spalding "Official League" baseball had been adopted by several professional and amateur leagues, and was made available at retail (Betts, 1974, pp. 75–76). Baseball, cycling, and, later on, basketball equipment could be made to standard specifications and sold nationally at affordable prices.

The availability of electric lighting after the 1880s made indoor evening sporting activities possible, and armories and gymnasiums became the site of nighttime sporting activities. This paved the way for the rapid popularization of basketball during the first decades of the 20th century. Increasing spectator involvement and more widespread participation, of course, contributed to the ever growing regularization of sports activities.

Terry Furst (1971) identified several familiar factors as contributing to the rise of highly organized sports. The decline in the length of the work week during the late 19th century, along with a general if uneven rise in industrial wages, facilitated sports participation. Furst also contended that religious resistance to sporting activity weakened during the late 1800s. He suggested that the rationalization of business that took place during the late decades of the 19th century affected the organization of sports. Just as highly organized "big business" began to supplant small, local business enterprises, "big sports" began to replace "small time," localistic sports (Furst, 1971, p. 157).

Furst's idea that the organization of big business somehow "transferred" to sports seems unlikely. Sports did change, but the change was most likely produced by conditions reviewed by Betts—urbanization and improvements in transportation and communication—which encouraged the growth of "big sports" just as they encouraged big business.

Paul Hoch (1972, pp. 70–79) made the rather startling claim that American wars of the 19th and 20th centuries correlated "with the rise of the American sports industry" (p. 70). Hoch argued that the periods following the 1860–1865 U.S. Civil War, the Spanish-American War (1898), World War I (1917–1918 for the U.S.), and World War II (1941–1945 for the U.S.) all produced booms in organized sports. Major league baseball was founded shortly after the Civil War. Auto racing as a sport arose after the Spanish-American War. The golden age of sports followed World War I, and the expansion of the big-time professional sports followed World War II.

Marxists like Hoch argue that capitalism cannot thrive without periodic imperialist wars in which new markets and new sources of raw materials are seized. The truth or falsehood of this argument for European countries may be left to economists, but a few comments are appropriate. The United States and Canada enjoy an ample supply of raw materials even to this day. Indeed, both countries eschew the exploitation of a large share of their resources because of environmental and other concerns. Neither country could be expected to gain economically from the seizure of foreign markets. Canada, of course, never has seized any foreign territory.

Irrespective of the "war leads to economic expansion" argument, what about the "war leads to sports expansion" argument? The reader may already have spotted flaws in Hoch's contention. Just because two things happen at approximately the same time does not mean one has any causal influence on the other. A sad fact of American history is that *everything* followed a war, simply because wars have been so frequent. Hoch provides no information on *how* wars "produced" sports booms, he just claims they did.

At least one major sports boom did not follow a war. A major nationwide bicycling rage swept the United States during the mid-1890s. Competitive races boomed and sales of bicycles to pleasure riders boomed (Snow, 1975). This boom occurred three decades after the Civil War and before the Spanish-American War. Indeed one could argue that football boomed in the years prior to WWI, and, thanks to radio, national interest in sports boomed during the 1930s, just prior to WWII—witness the Schmeling-Louis fight. Simple *post hoc ergo propter hoc* arguments like those provided by Hoch contribute little to our understanding of the growth of sport.

One final source of the growth and formalization of sport deserves mention—physical education. Thomas Arnold's idea that sport is a proper part of a good education was quickly adopted by leaders of elite schools of Canada and the United States (Brown, 1988) and shortly thereafter by regular schools and organizations like the YMCA. If the working class youth could not learn sports in school or in a private athletic club, the YMCA was there to provide training facilities and competition (Betts, 1974, pp. 107–108). Even the 19th century prison reformer Zebulon Brockway called for proper gymnasium and athletic facilities as a part in an overall reformatory program and provided such facilities, albeit on a limited basis, in the Elmira reformatory opened in 1876 (Barnes & Teeters, 1959, p. 426).

Finally, the late decades of the 19th century saw the establishment of many national athletic associations that were products of the rationalization of sports—some organization was needed to promulgate rules, certify officials, and arrange tournaments. The tumultuous business of professional baseball was tamed somewhat when the National League was founded in 1876. The National Association of Amateur Oarsmen (1872), the National Rifle Association (1871), the Intercollegiate Association of Amateur Athletics of America regulating track and field (1875), and the U.S. Lawn Tennis Association (1881), along with other national regulatory bodies, came to promote sports through highly visible spectator events and to standardize sports by providing a "correct" or "official" version of a sport (Betts, 1974, pp. 109–111).

Are Folk Sports Dead?

Anyone can play informal beach volleyball, picnic softball, or touch football. However, these games are modified versions of "real" games and not folk sports. These games may themselves be formalized, as with highly competitive touch football and beach volleyball leagues. Even naturally noncompetitive sports such as surfing and frisbee-tossing have developed highly competitive, highly formalized, highly commercialized championships. These competitive organizations can influence casual players through their rules and the model of excellence they provide, much as earlier sports organizations did in the last century. Children's sandlot sports might be considered folk sports because they are locally organized with local rules. But sandlot sports, mainly baseball, appear to have suffered a decline because of the dominance of "official" youth sports (Coakley, 1990, p. 100).

There seems to be one sport, or rather one version of a sport, that is played on a regular basis and is governed more or less by local traditions, in which players enforce the informal rules, and which loses its character when played in its "official" form. This is playground basketball, and it conforms to the definition of "folk games" discussed at the beginning of this chapter. Venerable games played by young players may be observed any day on indoor and outdoor courts across North America. Other games like "Horse" or "21" are played as well.

Teams may vary in size from one (one-on-one) to more than five. Games may be played on a half court or a full court. The "playground" may be outdoors or in a gymnasium. Some areas play losers outs, most play winners outs. Suburban players often require "clearing" (taking the ball about fifteen feet from the basket) after a rebound or air ball by the opposition. "City rules" allow a missed basket by anybody to be put back up immediately. There are no official rules in playground basketball. Rules are flexible and learned by tradition. Disputes are settled by arguments or "shooting fingers" or alternating outs. There are no jump balls in playground basketball. Instead, opposing teams alternate outs. This practice has been adopted by college basketball rules. Fouls are called by players committing them or by the fouled players themselves. Players who call too many fouls are not appreciated. Good players, after all, should be able to score whether fouled or not. (See Wielgus & Wolff, 1980, for a delightful look at playground basketball.)

Playground basketball is played throughout the country, but only against local competition. Rules are variable according to local tradition. Rules are enforced by the players themselves. There are no official rules, no national governing body, and no intersectional contests, yet playground basketball in its several locally defined forms continues to coexist with official basketball. A few years ago a former graduate student returned to the University of the Pacific after a 15-year absence. He was able to rejoin a noon basketball game that had changed little during his absence. There is no noon basketball association, no noon rules, and no officials, yet this game has survived since the 1960s and it shows no sign of weakening.

Notwithstanding the vitality of playground basketball, sports in general have grown widely, but have changed in character through the last century or so. Sport, like many other social institutions, was modified by changes in general social conditions that facilitated growth and rationalization—urbanization, technological progress and increasing leisure time—as well as by more direct causes such as the inclusion of sports in school programs and the efforts of YMCA organizations and various national sports associations.

While this chapter focuses on the past, it will be interesting to watch contemporary social conditions shape sports in the future. The outlandish commercial value of major sports franchises and events, along with the increasing cost of conducting the noncommercial sports (at school and youth levels) that provide talent for major sports, comes to mind as a source of tension in contemporary sports. Will corporate sponsors allocate more funds to development? Will fewer and fewer players have the opportunity to compete at a high level? Will profitable major leagues provide funds for low level youth and school feeder programs? Or will cash short schools and colleges deemphasize high cost commercial sports like football and basketball and emphasize low level "minor" sports, which allow lesser athletes to participate and which require less expensive staffing and facilities? Some future sport sociologist will be able to answer these questions.

Summary

One of the most important ideas in sociology is the gradual rationalization and formalization that is changing modern societies throughout the world. The game of football has changed from a local game with vague rules based on tradition. Folk football didn't even have a real definition of winner and loser. Modern football is a highly formalized game with strict rules and well-trained professionals assigned to enforce them. The history of football reflects the general formalization of all social institutions in Western states.

A review of changes in modern football rules illustrates football's transformation from a player-run sport for the enjoyment of players, to a sport controlled by a highly developed bureaucracy in which profit, safety, and spectator appeal take precedence over player enjoyment.

This rationalization and formalization was stimulated by 19th-century technical and social changes, which allowed widespread communication and movement between people from different towns and, most importantly, the rise of big cities. Local rules had to be standardized if players from different areas were to play each other.

One informal, "not-bureaucratized" sport appears to retain its popularity in the United States. This is playground basketball. Rules are traditional (albeit informed by official basketball rules); rules are enforced by the immediate players; and games are played only among "in-group" members. With no official regulatory organization nor any official rules, this sport has retained its vitality throughout the United States for several decades.

Notes

1. These and later changes are listed in the *Encyclopedia Britannica* (1967, vol. 3, p. 248), "Basketball" entry. The interpretation of the "goals" of the rule changes are mine.

2. This number, shocking as it is, might be put into perspective. Professional rugby football in Yorkshire, England, had an *average* of 24 fatalities during the early 1890s (Dunning & Sheard, 1979, p. 220).

3. Most of the changes are listed in Danzig, 1956, pp. 71–74. Later changes come from current football rules. The reasons for the rules are the author's interpretations.

References

Barnes, H. E., and Teeters, N. K. (1959). *New Horizons in Criminology,* 3rd ed. Englewood Cliffs, NJ: Prentice-Hall.

Betts, J. R. (1974). *America's Sporting Heritage: 1850–1950.* Reading, MA: Addison-Wesley.

Brown, D. (1988). Social Darwinism, private schooling and sport in Victorian and Edwardian Canada. In J. A. Mangan, Ed. *Pleasure, Profit, Proselytism.* London: Frank Cass, pp. 215–230.

Carew, R. (1602). *A Survey of Cornwall.* London.

Coakley, J. J. (1990). *Sport in Society: Issues and Controversies,* 4th Ed. St. Louis: Times Mirror/Mosby.

Danzig, A. (1956). *The History of American Football.* Englewood Cliffs, NJ: Prentice-Hall.

Dunning, E. (1971). The development of modern football. In E. Dunning, Ed. *Sport: Readings from a Sociological Perspective.* Toronto: University of Toronto, pp. 133–151.

Dunning, E., and Sheard, K. (1979). *Barbarians, Gentlemen and Players.* New York: New York University.

Durkheim, E. (1947). *The Division of Labor in Society,* trans. by G. Simpson. New York: Free Press. (Original work published 1893.)

Elias, N., and Dunning, E. (1971). Folk football in medieval and early modern Britain. In E. Dunning, Ed. *Sport: Readings from a Sociological Perspective.* Toronto: University of Toronto, pp. 116–132.

Encyclopedia Britannica (1967). Basketball. Chicago: Wm. Benton, pp. 247–250.

Furst, R. T. (1971). Social change and the commercialization of professional sports. *International Review of Sport Sociology, 6,* 153–170.

Hobson, H. A. (1984). *Shooting Ducks: A History of University of Oregon Basketball.* Portland, OR: Western Imprints.

Hoch, R. (1972). *Rip Off the Big Game.* Garden City, NY: Anchor.

Hodges, H. M. (1974). *Conflict and Consensus: An Introduction to Sociology,* 2nd ed. New York: Harper & Row.

Riesman, D., and Denney, R. (1954). Football in America: A study in culture diffusion. In D. Riesman, *Individualism Reconsidered.* New York: The Free Press, pp. 242–257.

Snow, R. F. (1975). The great bicycle delirium. *American Heritage,* XXVI (June), 61–72.

Stagg, A. A., and Stout, W. W. (1927). *Touchdown!* New York: Longmans, Green & Co.

Stagg, A. A., and Williams, H. L. (1893). *American Football.* Hartford, CT: Case, Lockwood & Brainard.

Vander Zanden, J. W. (1988). *The Sociological Experience: An Introduction to Sociology.* New York: Random House.

Watterson, J. S. (1988). Inventing modern football. *American Heritage, 39* (6), 102–113.

Wielgus, C., and Wolff, A. (1980). *The In-Your-Face Basketball Book.* New York: Everest.

Chapter 5

Effects of Sports on the Participant

This chapter is about the socializing effects of sports participation. Are people "changed," for good or ill, by sports? Before we look at *how* sports might affect participants, a brief look at *who* participates is in order. Whatever the effects of sports, there will be no effects unless people participate.

Anyone interested in sociological aspects of sports has observed that participants in different sports come from different social origins. Certain sports are more popular in certain regions (e.g., volleyball, water polo, field hockey); some are dependent on geographic conditions (e.g., alpine skiing, surfing); some are limited by economic factors (e.g., tennis, gymnastics); some have more meaning to certain racial/ethnic groups than others (e.g., basketball, soccer, judo). In many ways patterns of sports participation reflect the ethnic, economic, racial, regional, and gender differences that characterize American and Canadian societies. We all know that part of the reason for black absence from tennis, swimming, and golf is economic. Another part, to use the term loosely, is cultural, and part is racial discrimination. Geography and climate help to explain the preeminence of sports like surfing, volleyball, and water polo in California and Hawaii, while hockey and skiing are concentrated in cold winter regions. Some sports are very important to members of certain ethnic groups (soccer comes to mind), while not so important to other groups. A few sports are more accessible to young girls than boys—baton twirling? gymnastics?—but girls have much less access to most sports than boys. I have called these differences the "sports opportunity structure" (Phillips, 1976). While the broad outlines of the sports opportunity structure are obvious, little research has been done to fill in the details, especially for younger participants, who are the focus of this chapter.

Who Plays What? Getting Involved

A theory about crime and delinquency can help us identify factors that influence the likelihood of a young person becoming involved in sports. Lawrence Cohen and Marcus Felson (1979) recognized the need to go beyond the what's-wrong-with-those-people theories of criminal behavior to look at criminal opportunities and deterrents to crime as well. Accordingly, they argued that the level of crime in a community would be determined by: 1) the number of motivated offenders who might get involved in crime; 2) the prevalence of opportunities to commit crimes; and 3) the presence or absence of barriers or deterrents to the commission of crimes. As with most theories of deviant behavior, we can use this one to explain participation in types of conforming behavior (i.e., sports) as well.

Motivated Individuals

The first consideration in the Cohen-Felson approach is how many people want to participate in competitive sports. As one would expect, children are more interested in sports when they receive encouragement from parents. In one study (Snyder & Spreitzer, 1989, p. 87), some 435 college students were asked to recall the degree to which their parents had encouraged them to participate in sports. Male and female respondents who had participated in varsity sports in high school recalled being encouraged by parents much more often than those who had only been involved in recreational (intramural) sports in school (see also Overman & Prakasa Rao, 1981). Other studies of successful athletes indicate that encouragement by parents and peers is an important factor in the motivation of participation (McPherson, 1975; Castine & Roberts, 1974; Stevenson, 1990). Yasuo Yamaguchi (1984) found that Canadian males list parental influence among the factors that got them involved in childhood sports, although this was not true for French (Montreal) or English (Toronto) speaking females.

Peer support would seem to be a second obvious source of encouragement to participate in sports, but the studies cited above do not always support this conclusion. While respondents frequently cite peers as an important source of childhood motivation, factors such as parental encouragement and the availability of organized teams to play on appear to be more important than peer influence (Yamaguchi, 1984).

The studies cited above have one important limitation. They are all *retrospective* in design. Older people in high school or college are asked to recall what it was that first influenced them to participate in sports some ten years or so in the past. Memories can be distorted by more recent events (Brehm & Kassin, 1989, pp. 61–66). Ask a divorced person to recall what it was that made their former spouse lovable. They may have a hard time remembering any good qualities—but they will recall many bad qualities. College students almost certainly distort their memories of childhood initiation into sports competition, especially regarding a process as complex as the influences provided by peers, teachers, parents, or coaches.

It appears that the memory distortion problem associated with the retrospective studies is not too bad. A handful of contemporary studies of young children currently involved in sports, rather than older people relating memories, are available, and they generally support the retrospective studies. One study investigated the experiences of Midwestern kids in grades 4, 5 and 6 via a written questionnaire (Greendorfer & Ewing, 1981). Black children differed a bit from their white classmates and boys differed from girls in their perceptions of who or what was encouraging them to participate. Black kids were more influenced by brothers (for males) or sisters (females) and more by what sports opportunities were available, whereas white children were more influenced by their fathers and teachers.

A similar study involved interviews with 764 Oakland, California, sixth graders. Interview subjects were randomly selected from schools throughout Oakland to provide a *representative sample* of all sixth graders in Oakland in terms of race, sex, income, and family background. This sample, like the population of Oakland, was about 60 percent black, 25 percent white, 10 percent Asian (Chinese/Japanese) and 7 percent Hispanic and "other" (Medrich et al., 1982, p. 52). The study found some evidence of peer support for participation (p. 74), in contrast to the findings of the retrospective studies. No effort was made to assess the importance of parental encouragement, but given the number of children involved in sports lessons outside the school setting, it seems clear that parental interest played a role.

Aside from parental and peer encouragement, a rather vague factor, "tradition" or ethnic influence, appears to play a role in the creation of interest in sports. In Oakland, black kids were somewhat more involved in sports than whites, and whites were more involved than Asians. Medrich et al. found that this difference held across all income and social class levels. Others (e.g., Edwards, 1973; Greendorfer & Ewing, 1981) have found a similar pattern in the comparison of black and white interest in sports.

The concept of black culture or, more correctly, black subculture, may help explain these differences. Black and white Americans are remarkably similar in values and aspirations, but they differ in areas of language, popular culture, religion, and sports. These differences were produced by historical experiences of blacks and whites and are sustained by present social and economic conditions. Sociologists have a lot of ideas about the conditions that have shaped and continue to sustain black culture, but for present purposes let us accept that it exists. Skeptics are invited to acquire and then compare 1950s versions of *Tutti Frutti* sung by Little Richard and Pat Boone.

Blacks have long valued sports excellence (Edwards, 1973), and blacks participate in sports more than whites. Black culture may be seen as a source of encouragement for sports participation. The idea of culture does not appear in the studies cited above because it is not amenable to questionnaire research. How do you "measure" a concept like culture in a few short-answer questions? Culture is transmitted to children through family and friends, so it is probably reflected in the family and peer influences discussed above. (Fine, 1987, provides an excellent discussion of children's peer culture.) A recent study of French- and English-speaking Canadians provides some support for the thesis that culture can motivate participation in sport. White and Curtis (1990a, 1990b) surveyed several thousand Canadian adults, comparing French and English speakers on levels of sports participation and on reasons for participation. English speakers reported substantially more sports participation. Importantly the two language groups expressed different reasons (sources of motivation) for participation. The English speakers rated *competition* and *challenge* more highly, while French speakers rated *health* more highly. These ethnic differences persisted among respondents of comparable education, income, and community size. That is, the differences are not explained by differences in community residence, education, or income. The researchers suggest that the cultural traditions of English-speaking Canada place more emphasis on the values related to achievement, and this achievement orientation, obviously along with other factors, serves to motivate more people to participate in competitive sports (see also Lueschen, 1967).

Along with parents, friends, and broad cultural influences, success in sports has been identified as a motivator. Success in youth sports produces two kinds of incentives for continued participation. First, success in sports is rewarding. Peers and adults reward successful play; and it is more fun to win or play well than to play poorly. Second, success appears to contribute to the creation of a self-image as a good athlete (Snyder & Spreitzer, 1989, pp. 86–87; Stevenson, 1990; Yamaguchi, 1984; Gras, 1974). Decades of research indicate that, just as rewarding experiences tend to encourage more of the behavior (sports) associated with the rewards, so does a positive self-image (as a good athlete) motivate further involvement in the activity that produced the self-image. Once a person adopts or, more correctly, internalizes a self-image, the person will resist change and seek to reaffirm the self-image (Aronson, 1988, Ch. 4).

Please note that "role models" are ***not*** included here as motivators of sports participation, except for parents and peers. Parents and peers are real role models. They are close to the child. They exert a day-to-day influence on him or her. However, many people think of nationally famous individuals like boxing champions or football stars when they think of role models. When a famous athlete (or actor, politician, or TV evangelist for that matter) is exposed as a drinker or a drug user, or involved in a sexual escapade, many people wring their hands in fear that these role models might have a negative impact on young people.

I believe that they are worrying about little or nothing. Role models are effective in proportion to the intensity of the relationship with the person being socialized (Maccoby, 1959). Parents, siblings, and friends are important. Can the influence of a distant TV image rival that of one's closest associations? Count the number of famous athletes who have been exposed as drug users in recent years. What effect has this had on impressionable youth in the United States? Drug use *declined* throughout the 1980s. It declined sharply for high schoolers and college students alike (Jamieson & Flanagan, 1989, pp. 359–361). Have Arnold Schwarzenegger and company created a rash of violent crime? Violent crime *declined* steadily throughout the 1980s according to annual victim surveys conducted throughout the United States by the U.S. Bureau of the Census (Bureau of Justice Statistics, 1990). The key factor in the incidence of violent behavior appears to be the *style of interaction* employed by violent people (Toch, 1969), but "violent role models" in movies and television do not appear to interact much at all! When *real* violent behavior such as fighting or criminal assault (as opposed to experimental simulation of violence) is used to measure behavior, no connection between television watching and actual violent behavior has been observed (Hartnagel, Teevan, & McIntyre, 1975; Henningon et al., 1982).

National role models may influence the technique for administering a high five or what kind of socks to wear but, aside from these shallow influences, distant role models can do little to influence a child's life. Furthermore, it is most likely that any influence a nationally prominent role model might have comes *after* young people have become committed to sports participation, not before.

Opportunity to Play

The second "determinant" of sports participation is the *supply of opportunities* to participate. This involves the availability of facilities, coaching, and competition. Opportunity is a special kind of "cause" determining the level of participation. Just providing playing fields, coaches, and leagues does not guarantee that there will be young people using them. But *not* providing these facilities ensures that there will *not* be young people using them! This is an example of a *necessary cause,* something without which an effect will not take place (Cohen & Nagel, 1934, p. 271). We tend to think of causation in terms of *sufficient causes,* conditions that produce an increase in a given effect, but an understanding of necessary conditions is equally important.

Without pools, coaches, and competition a community cannot be expected to produce many competitive swimmers or water polo players, no matter how badly some people would like to participate. Without year-round competition against quality competition few people, no matter how motivated, can become good at basketball or tennis. The presence or absence of facilities, coaching, and quality competition is an important determinant of the number of skilled athletes in a community.

Opportunity is reflected in a number of racial and regional variations in sport. Boxers have always come from inner-city origins, even though the dominant ethnicity of boxers has changed over the years from Irish to Jewish to Italian to black. Whatever ethnic groups have occupied these areas have produced the best boxers, because boxing gyms with trainers and other boxers are located in inner-city areas (Weinberg and Arond, 1952).

Susan Greendorfer and Martha Ewing (1981) found that opportunity was an important influence on the kinds of sports black kids played, but not for whites, whose choices were not limited. Medrich and colleagues (1982) also found that disparities in kinds of sport participation between racial/ethnic groups in Oakland were produced as much by opportunity as by motivation.

> It is not surprising . . . that the sports favored by black boys in our sample were the team sports that emulate professional leagues in which blacks play a

> prominent role. These sports were also the ones most often provided by schools and recreation agencies in moderate- and low-income areas. This suggests another reason why ethnic differences were so significant. . . . Since support for facilities and instruction in many sports activities was based at the neighborhood or municipal level, an ecological factor influenced the availability of programs to children regardless of individual family characteristics. For example, the costs of providing facilities and instruction needed for youth programs in skating, swimming, or tennis are very high. By comparison, facilities for team sports, such as basketball and baseball, are much less costly on a per child basis. Not surprisingly, most of the highly developed programs in individualized sports are located in affluent, mostly white suburbs. (Medrich et al., 1982, p. 190)

A similar argument is found in an article I wrote some 16 years ago.

> One thing that distinguishes the sports in which blacks excel is that the best facilities, coaching and competition in these sports are available in the schools. For sports in which blacks are rare, the best facilities, coaching and competition are found in private clubs. It is my thesis that good black athletes are concentrated in those sports to which blacks in general have access. (Phillips, 1976, p. 49)

Geographical distribution of successful athletes in certain sports is affected by opportunity. Geographer John Rooney has shown that the distribution of participants in certain sports such as skiing, hockey, and curling in the United States is influenced by proximity to slopes (skiing) and, in the case of hockey and curling, proximity to Canadian influences (Rooney, 1974, p. 276). Outside certain regions, would-be participants have to find another sport or move to where the opportunities are.

Barriers to Participation

Suppose a lot of potential athletes are motivated to play and sufficient facilities, coaching, and competition are available. Some people may be prevented from participating by other barriers—conditions which make participation difficult.

The most obvious barrier to participation is discrimination. A part of the historic black absence from the "country club" sports of swimming, tennis, and golf has been produced by undisguised racial discrimination (Henry, 1991). Even in major professional sports, black athletes have often been excluded from opportunities. Weak black players have historically been denied opportunities in favor of weak white players; although, this phenomenon has shown a decline in professional football and baseball in the last 25 years (Loy & McElvogue, 1970; Phillips, 1991).

Females have been unfairly excluded from many sports opportunities. The first female participants in the Boston Marathon had to sneak into the crowd at the starting line and count on friends among the male runners to fend off officials attempting to remove the "illegal" female runners. Until the institution (in 1972) of a federal law mandating equal access to sports for females in American schools, few competitive opportunities were available to women in secondary schools or colleges. After this law took effect (i.e., after opportunity expanded), female participation jumped dramatically (Leonard, 1988, p. 276), suggesting that the barrier of discrimination did, indeed, reduce participation by female students.

Lack of money may also prevent would-be athletes from participating. The simplest of recreational sports may carry costs that exclude some children. A recreational soccer league may charge $30 per child for registration and shirt, but shoes may run another $15–$20 and transportation costs, along with the cost of providing refreshments for the team once or twice can add another $20–$30 during a season. The total cost for one child adds up to roughly $70. Some families cannot afford this, especially if the family has more than one child. If the child is going to become a good player, he or she will probably need a ball at home ($15) to practice, pushing the cost even higher. Even among families who can afford this modest cost, some choose not to pay it, leaving the children with one less sports opportunity. Exhibits 5–1 and 5–2 illustrate some of these barriers to sports participation.

A final deterrent to participation involves psychic costs. Studies of youth sport dropouts indicate that some children are simply not comfortable with the competitive atmosphere (Martens, 1978; Orlick & Botterill, 1925; Yablonsky & Brower, 1979). A later section of this chapter will argue that such problems are not as common as critics suggest, but they do happen. Good youth league programs strive to teach coaches to provide a supportive experience to weak players as well as the stars, and to emphasize "playing your best" over winning. Unfortunately, it doesn't always work out that way.

A variety of influences, then, determine the extent to which a young person becomes involved in sports. The following sections assess what impact this participation has as participants grow up.

EXHIBIT 5–1 So You Want to Be a Swimmer

Some sports—baseball, soccer, basketball—require little equipment. Good coaching and playing facilities are available in public parks and recreation programs; other sports cost money. Listed below are estimated costs of a moderately priced competitive swimming program in central California. It is easy to see how many families simply cannot afford the expenses of competitive swimming.

	Monthly	Annual
Coaching and pool use	$60	$ 720
Equipment (suits, warm-ups)	—	60
Travel (3 away overnight meets)	—	150
Daily travel (10 mile round trip)	75	900
Parents club expenses (treats at meets, donations, driving)		0–200
Estimated annual cost		2000

EXHIBIT 5–2 Cambodian Girls in California: Deterrents to Participation in Sports*

A recent series of interviews of 19 Cambodian girls attending high schools in Stockton, California revealed several reasons for their reluctance to participate in school sports. All the girls were refugees. All of their families were receiving welfare support. Most of the incentives and barriers to participation discussed in this section are reflected in the girls' responses. The influence of Cambodian cultural norms is especially clear.

1. If a woman chooses to play sports she is being disrespectful toward the men. Sport is a symbol of manliness.

This was the major source of parental opposition to the girls' participation, but even if parents approved, few of the girls would have participated because of several additional problems.

2. They didn't feel comfortable wearing sport shorts. It is not suitable for young girls to show off their legs.
3. They don't feel comfortable undressing in front of other girls in a gym, the naked body is a private and respectful soul.
4. They do not have reliable transportation.
5. They do not have money to purchase uniforms or go out of town for tournaments.
6. They do not have free time. They have responsibilities at home to their siblings and parents.
7. They do not understand English very well.
8. They are not familiar with Western sports.
9. They feel that they will experience prejudice and discrimination.

*Christine Muok, unpublished report, Department of Sociology, University of the Pacific.

Effects of Formal Games for Children

Little League baseball, first organized in Williamsport, Pennsylvania, in 1939, has grown to international prominence, involving about 50 thousand teams and over half a million nine to twelve year olds (Fine, 1987, p. 5). The size and impact of this program, with its "world series" on national television and local community organizations operating leagues and maintaining facilities, has made Little League a lightning rod for criticism of youth sports. Competitive hockey for children is highly developed in Canada and in several areas of the United States. Youth soccer rivals baseball in many American communities. Sports like tennis, swimming, and gymnastics can be far more demanding than baseball for participants (and their parents) who participate in competitive level programs, but it is Little League baseball that has received the most criticism in the United States, with minor league (youth) hockey receiving similar criticism in Canada.

Excessive Pressure

Perhaps the main criticism of Little League baseball is it is too competitive. For a nine to twelve year old boy, batting in a tight game in front of rival players and coaches, umpires, and vocal parents is just too much pressure. Competitive tennis, hockey, and especially swimming probably place even more pressure on young participants. Two incidents at Little League baseball games illustrate the kinds of pressures faced by participants, at least on some occasions.

> A timid eight-year-old reached first base on an error that was compounded by an overthrow at first base. He could easily have run to second, but he was so shocked by the trauma of reaching first that despite the shouting of his first base coach, every member of his team, and, especially, his mother in the stands, he stood rooted to first. His mother came out of the stands, and before the entire astonished audience hit the poor child, and then added, "Wait till your father gets you at home tonight." (Yablonsky & Brower, 1979, p. 90)
>
> The pressure was unbelievable; you know, if I was ever going to get an ulcer, I would have gotten it then. All that pressure, I think, gave us this killer instinct; it's like, you know, we just can't go out there and play a game, we had to go out there and win. So the only way to insure that we would win was for us to go out there and be as mean and as ruthless as we could; you know, we had a job to do, we had a mission to accomplish, and nobody, nobody, was going to prevent us from doing it. (Ralbovsky, 1987, p. 92)

The first illustration is an event at a low level Little League game. The second is the recollection of a man who had played on the 1954 Little League World Championship team. Both indicate that Little League can be so competitive that the fun associated with playing a game disappears.

The evidence contradicts the conclusions suggested by the above incidents. Gary Alan Fine (1987) found little dissatisfaction on the part of Little League players or parents (p. 208). Daniel Gould (1987) reviewed research on this issue and came to the same conclusion as Fine. Aside from infrequent individual cases, young athletes are not harmed by competitive pressure (p. 86).

As one might expect, competitive stress was found to be highest for children in individual sports, in more important events, and in critical game situations (Gould, 1987, pp. 86–87). Highly competitive kids, kids with low self-esteem, and kids who expect their team to lose tend to worry about failure and how it might look to parents and peers. Under these circumstances players are likely to experience a lot of stress (Scanlan, 1986, pp. 115–116). Significantly, Scanlan found in a series of studies that kids who felt they had fun during competition experienced less stress (Scanlan, 1986, p. 116), suggesting that coaches should emphasize fun as much as possible.

The studies cited above involved surveys of boys and girls who were participating in youth sports. A skeptic might suggest that such surveys should not be expected to uncover serious problems, because kids suffering serious problems of competitive pressure would have already quit. Interviews of dropouts suggest that while some kids quit because they could not live up to expectations, most quit for the opposite reason—not enough stress! Entering a contest you know you will lose or sitting on the sideline through most of the game is not stressful. Playing an evenly matched opponent in an important game is. Orlick and Botterill (1975) and Martens (1980) report not getting to play and lack of competitive ability (no chance to win, too small, lack of skills) are the main reasons why kids drop out of youth sports.

Martens summarizes the evidence on competitive stress, adding the point that children face stress in such activities as music just as they do in sports:

> Although on occasion a youngster may experience substantial stress when playing sports, it is the expectation rather than the rule. The vast majority of children find sports, and musical competition, to be exhilarating, challenging, and enjoyable, not stressful or frightening. Indeed, there is some evidence to suggest we should be less concerned about stress among young athletes and more concerned about stress among coaches and parents. (Martens, 1980, p. 384)

Overemphasis on Winning

Among the "founding" contributions to the Sociology of Sport as a field of study is the work of Harry Webb (1968). Webb anticipated that as boys and girls matured and were more and more exposed to competitive sports rather than recreational play activities, values such as skill and winning would come to take precedence over playing fairly. Specifically, Webb hypothesized that winning and playing well (a requirement for consistent winning) would be valued over fairness among teenagers (who have been exposed to competition in school activities), while grammar school children (whose school environment is much less competitive) would rate playing fairly as the most important value in games.

Webb surveyed a total of 1,274 students in the third, sixth, eighth, tenth and twelfth grades in public and parochial schools in a Michigan city. Students were asked to rank "playing well," "beat your opponent," and "play the game fairly" in order of their importance. A highly competitive person would rate "beat your opponent" first and "playing well" highly, but "play fairly" would probably finish a poor third. Noncompetitive children would be expected to rate fairness as the most important value but not care much for beating their opponent (1968, p. 166).

Webb found that younger children rated fairness far more highly than winning or playing well. This fit his expectations. He was surprised to learn, however, that fairness remained an important value as boys and girls matured. Even among high-school age respondents, fairness was a close second to playing well. Winning was rated a distant third of the three values by all age groups. Older children came to value playing skill highly, but not to the exclusion of fairness, and no age group appeared to buy the maxim "winning is everything."

Webb did not separate respondents who had experienced youth sports from those who had not. Perhaps children exposed to organized sports are socialized to value winning and skill, while others of the same age retain the high concern for fairness, with little concern for winning and playing skill. Richard Mantel and Lee Vander Velden (1974) sought to test this idea by comparing the responses of 73 fifth grade boys who had been involved in competitive sports to those of 60 classmates who had not participated in organized sports.

Boys who had been involved in organized sports were more likely (53 percent vs. 33 percent) to rank skill or winning above fairness and less likely (47 percent vs. 67 percent) to rate fairness as the most important value in playing a game. The authors did not provide information on how the boys rated winning as opposed to playing well (i.e., skill). Recall that Webb found that winning was rated last by all age groups, but that playing well replaced playing fairly as the number one value as respondents got older. It is safe to assume that Mantel and Vander Velden's respondents rated winning behind playing well. Had winning been the most important part of playing sports for the students, the authors would have given this finding a lot of attention. Given this assumption, we can draw some conclusions from the two studies.

1. Young kids (up to junior high-school age) rate fairness above winning or playing well as the most important part of playing a game. This includes children who have been involved in competitive sports.
2. Older (high-school age) youths rate playing well above fairness or winning as the most important part of playing a game.
3. Among all groups, winning ranks behind playing well and fairness.

The work of Annelies Knoppers and colleagues also indicates that boys and girls do not adopt a generalized "professional" attitude toward sport even when they are involved in competitive sports. They want to win important contests, but fun and fairness are important also (Knoppers, Schuiteman, & Love, 1986; Knoppers, Zuidema, & Meyer, 1989). This hardly supports the contention that young people in competitive sports adopt a "win at any cost" orientation toward sports. On the contrary, the data suggest that fairness remains an important value, and competitive activities teach a "play well" ethic, not a "just win, baby" attitude.

A related study of Canadian youth hockey players supports the contention that "winning" is not the main value learned by young competitors. Vaz (1974) surveyed 1,915 youth hockey players in an Ontario city. Vaz found that only about 10 percent of the players rated "trying to win at all costs" among the *first three* most important qualities, and as players gained more competitive experience their emphasis on winning *decreased.* Some 15 percent of the Tykes (ages seven to nine) thought winning was among the most important issues in playing hockey, while only 2 percent of the Midgets (ages 15 to 16) did (Vaz, 1974, p. 40)! Youth hockey is not a cream puff game, yet neither the players nor their coaches subscribed to a "win at any cost" view (Albinson, 1973; McPherson, 1974). Rather, they valued playing skill, much as their American counterparts did.

These studies are supported by the observational study of Little League teams conducted by Gary Fine (1987). Players and most coaches subscribed to a "play well" ethic most of the time. Boys were criticized for lack of hustle or failure to come to practice, but rarely was a team or player who played hard in a losing effort subjected to criticism (see Fine, 1987, pp. 75–77; see also Iso-Ahola, 1976).

Adult Misconduct

One of the more egregious cases of parental misconduct in youth sport involved the Soap Box Derby of 1973. A participant, or more correctly, his uncle, had secreted an electromagnet in his nephew's car to give the car an advantage by pulling the car forward at the start of the race. Soap box races are run on a downhill street. The cars were retained at the starting line by iron bars that automatically rolled down into the street, allowing gravity to take the cars down the hill to the finish line. A car with an electromagnet would be pulled slightly forward by the retracting retaining bar, giving the car an advantage over the competition. Even before this scandal broke it had become clear that the racers, supposedly built by young competitors for $75 or less, were being built by fathers out of high-tech materials costing considerably more than $75. The idea that "every driver is a champion" had been more or less replaced by, "if you don't cheat you can't win" (Woodley, 1974). This youth sport story is found more in criminology books than in sociology of sport books. What sort of business ethics were the cheating adults passing on to the boys and girls who drove the cars? Even kids who faithfully followed all the rules saw what their honesty got them—and what cheating got their opponents.

Others point to bad sportsmanship exhibited by parents and adult coaches. Underwood (1984) points to incidents such as mothers fighting at a New Jersey youth soccer match, parents assaulting opposing youth football coaches, and officials and players being berated by adults and coaches for real or imagined shortcomings.

These things happen in youth sports, and, when they do, they set a terrible example for the kids. I have a friend who, after refereeing an ***under eight years old*** soccer match, was beaten by a group of parents. After team coaches and parents refused to identify the individuals who assaulted my friend, the team was expelled from the league. This section is not about instances of terrible adult misconduct, though. It is about the overall effect of youth sports participation on the players. How often do these things happen and do they affect the players?

Anecdotes about adult misconduct appear to greatly overestimate the frequency with which such incidents occur. Gary Fine (1987) studied ten Little League baseball teams over a three-year period. As part of his research he asked the coaches of two leagues to enumerate all of the serious parental misconduct cases they could recall during their collective 63 years of Little League coaching. The responses indicated that only one serious incident happened to them every six seasons (Fine, 1987, p. 213)! Interviews with parents and observations of games confirmed the coaches' recollections. While parents yell, they rarely get out of hand. When they do, league officials can promptly rectify the situation (Fine, 1987, p. 213).

It seems unlikely that such rare, albeit notable, events can affect a child's development for good or ill. Other children's pastimes, such as television, comic books, and adventure games, have also been condemned with a confidence that exceeds by far the empirical evidence.

Regimentation

Baseball, soccer, basketball, hockey, and other sports are fun to play. Many critics, including young players themselves, contend that a coach can take the fun out of the game by overemphasizing drill and technique (Yablonsky & Brower, 1979; Orlick & Botterill, 1975; Martens, 1980). Indeed, coaches may inadvertently retard a player's development by over-organizing practices. Two-on-two basketball or short-goal soccer or pepper games in baseball, albeit not highly structured, can develop skills faster than more orderly drills. Players touch the ball far more frequently than in organized drills and they have to put skills together, whereas most skill drills teach skills one at a time.

For example, pepper practice in baseball involves perhaps five players including one batter. Players position themselves about five yards in front of the batter. One player pitches the ball softly (underhand or overhand) to the batter, who must make contact with the ball, hitting it forward to be fielded by another player, who picks it up and pitches it again. Pepper players get a *lot* of repetition at fielding ground balls, setting and throwing, and, especially, swinging the bat to make contact with the ball. There are several ways to decide when the hitter has had enough swings and should be replaced by another player. Pepper practice is a great way to develop hitting, fielding, and throwing skills, but it is not controllable by a coach, and kids may goof off. Consequently, coaches may emphasize more ordered drills, which, from the perspective of any one player, involves mainly standing in line with relatively little action.

The image of over-regimented children being put through their paces by coaches is rejected by Fine (1987) on two grounds. First, it does not happen. Second, the alternative, free play organized by children themselves, is not as attractive as the somewhat romanticized image presented by critics of "Little Leaguism."

Fine was clearly concerned about over-regulation of the boys in the leagues he observed. He discovered that *under*-regulation was more destructive of fun than the opposite. One team whose coach did not enforce strict rules wound up not practicing at all due to absences. His players bickered during games and openly showed contempt for less skilled opposing players (pp. 96–102). Fine provides an illustration of this team's antics at a late season game.

> The Giants have just allowed the Phils to score five runs in the bottom of the third to lead 8–0, and the team is angry and bickering with each other. Hal Brattle throws down his glove in disgust, and Rod holds his head in his hands, possibly in tears. Paul tries to reassert his moral authority by saying: "I'll do the bellyaching, not the players. You're a team. You got about as much spirit as a dead horse. Let's quit complaining." However, by this point late in the season, Paul has almost no credibility, and after Paul finishes his talk, Rod whispers, "Fuck you" and gives

> him the "finger" to his back. Rich sneers, "Bite my bag." Bill Anders adds sarcastically, "Let's put this game in the Hall of Fame," and he refuses to coach the bases. (Fine, 1987, p. 101)

Fine argues, "A coach like Paul who lets players have a good time often finds that players are not having a good time and are blaming it on him" (p. 101).

Even the more regimented teams mixed work with play. Players kidded, played side games, ate, talked to nonplayers, and even interrupted games to goof off (see pp. 52–58). Even professional players occasionally goof off during games rather than stay focused on the game (Bouton, 1970). Coaches may demand more or less discipline from their young players but, just as in a well-ordered classroom, there is always room for informal interaction that undercuts whatever discipline a coach may be able to impose.

Free Play: Sandlot Sports

One important theme of the criticisms of Little League baseball and of youth sports in general is that unorganized or, more correctly, child-organized play activities are better for the development of the players (Devereux, 1976; Yablonsky & Brower, 1979; Opie & Opie, 1969; Orlick & Botterill, 1975). Critics speak of sandlot baseball or "horse apple hockey" (the horse apple frozen solid, thankfully) in glowing terms while highlighting the defects of adult-sponsored events, some of which are enumerated above.

I can sympathize with them. There were no adult-sponsored sports outside of school teams in the towns where I grew up. I can recall a tackle football game in which players ranging in age from high schoolers to sixth graders played in a cow pasture, cows included. The east side of town was matched against the west side. Anybody who wanted to play got to play thanks to lack of numbers. Younger kids were not expected to block or tackle older kids. Rather, players matched up against opponents of comparable size. Everyone had fun, even those who fell on freshly deposited cow manure. People got hurt but no one was seriously injured, in spite of an absence of pads and helmets.

But there was a downside to our games, too. I remember two older boys settling a dispute, this time in a basketball game, with a fist fight. I can recall boys being excluded from games or sharply rebuked for the lack of playing skill. I can recall players "working over" opponents in sandlot football to settle scores from disputes that arose in school or social life. If adult-sponsored youth sports are not as *bad* as some say, sandlot sports organized by the kids themselves probably are not as *good* as some say.

The main advantage of sandlot games is thought to be the organizing experience children get. How to organize teams, enunciate ground rules, and settle disputes? Suppose only ten players are available for a baseball game. Teams can pitch to themselves and cover only the left half of the ball field. A hit to right field would be a foul ball—three fouls are an out. The pitcher can move to the third base line for left-handed batters to allow them to hit to left field. The batter can be called out if an infielder throws the ball to the pitcher before the batter reaches first base. "Ghost runners" may be used if players do not feel like running the bases. Players who do not want to swing the bat can be induced to do so via ridicule ("Jesus Christ! Whaddaya want?"). Close plays can be settled by arguing or by taking turns giving in on arguments about close plays. New players may be integrated into the game at any point. Sides may be changed if one team begins to dominate too much.

Janet Lever (1976, 1978) studied 181 fifth grade boys and girls at play in school and at home through direct observation and interviews. She found that boys, much more than girls, engaged in complex games like baseball, while girls tended to play in small groups in activities that, while demanding interpersonal skills, did not have the complex organization of the sports boys played (see also Klieber & Roberts, 1983; Medrich et al., 1982). Boys experienced play in bigger groups, in more competitive activities, and with much more complex rules. Boys, much more than girls, had to organize games and settle disputes. Lever suggested that these preadolescent game experiences may prepare boys for effective functioning in impersonal, competitive work settings, while most of their female classmates missed out on these experiences.

> Boys' experience in controlled and socially approved competitive situations may improve their ability to deal with interpersonal competition in a forthright manner. And experience in situations demanding interdependence between teammates should help boys incorporate more general cooperative skills, as well as giving some team members (especially the older boys during age-mixed play) very specific training in leadership skills. (Lever, 1976, p. 484)

Jay Coakley (1980, 1990) and students in his Sociology of Sport classes observed some 84 informal children's games and 121 adult-sponsored and controlled games.[1] Like Lever, Coakley suggested that the two types of experiences might have implications for the development of the children. In informal, child-organized games the players tried to maximize *action* by reducing unnecessary stoppages in play. They wanted to be *involved* in the action. This was accomplished via rule modifications like "do-over" or pitching easier balls to lesser players. Special rules could also maintain a *close game*, which was another "goal" of informal sports contests—changing players might even up a lopsided game. Play was seen as a way to *reaffirm friendships* among players. Older players used their status to enforce a modicum of order and, surprisingly, arguments rarely lasted long enough to disrupt the games (Coakley, 1990, p. 90; see also Lever, 1976, p. 482).

Coakley found a number of contrasts between child-organized games and adult-sponsored games. Adult-sponsored games were governed by *formal rules,* which were enforced by coaches and referees or umpires. Players were required to play at specific *positions, assigned* by coaches. When and where play occurred were governed by schedules. Who played was determined by team rosters, the composition of which was determined by coaches and league officials, not by patterns of friendship. If there was arguing to be done it was done by adults, not the players. Unskilled players were often limited to a minimum amount of playing time and, if my own observations are a guide, in positions that got the least amount of action (e.g., right field, outside fullback).

In that all of the organization was done by adults Coakley, along with others, suspected that the benefits of working out problems and opportunities for self-expression available to participants in informal games might not be available to kids who played in adult-sponsored sports. Coakley (1990) observed, however, that the evidence does not support this suspicion (p. 100). Two studies of grade school kids have found that participants in adult-sponsored sports are *more* likely to engage in sandlot sports activities than their peers who do not engage in "official" youth sports.

Klieber and Roberts (1983) studied 80 boys and 80 girls in fourth and fifth grades in Urbana, Illinois. They found that participants in formal sports were slightly more likely to be involved in informal sports. Medrich and colleagues (1982) interviewed 764 sixth graders in Oakland, California, schools. Boys who were involved in two or more formal youth sports activities were somewhat more likely to engage in informal sports with their friends than boys who did not play in formal youth sports (84 percent vs. 66 percent). Girls who participated in formal sports were slightly more likely to report informal sports activity.[2] These two studies provide solid evidence against the argument that adult-sponsored sports somehow rob children of the social benefits of sandlot sports. Critics also overlook the tremendous amount of informal, child-controlled interaction (not always admirable, but child-controlled nonetheless) that goes on among players during games and practices of adult-run sports teams (Fine, 1987). A lack of sandlot play does not necessarily imply an absence of opportunities to develop social skills.

Informal games probably do not live up to the almost romantic image suggested by critics of "Little Leaguism." Indeed, informal games may have an "ugly" side to them. Not everybody is included in informal games, which we know are limited to members of friendship groups. A study of informal school playground games at an Illinois school reported that kids picked last in playground games (usually those with the least skill) felt rejected, were placed in low action positions and tended to withdraw from games to avoid being reminded they weren't wanted (Evans, 1988). Gary Alan Fine (1987) found that most of the Little League ballplayers he studied preferred organized to sandlot baseball mainly because of the arguments so common in sandlot play (p. 217).

For all their potentially positive outcomes, informal play groups have long been recognized as a potential source of negative outcomes as well.

> To a very great extent these traditions of delinquency are preserved and transmitted through the medium of social contact within the *unsupervised play*

> *group* and the more highly organized delinquent and criminal gangs. (Shaw & McKay, 1931, p. 222; emphasis added)

Delinquency itself may be playful. An interviewee describes the "game" of theft:

> When we were shoplifting we always made a game of it. For example, we might gamble on who could steal the most caps in a day, or who could steal caps from the largest number of stores in a day, or who could steal in the presence of a detective and then get away. We were always daring each other that way and thinking up new schemes. This was the best part of the game. I would go into a store to steal a cap, by trying one on and when the clerk was not watching walk out of the store, leaving the old cap. With the new cap on my head I would go into another store, do the same thing as in the other store, getting a new hat and leave the one I had taken from the other place. I might do this all day and have one hat at night. It was the fun I wanted, not the hat. (Shaw & McKay, 1931, p. 251)

James Short and Fred Strodtbeck (1965), who studied several hundred adolescent delinquent gang members in Chicago, found that informal sports involving these youths could end in serious fighting or rather unsportsmanlike conduct.

> Among our gang of boys the threat of violence during and after athletic contests was ever present, among participants and spectators alike. After one particularly heated contest, twenty shots were fired by members of one gang at their rivals, as a result of an altercation over basketball officiating. No one was arrested for the incident, and fortunately, no one was hurt. (Short & Strodtbeck, 1965, p. 244)

One researcher even argued that the social dynamics of the pick-up game were the same as those that lead to minor delinquent behavior by adolescents—friends looking for something exciting to do (Gold, 1970, pp. 92–99).

Conclusions

Perhaps the best conclusion about the relative merits of adult-sponsored and child-organized sandlot sports is that the one is not as bad as some say and the other is not as good as some say. Those who praise youth sports and those who criticize it can offer little more than anecdotes and speculation to support their contentions. Both sides probably overemphasize the role of sport in the lives of young players. These players are involved in a variety of groups—school, scouts, neighborhood, friends, family, and church. Sports is not separate from these associations, nor is it unique in its influence (McCormack & Chalip, 1988). Sports are fun. Players develop skills that may provide some enjoyment in later years, but aside from these obvious outcomes youth sports have little demonstrable impact on participants.

Effects of School Sports

As young people mature many drop out of competitive sports. Rather than emphasizing fun and participation, high-school sports, especially at the varsity level, demand intense effort and high levels of skill. Many players, including some good athletes, experience being cut for the first time. Others avoid this kind of rejection by not trying out in the first place. Consequently, high-school varsity sports teams provide a highly competitive experience for a selected group of young athletes. Observers have long believed that the special experiences associated with varsity sports might "build character."

The precise meaning of "character" is not defined, but it clearly refers to good conduct and "good" attitudes which presumably will help the athletes to succeed in school and in later life. Sports sociologists have accumulated a considerable amount of research on the behavior, attitudes, academic performance and adult careers of high school athletes and nonparticipants. The following sections will look at the first two of these presumed outcomes of sports participation. The subjects of academic performance and adult careers will be reserved for the next chapter which centers on sport in the schools.

Some General Problems

When we speak of the "effects" of sports participation we are implying that participation is the *cause* of the effects. The standard method of discovering whether one condition (e.g., varsity sports) is a cause of something (e.g., different behavior or attitudes) is the *experiment* (see Table 5–2). The key to any experiment is the availability of two identical groups at Time 1. In animal research this may mean two groups of mice housed and fed the same and so inbred that all are virtual "identical twins." One group is given a treatment, perhaps a hormone that is supposed to promote growth. Sometime later, Time 2, the two groups, *still exactly the same except for the treatment administered to the experimental group,* may be different (perhaps

TABLE 5–2 A Model of an Experiment

	Experimental Group	Control Group
Time 1	X_1	X_1'
Treatment →		
Time 2	X_2	X_2'

The key to any experiment is that two or more *identical groups* must be available. A *treatment* is administered to one of the groups making it the *experimental group*. The "no treatment" group becomes the *control group*. Since the only difference between the groups is whether the treatment was administered, any differences between the groups at Time 2 must have been produced by the treatment.

the experimental group will weigh more). Since the treatment administered at Time 1 is the only difference between the groups, the treatment must be the only possible cause of the Time 2 differences. The difference is seen as the *effect.*

It is hard to imagine a mouse experiment that would duplicate membership in a varsity high school sports team. Mice are different than people, after all. Human experiments are also possible, but human beings are not as easy as rodents to use in experimental studies. Humans have more brains than mice. They also have more rights. Suppose a sociologist decided to randomly select names of incoming freshmen at a high school and assign some students to play on school teams, while denying this opportunity to the others. The *design* of this experiment looks OK. By randomly assigning some students to participate in sports and some not to participate, the effects of sports participation could be assessed. Thanks to random assignment to "sports" and "nonparticipant" groups, family background, academic talent, racial composition, and any other characteristics of the two groups could be expected to be the same, or nearly so. The only difference between the two groups would be the experience of playing on sports teams. Differences between athletes and nonathletes observed in future years could only be seen as effects of sports participation.

This neat, logical experiment could never be performed, of course. Parents and students would rebel against such a capricious restriction on their freedom. Students want to choose for themselves whether or not they participate in sports. Even if forced to conform to the experiment, unwilling students would almost surely react against being forced into sports by merely going through the motions of participating, and those kept out might react by forming off-campus teams to rival the school teams. In short, the proposed experiment would be a fiasco. Nothing about the effects of sports would be learned. Experiments somewhat like this imaginary one have been attempted, with real results somewhat like our imaginary ones (Hackler, 1978).

Like many important aspects of social life the effects of sports cannot be assessed just through the experimental method. Instead, the *correlational method* has been employed. Athletes and nonathletes are compared, even though it is known that they differ in many ways besides participation in sports. That is, differences may be produced by sports, *or* or by a multitude of other differences between athletes and nonathletes (see Table 5–3). The correlational method seeks to isolate any effects by applying statistical controls to remove the effects of "other" differences, leaving only sports as a possible "cause."

Walter Schafer (1969) sought to determine whether participation in high-school athletics reduced delinquent behavior—defined as having appeared in juvenile court for an offense other than traffic violations. Schafer found that athletes at two Midwestern high schools were substantially less likely, 7 percent vs. 17 percent, than nonathletes to have appeared in juvenile court (p. 76). This difference could have been produced by varsity sports, but it might also have been produced by some other differences that distinguished athletes from nonathletes. Future athletes had earned higher grades than nonathletes when they were in junior high school. Athletes were more likely than nonathletes to come from white-collar (middle-class) family origins, while nonathletes were more likely to come from blue-collar (working-class) origins.

TABLE 5–3 Some Preexisting and Collateral Confounding Variables Regarding the Effects of High School Sports

Preexisting differences (athletes vs. nonathletes):	*Collateral differences* (produced at least in part by sports):
IQ	Friendship patterns
Social class	Attitude toward school
Race	Time use
Academic achievement	Relationship with teachers
Family interest	Peer status
Academic self-image	

Was it sports or the preexisting differences that produced the difference between athletes and nonathletes? Schafer sought to answer this question by *stratifying* his data according to social class and ninth grade academic achievement. Whereas the original comparison was between all athletes and all nonathletes, Table 5–4 compares athletes to nonathletes *at a similar level* of social class background and the ninth grade GPA. Preexisting differences have been *statistically controlled.* When athletes and nonathletes of comparable backgrounds are compared, the sports-delinquency

TABLE 5–4 Delinquency by Athletic Participation with Social Class and Previous Achievement Controlled

	Percentage Delinquent	Difference (athlete minus nonathlete)	*N*
White Collar			
High 9B GPA			
Athlete	4%	–4	(74)
Nonathlete	8%		(113)
Low 9B GPA			
Athlete	11%	6	(27)
Nonathlete	5%		(94)
Blue Collar			
High 9B GPA			
Athlete	8%	–3	(36)
Nonathlete	11%		(57)
Low 9B GPA			
Athlete	10%	–13	(20)
Nonathlete	23%		(126)

relationship just about disappears except among boys from "blue collar" families and low ninth grade GPA. Among this group, athletes are substantially less likely than nonathletes to be involved in delinquency (see also Landers & Landers, 1978; Segave & Chu, 1978). Schafer did not control for several other differences that might have produced the difference between athletes. Race comes to mind immediately, as does previous delinquency—how about ninth grade delinquency to go along with ninth grade GPA? Schafer believed ninth grade GPA provided a control for more than academic achievement alone. Grades partly reflect parental interest and support. They reflect student interest in school. They reflect to some degree how well the student gets along with teachers. That is, whatever factors contributed to academic success (or failure) in the ninth grade probably continued to influence most of the subjects through the high-school years. Nonetheless, it remains entirely possible that the athletes' better behavior was produced by selection factors—preexisting differences between athletes and nonathletes—and not by the experience of playing on school teams.

Correlational research can never match the precision and control possible in an experimental study. None of the uncertainties faced by Schafer would have existed had he conducted an experiment like the one described at the beginning of this section. On the other hand, Schafer was able to *do* his study, however imperfectly, whereas he could only have imagined an experimental study. Unanswered questions about the influence of selection factors would be examined by future research.

Studies of Sports and Delinquency

Schafer's study has led researchers to study the topic of sports and delinquency further, paying special attention to Schafer's main findings—athletes are less delinquent than nonathletes, and this relationship is most pronounced among boys who are the least disposed toward educational success (low ninth grade GPA, working-class family background)—and Schafer's main oversights—no control for prior delinquent behavior, no attention to racial differences, and no attention to the sports-delinquency relationship among females.

Virtually every subsequent study has confirmed Schafer's finding that athletes are slightly less likely than comparable nonathletes to be involved in minor forms of delinquent behavior. Evidence about the degree to which the relationship is concentrated among less successful students is mixed. One study found that the negative sports-delinquency relationship occurred most among blacks. The authors of the study suggested that sports were more important in the black community than in the white and that this is why sports provided a more effective deterrent among blacks (Stark et al., pp. 119–122).

Black students, on average, are somewhat less advantaged than their white classmates in terms of education but, aside from this rather weak point, Stark and colleagues did not replicate Schafer's finding that students of low academic achievement and socioeconomic status are most influenced by sports participation.

Stark and colleagues did apply statistical controls for prior delinquency. They found that among subgroups in which sports were associated with delinquency (blacks and whites from small towns), level of delinquency declined more among athletes than nonathletes. In the case of blacks, athletes were *more* delinquent than nonathletes in the 10th grade but by the 12th grade they were about the same.

Segave and Hasted (1982), in a study of students at eight high schools, failed to replicate the finding that the sports-delinquency relationship was most pronounced among blacks or among students from low social-class backgrounds. They did find the general deterrent effect of sports.

Importantly, Segave and Hasted included female athletes in their analysis. The earlier studies had been done prior to the effects of Title IX, which provided females access to competitive sports programs in American schools. Sports had the same effect among females as among males—athletes were less involved in delinquent behavior. Others (Buhrman, 1977; Buhrman & Bratton, 1978; Melnick, Vanfossen, & Sabo, 1988) have found a slight reduction in delinquent behavior among females. Melnick, Vanfossen, and Sabo found a weak negative relationship between athletic participation and minor delinquency after prior delinquency was statistically controlled, suggesting that at least some of the reduction in delinquent behavior was produced by participation, not simply by the selection of more conforming girls.

While some questions are still unanswered, the general conclusion that athletes are slightly less involved in minor delinquency most of the time is well documented. Although more work remains to be done, it appears that this finding is only partly explained by the recruitment of more conforming students into sports in the first place. That is, sports do appear to exert a weak deterrent influence on participants. Future research should concentrate on the selection problem, as this seems to be the most important unanswered question on this topic.

Attitudes

School sports programs have often been justified on the ground that qualities such as fairness, sacrifice, respect for others, and teamwork are cultivated in sports. These good qualities are thought to "carry over" into other aspects of athletes' lives. Attitudes are technically ways of *thinking* or *feeling* about things. Decades of research have demonstrated that attitudes do not produce behavior (Deutscher, 1973), but the way people feel is important in its own right.

Athletic participation might be expected to reduce racial and religious prejudice in that sports brings members of different groups together in a cooperative effort (Aronson, 1988, Ch. 6). Expectations aside, the best evidence suggests that athletes are not affected for good or ill. Hilmi Ibrihim (1968) administered a prejudice questionnaire to 92 athletes and 74 nonathletes, all students at Whittier College in California. No differences appeared between the two groups in antiblack or anti-Semitic prejudice. Subsequent researchers have found high-school athletes and nonathletes to be about equal in various measures of racial prejudice (Chu & Griffey, 1985).

Fine's study of Little League baseball players and Charnofsky's study of major-league players found clear evidence of racial prejudice among players. Others have found racial stereotyping among coaches (Brower, 1972; Edwards, 1973, pp. 224–226; Williams & Youssef, 1975). The notorious Al Campanis and Jimmy "The Greek" television interviews in the late 1980s demonstrated that stereotyping was not a figment of the researchers' imaginations. Campanis, a Los Angeles Dodger Vice President, said on national television, "I truly believe that they [meaning blacks] may not have some of the necessities to be, let's say a field manager or perhaps a general manager. . . . Well I don't say all of them, but they certainly are short" (Scully, 1989, p. 171). Less than a year later, sportscaster Jimmy "The Greek" Snyder attributed black success to "big thighs" and "being bred to be that way" (Scully, 1989, p. 171). Both of these men were promptly dismissed, but the existence of stereotyping, a kind of racial prejudice, in high places was made manifest. This thinking might be expected to "trickle down" to the high-school level. Importantly, neither of these men is known as being hostile to blacks nor for overt discrimination. Racial prejudice may be quite pronounced even in a person who does not discriminate (Deutscher, 1973).

Although racial prejudice in its various manifestations appears to be alive and well in the world of sports, it is also alive and well outside the world of sports. The evidence suggests that racial prejudice in a person is neither increased nor decreased by the experience of sports participation.

Some observers have expressed concern over the possible effects of competitive sports on attitudes of young women. The best evidence suggests that besides being more physically fit and feeling popular in school, female athletes in high school are affected very little by sports participation. Melnick, Vanfossen, and Sabo (1988) analyzed data from a nationally representative sample of 5,669 female high-school students. The respondents were surveyed first in the 10th grade and then two years later in the 12th grade. No less than 47 percent of the girls had participated in sports in their sophomore year, while about 26 percent were on varsity teams in their senior year. Two years of experience in sports (from 10th to 12th grades) had no impact on the athletes' sex-role attitudes (ideas about a woman's role in the family) or self-esteem or out-of-school interaction with friends (this, of course, is a behavior not an attitude).

The convincing "no effect" finding is important given the folklore about good or bad effects of sports for girls. An earlier national level study of top caliber college athletes and other college women (athletes presumably had been thoroughly exposed to high-school sports) showed that sports were related to a variety of outcomes (Snyder & Kilvin, 1977). The athletes were a bit more conservative about sex role issues and about sexual behavior, in sharp contrast to the "rebel" or "lesbian" stereotypes that existed then, and they were more satisfied with their body image and with their life in general.

Eldon Snyder and Elmer Spreitzer (1978b, pp. 93–96) report data from a national survey of college students. Women and men involved with sports (ranging from intramural to varsity teams) were rather similar to nonparticipating students in most areas. Participants were more likely to be members of social fraternities or sororities, possibly because such organizations provide opportunity to participate in intramural sports teams. Aside from this one difference male athletes were remarkably similar to nonathletes, especially given the fact that background differences that might produce differences between athletes and nonathletes were not statistically controlled. Women athletes were also similar to their classmates in such factors as drug and alcohol use, religion, politics, leisure use, and educational plans. They were a bit more conventional than other women in their sexual behavior. A more recent study of female college athletes also found athletes to be somewhat more conventional than other college women (Apostolopoulos & Gibson, 1991). If the experience of high-school sports has a lasting effect on female athletes, some clear differences between athletes and nonathletes should have been evident, but there were none.

In summary, the experience of playing on school sports teams, or other teams for that matter, appears to have no major effects on men or women save for the fact that women athletes seem more conventional about their sex role behavior. This suggests that school sports do not change the lives of participants outside of sports itself.

A recent study of leisure time use among Canadian adults supports the "no effect" findings of the American studies (McTeer & Curtis, 1990). Drawing on data from a 1981 national fitness survey of 9,258 Canadian adults, the researchers examined the relationship between reported physical activity and actual level of fitness on feelings of well being. If sports participation influences self-concept, active adults should have higher feelings of well being. After controls for such background variables as age, region of residence, income, and education were applied, knowledge of a person's sports activity level added virtually nothing to the prediction of feelings of psychological well being. Thus, Canadian adults, like American students, appear to be unaffected by sports participation, except for the obvious physical-fitness advantages of physical activity (Figure 5–1).

The following section examines another supposed effect of sports, personality development. The evidence reviewed so far suggests that sports participation has little or no lasting effect on the way participants act, think, or feel. It is possible that detailed instruments designed to assess personality can detect subtle effects that less detailed measures, like those used in the studies reviewed in the sections above, might miss.

Psychological Effects of Competitive Sports

Psychiatrist Arnold Mandell (1976) spent two years observing the San Diego Chargers, a National Football League team. Mandell came away from the experience with the impression that occupants of different positions have distinctive personalities. Offensive players were said to like structure and take well to discipline, while their defensive teammates were not amenable to structure. Members of the offense tried to create successful plays, while defenders tried to disrupt such creation. Wide receivers were

FIGURE 5–1 Common sense suggests that serious competition should have some effects on the personality and social adjustment of athletes. However, no clear differences between athletes and nonathletes have been observed.

(Courtesy Janelle Day)

seen as "narcissistic and vain" (p. 90), while defensive linemen were "basically angry, restless, intolerant of detail, barely under control" (p. 91).

Another therapist (Letchworth, 1968) also observed distinctive personality patterns—mostly maladaptive—among college athletes. Letchworth argues that poor preparation for the intellectual side of college life, coupled with an inflated ego produced by the recruiting process and limitations on personal growth because of the demands and restrictions of athletic life on campus, caused many athletes to develop feelings of insecurity, inferiority, and inadequacy. Letchworth argued that these influences led to personality difficulties relating to the expression of hostility off the field.

Do the impressions of these two therapists reflect reality? Do athletes have distinctive personalities related to their sporting activities? If they do, does the experience of involvement in highly competitive sports produce personality changes?[3]

TABLE 5–5 Personality Factors on Two Personality Tests*

California Psychological Inventory	16 Personality Factor Questionnaire
Dominance	Reserved—Outgoing
Capacity for status	Less intelligent—More intelligent
Sociability	Affected by feelings—Emotionally stable
Social presence	Humble—Assertive
Self-acceptance	Sober—Happy-go-lucky
Well-being	Expedient—Conscientious
Responsibility	Shy—Venturesome
Socialization	Tough-minded—Tender-minded
Self-control	Trusting—Suspicious
Tolerance	Practical—Imaginative
Good impression	Forthright—Shrewd
Communality	Placid—Apprehensive
Achievement via conformance	Conservative—Experimenting
Achievement via independence	Group-dependent—Self-sufficient
Intellectual efficiency	Undisciplined—Controlled
Psychological mindedness	Relaxed—Tense
Flexibility	
Femininity	

*From Edwards, 1970, pp. 57–58.

Or are certain personality types "screened out" of competitive sports, leaving a preponderance of people who possess the necessary character to succeed? During the 1960s and early 1970s dozens of researchers examined these questions.

Searching for the "Sports Personality"

Examine Tables 5–5 and 5–6. A researcher interested in personality differences between athletes and nonathletes, between superior athletes and average athletes, or between athletes from different sports might administer personality tests to college men and women involved in different sports to see if such differences exist. Each personality test has several scales that measure various personality traits much as a yardstick measures height. The first test on Table 5–5 is the California Personality Inventory (CPI), which has 18 scales. Another popular test, the 16 Personality Factor Questionnaire, (16PF) has, not surprisingly, 16 separate scales. A sports oriented researcher would probably want to compare athletes to nonathletes who are reasonably similar to the athletes in terms of age, college major, and family background. The researcher also would be interested in any differences between "superior" athletes (defined one way or another) and average athletes.

For each sport, four comparisons could be made, male athletes to nonathletes, male average athletes to superior athletes, female athletes to nonathletes, and average female athletes to superior female athletes. The researcher has three sports, so 12

TABLE 5–6 A Sample Personality Test Study Design

Swimmers						Soccer Players						Gymnasts					
Male			Female			Male			Female			Male			Female		
S	A	N	S	A	N	S	A	N	S	A	N	S	A	N	S	A	N

Comparisons: Superior athlete vs. Average athlete (6)
Athletes vs. Nonathletes (6)
Swimmers vs. Gymnasts (2)
Swimmers vs. Soccer players (2)
Gymnasts vs. Soccer players (2)

*S = Superior athlete; A = average athlete; N = nonathlete (perhaps comparable to athlete in age, social class, and college major).

comparisons (three sports × four comparisons) will be made. Our researcher will probably be interested in any differences between participants in different sports, so at least six more comparisons will be necessary—soccer vs. gymnastics, soccer vs. swimming, and swimming vs. gymnastics, for both men and women. This brings the total number of comparisons to 18. There could be more than 18. Our researcher might want to compare males to females or superior athletes to nonathletes, but for our sake and the researcher's we will assume only the 18 obvious comparisons.

Assume our researcher has administered both the CPI and the 16PF tests, which are composed of 34 (18 + 16) separate scales. The names of scales on the two tests suggest a lot of overlap between the two. For example, a person high on "sociability" on the CPI will probably be "outgoing" vs. "reserved" on the 16PF. Nonetheless, our researcher would have 34 scale scores with which he or she could compare superior athletes, average athletes and nonathletes across the three sports. Eighteen comparisons times 34 scales provides *612* (18 × 34) potential differences.

A "significant" difference between two groups is traditionally one that would be expected to occur by chance fewer than five times in 100 (i.e., < .05). *By chance alone* our researcher could expect to find about 5 percent, or 31, of the 612 comparisons to be "significant" at the .05 level. If our researcher is like some, he or she might publish a paper about the 31 differences between athletes and nonathletes, average and superior athletes, and/or athletes in different sports.

The test of "significance" in this sort of research, indeed in all research, does not lie in mathematical tests of "significance of differences between means." Rather it lies in *replication*. If the same 31 differences keep appearing in study after study on a variety of campuses and in a variety of sports, some systematic causes are at work. If no consistent differences appear from study to study, the differences are best regarded as the result of chance, and the hypothesis that sports participation, or excellence in performance, is related to personality should be abandoned.

Many studies in the 1960s and '70s found personality differences between athletes and nonathletes. Bruce Ogilvie and Thomas Tutko administered batteries of personality tests to athletes ranging from major-league professionals to youth league participants. In one study of top class-male athletes they found the athletes differed in many ways from other college students. Athletes tended to be more outgoing, more trusting, more controlled or serious, and more able to endure than college students not engaged in sports (reported in Edwards, 1973, pp. 218–227). Others have found that athletes scored higher or lower than nonathletes on various scales of personality tests (e.g., Warburton & Kane, 1966; Ogilvie, 1968), which suggested that a certain kind of personality "fit" into the rigorous world of high level sport or, perhaps, was able to muster the effort to perform at peak levels day after day, year after year.

While many individual studies discovered differences between athletes and nonathletes or between top level and average athletes, much (too much) like our imaginary researcher, the promise of the early work proved to be illusory. As more and more studies came in, it became more and more apparent that there were no personality characteristics that *consistently* distinguished athletes from nonathletes. Some years ago a student of mine reviewed 13 studies of personality tests of male high-school athletes and their classmates. Each study found differences, but not the same differences as the other studies. In some studies athletes were more intelligent, outgoing, or whatever, while in others they were *less* intelligent, outgoing, and so forth. In the majority of the studies athletes and nonathletes scored approximately the same on the majority of the personality scales.

Personality test scores do not appear to distinguish between quality or type of athletes. Superior athletes score about the same on personality tests as average athletes. Athletes in one sport do not appear to differ from athletes in other sports (Singer, 1975, pp. 94–95). George Sage (1976) administered a personality test to several hundred male college athletes in eight different sports. He could find no patterns of personality scale scores to distinguish one sport from another. Sage reported that several similar studies had failed to distinguish between athletes involved in different sports. Rushall (1972) studied several collegiate and high-school teams. His findings led to two rather blunt conclusions: there is no evidence of a "football player" personality, supporting Sage's findings; and there is no evidence that level of performance is related to personality scores. (See Fisher, 1976, Ch. 4; and Stevenson, 1975, for a thorough review of the sports-personality issue.)

Harry Edwards (1973) examined the possibility that black-white personality differences might explain black-white performance differences. Comparing highly successful black (N = 136) and white (N = 396) athletes (from an Ogilvie-Tutko study), Edwards observed that, where athletes' scale scores differed from the norm, black athletes usually were a bit farther from the norm. The personality test results disproved the stereotype of the black athlete as suspicious of whites, with a flamboyant, happy-go-lucky approach to life. Black athletes tended to be serious, organized, and "steady" people according to the personality test results for this sample (Edwards, 1973, p. 225).

Can the black-white personality differences observed by Edwards explain black-white performance differences? No. Other studies show that personality test profiles do not appear to distinguish consistently between better and lesser athletes. Even if we assume that the study cited by Edwards found more than chance personality differences, it does little to explain black excellence. The whites in this study were as good as the blacks. All 532 subjects in this study had been drafted by a professional team at the end of their collegiate careers (Edwards, 1973, p. 218). Given no difference in performance quality between black and white subjects in this study, the apparent black-white personality differences can hardly explain differences in performance quality (Phillips, 1976, p. 45).

The limited literature on female athletes in the early 1970s yielded results similar to studies of males. No particular personality profile distinguished athletes from nonathletes, superior athletes from average athletes, or athletes in one sport from those in another. Although several individual studies found such differences, no *consistent* differences were found (Berlin, 1974).

Summary

Access to sports opportunities is affected by race, social class, and gender, as well as the environmental influences of family and neighborhood. This chapter questions the character shaping of sports. Personality "profiles" provided by paper and pencil tests are probably the most believable measure of "character" available. These tests have been carefully developed and standardized on thousands of individuals. If character is affected for good or ill by sports participation, then athletes should obtain different scores than nonathletes on these personality tests. They do not. Therefore, the notion that sports build character is untenable if "character" is defined as personality. Likewise any idea that sports harm character must be rejected.

The contention that certain types of people are attracted to sports, or that the "autocratic conditions prevalent in the sporting sphere" (Edwards, 1973, p. 223) screen out individuals who are uncomfortable with a competitive, somewhat authoritarian setting, must also be rejected. If a "personality screening" process was going on, personalities of athletes should be different than those of nonathletes. The same goes for personality types associated with different sports. No differences exist, so any ideas that sports attract different personalities or help to create different personalities must be rejected.

This review of the effects of sports participation on behavior, attitudes, and personality of athletes supports the earlier conclusion of Christopher Stevenson (1975). Athletes, while clearly exceptional in physical ability and skills, are otherwise "regular people" who must occasionally cope with being treated by other people as if they were exceptional people. Sport is not an important source of character training. Rather, it is an important source of enjoyment for many people. We would do well to remember this.

Notes

1. This illustrates an important aspect of sport sociology. Students can do meaningful research in the field, whereas other fields of sociology require so much advanced knowledge, such expensive facilities, or such inaccessible samples that undergraduates are unqualified to perform more than clerical tasks. Who is better qualified to observe cheating in big-time college sports, race relations on a college team, or friendships between intramural teammates?

2. These studies, taken together, also represent good sociology. The researchers observed male and female children whose sports involvement ranged from none to several hours a week. Samples included white, middle-class Midwesterners as well as blacks, Hispanics, and Asians, mostly lower/working-class kids in Oakland. Any time you see consistent findings in studies of diverse populations, pay attention.

3. One wonders what kind of personality players had in the days of one-platoon football when all players played both offense and defense. Or what kind of personality a multiple sport athlete like Bo Jackson or Jackie Joyner-Kersee might have.

References

Albinson, J. G. (1973). Professionalized attitudes of volunteer coaches toward playing a game. *International Review of Sport Sociology, 8*(2), 77–86.

Apostolopoulos, Y., and Gibson, H. (1991, November). *Intercollegiate Athletics and Conservatism: Implications for Understanding Role Conflict Among Female Athletes.* Paper presented at the meeting of the North American Society for the Sociology of Sport, Milwaukee, WI.

Aronson, E. (1988). *The Social Animal.* New York: Freeman.

Berlin, P. (1974). Personality Traits. In E. W. Gerber, J. Felshin, P. Berlin, and W. Wyrick. *The American Woman in Sport.* Reading, MA: Addison-Wesley, Ch. 9.

Bouton, J. (1970). *Ball Four.* New York: Dell.

Brehm, S. S., and Kassin, S. M. (1989). *Social Psychology.* Boston: Houghton Mifflin.

Brower, J. J. (1972). *The Racial Basis of the Division of Labor among Players in the National Football League as a Function of Stereotypes.* Paper presented at the annual meeting of the Pacific Sociological Association, Portland, OR.

Buhrman, H. G. (1977). Athletics and deviancy. *Review of Sports and Leisure, 2,* 17–35.

Buhrman, H. G., and Bratton, R. D. (1978). Athletic participation and deviant behavior of high school girls in Alberta. *Review of Sports and Leisure, 3,* 25–41.

Bureau of Justice Statistics (1990). *Violent Crime in the United States.* Washington, DC: U.S. Department of Justice.

Castine, S. A., and Roberts, G. C. (1974). Modelling in the socialization process of the black athlete. *International Review of Sport Sociology, 9*(3–4), 59–73.

Charnofsky, H. (1968). The major league professional baseball player: Self conception versus the popular image. *International Review of Sport Sociology, 3,* 39–53.

Chu, D. B., and Griffey, D. C. (1985). The contact theory of racial integration: The case of sport. *Sociology of Sport Journal, 2,* 323–333.

Coakley, J. J. (1980). Play games and sport: Developmental implications for young people. *Journal of Sport Behavior, 3*(3), 99–118.

Coakley, J. J. (1990). *Sport in Society: Issues and Controversies,* 4th ed. St. Louis: Times Mirror/Mosby.

Cohen, L. E., and Felson, M. (1979). Social change and crime rate trends: A routine activities approach. *American Sociological Review, 44,* 588–607.

Cohen, M. R., and Nagel, E. (1934). An introduction to logic and scientific method. London: Routledge and Kegan Paul.

Deutscher, I. (1973). *What We Say/What We Do.* Glenview, IL: Scott Foresman.

Devereux, E. C. (1976). Backyard vs. Little League baseball: The impoverishment of children's games. In D. M. Landers, Ed. *Social Problems in Athletics.* Urbana, IL: University of Illinois, pp. 37–56.

Edwards, A. L. (1970). *The Measurement of Personality Traits By Scales and Inventories.* New York: Holt, Rinehart, & Winston.

Edwards, H. (1973). *Sociology of Sport.* Homewood, IL: Dorsey.

Evans, J. R. (1988). Team selection in children's games. *The Social Science Journal, 25,* 93–104.

Fine, G. A. (1987). *With the Boys.* Chicago: University of Chicago.

Fisher, A. C. (1976). *Psychology of Sport.* Palo Alto, CA: Mayfield.

Gold, M. (1970). *Delinquent Behavior in an American City.* Belmont, CA: Brooks/Cole.

Gould, D. (1987). Promoting positive sport experiences for children. In J. R. May and M. J. Asken, Eds. *Sport Psychology.* New York: PMA, Ch. 5.

Gras, F. (1974). The shaping of the interest in and the need for sport. *International Review of Sport Sociology, 9* (3–4), 75–80.

Greendorfer, S., and Ewing, M. (1981). Race and gender differences in children's socialization into sport. *Research Quarterly, 52,* 301–310.

Hackler, J. C. (1978). *The Prevention of Youthful Crime: The Great Stumble Forward.* Toronto: Methuen.

Hartnagel, T. F., Teevan, J. J., and McIntyre, J. J. (1975). Television violence and violent behavior. *Social Forces, 54,* 341–351.

Hennigan, K. M., et al. (1982). Impact of the introduction of television on crime in the United States: Empirical findings and theoretical implications. *Journal of Personality and Social Psychology, 42,* 461–477.

Henry, W. A. (1991). The last bastions of bigotry. *Time, 138* (July 22), 66–67.

Ibrihim, H. (1968). Prejudice among college athletes. *Research Quarterly, 39,* 556–559.

Iso-Ahola, S. (1976). Evaluations of self and team performance and feelings of satisfaction after success or failure. *International Review of Sport Sociology, 11* (4), 33–44.

Jamieson, K. M., and Flanagan, T. J. (1989). Sourcebook of criminal justice statistics. Washington, DC: USGPO.

Klieber, D., and Roberts, G. (1983). The relationship between game and sport involvement in later childhood: A preliminary investigation. *Research Quarterly for Exercise and Sport, 54,* 200–203.

Knoppers, A., Schuiteman, J., and Love, B. (1986). Winning is not the only thing. *Sociology of Sport Journal, 3,* 43–56.

Knoppers, A., Zuidema, M., and Meyer, B. B. (1989). Playing to win or playing to play? *Sociology of Sport Journal, 6,* 70–76.

Landers, D. M., and Landers, D. M. (1978). Socialization via interscholastic athletics: Its effects on delinquency. *Sociology of Education, 51,* 299–303.

Leonard, W. M. (1988). *A Sociological Perspective on Sport,* 3rd ed. New York: Macmillan.

Letchworth, G. E. (1968). The mystique of the college athlete. *Journal of College Student Personnel, 9* (January), 55–59.

Lever, J. (1976). Sex differences in games children play. *Social Problems, 23,* 478–487.

Lever, J. (1978). Sex differences in the complexity of children's play. *American Sociological Review, 43,* 471–483.

Loy, J. W., and McElvogue, J. (1970). Racial segregation of American sport. *International Review of Sport Sociology, 5,* 1–23.

Lueschen, G. (1967). The interdependence of sport and culture. *International Review of Sport Sociology, 2,* 127–139.

McCormack, J. B., and Chalip, J. H. (1988). Sport as socialization: A critique of methodological problems. *Social Science Journal, 25* (1), 83–92.

McPherson, B. D. (1974). *Career Patterns of a Voluntary Role: The Minor Hockey Coach.* Paper presented at the annual meeting of the Canadian Sociology and Anthropology Association, Toronto.

McPherson, B. D. (1975). The segregation of playing position hypothesis in sport: An alternative explanation. *Social Science Quarterly, 55,* 960–966.

McTeer, W., and Curtis, J. E. (1990). Physical activity and psychological well-being: Testing alternative sociological interpretations. *Sociology of Sport Journal, 7,* 329–346.

Maccoby, E. E. (1959). Role taking in childhood and its consequences for social learning. *Child Development, 30,* 239–252.

Mandell, A. (1976). A psychiatrist looks at pro football. *Readers Digest, 106* (January), 89–92.

Mantel, R. C., and Vander Velden, L. (1974). The relationship between professionalization of attitude toward play of preadolescent boys and participation in organized sport. In G. H. Sage, Ed. *Sport and American Society.* Reading, MA: Addison-Wesley, pp. 172–178.

Martens, R., Ed. (1978). *Joy and Sadness in Children's Sports.* Champaign, IL: Human Kinetics.

Martens, R. (1980). The uniqueness of the young athlete: Psychologic considerations. *American Journal of Sports Medicine, 8,* 382–385.

Medrich, E., Roizen, J., Rubin, V., and Buckley, S. (1982). *The Serious Business of Growing Up.* Berkeley: University of California.

Melnick, M. J., Vanfossen, B. E., and Sabo, D. F. (1988). Developmental effects of athletic participation among high school girls. *Sociology of Sport Journal, 5,* 22–36.

Ogilvie, B. (1968). Psychological consistencies within the personality of high level competitors. *Journal of the American Medical Association, 205,* 156–162.

Opie, I., and Opie, P. (1969). *Children's Games in Street and Playground.* Fair Lawn, NJ: Oxford University Press.

Orlick, T., and Botterill, C. (1975). *Every Kid Can Win.* Chicago: Nelson Hall.

Overman, S. J., and Prakasa Rao, V. V. (1981). Motivation for and extent of participation in organized sports by high school seniors. *Research Quarterly, 52,* 228–237.

Phillips, J. C. (1976). Toward an explanation of racial variations in top-level sports participation. *International Review of Sport Sociology, 11* (3), 39–53.

Phillips, J. C. (1991). The integration of central positions in baseball: The black shortstop. *Sociology of Sport Journal, 8,* 161–167.

Ralbovsky, M. (1987). Destiny's forgotten darlings! In A. Yiannakis, T. D. McIntyre, M. J. Melnick, and D. P. Hart, Eds. *Sport Sociology: Contemporary Themes.* Dubuque, LA: Kendall/Hunt, pp. 90–97.

Rees, C. R., and Miracle, A. W. (1984). Participation in sport and the reduction of racial prejudices: Contact theory, superiordinate goals hypothesis or wishful thinking? In N. Theberge and P. Donnelly, Eds. *Sport and the Sociological Imagination.* Fort Worth: Texas University, pp. 140–152.

Rooney, J. F. (1974). *A Geography of American Sport.* Reading, MA: Addison-Wesley.

Rushall, B. S. (1972). Three studies relating personality variables to football performance. *International Journal of Sport Psychology, 3,* 12–24.

Sage, G. H. (1976). An assessment of personality profiles between and within intercollegiate athletes from eight different sports. In A. C. Fisher, Ed. *Psychology of Sport.* Palo Alto, CA: Mayfield, pp. 366–370.

Scanlan, T. K. (1986). Sources of stress in youth sport athletes. In M. R. Weiss and D. Gould, Eds. *Sport for Children and Youth.* Champaign, IL: Human Kinetics, Ch. 16.

Schafer, W. E. (1969). Some social sources and consequences of interscholastic athletics: The case of participation and delinquency. *International Review of Sport Sociology, 4,* 63–79.

Scully, G. W. (1989). *The Business of Major League Baseball.* Chicago: University of Chicago.

Segave, J. O., and Chu, D. B. (1978). Athletics and juvenile delinquency. *Review of Sport and Leisure, 3,* 1–24.

Segave, J. O., and Hastad, D. N. (1982). Delinquent behavior and interscholastic participation. *Journal of Sport Behavior, 5,* 96–111.

Shaw, C. R., and McKay, H. D. (1931). Social factors in juvenile delinquency. Volume II of the *Report on the Causes of Crime.* National Commission of Law Observance and Enforcement. Washington, DC: USGPO.

Short, J. F., and Strodtbeck, F. L. (1965). *Group Process and Gang Delinquency.* Chicago: University of Chicago.

Singer, R. N. (1975). *Myths and Truths in Sports Psychology.* New York: Harper & Row.

Snyder, E. E., and Kivlin, J. E. (1977). Perceptions of sex role among female athletes and non-athletes. *Adolescence, 45* (Spring), 23–29.

Snyder, E. E., and Spreitzer, E. (1978a). Socialization comparisons of adolescent female athletes and musicians. *Research Quarterly, 49,* 342–350.

Snyder, E. E., and Spreitzer, E. A. (1978b). *Social Aspects of Sport.* Englewood Cliffs, NJ: Prentice Hall.

Snyder, E. E., and Spreitzer, E. A. (1989). *Social Aspects of Sport,* 3rd ed. Englewood Cliffs, NJ: Prentice Hall.

Stark, R., Kent, L., and Finke, R. (1987). Sports and delinquency. In T. Hirschi and M. R. Gottredson, Eds. *Positive Criminology.* Newbury Park, CA: Sage, pp. 115–124.

Stevenson, C. L. (1975). Socialization effects of participation in sports: A critical review of the research. *Research Quarterly, 46,* 287–301.

Stevenson, C. L. (1990). The early careers of international athletes. *Sociology of Sport Journal, 7,* 238–253.

Toch, H. (1969). *Violent Men.* Chicago: Aldine.

Underwood, J. (1984). What's wrong with organized youth sport and what we should do about it? In J. Underwood, *Spoiled Sport.* Boston: Little Brown, pp. 154–173. Reprinted in D. S. Eitzen, Ed. (1989). *Sport in Contemporary Society.* New York: St. Martins, Ch. 12.

Vaz, E. W. (1974). What price victory? An analysis of minor league players attitudes towards winning. *International Review of Sport Sociology, 9* (2), 33–53.

Warburton, F. W., and Kane, J. E. (1966). Personality related to sport and physical activity. In J. E. Kane, Ed. *Readings in Physical Education.* London: The Physical Education Association, Ch. 4.

Webb, H. (1968). Profesisonalization of attitudes toward play among adolescents. In G. S. Kenyon, Ed. *Aspects of Contemporary Sport Sociology.* Chicago: Athletic Institute, pp. 161–178.

Weinberg, S. K., and Arond, H. (1952). The occupational culture of the boxer. *American Journal of Sociology, 57,* 460–469.

White, P. G., and Curtis, J. E. (1990a). Participation in competitive sport among Anglophones and Francophones in Canada: Testing competing hypotheses. *International Review for the Sociology of Sport, 25,* 127–138.

White, P. G., and Curtis, J. E. (1990b). English/French Canadian differences in types of sports participation: Testing the school socialization explanation. *Sociology of Sport Journal, 7,* 347–368.

Williams, R. L., and Youssef, Z. I. (1975). Division of labor in college football along racial lines. *International Review of Sport Psychology, 6* (1), 3–13.

Woodley, R. (1974). How to win the soap box derby. *Harper's, 246* (August), 62–69.

Yablonsky, L., and Brower, J. (1979). *The Little League Game.* New York: Times Books.

Yamaguchi, Y. (1984). A comparative study of adolescent socialization into sport: The case of Japan and Canada. *International Review for the Sociology of Sport, 19,* 63–81.

Chapter 6

Sports in Educational Institutions

High-School Sports Participation and Academic Achievement

James Coleman, the eminent scholar of the American educational system, has commented:

> A visitor entering a high school would likely be confronted, first of all, with a trophy case. His examination of the trophies would reveal a curious fact: the gold and silver cups, with rare exception, symbolize victory in athletic contests, not scholastic ones. The figures adorning these trophies represent men passing footballs, shooting basketballs, holding out batons; they are not replicas of "The Thinker." The concrete symbols of victory are old footballs, basketballs and baseballs, not works of art or first editions of books won as literary prizes. Altogether, the trophy case would suggest to the innocent visitor that he was entering an athletic club not an educational institution. (Coleman, 1961a, p. 34)

Critics have argued that this "overemphasis" on sport affects more than the feelings of the hypothetical visitor. Many believe that the pursuit of sporting success somehow diminishes academic excellence. Many others believe sports help academic achievement. This chapter examines the evidence on this topic.

The Adolescent Society

Among the many studies of the connection between sport and academics, James Coleman's *The Adolescent Society* (1961b) stands as the basic work on the subject. Coleman studied ten different American secondary schools of varying sizes and in different Illinois communities, ranging from small towns to suburbs of a major city. Coleman sought to determine the impact of a variety of influences on the educational performance of teenagers.

Coleman's study observed the now familiar "adolescent culture," somewhat divorced from the influence of family and community but greatly influenced by the school—where every teenager spent some six hours per day, not to mention a goodly amount of his or her leisure time. The adolescent culture was centered in the school and school-related activities. Hence, he argued, the educational performance of teenagers in general could be explained best by school conditions, not by social forces outside the school.

What was there to be explained? In 1961 Americans had, perhaps unjustly, experienced a sharp decline in their faith in American education. In 1957 the Soviet Union orbited the first Sputnik space satellite. Soon thereafter, Americans watched on television the efforts to launch the first American satellite, only to see the Vanguard rocket lift off, turn on its side, and explode—on two successive occasions. Seeing their technology "outdone" by their chief rival, Americans sought to fix the blame and to "catch up." Clearly (albeit wrongly) American schools were responsible in that they had failed to produce the engineers who could create a reliable launching vehicle. The Sputnik episode served to focus attention on long-felt unease about the quality of American education, much as concern for American "competitiveness" with Japan and other industrial nations does today. It was at the height of this concern for educational excellence that *The Adolescent Society* appeared. To be explained was the alleged absence of academic excellence in American secondary schools.

Coleman began his argument with the contention that all students seek *status*—respect and recognition in the eyes of their peers and teachers. Ascribed characteristics such as father's occupation or ethnicity had little impact on status in school, according to Coleman's data. Rather, status could be achieved through two main activities. The first was academic excellence; the second, athletic [sports] participation. True, there were other factors—having a car or a good "personality"—but these were far less important than academics and athletics. As indicated by the comment quoted at the beginning of this chapter, Coleman found that students clearly valued athletics more highly than academics.

He believed that the effect of this overvaluation of athletics was a minimization of effort devoted to academic pursuits. While Coleman did not choose to elaborate on his theory per se, it can be applied at both the individual and organizational levels (see Figure 6–1).

The individual student would see how to become a member of the "leading crowd" in school and devote himself or herself to the most rewarding activity available. Suppose, for example, a student excelled in mathematics and in basketball. Observing the high level of status accorded basketball players and the limited status enjoyed by student mathematicians, he or she would devote maximum time and effort to the cultivation of basketball skills—presumably at the expense of mathematics.

On the organizational level the mechanism by which an overemphasis on athletic participation may inhibit academic success becomes clear. In any school the most

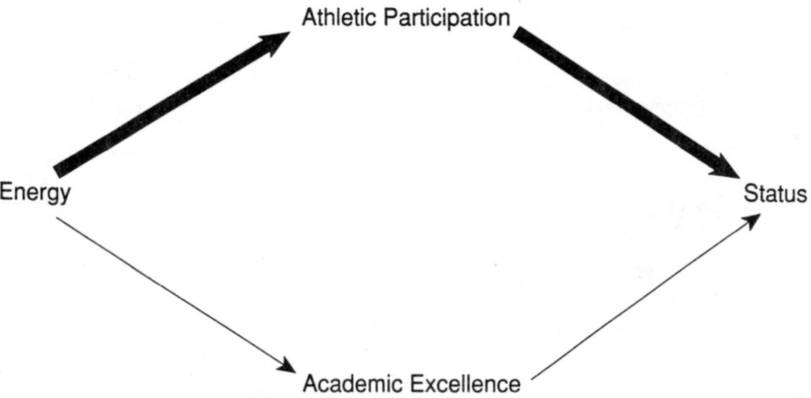

FIGURE 6–1 The Effect of Overvaluation of Athletics on Energy Allocation

talented athletes tend to be drawn into the pursuit of athletic excellence. What of the best scholars? Potentially excellent scholars will not be drawn into scholarship as athletes are drawn into athletic pursuits for two reasons. First, the "draw" (status to be gained) for scholars is less than the "draw" for athletes. Second, many potentially excellent scholars are also potentially excellent athletes who have chosen to devote their energies to athletic participation. Thus, the American high school was seen as highly effective in optimizing the selection and development of athletic talent, but inefficient in the development of intellectual talent. The best athletic talent would be cultivated, while only some of the best academic talent would be cultivated (Coleman, 1961b, Ch. 5).

A similar theory was proposed by K. B. Start (1966) in his study of a sample of English students. In contrast to the preeminent status given sports achievement in American secondary schools, academic achievement is the most important area in which a typical British secondary school student can achieve status. Start suggested that low achieving students would be attracted to sport as a compensation for poor performance in academics—in contrast to Coleman's students, who might turn to academics in response to failure in sport.

In this and a subsequent study (1967), Start discovered what his colleagues across the Atlantic were discovering—the theory that sports participation and academic pursuits compete for the energy of students is not supported by the data. If, as Coleman proposed, success in sport somehow inhibits academics or, as Start suggested, success in academics somehow inhibits sports participation, poor students should predominate and better students should be underrepresented on sports teams.

Start (1967) cited a study of London secondary school students (McIntosh, 1966) and his own studies of Manchester students, all of which examined the connection between academics and success in sports. The data clearly indicated that success in academics was *positively* related to success in school sport, in contrast to Start's and Coleman's prediction.

Testing Coleman

The first direct examination of Coleman's thesis was performed by Walter Schafer and Michael Armer (1968). Schafer and Armer reasoned that, if Coleman's thesis was correct:

> **1.** Athletes [boys participating on sports teams] should not perform as well scholastically as nonathletes.
> **2.** The greater the student's participation in sports, the greater the detriment to his studies.
> **3.** A student's participation in those sports that are given the greatest recognition and attention—generally football and basketball—should harm his academic performance more than the minor sports that do not . . . give as great social rewards. (Schafer & Armer, 1968, p. 23)

Employing a *matched pairs design* (boys were matched on IQ, fathers' occupation, curriculum level or "track," and grades in the semester immediately preceding entry into high school), Schafer and Armer compared the academic performance of 152 athletes with that of 152 "matches." The data contradicted the hypotheses suggested by Coleman's theory. That is, athletes generally received slightly better grades than their matches. This advantage increased the more seasons a boy had been involved, and the advantage increased for athletes engaged in the "high reward" sports. While the overall advantage of athletes was slight (average grade 2.35 vs. 2.24 on a scale of 0–4), the advantage increased precisely where Coleman predicted a decrease. Athletes involved in three or more seasons exceeded their matches by .21 grade points (2.45 vs. 2.24), while athletes involved in only one or two seasons showed no real advantage compared to their matches (2.26 vs. 2.23). Athletes involved in "high reward" sports of football and basketball exceeded their matches by .18 grade points (2.20 vs. 2.02), while athletes involved in less prestigious sports barely exceeded their matches (2.53 vs. 2.50) (Schafer & Armer, 1968, p. 24). Schafer and Armer pointed out that even Coleman's own data did not clearly support the "diversion of energy" thesis.

While the Schafer-Armer study provided a rigorous test of Coleman's thesis, the issue was far from settled given the small sample size of the Schafer-Armer study. Recognizing this, Schafer and Armer cited data from another study (Rehberg & Schafer, 1968), which involved a larger sample (785) from high schools in a different region of the country. This study employed a survey design in contrast to the matched-pairs design employed in the Schafer-Armer study. The results supported the Schafer-Armer study. Athletes received better grades than comparable nonathletes. Athletes were also found to exceed nonathletes in another measure of educational success, plans to attend college. This tendency for athletes to excel over comparable nonathletes in scholastic achievement (grades) and/or college expectations has been widely replicated (e.g., Schafer & Rehberg, 1970; Picou & Curry, 1974; Spreitzer & Pugh, 1973; Snyder, 1972; Otto & Alwin, 1977; Bend, 1968).

A more recent study involving a much larger sample confirms the Schafer-Armer findings. Don Sabo, Merrill Melnick, and Beth Vanfossen (1989) analyzed data from a nationally representative study of high school students, starting during their sophomore year in 1980 and following them at two year intervals to four years after high school graduation. Sample size ranged from some 30,000 in the initial 1980 survey of sophomores to 25,500 in the 1982 survey of seniors (85 percent of the original 30,000) to smaller, selected samples in later years (14,825 in 1984 and 13,481 in 1986) (Sabo, Melnick, & Vanfossen, 1989, p. 6).

The authors examined a variety of educational and career outcomes for students involved in the study. The sample was stratified (broken down) by racial/ethnic group (black, white, Hispanic), by residence (rural, suburban, urban), and by sex (male, female). This yielded 18 subgroups—for example, black rural females, Hispanic urban males—that could be analyzed separately. The authors applied statistical controls to assure that differences between athletes and nonathletes could not be explained by previously existing differences in social class background, school grades, or achievement test scores. *Athletes in every subgroup equalled or excelled comparable nonathletes in every measure of educational achievement.* Athletes generally earned better grades, dropped out less, had higher aspirations, attended college more often, and attained more years of college education (Sabo, Melnick, & Vanfossen, 1989, pp. 22–32). This is hardly the outcome to be expected if Coleman's theory were correct.

It has been suggested that the higher educational aspiration of athletes might do some harm to some athletes (Spady, 1970). Spady found that some athletes, who felt that they were members of their school's "leading crowd," aped their friends' college plans but lacked the academic preparation of their more academically oriented friends. The result, according to Spady, was an experience of failure once the unprepared athlete entered college. There is, however, another side of this "problem." Some unprepared athletes attend college and fail, but some manage to succeed, thereby achieving more than they would have had they not been influenced by unrealistic aspirations created by their secondary school athletic participation. Several studies have found a tendency for high-school athletes to finally attain more years of education than comparable nonathletes (Bend, 1968; Hanks & Eckland, 1976; Otto & Alwin, 1977; Sabo, Melnick, & Vanfossen, 1989).

A final aspect of these studies of sport and academic achievement is worthy of mention. The positive effect of athletic participation appears to be most pronounced among athletes who are *least disposed toward educational success* (low IQ, blue collar, low curriculum track). For example, Schafer and Armer (1968) found that the "grade point" advantage of athletes over their matches was consistently greater among blue-collar students. White-collar athletes achieved an overall grade average of 2.53, compared to 2.48 for their matches (advantage .05, virtually nil); blue-collar athletes achieved a grade average of 2.05, compared to 1.84 for their non-athlete matches (advantage .21) (p. 25). Data on college expectations (from Rehberg & Schafer, 1968) are also reported by Schafer and Armer (p. 26). Among middle-class males, some 91 percent of the athletes anticipated at least two years of college, compared to 89 percent of nonathletes, whereas blue-collar athletes enjoyed a much greater advantage, 78 percent vs. 69 percent, over comparable nonathletes (see also Picou & Curry, 1974, pp. 774–776; Bend, 1968).

In summary, the present empirical evidence indicates the following, at least in the case of American high-school students:

1. Athletes get slightly better grades than comparable nonathletes.
2. Athletes drop out of school less.
3. Athletes are more likely to aspire to a college education, and more likely to actually attend college.
4. These relationships generally are more pronounced among those who are least disposed toward educational success—low IQ and/or lower social-class background. This final fact has not been established in the few studies comparing female athletes and nonathletes.

Research on the academic effects of high-school sports has clearly falsified Coleman's reasonable contention that sports participation somehow diverts energy from academic pursuits. Indeed, with a few notable exceptions, sport appears to *enhance* academic achievement by athletes. This is one of the things that makes social science fun. A failed theory may lead to new facts (which, of course, must be judged for reliability) and the new facts demand the construction of a new theory that makes sense of the facts. The next section examines the adequacy of several theories that attempt to explain the facts about athletics and academic achievement.

Explanations of the Academic Advantages of Athletes[1]

Many of the studies uncovering evidence of the favorable effects of athletic participation have suggested explanations (Schafer & Armer, 1968; Buhrmann, 1972). This section reviews proposed explanations and evaluates their tenability given the present data. The following list summarizes virtually all of the explanations that have been offered:

1. Selection—better students go out for sports, hence the higher achievement of athletes.
2. Spillover of values—excellence and hard work learned in sport are transferred to academic pursuits.
3. Efficient use of time—the athlete must organize his otherwise limited time, thus doing more systematic, concentrated work.
4. Superior physical fitness somehow leads to better academic work.
5. Lure of a college career provides an incentive for athletes to improve their academic work.
6. Special treatment—the athlete is given better grades and extra help. Hence their better performance is artificial.

7. Special rewards (status) enjoyed by athletes lead to high self-esteem, which leads to better academic performance and higher aspirations.
8. Special rewards lead to an attraction to the source of those rewards, the school, and this enhances academic performance and aspirations.
9. Special rewards lead to association with (liking) proschool persons (students, teachers), who in turn influence the athlete toward better academic performance and higher aspirations.

How well do these explanations stand up in the light of the available evidence? Most do not stand up at all. "Selection" may be ruled out on the basis of controls applied by researchers. No competent researcher would compare athletes to other students without testing as much as possible to assure that the differences between the two groups were not produced by preexisting differences, such as IQ, social-class background, or earlier educational achievement. Probable selection factors were controlled in all of the research cited in this section.

Explanations 2, 3, 4, and 5 suggest a direct relationship between sports participation and various academic outcomes. A number of recent studies have cast grave doubt on all such explanations. Wendy Jerome and I (1971) examined such explanations in a comparison of the athletics-academics relationship in Canadian and American high schools. High schools in both countries are quite similar in organization, and this similarity extends to interscholastic sports. The one key difference is the high prestige accorded to sports in American schools. Academic achievement, far more than athletic achievement, was the way to gain peer status in Canadian high schools, while the reverse was and is true in American high schools, at least for boys (see Eitzen, 1975; Chandler & Goldberg, 1990; Sabo, Melnick, & Vanfossen, 1989). Sport does not appear to be the important source of status for girls that it is for boys, but it is a small source of status. In any event, girls appear to benefit from participation much as their male counterparts do. The widely reported educational advantages of American athletes were not evident among Canadian students. If participation in sports directly enhanced educational performance through a direct "spillover" of values, efficient use of time, or superior physical fitness, the Canadian athletes should have excelled over their peers as did their American counterparts. They did not.

A later study of educational aspirations (Spreitzer & Pugh, 1973) supported the findings of the Jerome-Phillips study. Spreitzer and Pugh surveyed a number of American high schools. They found that in schools where athletics was not highly valued relative to academic achievement (as in Canadian schools), athletes had no higher aspirations than other students, but in schools where athletic participation was highly valued, the athletes had substantially higher educational aspirations than other boys. Thus, "cross-cultural" and cross-school studies have both suggested that a key consideration is the high value generally placed on athletic participation or, more likely, the associated rewards in the form of status accorded to participants in interscholastic sports activities.

A second form of reasoning has also contributed to the rejection of the "direct relationship" explanations. William Spady (1970) was the first to distinguish between athletes who participate in a variety of school activities and "pure" athletes, who limit themselves to sports alone. Pure athletes appear not to exceed comparable students in any measure of educational outcomes (Rehberg & Cohen, 1975; Spady, 1970). If athletic participation directly produces various educational outcomes (e.g., "spillover" of values or efficient use of time), pure athletes should do better than comparable nonathletes, but they do not.

In short, the positive effects of athletic participation appear to be contingent on factors beyond participation itself. In schools with value climates that do not accord special rewards to athletes, the athletes do not outperform other students in academic achievement. Athletes who do not engage in other forms of extracurricular activities do not outperform comparable students. Given these facts, explanations 1 through 5 in the list given previously may be rejected. The remaining explanations have in common the importance of special rewards—status accorded participants in athletics.

Explanation 6 implies that high-school athletes are given higher grades than they deserve. There is little doubt that this is done occasionally, but does it explain the generally better performance of athletes? The pure athlete provides a problem for this explanation. The pure athlete does *not* exceed the comparable student as the explanation would suggest. Other positive outcomes, such as extracurricular participation and higher aspirations, cannot be "given" by teachers. Neither can actual attainment in later years be given by high-school teachers.

Explanation 8 suggests that *self-esteem* mediates the relationship between athletics and academic outcomes. It is certainly reasonable to expect successful athletes in American high schools to enjoy considerable self-esteem. These are the boys who are succeeding in the most important aspect of their school status system and the girls who are succeeding in an activity that is an important source of status. Furthermore, there is empirical evidence that "self-concept of school ability" is related (for obvious reasons) to various forms of educational success (Bachman, Green, & Wirtanen, 1971, pp. 58–60).

However, Jay Coakley (1990, pp. 325–326) questions the veracity of the athletics →self-esteem→academic success model. Coakley cites four objections, some of which are more justified than others. First, one may question the assertion that participation in sports is always a success experience—what of consistent losers? Second, even successful athletes may have their confidence shaken by new responsibilities associated with their success. Third, an enhanced self-concept based on athletic success may be limited to athletics. That a girl feels she can defeat anyone in tennis does not imply that she thinks of herself as a good student. A final point questions whether it is a high self-concept that leads to academic success or academic success that leads to high self-concept. To add a bit to Coakley's discussion, it is entirely possible that academic success causes high "academic self-concept." Should this causal order be correct, the model under consideration, which places self-concept prior to academic success, would be impossible.

The reader has probably noted that the above discussion is primarily speculative. There is little hard evidence available regarding the athletics→self-esteem→academic success model, and the questionable placement of self-esteem as causally prior to academic success is not justified by any analysis, it is assumed. A variable similar to self-esteem, called "perceived peer status" (a person's belief that others think well of him or her), has been employed in three studies with mixed results.

Melnick, Vanfossen, and Sabo (1988, p. 29) found that athletic participation had no effect on self-esteem but that "perceived popularity" was affected. This reflects findings of earlier studies. Spady (1970) and Spreitzer and Pugh (1973) found that perceived peer status had a positive effect on educational aspirations (a form of academic success). It should be noted that Spady found that perceived peer status was often inflated compared to "actual peer status," especially among pure athletes. Boys (Spady's study was limited to boys) who overestimated their status had high aspirations but slightly lower actual attainment (years completed) than boys who accurately estimated their status. On balance, however, the pure athletes attained slightly more years of schooling than comparable nonathletes (Spady, 1970, p. 695).

Spreitzer and Pugh found that athletes who reported low perceived peer status were no more likely to aspire to a college education than comparable nonathletes. This finding suggests that the athletics→academic success (aspirations) relationship is contingent on the presence of self-esteem as an intervening variable. However, a later study (Otto & Alwin, 1977) failed to replicate the finding that perceived peer status mediated the relationship between athletic participation and academic success. In summary, explanation 7 is questionable in terms of the causal order it assumes, and the empirical evidence is limited and equivocal.

Explanations 8 and 9 may be taken together. Special rewards (status) may be expected to produce a "positive attachment" toward the school and what it stands for. This contention stems from a school of thought in social psychology called "balance theory" (Heider, 1958; Newcomb, 1961). The argument is that people tend to like others who like them (e.g., a teacher complimenting an athlete for his success on the field), and that people tend to "like" characteristics that they associate with the people they like. This liking of people may be extended to social entities such as the school.

The vast majority of American high schools provide special rewards to athletes in the form of mention in school publications, special "letter sweaters," cheers at games, and special attention ("You played well in your game") in the classroom. Balance theory suggests that athletes should develop feelings of liking not only toward the rewarding experiences themselves but toward the *source* of the rewards, the school, and to *what the school stands for* as well. It is true, as Coleman (1961a) argued, that the school "stands for" athletic excellence (hence, the trophy case described at the beginning of this chapter), but it also stands for scholarship. Boys who "like" the school, then, should tend to "like" the scholastic aspect as well. Most studies of the athletics-academics relationship suggest this, but only one study (Phillips & Schafer, 1970) has examined it directly. Phillips and Schafer found clear evidence that athletes were more supportive than other students of the school, its traditions and objectives. Presumably this "liking" is translated into greater effort, which results in greater achievement.

Explanation 9 adds an extra step to explanation 8, specifying how a person who is attracted to the school and what it stands for is induced to actually accomplish higher academic achievement through the influence of teachers and academically oriented students. Indeed, "attraction to the school" may best be seen as attraction to individuals who represent (in the eyes of the beholder) the school and its objectives.

Imagine an athlete of limited academic talent and a comparably limited nonathlete. The athlete is known and respected by his or her teachers. The athlete's school work will probably seem less onerous because of the good relationship with his or her teachers (at least some of them). The nonathlete is not so lucky. The nonathlete's access to teachers' approval is limited. All this student receives from teachers is bad grades. A well-developed body of literature indicates that school failures tend to become progressively alienated from the school and what it stands for (e.g., Wicker, 1968; Phillips, 1980; Willems, 1967; Bachman, Green, & Wirtanen, 1971; Alexander & McDill, 1976).

There is ample evidence that athletes are favorably influenced (encouraged to do well) by teachers (Rehberg & Schafer, 1968; Spreitzer & Pugh, 1973) and their coaches, who are teachers as well (Snyder, 1972). This influence was found to grow stronger among students who were less disposed (lower IQ, lower SES, lower grades) toward educational success (Picou & Curry, 1974).

Friends also appear to exert a positive influence on athletes compared to nonathletes. Otto and Alwin (1977), in a longitudinal study of Michigan students, found that male athletes aspired to more years of education and higher level occupations relative to nonathletes of comparable IQ, social class and grades; they also achieved more years of education and higher occupational and income levels after 15 years. Much of this advantage was due to the influence of significant others—best friends, girl friend, and parents.

A recent study that was based on the same national level data as the Sabo, Melnick, and Vanfossen studies found clear evidence that friends can exert a substantial influence on a student's academic aspirations and achievement (Hallinan & Williams, 1990). While this study did not attempt to demonstrate the impact of sports on friendships, it did show the impact of friendships on achievement. Melnick, Vanfossen, and Sabo (1988) found a strong tendency for athletes to be involved in extracurricular activity (p. 30). Data from Spady (1970) also indicated that athletes were far more likely than comparable nonathletes to participate in extracurricular service activities. Spady found that this participation enhanced educational aspirations and attainment of participants. Thus, Spady's data support a model leading from athletic participation to participation in service activities in school (involving peer contact) to higher aspirations and attainment. Steven Picou (1978) also found that peer influence explained much of the better performance of athletes.

In summary, the available evidence supports explanation 9, the athletics→peer influence→enhanced performance model, far more convincingly than any of the other explanations proposed. This explanation is consistent with data regarding the better educational performance of athletes. More importantly, this explanation is consistent with the evidence that the positive impact of athletic participation is usually concentrated among students who are generally poorly disposed toward educational success, and that athletic participation does not improve educational performance in schools in which athletics is not highly rewarded.

Female Athletes

The early research on the academic effects of school sports was conducted during an era in which girls were excluded from school sports in the United States. Consequently, few of the early studies—prior to about 1975—included female athletes. Recent work suggests that participation in sports improves the achievement of females much as it does males, but the way sports help is unclear.

Sports participation appears to enhance the status of female athletes (Melnick, Vanfossen, & Sabo, 1988; Feltz, 1979; Buhrmann & Jarvis, 1971; Buhrmann & Bratton, 1978; Thirer & Wright, 1985; Chandler & Goldberg, 1990; MacKillop & Snyder, 1987), but other factors, such as being in the leading crowd or a leader in activities or academic achievement, appear to be more important. Hence the role of special rewards (status) may be less important in the explanation of the success of female athletes than it is in the case of males. In spite of this relative lack of status female athletes earn grades equal to or higher than comparable nonathletes, they have slightly higher academic aspirations, and they are more involved in extracurricular activities (Snyder & Spreitzer, 1977; Melnick, Vanfossen, & Sabo, 1988; Sabo, Melnick, & Vanfossen, 1989).

Perhaps the better performance of female athletes is produced the same way it is for boys—contact with academically oriented peers who are teammates or colleagues in extracurricular activities. Perhaps coaches influence female athletes to do better. Understanding the process by which the educational performance of female high school athletes is enhanced remains "unfinished business" in the sociology of sport.

Black Athletes

The apparent educational benefits of sports participation do not appear to apply to black students, especially black female athletes, nearly as much as they do to other groups. This was first observed by Picou (1978). Picou analyzed information from a statewide sample of 1,506 Louisiana male high-school students. Grades of black athletes were not significantly higher than black nonathletes, while white athletes did achieve slightly higher grades than white nonathletes. Black athletes, like whites, had higher educational aspirations than comparable nonathletes, but the data analysis indicated that black athletes did not receive the benefit of positive peer influence received by whites. Picou suggested that the process by which sports led to academic ambition deserved further research because neither peer, nor teacher, nor parental influence could explain the higher aspirations of black athletes (p. 436). Another study (Braddock, 1981) did find positive outcomes for black male athletes. The more recent national study of male and female athletes reported by Sabo, Melnick, and Vanfossen (1989) found that aside from greater extracurricular participation among males, black athletes ***gained no academic benefit*** from athletic participation. Black athletes did no better than comparable nonathletes in academic achievement, graduation rates, educational aspirations, college attendance, or test score achievement (see Table 6–1).

This is a perplexing finding. First, it appears to be reliable. Both Picou and Sabo, Melnick, and Vanfossen had large, widely representative samples. Both conducted a "state of the art" data analysis. Had these studies involved small samples of one or two schools we could say many more such studies would be required before we would "trust" the findings. But these studies were "big," and representative of a wide variety of high schools. It is time to ask why black athletes do not benefit like whites and Hispanics do, and, of course, how schools might help them benefit. Recall that one "official" reason for school sports is the enhancement of academic achievement.

Given what we know (or think we know), black athletes should benefit more than whites, not less. Blacks are more likely than whites to come from economically disadvantaged backgrounds. Blacks are more likely than whites to have poor previous academic achievement. Recall that the benefit of athletic participation is supposed to be *strongest* for weaker students from lower socioeconomic backgrounds, and that athletes are supposed to be influenced by academically oriented peers and teachers. The limited evidence indicates that black males, at least, do not receive the benefit of positive peer influence, while their white teammates do (Picou, 1978; Thirer & Wieczorek, 1984).

We can only speculate about other reasons why blacks do not benefit from sports. (Importantly, they do not suffer any damage to academic achievement either.) The first possibility that comes to mind is discrimination. Perhaps blacks are not quickly accepted into leadership roles in extracurricular groups. Perhaps blacks perceive less future opportunity, and so are uninterested in academic achievement because of a lack of apparent future "payoffs." Perhaps there exists in some schools an anti-academic subculture among blacks that cancels out any positive benefits of

TABLE 6–1 Educational Advantages of Athletes over Comparable Nonathletes by Race/Ethnic Group, Gender, and Residence*

	Hispanic		Black		White	
	Females	Males	Females	Males	Females	Males
Extracurricular Activity	R S U	R S U	R S U	R S U	R S U	R S U
Grades	R			S		R
Test Scores	R			U		
Dropout Rate	R	S		R	R S	R S
College Attendance	R	R U			R S	R S U

R = Rural residence; *S* = suburban residence; *U* = urban residence.

*Compiled from Sabo, Melnick, and Vanfossen (1989), Appendix A. These represent advantages that were statistically significant after controls for background factors were applied.

athletics. Perhaps a self-fulfilling prophecy effect reduces black achievement (Rosenthal & Jacobson, 1968). That is, teachers and peers may subtly communicate a "You can't do it" message to aspiring black scholars. Being perplexed about educational effects of sports on black students is one of the things that makes sport sociology so interesting. Nobody knows much of anything about why things are the way they are, but a modicum of creative thought, combined with a lot of hard work in research, will begin to provide an understanding of this important issue.

The C-Average Rule

German Chancellor Otto von Bismarck is said to have warned consumers away from seeing two products in the process of being manufactured. These were laws and sausages. The establishment of state laws requiring a minimum C average (2.0 GPA) to participate in extracurricular activities was not a pretty process. A Texas governor was defeated in a reelection bid partly because of his stance in favor of this requirement. The law was challenged in Texas courts and an appeal, which was rejected, went all the way to the United States Supreme Court. A similar controversy accompanied the establishment of this rule in California (Lapchick, 1987). When "outsiders" disturb sports programs, sparks are liable to fly.

The idea behind the C-average rule is stated in California Assembly Bill No 2613, passed July 21, 1986. By limiting sports participation to students earning a 2.0 average or higher, the legislature hoped to "emphasize to all pupils in California that each pupil's primary responsibility is to meet the academic challenge of learning" (p. 1). The act was intended not "as a means to exclude students from participation . . . but rather a means to encourage and promote academic excellence" (p. 2). By excluding poor students from extracurricular activities, including sports, the legislators hoped two things would happen. First, excluded students would work harder in the classroom to get back on the team. Second, the overall climate of the school might improve, with more attention paid by all students to their academic work. The second goal might be measured by improved grades of students in general or by improved achievement test scores. The first would be demonstrated if excluded students upped their grades *more than they would have* if the C-average rule not been in effect.

I know of no evidence of any jump in overall academic performance in California and Texas after the adoption of the C-average rule in these states. In California, achievement test scores have generally declined during the 1980s. There is some evidence that, where the rule has been instituted, the percentage of students in activities who were ineligible because of poor grades declined during the first year or so of the institution of the rule. This occurred in Texas and in several other districts across the United States (Lapchick, 1987). Patricia Ashby (1984) found a clear decline in the proportion of students dropped from activities during the initial year of the rule in Los Angeles.

There is some evidence on the other side of this issue, though. Table 6–2 shows more recent data from the Los Angeles Unified School District (B. Mostovoy, personal communication, 1986). It appears that after the spring of 1983, the first year of the

TABLE 6–2 Rate of Ineligibility for Activities in Los Angeles School District High Schools, 1983–1985

Semester	Ineligible (%)
Spring 1983, midterm	20.5
Spring 1983, final	8.1
Fall 1983, midterm	19.4
Fall 1983, final	18.8
Spring 1984, midterm	18.5
Spring 1984, final	16.2
Fall 1984, midterm	20.8
Fall 1984, final	19.6
Spring 1985, midterm	18.2
Spring 1985, final	16.3

C-average rule there, the percentage of students academically ineligible for participation returned to prerule levels. Jean Fitzgibbons (1989) studied the effect of the C-average rule in a single California high school. Fitzgibbons found no improvement in participants' grades after the policy was implemented, and a slight *increase* in absences in the two years following implementation. Thus, the long-term effect of the C-average rule appears to be nil in regard to academic achievement.

The California data, albeit limited, suggest a somber assessment of the effects of the rule. The rule requires the exclusion of weak students to motivate them toward greater effort and achievement. The rule has successfully excluded weak students. However, what little evidence we have suggests that in the long run there is no improvement in effort or achievement. The net effect of this policy has been to deny some students the opportunity to participate—with no benefit whatsoever.

Recall that there is ample evidence that sport helps the academic achievement of participants, and that it helps weak students the most. The C-average rule calls for the exclusion of weak students from a program that is likely to help their achievement, and almost certainly will not harm it, in favor of one that may harm the academic achievement of excluded students and almost certainly will not help it.

College Athletic Programs

The topic of college sports may well belong somewhere other than a chapter on sports and education. There is no reason other than historical happenstance for colleges and universities to sponsor sports teams. Chapter 4 of this book relates how Midwestern college officials wrested control of football from the "big four" (Harvard, Yale, Princeton, Pennsylvania) football rules committee, which was run by representatives of student clubs, in order to curb abuses such as roughness and use of ineligible players (Danzig, 1956). Others have argued that when college officials smelled the money earned at the gate of football games they sought to impose control.

The chance to enhance enrollment also served as a financial incentive to embrace commercial spectator sports (Chu, 1982, Ch. 9).

College sport has developed a great deal since the formation of the NCAA in the early 20th century. Programs vary widely, so no blanket statements may be made about college sports. The NCAA divides athletic programs into three divisions. Division I is the top competitive level. Schools at this level are required to schedule most of their games with other Division I teams and to sponsor a minimum number of sports. For example, schools that sponsor Division I football teams must also sponsor at least six men's and six women's teams. These programs may offer "full ride" scholarships to defray the costs of tuition, books, room, and board. One of the key differences between Division I and Division II programs is the number of grants allowed per sport. For example, Division I football programs may award 95 (Division IA) or 65 (Division IAA) football grants, while Division II teams are limited to 40 and Division III programs may award aid only on the basis of financial need. Numbers in other sports are fairly close. Division I programs may award 15 grants for men's and women's basketball, 14 for track, and 11 for soccer, while comparable Division II programs may award one or two fewer grants in most sports.

Formal rules, then, don't sharply distinguish Division I and Division II programs outside of football, but sharp differences may exist in unofficial matters like recruiting practices and perquisites to players. These may range from "lawful" inducements (e.g., quality of competition and travel opportunities) to "illegal" inducements (e.g., sham jobs, phony academic courses, or under-the-table payments). Division II and III programs may vary widely in scholarship support—some give none, some award the maximum—and unofficial inducements. Even some Division I programs, mainly in the Ivy League, restrict awards to need, although admission at these institutions may constitute an important award in itself.

Students Are Not Fools: Illegal Payments

The main thrust of this chapter is the academic effects of sports, but a few words on dishonest practices by athletic departments are appropriate. Amos Alonzo Stagg remarked, "Students are not fools. The faculty that winks at crooked work by a coach . . . can save its breath in preaching ideals in the classroom" (Stagg & Stoudt, 1927, p. 178). Crooked sports programs can affect the academic programs of universities.

NCAA athletic programs, especially basketball and football, rely on ticket and radio and television revenues for funding. Consistently losing programs tend to lose out on both of these sources of revenue. Losing coaches are routinely fired. Coaches of bowl or tournament teams may be paid a bonus, ostensibly for the extra month of work they do for the bowl game or tournament, but really because of their success on the field. The money incentive for the coaches and athletic departments *encourages* cheating. How many coaches or ADs have been dismissed for recruiting violations or lack of academic progress by scholarship athletes? How many have been fired for winning too few games? Coaches, like the rest of us, can compare these numbers and come to an appropriate decision whether to adhere to the NCAA rules and have a potentially weaker team, or cheat and have a stronger team. The very existence of a 400-page *NCAA Manual* testifies to the manifold ways coaches and boosters may "cheat" to gain a competitive advantage over their opposition.

There is a certain irony to the term "illegal payments" as there is nothing illegal whatsoever about paying people to do a job like playing football. Indeed, if anything is illegal under public law it is the banding together of hundreds of colleges in effect to restrict the freedom of athletes to sell their services. Ironic or not, the NCAA has legislated a sophisticated set of regulations designed to promote conformity to fair practices. However, rules were made to be broken, and rule breakers stand to gain a lot while risking little. From the point of view of the hypothetical coach, the risks of scrupulous adherence to NCAA rules (losing games and losing one's job) almost certainly outweigh the risks of cheating (possibly getting caught and, even if caught, probably getting a better paying job thanks to a favorable win-loss record). *The system encourages* the use of illegal inducements in major college programs in the United States.

A recent survey of retired National Football League players revealed a veritable "underground economy" of unsanctioned financial inducements in major college football programs. Allen Sack (1991) mailed a questionnaire to 3,500 former NFL players, receiving a return of 1,182 or about one-third of the "target" group. This kind of return rate is not bad for a "mail away" survey. While some doubts remain about how well the 1,182 represent the original 3,500, Sack did obtain information from a large number of former players, and the information they provided is important no matter *how* well they represent the target group. This study adds some systematic evidence to the frequent cases in which a renowned football or basketball school is caught granting unsanctioned financial inducements to players and punished by the NCAA.

Two-fifths of Sack's respondents reported receiving some form of under-the-table payment for their football services. A few received virtual salaries, but most received cash in small quantities after games or at other times. Many reported receiving clothing, free meals at restaurants, and travel money (or tickets), as well as being able to make free long-distance telephone calls and having use of expensive cars. The main source of income was selling high-demand complimentary game tickets at huge markups. Another important source of income was "no show" jobs wherein a player was paid for summer work not performed (Sack, 1991, pp. 7–8). Sack also points to jobs for players' relatives as a financial inducement for some players (p. 2).

Athletes to whom I have spoken suggest the existence of two more inducements that may be used by colleges to obtain or retain top-flight athletes. The first is payoffs to crime victims (ranging from date rape victims to victims in traffic accidents) to avoid prosecution and its attendant bad publicity. The second is sexual inducements. "Sports hostesses" at some institutions may provide hospitality beyond what is officially expected, or strongly imply they will when the player arrives at school in the fall. My sources do not suggest that this is common, but that it does happen. A recent news item relates the story of a booster paying for the services of a prostitute for a star basketball player. Readers may recall a theme of "The Best Little Whorehouse in Texas," a nonfiction magazine article that was elaborated into a stage musical play and later a movie. Members of a winning football team were treated to an evening at the "Chicken Ranch." These sorts of inducements are unusual and probably exaggerated when they happen, but they are related by a variety of sources, so it is likely that they really happen from time to time.

Sack's data suggest that the term "underground economy" is very appropriate. There appears to be a sort of market system that influences trade in under-the-table inducements. Inducements appeared to be more common in some conferences than in others, with the Southeast, Big Eight, Southwest and Western Athletic conferences the most generous. This suggests a competitive market for players in these conferences. Where some programs pay higher prices for talent, others find they must do it if they are to stay competitive. Highly talented athletes were substantially more likely to receive special inducements than less talented ones. Recall that all respondents were good enough to make the NFL! (Sack, 1991, p. 9). This suggests a supply effect on prices. Good players are in short supply so they can command higher compensation. Players from low-income families were more likely than others to have received inducements (p. 10). This suggests that payments were affected by financial need of athletes, not just their market value.

Sack observes that financial inducements have been widely used by college sports programs from the earliest years (Sack, 1991, p. 1). Many schools employed "ringers" to strengthen their sports teams (Betts, 1974, pp. 126–127). Stagg relates the case of a ringer who played for Harvard in the 1880s:

> One of the men playing for the Crimson was said to have been a Boston and Maine brakeman in private life. Professionally, he was a tower of strength in the Harvard line. (Stagg & Stout, 1927, p. 177)

Yale, Stagg's *alma mater,* was not without fault. Renowned turn-of-the-century tackle Jim Hogan was accused of accepting a suite in exclusive Vanderbilt Hall, meals at the University Club, a ten-day trip to Cuba paid by the athletic association, the $100 John Bennett scholarship, free tuition, a monopoly on the sale of score cards, and a position as cigarette agent of the American Tobacco Company (Betts, 1974, p. 127).

Many critics have suggested that the best way to deal with "illegal" professionalism in college football is to make it legal—put an end to the hypocrisy and pay athletes above the table not under it (Michener, 1976, pp. 251–255). Colleges unable or unwilling to pay salaries would form separate competitive divisions, playing only unpaid athletes who were also attending classes. The "legalization" of payments to amateur track and field, and later tennis, athletes may serve as a model for what might happen in college football and basketball. Neither sport really experienced any problems. Payments were being made anyway, so costs to meet directors did not change much. Athletes benefitted a lot from being able to accept money openly. This was especially advantageous to athletes from poor families.

Oftentimes efforts to suppress a "vice" like professionalism create more problems than the vice itself. The best model of the harm caused by suppression and the benefits of legalization of a vice is the American experience with alcohol prohibition (Tappan, 1960, pp. 232–234). Vices such as drug use, prostitution, and gambling might be far less harmful if legalized than they are when criminalized. The legalization of abortion solved many severe problems that existed in jurisdictions where it was illegal. Likewise the "vice" of openly paying athletes to play in "amateur" competition is far less destructive than the dishonesty required of officials who must make such payments while pretending not to.

Students Are Not Fools—Academic Abuses

Far more important than professionalism in college sports is the compromising of the academic integrity of colleges and universities. Amos Alonzo Stagg outlined the basic ways sports officials could circumvent academic requirements back in 1927:

> Playing ringers fell into three types: first, those who did not even take the pains to register for courses; second, those who registered for courses which they seldom attended; and third, those who registered for snap courses in some department where the work was easy and little or no work was required. There are no self respecting colleges now where the first and second cases can happen. There are still quite a number of colleges and universities where the third case can and does happen. (Stagg & Stout, 1927, p. 180)

It would appear that only the first practice has been eradicated by NCAA regulations.

Snap Courses

Athletes at many colleges may register for courses they never attend and receive credit, most likely an A grade. I am sure students in a Sociology of Sport class in almost any university with a "big time" sports program could identify three "no show" classes commonly used by athletes in need of easy credits.

No sane college official is going to help a researcher identify courses at his or her institution in which athletes may gain credit without taking the course, but the number of exposés in newspapers and sports magazines indicates that it is widely practiced. Leonard (1988) lists five such incidents, including cases in which athletes received credit for courses they never attended. These courses are usually summer or extension courses "taught" by friends of coaches who need to keep their players eligible (p. 309).

A recent study of a single Big Eight school reveals some statistical evidence of the kinds of academic abuses just mentioned. Brede and Camp (1987) traced the academic progress of 167 male football and basketball players through one year. Athletes who were academically qualified to attend college earned satisfactory grades and made progress toward their degrees. But for the 44 athletes who had not been academically qualified, the story was different. These athletes frequently failed courses. For example, the average "low academic ability" athlete attempted 13.6 units, but passed only 7.1, for a GPA of 1.8 (Brede & Camp, 1987, p. 253). The picture was really worse. Many of these athletes had been helped by what appears to be remarkably generous grade changes. Their initial grades had indicated only 5.1 passing credit hours with a GPA of 1.1! Either the faculty at this institution were sloppy record-keepers or they accorded some generous consideration to these athletes. No comparable improvement from grade changes was apparent for the academically qualified athletes.

An additional phenomenon is apparent. Table 6–3 is constructed from the Brede-Camp data. It reveals that the "low academic ability" athletes earned 11 percent of their passing units during winter and spring intersessions and summer sessions. Their GPA during these sessions jumped from about 1.8 to 2.3 during intersessions and to 2.9 during summer! Brede and Camp do not suggest it, but a suspicious person might interpret these grade jumps and the change-of-grade benefits as unearned college credit given athletes by faculty members to help coaches keep the athletes eligible. Exhibit 6–1 illustrates an extreme instance of this sort of academic abuse.

A recent study of faculty at universities with big time football programs revealed that few faculty members ever felt pressured to help an athlete by changing a grade (Weber, Sherman, & Tegano, 1990, p. 391). But it only takes a handful of compliant faculty members to provide enough phony course credits or inflated grades to keep a few athletes eligible.

Research indicates that male football and basketball players in big time programs often find athletic responsibilities interfering with their classroom responsibilities to the detriment of their academic achievement (Sack, 1987; Adler & Adler, 1985). The problem is particularly acute for blacks, who are more likely than their teammates to be ill-prepared and to be "protected" from campus resources that might help them succeed (Eitzen, 1987, pp. 24–25). This results in many such individuals providing four years of valuable service as athletes and receiving little education in return—an

TABLE 6–3 Academic Achievement among Male Football and Basketball Players of Low Academic Ability*

	Fall Semester	Spring Semester	Spring and Winter Intersessions	Summer Sessions
GPA	01.84	1.83	2.32	2.94
Units Earned	8	11	2.5†	5.2
Number of Athletes Enrolled	44	40	17‡	11

*Adapted from Tables 1 and 2 of Brede and Camp (1987, pp. 250–251).

†This represents a single average student enrolling in one session.

‡This is an average of the two intersessions. Enrollments were: Winter intersession, 20; Spring intersession, 15.

EXHIBIT 6–1 Academic Fraud: A Case in Point

The most conspicuous case of academic abuse by an athletic department in recent years involved Dr. Jan Kemp, a professor at the University of Georgia who was fired for doing her job. Unfortunately for Professor Kemp, her job responsibilities conflicted with the interests of the University of Georgia Athletic Department.

Dr. Kemp was an assistant professor of English in the University of Georgia's Developmental Studies Program. After nine football players were passed even though they had not passed their final quarter of English, Dr. Kemp objected. The University officials who ordered the passing of the athletes contended that they had made progress and deserved admission into the regular University of Georgia curriculum. Others thought they were being given sham passes to keep them eligible for football, especially the upcoming 1982 Sugar Bowl game. Dr. Kemp argued that if these nine could be passed without doing the required work, a message would be sent to all remedial students, at least athletes, that they did not have to try and that they could expect to be passed whether they accomplished anything in the classroom or not.*

For her abrasiveness, Dr. Kemp was demoted and later fired. After a very difficult post-dismissal period, Dr. Kemp decided to sue the University on the ground that professors ought not to be fired for objecting to administrators passing athletes who had not passed their courses.

The jury at Kemp's civil trial did not believe the University of Georgia's rather lame reasons for Kemp's dismissal. They were outraged to learn from university officials that the University routinely admitted athletes who could barely read and that these individuals virtually never graduated nor, for that matter, went on to become professional athletes. Rather, they played for four years and went on to careers that required little or no education. University officials said they admitted such players because other teams in the Southeast Conference did.

The jury awarded $2.5 million to Kemp, mostly punitive damages against the officials who had wrongly dismissed her. Kemp said she hoped the lawsuit would create reforms at Georgia. Prior to the lawsuit about 17 percent of Georgia's black football players graduated. The recent Chronicle of Higher Education (1991) report on graduation rates after five years for athletes recruited as freshmen in 1984 (shortly after the Kemp dismissal) indicates that about 32 percent of white and black Georgia football players graduated, and none of three basketball recruits graduated. No reports of faculty members being fired for doing their job honestly have come out of the University of Georgia in recent years.

Compiled from Nack (1986); Bowen (1986); Clendinen (1986).

**A personal note.* Your author has been involved in a college program in a California prison. Good remedial courses *work* when the students, who in this case had been expelled from schools more often than in them, have ability and are *motivated* to learn. Most of my students went from fifth or sixth grade mathematics to college level in a matter of a few months.

economic exploitation that has prompted sociologist Harry Edwards to complain that colleges have "simply moved [blacks] from the cotton fields to the football fields" (Wiley, 1989, p. 12).

Easy Majors

Stagg's third dodge for athletes who would avoid academics is for athletes to enroll in easy majors or in departments that grant easy grades. Two recent studies indicate that this is done at several schools. Raney, Knapp, and Small (1986) examined transcripts of male football, basketball, and baseball players at the University of Nevada at Las Vegas, an institution that has been widely criticized for its alleged inattention to the academic qualifications and achievement of scholarship athletes. Baseball players did about as well as nonathletes on the UNLV campus, but football and basketball players were a different story. These players took most of their units in PE and Ethnic Studies (33 percent for football, 48 percent for basketball), earning respectable grades (GPA of 3.1 for football and 2.7 for basketball). One assumes these athletes avoided the demanding courses in PE and Ethnic Studies, thereby avoiding progress toward a degree. Outside these friendly departments the football players earned a GPA of 1.9, while basketball players earned a 1.6 (my calculations from Raney, Knapp, & Small, p. 57).

A study of several NCAA Division I schools revealed that this "clustering" of athletes into certain majors—taking a disproportionate number of courses in a particular department whether or not one is enrolled as a major—was evident at many universities. Clustering was most pronounced at big time schools, among black athletes, and at the elite academic schools. Male athletes also were more likely to be involved in clustering than women (Case, Greer, & Brown, 1987).

It is important to note that some big time athletic programs are able to win on the field and still provide a good education to athletes (Eitzen, 1987, p. 21). Indeed, a national survey of Division I colleges found that athletes generally appear to graduate at about the same rate as other students, and female athletes are somewhat *more* likely to graduate than other students (Chronicle, 1991, p. A44). The only sport that clearly fails to produce its share of graduates is men's basketball. All this suggests several conclusions about academic dishonesty by athletic departments:

1. Since women athletes and men in "nonrevenue" sports work just as hard as football and basketball players (Meyer, 1990), poor academic performance by male football and basketball players should not simply be blamed on time demands associated with football and basketball.

2. Many schools and even some major conferences graduate a respectable percentage of men's basketball players. In the Pac 10, 50 percent of all students graduate in five years vs. 41 percent of men's basketball players. Big 10 percentages are 59 percent vs. 44 percent (Chronicle, 1991, pp. A42–43). Top-caliber sports programs may coexist with respectable academic performance by athletes.

3. It appears that several universities do not give a hoot about the academic success of athletes. At these schools the term student-athlete is a farce. Southeastern Conference football and basketball players graduated at rates of 32 percent and 14 percent, while 46 percent of all students at these schools graduated. The Southwest Conference graduated 33 percent and 24 percent of its football and basketball players compared to 49 percent of all students at these institutions (Chronicle, p. A43). Nonathletes more frequently transfer to other schools and graduate from them, so the graduation rates for all students is probably understated. Thus, the low graduation rate for athletes is probably worse than it appears.

The practice of keeping athletes eligible by steering them to easy courses and easy departments probably contributes to the lack of success of many athletes. Chances are that some of the poorly prepared athletes could, given support, succeed in a "real" educational program.

Solutions?

Some schools cheat a lot. Some cheat a little. Some hardly cheat at all on academic qualifications of football and basketball players. The NCAA and its critics have proposed a lot of reforms, ranging from James Michener's suggestion that big time colleges ought to come clean and openly pay athletes to play without regard to academics, to others who argue that scholarships should be given on a need basis only and limited to students who are admitted through the same process as all students at the university. This latter situation *never* existed in the United States. Some schools have always sought to gain an advantage by recruiting superior players who often had neither the talent nor the will to pursue an education. Insofar as American colleges remain committed to providing big time sports, reform efforts can only hope to minimize rewards to cheaters and minimize the harm done to coaches and institutions that lose because they do not cheat. Further reforms would encourage educational progress by athletes, especially those who are underprepared for college work.

Whatever national policy the NCAA institutes, individual colleges can and do effect academic reforms. In 1982 athletic director Ced Dempsy and academic coordinator Lee McElroy instituted an academic support program at the University of Houston. This program monitored class attendance by at-risk athletes and instituted a mandatory study-hall program for these students. Incoming freshmen were tested for study skills and reading, receiving remedial instruction where appropriate. They were also tested for career orientation to help them select an appropriate course of study. Coaches' budgets and salary increments were linked to how well the players participated in this program. Graduation rates for male football and basketball players tripled from an abysmal 10 percent to about 30 percent. These gains were not created by increasing admission standards. Many of the athletes were unqualified for college work, but with good support some of the "lost causes" were able to "do the impossible" and complete a degree. It is likely that many who did not complete degrees still achieved significant improvement in their skills (Lee McElroy, personal communication).

The most prominent reform in recent years was the adoption by the NCAA of Proposition 48, a rule that requires potential scholarship athletes to have a C average in selected high-school courses and to score a minimum combined SAT score of 700 or a composite score of 15 on the ACT. Both of these requirements are, of course, minimal. If a recruit cannot get the required test score but does have a C average in required high-school work, he or she may receive a scholarship and may attend his or her university of choice, but the athlete may not participate in intercollegiate athletics during the freshman year.

This seemingly innocuous piece of legislation caused a storm of controversy. The main criticism of the proposal was that it would affect black male athletes much more than others. Harry Edwards (1984) found that 51 percent of black males would be ineligible under the proposed rule compared to 26 percent for other minority males and only 9 percent of white males. Richard Lapchick (1987) found that fully 54 percent of black athletes who would have been limited by the rule if it had been in effect in 1981 (it was adopted in 1986) had been able to earn degrees (Washington et al., 1991, p. 51). That is, it appears that the rule, not unlike the high-school C-average rule, disproportionately affects blacks and may screen out future graduates as often as future failures. Indeed, there is some evidence that SAT or ACT scores predict little about future success that is not apparent from high school grades (Bauman & Henschen, 1986; Sellers, 1992).

It would appear that a C average or higher in a core of high-school courses could suffice as a minimum requirement for athletic scholarships, and the SAT/ACT minimum could be dropped with little harm to entrance standards for athletes. The academic audit proposal by the Knight Commission (see Exhibit 6–2) could assure that athletes receive educational support as needed and are really progressing toward degrees. Athletic departments could still cheat, but it would be harder to do so without being exposed.

It would make economic sense to provide coaches long-term contracts if not the tenure that successful faculty members earn. University regulation of coaches' compensation, including funds provided by boosters (another Knight commission proposal), might reduce the financial incentive to cheat. Another such measure might involve revenue sharing. Big bowl, tournament and TV payoffs might be shared equally among all schools in the NCAA Division I. For winning teams to earn this money, they had to defeat other teams who did not earn TV contracts largely because TV fans tend not to follow losing teams. The risk of being fired for losing and the chance to earn money for oneself and one's program are powerful incentives to cheat. Reduce these incentives and cheating might be reduced too.

College Sports and Alumni Support

One traditional argument in support of big time sport is that colleges that conduct such programs generate funds that can be used to advance the educational programs of the college. The fact is only a dozen or so athletic programs make money, and those profits are invested in athletics. Virtually every big time athletic program operates at a loss, diverting funds from educational programs and detracting from the educational mission of the university (Sperber, 1990).

Neither does athletic success appear to contribute to alumni giving. Several studies of the connection between alumni and corporate donations on the one hand and

EXHIBIT 6–2 Principles for Action: A Proposed Statement of Principles by All NCAA Institutions

I. The educational values, practices, and mission of this institution determine the standards by which we conduct our intercollegiate athletics program.

II. The responsibility and authority for the administration of the athletics department, including all basic policies, personnel, and finances, are vested in the president.

III. The welfare, health, and safety of student-athletes are primary concerns of athletics administration on this campus. This institution will provide student-athletes with the opportunity for academic experiences as close as possible to the experiences of their classmates.

IV. Every student-athlete—male and female, majority and minority, and all sports—will receive equitable and fair treatment.

V. The admission of student-athletes—including junior college transfers—will be based on their showing reasonable promise of being successful in a course of study leading to an academic degree. That judgment will be made by admissions officials.

VI. Continuing eligibility to participate in intercollegiate athletics will be based on students being able to demonstrate each academic term that they will graduate within five years of their enrolling. Students who do not pass this test will not play.

VII. Student-athletes, in each sport, will be graduated in at least the same proportion as nonathletes who have spent comparable time as full-time students.

VIII. All funds raised and spent in connection with intercollegiate athletics programs will be channeled through the institution's general treasury, not through independent groups, whether internal or external. The athletics department budget will be developed and monitored in accordance with general budgeting procedures on campus.

IX. All athletics-related income from nonuniversity sources for coaches and athletics administrators will be reviewed and approved by the university. In cases where the income involves the university's functions, facilities, or name, contracts will be negotiated with the institution.

X. We will conduct annual academic and fiscal audits of the athletics program. Moreover, we intend to see NCAA certification that our athletics program complies with the principles herein. We will promptly correct any deficiencies and will conduct our athletics program in a manner worthy of this distinction (Lederman, 1991, p. 36).

The Knight Foundation Commission asks that all NCAA institutions adopt these ten principles for the operation of sports programs. Would abuses end if every president of every NCAA university sincerely embraced these principles?

(Adapted from Lederman, 1991, p. 36)

athletic, especially football, success on the other, reveal no correlation between the two. Successful sports programs do not stimulate donations to universities, except to the athletic programs themselves (Frey, 1985). James Michener (1976) reports on a 1974 study by Felix Springer of the fate of 151 colleges that terminated their football programs between 1939 and 1974. Springer's conclusion: no effect. Enrollments stayed the same and alumni giving was unaffected (Michener, 1976, p. 271).

Critics of big time college athletics ask whether the educational benefits inherent in sports, particularly expensive ones like football, can justify the financial drain on educational institutions. Perhaps professional football and basketball leagues should join hockey, soccer, and baseball and provide professional developmental leagues for athletes who want to try for a professional career but do not want to pursue a college education. As with collegiate hockey, soccer, and baseball, the quality of competition would still be high, even if limited to genuine college students.

Summary

A long tradition of research on the effect of high-school sports participation on academic achievement reveals a slight academic advantage for athletes. Most explanations of this advantage emphasize the role of high status (respect and recognition in the eyes of others) that athletes enjoy in most high schools in the United States. The educational advantage appears to result from positive peer associations facilitated by athletic participation.

The academic advantages associated with high-school athletic participation do not appear to benefit black athletes. Why white and Hispanic athletes are helped while blacks are not is an important issue for future sport sociologists. Another unanswered question involves the academic success of female athletes. Participation brings status to female athletes but other activities, including scholarship, are more important than sports at most schools. With sports-related status a relatively unimportant factor in the case of females the status→pro-school associations→academic success explanation probably does not apply to the case of females. Why female athletes do better than comparable students remains to be explained.

Many school districts and a few states have adopted laws requiring aspiring high-school athletes to maintain a C average or be dropped until they bring their grades up. No research to date has demonstrated that this rule actually improves the academic performance of athletes. At present many marginal students who, according to present knowledge about academics and athletics, might be helped by participation are being excluded.

Most college and university athletes succeed about as well as comparably qualified students. Women in all sports appear to perform a bit better than other women. Academic failure is limited to male football and basketball players at most, but not all, big time sports programs. Such failures can be blamed on a combination of factors, including the admission of unqualified students, pressures of big time sports, and lack of interest in academics by some athletes. Where efforts have been made to support at-risk students, academic achievement has improved. An effort by the NCAA to create national minimum admission standards for scholarship athletes (Proposition 48) has been sharply criticized. Critics argue that a minimum score on a standard achievement test is biased against blacks and other minorities, and does not predict college success any better than high-school grades alone do. Supporters argue that athletes affected by this rule may still attend college. They just cannot play during their freshman year.

It is no wonder that many college athletic programs cheat by offering financial inducements to prospective recruits and by encouraging dishonest academic practices. Coaches are expected to win. They gain financial benefits and professional advancement when they win, but receive little when student-athletes succeed in their academic pursuits. Reform proposals range from increasing requirements and monitoring athletic departments for compliance to eliminating requirements and allowing programs to openly pay athletes who may or may not be required to attend the universities they play for. Some argue that big time sports programs might best be dropped at universities because they divert funds from academic programs. There is no evidence that success in sports stimulates university fund raising.

Note

1. This section is a revision of an earlier paper by the author (see Phillips, 1979).

References

AB 2613 (1986). Section 35160.5, Chapter 422, *California Education Code.*

Adler, P., and Adler, P. (1985). From idealism to pragmatic detachment: The academic performance of college athletes. *Sociology of Education, 58,* 241–250.

Alexander, K. L., and McDill, E. L. (1976). Selection and allocation within schools: Some causes and consequences of curriculum placement. *American Sociological Review, 41* (December), 963–980.

Ashby, P. G. (1984). The impact of the Los Angeles Unified School District C-average/no fail policy on student academic progress. *Dissertation Abstracts International, 46,* 337A–338A.

Bachman, J. G., Green, S., and Wirtanen, I. D. (1971). *Youth in Transition, Volume III: Dropping Out—Problem or Symptom?* Ann Arbor, MI: Institute for Social Research.

Baumann, S., and Henschen, K. (1986). A cross-validation study of selected performance measures in predicting academic success among college athletes. *Sociology of Sport Journal, 3,* 366–371.

Bend, E. (1968). *The Impact of Athletic Participation on Academic and Career Aspiration and Achievement.* New Brunswick, NJ: National Football Hall of Fame.

Betts, J. R. (1984). *America's Sporting Heritage—1850–1950.* Reading, MA: Addison-Wesley.

Bowen, E. (1986). Blowing the whistle on Georgia. *Time, 127* (February 24), 65.

Braddock, J. H. (1981). Race athletics and educational attainment: Dispelling the myths. *Youth and Society, 12,* 335–350.

Brede, R. M., and Camp, H. J. (1987). The education of college student-athletes. *Sociology of Sport Journal, 4,* 245–257.

Buhrmann, H. G. (1972). Scholarship and athletics

in junior high school. *International Review of Sport Sociology, 1,* 119–128.

Buhrmann, H. G., and Bratton, R. D. (1978). Athletic participation and status of Alberta high school girls. *International Review of Sport Sociology, 1* (12), 57–69.

Buhrmann, H. G., and Jarvis, M. S. (1971). Athletics and status. *CAHPER Journal, 37* (January-February), 14–17.

Case, B., Greer, H. S., and Brown, J. (1987). Academic clustering in athletics: Myth or reality? *ARENA Review, 11* (2), 48–56.

Chandler, T. J. L., and Goldberg, A. D. (1990). The academic all-American as vaunted adolescent role identity. *Sociology of Sport Journal, 7,* 287–293.

Chronicle of Higher Education (1991). Graduation rates of athletes and other students at Division I colleges, *37* (March 27), 39–44.

Chu, D. (1982). *Dimensions of Sport Studies.* New York: Wiley.

Clendinen, D. (1986). State survey of Georgia University cites preferential grading for athletes. *New York Times* (April 4), I: 1, 26.

Coakley, J. J. (1990). *Sport in Society,* 4th ed. St. Louis: Times Mirror/Mosby.

Coleman, J. S. (1961a). Athletics in high school. *The Annals of the American Academy of Political and Social Science, 338* (November): 33–34.

Coleman, J. S. (1961b). *The Adolescent Society.* New York: The Free Press.

Danzig, A. (1956). *The History of American Football.* Englewood Cliffs, NJ: Prentice Hall.

Edwards, H. (1984). The collegiate athletic arms race: Origins and implications of the Rule 48 controversy. *Journal of Sport and Social Issues, 8* (1), 4–22.

Eitzen, D. S. (1975). Athletics in the status system of male adolescents: A replication of Coleman's *The Adolescent Society. Adolescence, 10,* pp. 268–276.

Eitzen, D. S. (1987). The educational experiences of intercollegiate student-athletes. *Journal of Sport and Social Issues, 11,* 15–30.

Elder, D., and Parker, S. (1987). The cultural production and reproduction of gender: The effect of extracurricular activities on peer group culture. *Sociology of Education, 60,* 200–213.

Feltz, D. L. (1979). Athletics in the status system of female adolescents. *Review of Sport and Leisure, 4* (1), 110–118.

Fitzgibbons, J. K. (1989). The impact of the C-average policy on the academic achievement and attendance of student athletes at Stagg High School between 1981 and 1983. *Dissertation Abstracts International, 50,* 2446A. (University Microfilms No. DA 9002104).

Frey, J. (1985). The winning team myth. *Currents: Journal of the Council for Advancement and Support of Education, 11* (1), 32–35.

Hallinan, M. T., and Williams, R. A. (1990). Student's characteristics and the peer influence process. *Sociology of Education, 63,* 122–132.

Hanks, M. P., and Eckland, B. K. (1976). Athletics and social participation in the educational attainment process. *Sociology of Education, 49* (October), 271–294.

Heider, F. (1958). *The Psychology of Interpersonal Relations.* New York: Wiley.

Jerome, W. C., and Phillips, J. C. (1971). Academic achievement and interscholastic athletic participation: A comparison of Canadian and American high schools. *CAHPER Journal, 37* (January-February), 19–21.

Lapchick, R. (1987). The high school athlete as the future college student-athlete. *Journal of Sport and Social Issues, 11,* 104–124.

Lederman, D. (1991). Knight Commission tells presidents to use their power to reform the "fundamental premises" of college sport. *Chronicle of Higher Education, 37* (March 27), 1, 33–37.

Leonard, W. M. (1988). *A Sociological Perspective of Sport,* 3rd ed. New York: Macmillan.

MacKillop, A., and Snyder, E. E. (1987). *An Analysis of Jocks and Other Subgroups within the High School Status Structure.* Paper presented at the Fifth Canadian Congress on Leisure Research, Halifax, Nova Scotia.

McIntosh, P. C. (1966). Mental ability and success in school sport. *Research in Physical Education, 1* (1).

Melnick, M. J., Vanfossen, B. E., and Sabo, D. F. (1988). Developmental effects of athletic participation among high school girls. *Sociology of Sport Journal, 5,* 22–36.

Meyer, B. B. (1990). From idealism to actualization: The academic performance of female collegiate athletes. *Sociology of Sport Journal, 7,* 44–57.

Michener, J. A. (1976). *Sports in America.* Greenwich, CT: Fawcett.

NCAA Manual (1989, 1991). Mission, KS: NCAA.

Nack, W. (1986). This case was one for the books. *Sports Illustrated, 64* (February 24), 34–37, 42.

Newcomb, T. M. (1961). *The Acquaintance Process.* New York: Holt, Rinehart, & Winston.

Otto, L. B., and Alwin, D. F. (1977). Athletics, aspirations and attainments. *Sociology of Education, 42* (April), 102–113.

Phillips, J. C. (1979). *The Educational Consequences of School Sports Participation.* Paper presented at the annual meeting of the American Sociological Association, Boston, MA.

Phillips, J. C. (1980). The creation of deviant behavior in American high schools. In K. Baker and R. J. Rubel, Eds. *Violence and Crime in the Schools.* Lexington, MA: Lexington Books, Ch. 10.

Phillips, J. C., and Schafer, W. E. (1970). *The Athletic Subculture: A Preliminary Study.* Paper presented at the annual meeting of the American Sociological Association, Washington, DC.

Picou, J. S. (1978). Race athletic achievement and educational aspiration. *The Sociological Quarterly, 19,* 429–438.

Picou, J. S., and Curry, E. W. (1974). Residence and the athletic participation-educational aspiration hypothesis. *Social Science Quarterly, 55,* 768–776.

Raney, J., Knapp, T., and Small, M. (1986). Pass one for the gipper: student-athletes and university coursework. In R. E. Lapchick, Ed. *Fractured Focus.* Lexington, MA: Lexington Books, pp. 53–61.

Rehberg, R. A., and Cohen, M. (1975). Athletes and scholars: An analysis of the compositional characteristics of and image of these two youth culture categories. *International Review of Sport Sociology, 1* (10), 91–107.

Rehberg, R. A., and Schafer, W. E. (1968). Participation in interscholastic athletics and college expectations. *The American Journal of Sociology, 73* (May), 732–740.

Rosenthal, R., and Jacobson, L. (1968). *Pygmalion in the Classroom.* New York: Holt, Rinehart, & Winston.

Sabo, D., Melnick, M. M., and Vanfossen, B. (1989). *Minorities in Sport.* New York: Women's Sports Foundation.

Sack, A. L. (1987). College sport and the student-athlete. *Journal of Sport and Social Issues, 11,* 31–48.

Sack, A. L. (1991). The underground economy of college football. *Sociology of Sport Journal, 8,* 1–15.

Schafer, W. E., and Armer, J. M. (1968). Athletes are not inferior students. *Trans-Action* (November), 21–26, 61–62.

Schafer, W. E., and Rehberg, R. A. (1970). Athletic participation college aspirations and college encouragement. *Pacific Sociological Review, 13* (Summer), 182–186.

Sellers, R. M. (1992). Racial differences in the predictors for academic achievement of student-athletes in Division I revenue producing sports. *Sociology of Sport Journal, 9,* 48–59.

Snyder, E. E. (1972). High school athletes and their coaches: Educational plans and advice. *Sociology of Education, 45* (Summer), 313–325.

Snyder, E. E., and Spreitzer, E. (1977). Participation in sport as related to educational expectations among high school girls. *Sociology of Education, 50* (January), 47–55.

Spady, W. G. (1970). Lament for the letterman: Effects of peer status and extracurricular activities on goals and achievement. *American Journal of Sociology, 75* (January), 680–702.

Sperber, M. (1990). *College Sports Inc.* New York: Henry Holt.

Spreitzer, E., and Pugh, M. (1973). Interscholastic athletics and educational expectations. *Sociology of Education, 46* (Spring), 171–182.

Stagg, A. A., and Stout, W. W. (1927). *Touchdown!* New York: Longmans, Green & Co.

Start, K. B. (1966). The substitution of games performance for academic achievement as a means of achieving status among secondary school children. *British Journal of Sociology, 17*(3), 300–305.

Start, K. B. (1967). Sporting and intellectual success among English secondary school children. *International Review of Sport Sociology, 2,* 47–53.

Tappan, P. W. (1960). *Crime, Justice and Correction.* New York: McGraw-Hill.

Thirer, J., and Wieczorek, P. J. (1984). On and off

field social interaction patterns of black and white high school athletes. *Journal of Sport Behavior, 7,* 105–114.

Thirer, J., and Wright, S. D. (1985). Sport and social status for adolescent males and females. *Sociology of Sport Journal, 2,* 164–171.

Washington, R., et al. (1991). Things seem better but . . . *Sports Illustrated, 5* (August 5), 48–53.

Weber, L. J., Sherman, T. M., and Tegano, C. (1990). Faculty perceptions of the sources and types of pressure to assist student athletes. *Sociology of Sport Journal, 7,* 389–393.

Wicker, A. W. (1968). Undermanning, performances, and students subjective experiences in behavior settings of large and small high schools. *Journal of Personality and Social Psychology, 10* (November), 255–261.

Wiley, E. (1989). Sociologist Edwards derides "plantation system" of college athletics. *Black Issues in Higher Education,* April 27, 12.

Willems, E. P. (1967). Sense of obligation to high school activities as related to school size and marginality of student. *Child Development, 38* (December), 1247–1260.

Chapter 7

Race and Sport: Physical Causes?

The idea that some race-linked physical differences may explain racial differences in athletic performance has a long, and sometimes ugly, history. The ugly part of this history affects thinking in social science to this day. Nazi racial theories were used as part of the justification for the genocidal campaign against European Jews as well as mass murder and expulsions of whole populations in regions of Eastern Europe. In the United States, racial differences were used to justify slavery before the Civil War and racial segregation after the Civil War. Not surprisingly, social scientists in the middle of this century saw a need to explode these crude and demonstrably false theories.

Many sport sociologists have gone overboard on this. It is one thing to reject false ideas. It is quite another to replace them with other false ideas. For example, a theory of why black long jumpers can jump farther than their white or Asian compatriots should not be rejected if the only reason for the rejection is an objection to earlier racism. The old 19th century racial theories were rejected by social science because they were tested and proven false, not because they were immoral. Latter-day ideas about possible race-linked physical causes of racial performance differences should be tested also. This chapter considers ways sociologists can test such theories and try to assess the likelihood that such theories may be true. One widely known "physical" theory, *the self-paced reactive hypothesis,* is also carefully examined.

Before looking at how we might assess the truth of racial theories, it is appropriate to look at the confused state of current thinking among sport sociologists. This thinking discourages careful testing of "physical type" hypotheses. Consider the following thesis statement of a recent paper (Davis, 1990), which won the 1989 Student Paper Award of the North American Society for the Sociology of Sport.

> Whites appear to be threatened by black success in sport, and the common-sense preoccupation with the question of racially linked genetic differences between black and white athletes reflects this racist fear. The preoccupation itself is racist because it is founded on and naturalizes the categories of "black" and "white," categories that are crucial to the maintenance of white power structures. These categories are perceived to be biological categories that are fixed, unambiguous, and dichotomous. The perceived genetic differences between the categories of black and white are used to explain success in sport. This practice is problematic not only because unambiguous biological racial categories do not exist but also because the use of biological determinist arguments to explain human behavior obscure human agency and sociopolitical forces. When the sociopolitical world is obscured, racism is ignored and white power structures remain unchallenged. (Davis, 1990, p. 180)

Note that the first sentence refers to whites and blacks. Whether whites are or are not "preoccupied" with race-linked genetic differences is not at issue here. Just recall that the first sentence implies that the author can tell whites from blacks. A few sentences later we are informed that we should not think in terms of black and white because: 1) this helps maintain the "white power structure" (Oops! We are not supposed to think in terms of "white" and "black."); and 2) "unambiguous racial categories" do not exist. The author does not explain why she uses the categories black and white even though it is harmful to do so. Neither does she explain how she can tell blacks from whites even though an absence of "unambiguous racial categories" would make her distinction impossible.

It is true that the black-white racial distinction is much more a cultural than a biological reality. Many individuals and groups simply do not "fit" into these categories. Arabs, for example, are not black and they are not white. Neither are they a "race" unto themselves. Arabs are undefined by American racial categories. The reader may want to contemplate why such groups as Arabs or Polynesians are not defined under the traditional black-white-Asian racial scheme current in American thinking. On the other hand, most of us can distinguish blacks from whites on the basis of physical features. If this were not possible racial discrimination would be rendered difficult if not impossible. Caste discrimination among racially homogeneous societies such as Japan or India is facilitated by economic and cultural traits and, ultimately, by an appropriate entry on people's ID cards. Lower castes in these societies are perceived much as racial minorities are in North America. Would-be racists in the United States require no special means of identification to choose the people against whom they direct their racial discrimination. Asians, blacks, and whites can be easily distinguished, notwithstanding Davis' observation that the three races are not really separate biological categories.

Davis' argument that race-linked physical difference theories somehow "obscure human agency and sociopolitical forces" seems less a statement of fact than a justification for censorship against physical type theories. This censor-it-don't-test-it attitude is also evident in another recent *Sociology of Sport Journal* article (Mathisen & Mathisen, 1991).

Contrast the muddled thinking of the recent critiques of race-linked physical difference theories with that of Harry Edwards (1973, pp. 193–196) two decades prior. Edwards took up the *scientific* status of these theories, not their moral implications. Edwards asked "Is it true?" not "Is it proper to ask this question?" Edwards attacked these theories on two grounds. First, the samples upon which black and white racial characteristics are based are far too small and unrepresentative of the tens of millions of black and white people in the population. This problem is exacerbated by the fact that characteristics of *average* blacks and whites tell us little about possible racial differences among *elite* athletes, whose physical talents fall at the very top one-thousandth of their populations. For example, knowing about the height of the average white and the average black tells us little about how many blacks and whites are taller than seven feet (Phillips, 1976, pp. 42–43). Only an immense, scrupulously representative sample can provide this sort of information.

Edwards' second point takes up the problem of theory. There are black-white differences, but these differences must also distinguish good athletes from mediocre athletes. Edwards observed that great athletes, black and white, come in a variety of shapes and sizes, defying the creation of any "type" that can then be counted for its frequency among racial populations. Differences between East African distance runners (mainly Kenyans) and American and Caribbean sprinters defy any "black athletic type" theory. Years before Edwards' work, Dr. W. Montague Cobb (1936) pointed to a related problem of physical type theories, namely that some great sprinters do not look like sprinters. (Sprinting is often used as a basis for testing racial theories because blacks overwhelmingly excel over whites in the sprints.) Jesse Owens, who broke *four* world records in the sprints and long jump on one day, and later won four gold medals in the 1936 Olympic Games, did not fit the anatomical "mold" of top sprinters (Cobb, 1936, pp. 52–53).

More will be said about "physical type" theories later. At this point I want to say that the quality of inquiry has deteriorated sharply from the early work of Edwards to the present day moralism (let us be contemporary and say politically correct moralism) or at least some of the more recent writing on this topic. Exhibit 7–1 lists some traps that sports sociologists can fall into when studying the connection between race and sport.

Race-Linked Physical Differences

It is by no means surprising that many people, white and black, assume that black success in sports may be explained by some race-linked physical advantage. If an individual is to perform at the highest level of a sport, he or she must possess a high level of physical ability. Without this basic talent no one, no matter how well trained,

EXHIBIT 7–1 Three Logical Traps That May Confuse Thinking about Race and Sport

Thinking on the subject of race and sport would be improved if thinkers would discipline themselves better and observe what they have been taught about logic and the scientific method. One wonders if some recent commentators on the race and sport issue have been taught much of anything about logic and science. Discussed below are three ideas that could clarify debate on physical type theories of athletic achievement, if commentators would pay attention to them.

Necessary vs. Sufficient Causes

When we think of *cause and effect* we usually think about condition *a*, which, when present, produces or greatly increases the likelihood of effect *b*. "If you train hard you will be a better swimmer" expresses the idea of sufficient causation. Hard training is a *sufficient condition* to produce an effect, improved times in swimming. But what if a coach promises, "If you train hard you will win the city championship"? True, hard training increases an athlete's chances of winning a race, but other swimmers are training hard too. A would-be champion has to improve his or her stroke and, perhaps, have a "good day" in order to win.

The coach would be more logically precise to say, "If you don't train hard you will not win the city championship." This statement implies that hard training is a *necessary condition* of successful competition. Without hard training no championship is possible. With hard training a championship is possible, but not guaranteed. It may take a combination of talent, stroke improvement, peaking, good diet, psychological focusing, and even luck to be *sufficient* to create a victory in a championship event.

Physical ability theorists often imply that physical ability is a *sufficient* condition for the achievement of elite athletic status. Critics of physical ability theories seem to think that hard work or an abundance of playing opportunities are sufficient conditions for the achievement of elite athletic status. In fact these things are *necessary conditions.* Without hard work, without good facilities, without physical ability, without good competition, people cannot become elite athletes. When some of these conditions are met, people have a chance to become elite athletes. Heredity and environment are *both* necessary conditions for athletic success.

A talent-rich population will not produce many champions without favorable social conditions that encourage people to participate. Excellent coaching, facilities, and competition are also required. A population with little talent will not produce many champions even if opportunities to participate are plentiful.

Affirming the Consequent

If it rains the sidewalk will get wet.
The sidewalk is wet.
Therefore, it has just rained.

This statement appears reasonable enough, but it is flawed. Yes, if it rains the sidewalk will get wet, but if I water my lawn carelessly it will get wet too. If the street sweeper gets careless the sidewalk may get wet. Just because the sidewalk is wet does

EXHIBIT 7–1 *Continued*

not prove that it rained. Assuming that a result (a wet sidewalk) proves that a particular cause has happened is called ***affirming the consequent.***

Theorists who observe sharp racial differences in performance often assume that these differences "prove" their particular theory, but other theories might explain the differences instead. The fact that blacks excel in basketball in the United States does not prove that blacks see basketball as a way out of the ghetto, or that blacks have more natural ability, or that black kids imitate the role models of famous basketball players.

"Man on the street" beliefs about why black athletes excel in sprinting, basketball, football, and baseball assume that the black excellence they are explaining "proves" their particular explanation (see, for example, Kane, 1971). Far from it. The physical causes, whatever they may be, of black-white performance differences have to be shown to exist in the two populations in roughly the same proportion as athletic achievement. To complicate matters, the effects of sociological factors like incentives and opportunities to play must also be considered.

Adequate demonstration of any theory that considers some black-white physical or psychological differences as causes of black-white performance differences requires a long, arduous research agenda. Saying "this must be so because it is consistent with known performance differences" proves little about the truth of any particular explanation.

Tautology

Tautology means saying the same thing twice. Saying "The Chinese don't like milk because Chinese culture defines milk as unpalatable" is really saying "the Chinese don't like milk because the Chinese don't like milk." Some theories about physical causes of racial performance differences are tautological. "Blacks are better sprinters because they can run faster" is, of course, tautological.

Should a researcher discover certain morphological differences (say, longer legs and narrower hips in blacks) between racial groups, he or she would be wrong to believe the morphological differences necessarily explain performance differences. All that is being done is substituting two sets of morphological descriptors for the words black and white, saying "people who look like blacks can run faster than people who look like whites." This is no different than "blacks can run faster than whites."

To show that blacks have some anatomical advantage over whites that helps them achieve faster times in sprinting events, two "facts" must be demonstrated. First, there must be black-white physical differences that approximate in magnitude known black-white performance differences. Second, and more importantly, ***these same differences must distinguish good sprinters from less able sprinters.*** The best Japanese sprinters should have these physical characteristics more than less successful Japanese sprinters. The best white sprinters should have these characteristics more than less able white sprinters. The best black sprinters should have these characteristics more than less able black sprinters.

An adequate physical explanation of black sprinting superiority has to first

Continued

EXHIBIT 7–1 *Continued*

distinguish between good and bad sprinters. It has to show what better Russian sprinters have that slower Russians do not, and what better Arab sprinters have that slower Arabs do not, and so forth. Once an explanation of what physical characteristics distinguish better sprinters within any population is demonstrated, these same characteristics have to be shown to be distributed between races in approximately the same proportion as racial differences in performance. That is, world-class white sprinters should exhibit the same "sprinter profile" that top black sprinters have. Slower white and black athletes should not fit this profile.

can succeed. If blacks constitute 75 percent or so of the best basketball players, isn't this an indication that 75 percent of all basketball talent is concentrated in the black population?

The Natural East German Athletes

Until the reunification of East and West Germany in 1991, athletes from tiny East Germany, population about 17 million, were a force in international sports far out of proportion to their numbers. In track and field, for example, we might be amazed to see the East German men ranking second in the world (behind the United States) over the past several years, occasionally slipping to third behind the Soviet Union. East Germany was in some years better than the United States (population 250 million) in swimming, especially women's swimming. East Germany was a major force in most winter sports, leading the world in many sports and competitive in all.

The East Germans have dominated certain sports in Europe every bit as thoroughly as blacks do in America. Is this to be explained by some race-linked physical advantage enjoyed by East Germans? We can safely dismiss the old Nazi ideas about German racial superiority. West Germans do not seem to be nearly as good as their Eastern relatives; Americans of German descent do not seem to do especially well in sports in the United States. Perhaps the rigors of losing two major wars in this century culled the weak from the East German population, leaving a generation sired by the most hearty Germans, the postwar survivors. But what about the West Germans, who also suffered, or the Russians, who suffered even more?

We could take some time to explore racial theories that might explain East German success in sports, but this chapter is about black success in sport. Suffice it to say that if Germans had some racial advantage in sports, Germans everywhere would display this advantage, not just Germans who lived in East Germany. As for wartime survival of the fittest—who says the most athletic people survive? Wouldn't the best athletes be more likely to serve in combat, dying rather than surviving? Any sports fan knows why the East Germans have been good in sports: sophisticated selection and training of the available talent. Now that this system has been abandoned, athletes from what used to be East Germany may be expected to perform at a level similar to that of athletes from West Germany.

Curiously, many people tend to favor explanations of black success in sports that parallel the easily refuted "natural ability" arguments just made regarding East Germans. Do blacks everywhere excel in the traditional "black" sports? Do blacks have some observable physical advantage for certain kinds of sports?

The Natural African-American Athletes

There have been dozens of studies of black-white physical differences. Collected findings of several studies of these differences (see Table 7–1) suggest that certain race-linked physical factors may explain some racial differences in athletic performance. Arm and leg structure, musculature, and narrow hips are believed to suit blacks for activities that require speed, while a lack of body fat and small chest cavity presumably constitute a disadvantage to blacks who might want to swim, perform in cold-weather sports, or compete in endurance sports.

Some of these presumed explanations can be quickly dismissed. Lack of insulating body fat as protection in cold weather ceased to have importance with the invention of clothes. The lack of body fat causes a high proportion of blacks to lack natural buoyancy in the water, but this fact proves to have little import in the explanation of

TABLE 7–1 Some Black-White Comparisons That May Have Performance Implications*

Physical Attribute (black compared to white)	Presumed Implications for Sport
Increased body weight, decreased body fat.	Overall sturdier construction; advantageous for contact sports, e.g., football.
Increased muscular girth.	Suggests greater strength/body size ratio; advantageous in explosive events, e.g., jumping, sprinting.
High center of gravity.	Advantageous in jumping events.
Longer forearm and arm span.	Longer levers develop greater velocities. Advantageous for throwing events, e.g., discus.
Narrow hips, longer legs (shorter upper segment, longer lower segment), broader and longer feet.	Longer strides for running, jumping events (lever principle). Overall trunk and leg structure enhance events that require speed.
Shorter trunk, shallower chest.	Reduced thoracic volume and vital capacity; disadvantage for endurance events.
Faster patellar tendon reflex.	Enhanced spinal response; may increase sprinting ability.

*From Jordan (1969); de Garay, Levine, & Carter (1974); and Tanner (1964).

swimming performance—lack of opportunity for would-be black swimmers is clearly the main reason for the absence of black swimming success. Malachi Cunningham, a black swim coach, has shown that buoyancy has little importance for swimming performance once the swimmer has passed the beginner level (Cunningham, 1973). Other explanations may have a basis in truth. It is possible that leg morphology, for example, is different among blacks and whites and that this difference might influence sprinting ability.

It is no easy task to assess the "truth" (the likelihood that an explanation is correct) of any given physical factor explanation of racial differences in performance. Several questions must be addressed for such an assessment, including:

1. *Sampling*. Do the observed differences really exist in the black and white populations? That is, were the studies that found racial differences somehow biased, giving erroneous black-white comparisons?

2. *Magnitude.* Are the physical differences great enough to explain the sometimes huge racial differences in performance? Small physical differences cannot explain big performance differences.

3. *Theory.* Do the observed physical differences between blacks and whites explain performance differences? Many racial differences (e.g., hair texture) have nothing to do with athletic performance. Hence any black-white differences also have to produce top level performance in "black" events [using track and field as a case in point] such as sprinting and long jumping. Likewise white athletes will have to possess a physical advantage in "white" events such as discus, shot put, pole vault, and distance running.

4. *Consistency.* Do blacks throughout the world excel at the "black" events? Do blacks around the world do poorly in "white" events? We showed that West Germans did not share the amazing success of their East German cousins. This was used to dispel the argument that East Germans enjoy some physical advantage that has helped them succeed in a variety of international sports. Do all black populations achieve the amazing success of North American and Caribbean blacks? A physical factor explanation would suggest universal black excellence in "black" events and universal weakness in "white" events.

The next section deals at length with these issues. Simple physical factor explanations become very questionable when examined in depth.

Objections to Race-Linked Physical Factor Theories

Sampling

Perhaps the most common objection to race-linked physical factor explanations centers on the quality of the evidence. When one speaks of differences between blacks and whites in the United States, one is speaking of populations in excess of

30 million blacks and 200 million whites. Clearly, researchers must *infer* characteristics of the black and white populations from *samples* of black and white individuals. If these samples are either too small or unrepresentative of the total populations, evidence based on the samples is liable to be misleading.

Harry Edwards, a national leader in black resistance to racism in sports, flatly rejects the validity of studies that assert the existence of race-linked physical differences to explain racial differences in athletic performance. Edwards points out that:

> In no case was the evidence presented gathered from a random sample of subjects selected from the black population at large in America. . . . Therefore, the generalization of the research findings to the black population as a whole . . . constitutes a scientific blunder of the highest magnitude and invalidates the would-be scientific foundations of [this argument]. (Edwards, 1972, p. 59)

Edwards probably goes too far in his rejection of physical-type studies. It is true that some studies used samples that were far too small for any statistical reliability. For example, the often-cited study by Eleanor Metheny (1939) involved only 51 black and 51 white subjects, and the famous study of Olympic athletes by J. M. Tanner (1964) had only *15* black subjects! On the other hand, some studies involved many thousands, most notably those involving comparisons of black and white soldiers (e.g., Baker, 1959; Davenport & Love, 1921). Of equal importance, several black-white differences appear in study after study. These replicated findings *are* based on a large number of cases even though each individual study had employed a "small" sample.

On the other hand, even if problems associated with small samples can be overcome by replication studies, a major problem still remains. Standard statistics books declare the importance of random selection of subjects for study if the researcher is to avoid some form of *selection bias*. In practice, random sampling can only rarely be achieved and selection bias can only rarely be avoided. Studies of populations as large and diverse as black and white Americans cannot come close to achieving perfect random sampling. No one has a list of all black and white people and where they live. If such a list were available a "true" random sample still could not be selected, as a certain number of randomly selected people would be unable or unwilling to participate in whatever activities were required for the research. Couple this with the fact that researchers have limited resources (i.e., budgets). This forces them to seek not representative samples of blacks and whites, but samples of *available* blacks and whites, accepting whatever known and unknown biases might exist.

For example, a study comparing black and white college students would be far less expensive than a comparable study of general populations, but the study might reach conclusions far removed from those that might result from a study of the general black and white populations. College students are probably somewhat healthier and larger than the general population, and a substantial proportion of the black students may be in the student population precisely because of certain physical characteristics associated with athletic success. Thus, black-white differences discovered among small or large samples of college students (or fire fighters or soldiers) cannot be taken to accurately estimate differences that exist in the general population.

Magnitude of Racial Differences

The issue of magnitude of black-white differences is an important one for any physical-ability theory. If racial variations in sports achievement are the result of race-linked physical differences, the magnitude of the physical differences should approximate the magnitude of the racial differences in achievement. Thus, if some physical advantage (or, more likely, some combination of physical advantages) explains black-white performance differences in a given sport, for example the high jump, the particular physical advantage should appear in the black and white populations approximately as often as top level high jumpers appear among the black and white populations.

Roughly 12 percent of all males between the ages of 20 and 30 are black (Phillips, 1976, pp. 40–41), while about half of the best American high jumpers are black. To achieve this over-representation, blacks would have to possess the extreme physical advantages required for a "top 50" performance some eight or nine times as frequently as their white counterparts.

There simply is no evidence of any black-white physical difference of this magnitude that could possibly explain black success in the high jump. Let us take a more distinct case—sprinting. In a typical year about 90 percent of the top American sprinters are black (Hendershott, 1975). To achieve this sort of dominance blacks would have to enjoy a 66 to 1 advantage in whatever physical characteristics produce excellence in sprinting (Phillips, 1976, p. 41)! One would think that a physical advantage of this magnitude would have long ago been observed, but none has. Perhaps this inability to discover the physical cause of black-white performance differences results from the absence of such a cause.

Theory of Athletic Excellence

On the other hand, failure to discover the cause of racial performance differences may result from an ignorance of what to look for in the first place. Suppose it were possible to examine many thousands of black and white subjects who were randomly selected from the entire North American population. What sort of examination would you perform? What differences would you look for to explain black success in certain sports? We have shown that the physical differences between blacks and whites would have to be sizable, but what would these differences be? What physical characteristics make for success in sprinting? jumping? swimming? Harry Edwards' term, "scientific blunder of the highest magnitude," might better be applied to the lack of "theories" of sprinting, jumping, and hitting, rather than the absence of random sampling. With no theory or at least no educated guess about what physical characteristics "cause" excellence in various sports, a researcher cannot know what racial differences to look for!

As one would expect there has been a substantial amount of research directed at describing anatomical differences between athletes of various sports. A number of studies of international caliber athletes have shown clear differences in somatotype scores and a variety of body size and relative limb length (e.g., the ratio of leg length to trunk length) measurements (de Garay, Levine, & Carter, 1974, Ch. 2). Such differences constitute the beginning of a theory. Could it be that lighter calves, along with stronger muscles and a relatively short, slender trunk (and, according to de Garay, narrow hips allowing a more direct line of impulse from legs to the body's center of gravity), give the black athlete an advantage over his white counterpart in certain events?

This notion, although it does constitute the beginning of an explanation of black-white performance differences, is fraught with weaknesses and anomalies:

1. Tanner's track and field sample, for instance, consisted of some 137 competitors in the Rome Olympics, only *15* of whom were black. Three of the 15 were East Africans (two distance runners and one 400-meter runner) leaving some *12* North Americans, West Indians, and a single West African to constitute the sample on which the black advantages might correctly be assessed.

2. Of great interest in the case of this particular study of 1960 Olympians is the fact that white athletes dominated the sprint events, black athletes won no medals in the 100 meters, and only silver and bronze in the 200. Whites won the gold and silver medals in the high jump. That is, in many cases the black athletes, whose supposed structural advantages are suggested as a possible explanation of black success in certain events, were beaten by white athletes who may have lacked the structural advantages.

Whether or not black athletes are defeated by whites in events that blacks ordinarily dominate, racial comparisons among world-class athletes must be evaluated with the greatest reserve (Figure 7–1). All of the athletes studied by Tanner and de Garay, white and black, were world class. They all met an extremely high standard of performance. If the "black morphology" explains black excellence, how do we explain the excellence of the world-class white athletes who do not enjoy the supposed structural advantages of black morphology?

A satisfactory theory of black success in certain events has to show that all top performers, black and white, possess certain physical advantages that are not evident among ordinary performers, *and* that these advantages are found far more frequently among the black population than among the white population.

Table 7–2 provides an opportunity to compare sprinters to nonsprinters, and blacks to whites, on two measures that are thought to partly explain black success in sprinting and jumping events. White sprinters and jumpers have more narrow hips relative to leg length than do whites in other events, such as swimming or boxing.

FIGURE 7–1 While there are clear black-white performance differences in several sports, no "physical type" theory has been able to adequately explain the reasons for these differences.

(Courtesy of the University of the Pacific)

Likewise, white sprinters and jumpers seem to have longer legs relative to overall height than competitors in other events (the subjects of these measurements were competitors in the 1968 Olympic Games). Thus, for whites the notion that individuals with long legs and narrow hips are advantaged in the sprints and jumps is supported. But now examine the evidence for black athletes. Black sprinters and jumpers have long legs and narrow hips—longer and narrower than their white counterparts. But black boxers and middle-distance runners also possess the long legs and narrow hips that are supposed to characterize sprinters. Indeed, black sprinters are *not* distinguishable from black nonsprinters in these factors. Finally, white sprinters who are substantially faster than black basketball players, boxers, or middle-distance runners do not have longer legs or narrower hips. Black sprinters look more like black nonsprinters than white sprinters. If leg length and hip width contribute to sprinting

TABLE 7–2 Comparisons of Blacks to Whites and Sprinters to Nonsprinters on Ratios between Hip Width, Height, and Leg Length*

	Hip Width/ Height		Hip Width/ Leg Length		Leg Length/ Height	
	Black	White	Black	White	Black	White
Reference	—	.16	—	.35	—	.46
Sprinters	.15	.16	.31	.33	.48	.47
Basketball	.15	.16	.30	.34	.48	.47
Boxers (Welter-Lt. Middleweight)	.15	.17	.31	.36	.47	.46
Long Distance	.15	.16	.32	.34	.47	.46
Middle Distance	.15	.16	.30	.34	.49	.47
Jumpers (HJ, LJ, TJ)	.15	.16	.30	.33	.49	.47
Swimmers	—	.16	—	.34	—	.46

Conclusions:

1. Sprinters have narrower hips (relative to height or to leg length).
   a. Black sprinters do *not* have narrower hips than black nonsprinters.
   b. White sprinters do have narrower hips than white nonsprinters.
2. Black nonsprinters have narrower hips than white sprinters.

*Data from de Garay, Levine, & Carter (1974), Tables 3.100, 3.104, 3.106, 3.107, 3.109, 3.113, 3.122.

ability we should expect both black and white sprinters to have narrow hips and long legs, which distinguish them from nonsprinters, black and white. Instead we find that all black athletes are alike in their long legs and narrow hips, which distinguish them from nonblacks.

In summary, black and white sprinters (or jumpers) are not alike, at least in terms of hip width and leg length. Black sprinters are not distinguishable from black performers who are not good sprinters or jumpers. It would appear that narrow hips and long legs are found more frequently among blacks than whites, but this fact may not be relevant to the explanation of black success at sprinting, since black sprinters appear not to be distinguished from black nonsprinters in hip and leg measurements.

Many of the apparent black-white structural differences suggest that blacks should excel in events in which they are virtually absent at world-class levels. For example, Tanner argues, "The pole vault should be particularly attractive [to blacks], as the length and power of the arms would add to the advantage already present in the weight relations. . . . In the discus and perhaps the shot, the long arms should be an advantage, but they might well be offset by the lighter body" (1964, p. 107). If we assume that the lighter body results from less fat content, the lighter body should pose no problem for blacks. Further, a light body may be greatly modified via training, legally through weight training or illegally through artificial steroid use. If black-white performance differences may be explained by a race-linked physical ability theory, the absence of blacks in events such as the pole vault, discus throw, shot put, and javelin throw contradicts the theory.

Consistency

A related problem lies in the absence of black athletes from Brazil and West Africa in world-class sprinting and jumping circles. If some set of physical factors produce black domination of certain events, Brazilian blacks, whose racial heritage closely parallels the history of North American and Caribbean blacks, and West Africans, from the ancestral homeland of all American blacks, should have the same advantage. While many Brazilians simply do not fit into traditional American racial categories, more than 15 percent of the population, or about 20 million Brazilians, would be recognized by a typical American as black. The region of Africa from which the slave trade was conducted runs roughly from present day Zaire to Senegal. This region is populated by approximately 130 million people. Nigeria alone has more than 85 million people. Nigeria's ties to Britain include a tradition of track and field athletics. The Nigerian government has a ministry of sport. There are some five million youths in school. Nigeria, like Brazil, ought to produce a high proportion of the world's best sprinters, hurdlers, and jumpers *if the population enjoys some race-linked physical advantage.*

They do not. Neither Nigeria nor Brazil has produced more than a handful of world-class sprinters or jumpers. As of 1991, Brazil has one world-class male sprinter, Robson da Silva, and one world-class female sprinter, Maria Figuereido, who ranked eleventh in the world in the 400-meter run. No Brazilians appear among the top-20 best performers in the traditionally "black" events of long jump, high hurdles, or high jump.

Nigeria has produced a line of excellent long jumpers and quite a few world-class sprinters. Presently Nigeria has three male top-20 sprinters and three women who are among the top 20 in the 100-meter, 200-meter, and 400-meter distances. Nigerians are absent from the high hurdles, long jump, and high jump top-20 lists, although the redoubtable Yusuf Ali missed the long jump top 20 in 1991 by 1/2 inch. If sprinting and jumping success is to be explained by race-linked physical ability, the dearth of top-class Nigerians and Brazilians poses a problem. They have the talent, but they do not perform as well as they should if physical talent is the main cause of black success.

Could it be that poverty and the rural village lifestyle of these populations inhibits athletic achievement? Kenya, an African country that is poorer than Nigeria and far poorer than Brazil, with a smaller urban population than either, has throughout the years produced a high proportion of the world's best distance runners and a few of the world's best sprinters. Poverty and ruralism should not prevent the talent-rich populations of Nigeria and Brazil from dominating the world in the sprints and jumps if physical talent explains a population's success in these sports.

The problems discussed above do not disprove any particular physical-type theory, but they do indicate that such a theory has yet to be verified. Whether or not such a theory ever is verified (that is, whether or not there really is a physical type reason for black-white performance differences, and that reason is demonstrated) it can have little practical impact. Coaches would still ask athletes to run races to determine who was fastest. Prejudiced people would still believe black athletes succeed because of physical talent alone, not because of hard work. The cases of the East German athletic dominance, and black-white differences in adoption of the flop technique in high jumping (see Exhibit 7–2) demonstrate the powerful impact of

EXHIBIT 7–2 Adoption of the Flop Technique in the High Jump*

The 1968 Olympic victory of Dick Fosbury revolutionized the high jump technique. Prior to Fosbury jumpers employed a roll or straddle technique in which the lead leg was propelled over the bar and then down while the trail leg and arm were lifted, imparting a rolling motion as the jumper cleared the bar. In the flop the jumper runs quickly to the bar, executing a turn the last two steps that propels the body over the bar in a back layout position. Within 12 years this new technique had been all but universally adopted.

An interesting aspect of the adoption of the flop was that black jumpers did not appear among floppers in the early 1970s when more and more white floppers were appearing. As of the 1973 season only two black floppers had ever appeared among the top 50 high jumpers in the United States while about half, or 14, of the white jumpers on the top 50 list that year used the flop.

Here was a sharp black-white performance difference. Virtually all black jumpers used the older roll technique while more and more whites were moving to the flop, and with great success. Interviews with coaches and jumpers from that era reveal no evidence that "black culture" somehow influenced black jumpers' preference for the roll. Young aspiring jumpers do not study "role models" and attempt to imitate them in sandlot high jumping contests. Rather they are taught by a coach in school or in a recreation or club setting.

It would not be surprising if an observer during that era had concluded that blacks used the roll and eschewed the flop because, compared to whites, they were physically suited for the roll and had a physical disadvantage in the flop. How else could such a sharp difference happen? Perhaps some muscle attachment or morphological difference gave blacks an advantage in the roll and a disadvantage in the flop.

No physical explanation can explain the 1973 variations no matter how likely such an explanation might have appeared at that time. By 1978 virtually all black and white jumpers were floppers. If the black population enjoyed some physical advantage in the roll and suffered a disadvantage in the flop in 1973, how could they do so well at the flop just five years later?

Clearly, the sharp black-white performance difference in early 1970s high jumping was produced by environmental factors, not hereditary ones. The best guess is that young white jumpers had more access to the proper landing pit than blacks. The flop technique cannot be used in a sawdust pit. Modern landing pits, which look like a giant mattress, provide a safe cushion for floppers. It appears likely that with the forced integration of schools during the 1968–73 era many young black jumpers gained access to proper landing pits, learned the flop, and began to make the top 50 ranking some six or so years later when they matured.

*Adapted from Phillips & Boelter (1984).

environmental factors like opportunity and incentive to participate, whatever the influence of hereditary factors.

Occasionally a physical type theory is stated with sufficient precision to allow a thorough evaluation of its truth. A few years ago Margaret Ciccolella and I (Phillips & Ciccolella, 1989) examined the adequacy of one such theory, the "self-paced reactive hypothesis." The next section reviews the facts on which the theory was based, some research that tended to support the theory, and some facts and conceptual problems that led us to reject it, even though it had appeared to "make sense" at first.

*The Reactivity Hypothesis: The Fate of a "Natural Ability" Theory**

A rather bizarre association between race and athletic performance was discovered by Morgan Worthy, a psychologist interested in the explanation of success in sports. Worthy (1971) reported a remarkable association between the proportion of blacks occupying a given position in professional football and the *eye color* of whites occupying those same positions. White players in "black" positions such as defensive back, wide receiver, and running back were found to have dark eyes, while white players in predominantly "white" positions such as quarterback, linebacker, and offensive line tended to have light-colored eyes. The eye color of white players appeared to parallel the racial distribution of players' various positions in professional football! An initial reaction to the above might attribute it all to happenstance, but there exists at least an idea as to why such a relationship (eye color and playing position) might exist:

> Neuromelanin may function in vivo as an amorphous semiconductor switching device to speed the transmission of neural impulses. . . . If eye color is a good indicator of the degree of neuromelanization we may be able to infer greater neural transmission speed and the organism's capability for reactive behavior.†

Two experiments have shown that dark-eyed subjects really do have slightly faster reaction times than light-eyed subjects (Landers, Obermeier, & Wolfe, 1977; Wolfe & Landers, 1978). The experiments involved response to a stimulus (visual or auditory) by pushing an electrical switch. The experiments allowed separation of *reaction time* from *movement time*. Dark-eyed subjects were faster to react, but they were no faster in the movement of their finger to press the switch. Blacks, most of

*This section is based on a recent paper (Phillips & Ciccolella, 1989) that the author wrote with Dr. Margaret Ciccolella.

† From Eye Color and Reactivity in Motor Behavior by M. D. Wolf and D. M. Landers. In D. M. Landers and R. W. Christina, Eds. *Psychology of Motor Behavior and Sport—1977*. Champaign, IL: Human Kinetics, pp. 255–263. Copyright 1978 by Human Kinetics Publishers, Inc. Reprinted by permission.

whom have dark eyes, might be expected to have (on the average) faster reaction times than whites, only some of whom have dark eyes. This faster reaction time might be expected to provide an advantage for blacks at certain kinds of tasks in sports.

Worthy and his associate, Allen Markle (1970), set off a small controversy when they suggested that many performance differences between blacks and whites might be explained by a black advantage at *reactive* activities, whereas whites excelled at *self-paced* activities. It was the work of Worthy and Markle (1970) and Worthy (1971, 1974) that led to the experimental work of Landers and Wolfe discussed in the previous paragraph. *Self-paced* refers to activities in which "the individual responds when he chooses to a relatively static stimulus" (Worthy & Markle, 1970, p. 439). Shooting a free throw or pitching a baseball are self-paced in that the person chooses when he or she initiates the activity. *Reactive* activities require the individual to "respond appropriately and at the right time to changes in the stimulus situation" (Worthy & Markle, 1970, p. 439). Hitting a baseball thrown by a good pitcher or shooting baskets against a defender are examples of reactive tasks in that the person must act in response (reaction) to unexpected conditions produced by the opposing players. Worthy and Markle (1970) observed that black baseball players excelled over whites in hitting (a reactive task) while whites were better than blacks at pitching (a self-paced activity). A similar trend was evident in professional basketball. Blacks had slightly higher field-goal shooting percentages (a more reactive task) while white players achieved slightly better free-throw percentages (a self-paced activity). Worthy (1974) reported some other examples of a tendency for blacks to do better in reactive tasks, such as an experiment in which black fourth-grade boys performed better than their white peers in the reactive task of defending a soccer goal but were outperformed at the more self-paced task of attacking the goal (p. 28).

Recall that the self-paced reactive hypothesis deals with eye color, not race, except that blacks have dark eyes. Worthy (1974) reported studies that indicated greater success of light-eyed, white professional athletes at such self-paced tasks as pitching, free-throw shooting, and bowling, although the light-eyed advantage did not appear among amateur league bowlers (pp. 31–33).

Critique

The idea that blacks may have a genetic advantage in certain activities owing to something related to eye darkness was interesting if only for its eccentricity. Some evidence tended to support the theory, so it may not be as eccentric as it appeared. On the other hand, evidence developed after the Worthy-Markle thesis appeared tends to refute the self-paced reactive hypothesis.

Even the favorable evidence seems to be equivocal. James M. Jones and Adrian Ruth Hochner (1973) found that the better basketball shooting percentage observed by Worthy and Markle did not hold up over a four-season span (Worthy and Markle examined data from one season only). That is, blacks did not appear to do better than their white counterparts at the reactive task of field-goal shooting, at least in professional basketball. On the other hand, the over-representation of blacks in top level basketball suggests that a much higher proportion of blacks than whites in the general population can shoot well enough to be a professional. Thus, in spite of NBA statistics one could say blacks can shoot better than whites.

But field-goal shooting in basketball may be a poor example of a reactive task. In a good offense outside shooters are given sufficient time to shoot without interference from defensive players. Inside shooting results in a high percentage of baskets even against opposition. Shooters employ well-practiced "moves" to fake out the defense in inside shooting, producing a basket, or a defensive foul. A basketball shooter who has to react to the actions of a defender should not shoot; rather, he or she should pass off to set up an open shot. Furthermore, shooting is a highly trained skill. When and from where a player shoots is determined by the actions of the defense, but the act of shooting requires a highly routinized (hence, not reactive) motion.

Jones and Hochner supported the baseball findings of Worthy and Markle. Blacks are somewhat over-represented at the major-league level in baseball. The fraction of the black population who can hit major-league pitching is substantially larger than the fraction of the white population who can do so. Thus, the self-paced vs. reactive hypothesis is probably supported in the case of baseball, but not in the case of shooting in basketball.

Football is a far better testing ground than baseball or basketball for the self-paced reactive hypothesis. Football has a variety of positions that vary considerably in task, including the reactivity required of occupants. Do presumably more reactive blacks (and dark-eyed whites) occupy reactive positions while more self-paced whites occupy more self-paced positions? A careful examination of two studies involving football players at Pennsylvania State University (Landers, Obermeier, and Wolfe, 1977) casts doubt on this contention of the self-paced reactive hypothesis. The strong race-eye color connection across football positions observed by Worthy (1971) did not hold for the Penn State players. The Penn State data show the relationship to be weak and within the boundaries of chance association (Landers, Obermeier, & Wolfe, 1977, pp. 104–105).

The Penn State data allow us to go a step further. Table 7–3 lists the reaction times of players in various positions on the football team, allowing a ranking of football positions according to the reactivity required of each position. This assumes, of course, that the players were in the positions for which they were best suited. Given the national reputation of football at Pennsylvania State University, this assumption seems reasonable. Receiver is the least reactive position according to the table. Receivers, like all football players, must be able to react quickly to changing circumstances but, relative to other positions in football, this ability seems less important. Receivers, especially wide receivers, are required to run specific pass routes to arrive in a particular area at a specified time. This "job description" is more self-paced than that of linebackers, who must fulfill their assignments *only in response* to the actions of the opposing offensive players—blockers, runners, and receivers. Likewise, the quarterback, at least in the passing game, is required to react quickly

TABLE 7–3 Relationship between Reaction Time Required and Racial Representation at Various Football Positions*

Position	Reaction Time of Players†	Rank	Percent Black in Position‡	Rank
Linebacker	.2316	(1)	8	(5)
Quarterback	.2335	(2)	7	(6)
Running Back	.2338	(3)	26	(1)
Defensive Back	.2343	(4)	17	(3)
Offensive Line	.2346	(5)	4	(7)
Defensive Line	.2410	(6)	13	(4)
Receiver	.2517	(7)	22	(2)
	$r_s = -.25$			

*Adapted from The Influence of External Stimuli and Eye Color on Reactive Motor Behavior by D. M. Landers, G. E. Obermeier, and M. D. Wolf. In R. W. Christina and D. M. Landers, Eds. *Psychology of Motor Behavior and Sport—1976*, Vol. II. 1976. Champaign, IL: Human Kinetics, pp. 94–112. Copyright 1977 by Human Kinetics Publishers, Inc. Reprinted by permission.
†Penn State University football players, 1975.
‡Penn State University football players, 1971–1974.

and with precision to the fast-changing conditions produced by onrushing defensive players and the moves of his receivers and opposing defensive backs.

Arguments could be made for a reshuffling of the ranking in Table 7–3, and with good reason! The difference between reaction time of the most reactive position of linebacker and the offensive lineman, who ranks fifth out of seven positions, amounts to .003 seconds. Does this mean the assumption that football positions vary in their reactivity requirements is wrong? If so, Worthy's fascinating discovery of a parallel between percentage of blacks in different positions and eye darkness of whites in those positions cannot be explained in terms of the reactivity required of occupants of the positions. If one wishes to retain the assumption that the positions do vary in the reactivity required of players, a major problem arises. The reactivity hypothesis contends that there is a positive correlation between the degree of reactivity required of players in a position and the percentage of black players in the position. In fact, the correlation between reactivity of football positions and black representation in those positions is *negative*. The most reactive positions are quarterback and linebacker. But these positions are "white" positions. The least reactive of all positions, receiver, is a "black" position.

The Penn State data, then, refute the reactivity hypothesis. The prediction that positions requiring the highest degree of reactivity should be disproportionately occupied by black athletes is simply wrong. This, along with the Jones and Hochner (1973) data on black-white basketball field-goal shooting percentages (and the questionable utility of shooting as an example of reactivity), falsifies the reactivity hypothesis insofar as black-white performance in football and basketball are concerned. Baseball hitting statistics do not refute the hypothesis, but its failure in football, along with the availability of alternative explanations of black success in baseball and basketball, make the hypothesis very unlikely.

Let us take a brief look at the other side of the self-paced reactive hypothesis. Do light-eyed individuals excel in self-paced activities? We can point to self-paced sports in which whites dominate such as golf, shot put, and discus, but others at which blacks are outstanding, such as long jump and high jump. There are many reasons why blacks or whites might be good in one sport or another, so we would do well to consider only ***within-sport comparisons*** as Worthy and Markle did.

Jones and Hochner (1973), in their reexamination of the self-paced reactive hypothesis, found that black professional basketball players were not as accurate at free-throw shooting as their white counterparts. They suggested, however, that this difference may be produced by differences in style of play (i.e., how players learned to play the game) rather than some genetic advantage enjoyed by light-eyed whites. The authors challenged the Worthy-Markle contention that whites in baseball were better pitchers than blacks. Worthy and Markle (1970, p. 440) assumed that because few blacks were pitching in major-league baseball, few blacks were good enough to pitch in the major leagues. This straightforward interpretation ignores ample evidence of long-standing discriminatory practices in baseball that have kept all but the better black pitchers out of the major leagues (Pascal & Rapping, 1970; Rosenblatt, 1967; Scully, 1974). No explanation of black-white differences in sports performance can be taken seriously unless it accounts for obvious racial differences in opportunity to play a given sport or to learn certain positions in a sport. In summary, the available evidence does not support the self-paced reactive hypothesis. Careful consideration of other physical type theories may well yield a similar result.

Conclusions

The facts that there are sharp racial differences in athletic performance, and that physical talent is necessary for top-class performance, suggest that there ***may*** be race-linked physical differences that explain some of the performance differences between races. A variety of racial differences have been proposed as explanations of racial performance, but none of these explanations have been demonstrated to be "true."

Before any race-linked physical difference theory can be considered "true," several conditions will have to be satisfied. The race-linked differences that are thought to produce performance differences must be shown to exist in the total black, white, and Asian populations. This requires huge samples that accurately represent the populations. The magnitude of any differences has to approximate the magnitude of performance difference between races. The observed racial differences also have to be proven to be causes of athletic performance. This means that if white swimmers have some physical advantage over black swimmers, the few blacks who become top calibre swimmers should have this advantage too, even if most blacks do not.

Finally, since blacks all over the world enjoy the same race-linked physical advantages for certain activities and disadvantages in others, blacks from all over the world should excel in the same sports and do poorly in the other sports.

These are very challenging criteria, but no physical-type theory of racial performance differences can be accepted as tenable until the criteria are met. The available evidence on physical-type theories does not begin to meet these criteria, so such theories should be considered not proven.

A closer examination of a particular physical type theory, the self-paced reactive hypothesis, shows that some research contradicts the theory, and even some of the evidence that seemed to support it (the Penn State studies) contradicts it on closer examination. Specifically, football positions most occupied by black players do not appear to be the same positions that require the most reactive abilities.

Race-linked physical type theories can probably never be convincingly demonstrated given the prodigious task required to properly test them. Even if such a theory were suitably tested it would have little practical impact. Some people already believe in such ideas, evidence or no evidence. Racial differences in athletic achievement would be unchanged whether the reason for the differences were known or not. Athletic potential would still be best assessed by allowing aspiring athletes to compete against each other, not by carrying out some complex protocol of measurements.

Perhaps the most interesting aspect of this line of research is the reaction to it by some sport sociologists. Some sport sociologists have voluntarily assumed the burden of telling others what they ought to think and what subjects they should or should not investigate. In science good ideas are separated from bad ideas by reason and investigation, not by self-appointed censors or moral arbiters. Since race-linked physical differences are a possible source of differences in athletic performance, they should be treated accordingly, and given a fair test. Insofar as this chapter has provided a fair test, present-day physical type theories appear to be far from proven.

The next chapter examines the impact of sociological factors such as incentives and opportunity to participate on racial performance differences. Whatever the effect of physical ability, these sociological factors play an important role in the determination of who does or does not become an elite athlete.

Summary

Nineteenth-century racial oppression was rationalized in part by theories of innate racial differences. This history along with more recent racist beliefs has made sociologists reluctant to entertain any innate ability theory about racial differences in sports performance. Nonetheless, sharp racial differences in performance among athletes in some sports have led many to explore the possibility that the variations might be explained by race-linked physical differences.

No research has found racial differences that can satisfactorily explain performance differences. A successful race-linked physical ability theory will have to demonstrate a combination of physical differences between different racial groups. The differences will have to be linked to athletic performance. Environmental influences such as motivation and opportunity have been shown to produce tremendous intergroup performance differences; thus, the effects of environment will be ruled out in a successful theory.

Among the problems faced by any race-linked physical ability theory are the facts that

1. Many racial differences in performance have changed over time for some athletic events (e.g., high jumping, 800-meter run).
2. Brazilian and African blacks do not excel in the same events as those in which North American and Caribbean blacks excel.
3. Black athletes do not excel in certain events that they should dominate if the present data on racial differences are correct (e.g., pole vault, discus).

The reactivity hypothesis contends that a greater amount of neuromelanin allows blacks to excel in reactive activities, whereas whites excel in self-paced activities. This race-linked physical difference theory drew some early support, but on further review, it appears to be wrong. White professional basketball players shoot field goals (a reactive activity) as well as black players do. White players appear more often in football positions that require the most reactivity (e.g., linebacker, quarterback) than do blacks, whereas blacks are overrepresented in the least reactive positions. The reactivity hypothesis does not hold up when tested against the facts. Indeed, no theory based on race-linked physical differences has held up under close scrutiny.

References

Baker, P. T. (1959). American white and negro differences in thermal insulative aspects of body fat. *Human Biology, 31,* 316–324.

Cobb, W. M. (1936). Race and runners. *Journal of Health and Physical Education,* 7 (January), 3–7, 52–56.

Cunningham, M. (1973). Blacks in competitive swimming. *Swimming Technique, 9* (January), 107–108.

Davenport, C. B., and Love, A. G. (1921). *Army Anthropology, 15,* part 1. The Medical Department of the United States Army in the World War.

Davis, L. R. (1990). The articulation of difference: White preoccupation with the question of racially linked genetic differences among athletes. *Sociology of Sport Journal, 7,* 179–187.

de Garay, A. L., Levine, L., and Carter, J. E. L. (1974). *Genetic and Anthropological Studies of Olympic Athletes.* New York: Academic Press.

Edwards, H. (1972). The myth of the racially superior athlete. *Intellectual Digest, 2* (March), 58–60.

Edwards, H. (1973). *Sociology of Sport.* Homewood, IL: Dorsey.

Hendershott, J. (1975). Is black fastest? *Track and Field News, 28* (February), 56–58.

Jones, J. M., and Hochner, A. R. (1973). Racial differences in sports activities: A look at the self-paced versus reactive hypothesis. *Journal of Personality and Social Psychology, 27,* 86–95.

Jordan, J. (1969). Physiological and anthropometrical comparisons of negroes and whites. *Journal of Health, Physical Education, and Recreation, 40* (November-December), 93–99.

Kane, M. (1971). An assessment of black is best. *Sports Illustrated,* January 18, 73–83.

Landers, D. M., Obermeier, G. E., and Wolfe, M. D. (1977). The influence of external stimuli and eye color on reactive motor behavior. In R. W. Christina and D. M. Landers, Eds. *Psychology of Motor Behavior and Sport—1976,* vol. II. Champaign, IL: Human Kinetics Publishers, pp. 94–112.

Mathisen, J. A., and Mathisen, G. S. (1991). The rhetoric of racism in sports: Tom Brokaw revisited. *Sociology of Sport Journal, 8,* 168–177.

Metheny, E. (1939). Differences in bodily proportions between American negro and white male college students as related to physical performance. *Research Quarterly, 10,* 41–53.

Pascal, A. H., and Rapping, L. A. (1970). *Racial Discrimination in Organized Baseball.* Santa Monica, CA: Rand.

Phillips, J. C. (1976). Towards an explanation of racial variations in top-level sports participation. *International Review of Sport Sociology, 11* (3), 39–53.

Phillips, J. C., and Boelter, J. (1984, July). *Diffusion of the "Flop" Technique in the High Jump along Racial Lines.* Paper presented at the Olympic Scientific Congress, Eugene, OR.

Phillips, J. C., and Ciccolella, M. E. (1989, November). *Race, Physical Attributes and Athletic Performance: A Case Study of a Failed Theory.* Paper presented at the meeting of the North American Society for the Sociology of Sport, Washington, DC.

Rosenblatt, A. (1967). Negroes in baseball: The failure of success. *Trans-Action, 4,* 51–53.

Scully, G. (1974). Discrimination: The case of baseball. In R. Noll, Ed. *Government and the Sports Business.* Washington, DC: The Brookings Institution, pp. 221–273.

Tanner, J. M. (1964). *The Physique of the Olympic Athlete.* London: George Allen & Unwin.

Wolfe, M. D., and Landers, D. M. (1978). Eye color and reactivity in motor behavior. In D. M. Landers and R. W. Christina, Eds. *Psychology of Motor Behavior and Sport—1977.* Champaign, IL: Human Kinetics Publishers, pp. 255–263.

Worthy, M. (1971). *Eye Darkness, Race and Self-paced Athletic Performance.* Paper presented at the Southeastern Psychological Association Meeting, Miami.

Worthy, M. (1974). *Eye Color, Sex and Race.* Anderson, SC: Drake House/Hallux.

Worthy, M., and Markle, A. (1970). Racial differences in reactive versus self-paced sports activities. *Journal of Personality and Social Psychology, 16,* 439–443.

Chapter 8

Race and Sport: Social Sources of Variations in Performance

The previous chapter reviewed ideas about race-linked physical differences as an explanation of racial performance differences. This chapter focuses on environment rather than heredity. Are there economic, cultural, geographic, or social psychological factors that can help explain racial performance differences? Sport sociologists have proposed a variety of ideas, some of which have received more empirical support than others. Before reviewing theories of black-white sports performance differences, a review of what these differences are is appropriate. That is, before we review theories let us examine the facts.

Black-White Performance Differences

Race and Type of Sport

Some sports are clearly linked to certain racial-ethnic groups. It may not be difficult to explain why Japanese Americans, who constitute less than three-tenths of 1 percent of the United States population, regularly constitute about one-fifth of the top male judo competitors in the United States, or why Mexican Americans excel in soccer out of proportion to their representation in the United States population.

Black-white differences are not so easily explained, yet clear differences exist. The first step in any explanation of these differences is to examine the facts. Table

8–1 lists sports in which black athletes are over-represented and under-represented. The list of under-represented sports is not exhaustive. Sports like rowing, mountain climbing, or surfing could just as well be included as not; but the point remains the same—black athletes excel in a limited number of sports.

Table 8–1 is limited to men's sports in the United States. Black women excel at basketball and track and field. They do not appear in numbers in softball, a sport parallel to baseball. Otherwise, the table would be unchanged if it were keyed to women's sports. When an earlier version of the table was first published (Phillips, 1976, pp. 49–50) competitive sports were just beginning to be made available to women in schools and colleges. Country-club sports like swimming, tennis, and skiing were about the only competitive opportunities available to women. Not surprisingly, top performers in these sports were almost exclusively white and well-to-do, as only these women had easy access to the facilities and the money to afford the coaching required for training. A few black women had the opportunity to compete in track and field thanks to several city track programs and a handful of college programs, most notably that at Tennessee State.

A popular explanation for the black-white variations in Table 8–1 is based on economic opportunity. Harry Edwards (1973) argues that black athletes recognize the limited opportunity in other occupations and devote themselves to sports, while their white teammates have a much wider set of options and so are less likely to adopt a professional orientation toward sports.

> Black society, as does the dominant white society, teaches its members to strive for . . . the most desirable *among potentially achievable goals*. . . . [Hence] the

TABLE 8–1 Black Representation in Top-Level Sports*

Over-representation	Under-representation
Basketball	Swimming and Diving
Football	Golf
Track and Field	Tennis
Baseball	Hockey
Boxing†	Volleyball†
	Soccer
	Skiing
	Bowling

*Adapted from Phillips (1976, p. 49). This table represents players and teams in the United States.

†There are exceptions to this table. The U.S. National Women's Volleyball Team has five black women, so blacks are over-represented here. Blacks are under-represented on top collegiate volleyball teams, however. Boxing has many excellent Hispanic champions and contenders in the lighter weight classifications.

> talents of Afro-American males . . . are disproportionately concentrated toward achievement in this one area. In high prestige occupational positions outside of the sports realm, black role models are an all but insignificant few. . . . Thus, given the competition among athletic organizations for top-flight athletes, it is to be expected that a high proportion of the extremely gifted black individuals would be in sports. Whites, on the other hand, because they have visible alternative role models and greater potential access to alternative high-prestige positions, distribute their talents over a broader range of endeavors. (Edwards, 1973, pp. 201–202, emphasis in original. See also Bledsoe, 1973; Cashmore, 1982, Ch. 4.)

Recall James Coleman's theory (1961) discussed in Chapter 6 of this book. Coleman's theory was the same as that stated above. People devote their energies to activities that they believe to be linked to future payoffs. The theory is probably wrong in the present context much as it was in the context of athletics and academics.

Black access to a variety of occupations has increased dramatically since Edwards' 1973 statement (Wattenberg, 1985, Ch. 31), yet black representation in football, basketball, and baseball has increased. Edwards' "payoff" hypothesis would predict less black involvement as alternative opportunities become more available. Furthermore, the statement implies that black athletes gravitate toward professional sports, but black athletes have always been well represented in the "amateur" sport of track and field. Even in today's professionalized track and field only an elite few make any money, yet black athletes participate at all levels of the sport. Finally, the contention that white athletes do not devote themselves to sports is questionable. How many occupations offer the prestige and financial rewards that professional baseball, football, and basketball do? It is hard to imagine the vast majority of outstanding young white athletes forgoing athletic stardom to pursue more glamorous and rewarding career options.[1]

A further problem with the "blacks see sports as professional opportunities" thesis is the absence of black participants from all levels of the lucrative professional sports of golf, tennis, and bowling. All three of these sports offer excellent professional opportunities, yet only a handful of black athletes participate in them at top competitive levels. Why do blacks not excel in these sports? One may defend the "sports as profession" thesis by pointing to economic and social barriers that still prevent black aspirants from learning golf, tennis, or bowling (competitive bowling, for example, may cost more than $5,000 a year for lane fees, coaching, and travel expenses). This may help protect the professional opportunity thesis, but it also suggests a preferable alternative.

The Edwards quotation contends that the *general occupational opportunity structure* of the United States can explain racial variations in sports participation. A better explanation (in that it fits the facts better and is a lot "closer" to the phenomenon being explained) focuses on the *sports opportunity structure* (see Brown, 1969; Davis, 1966). The sports opportunity structure is the relative access that blacks, whites, and other groups have to *facilities, coaching,* and *competition.* Without access to these three necessary conditions for athletic success no one can succeed at a highly competitive sport. The absence of good black swimmers may be understood in terms of limited access to: 1) a pool; 2) a competent coaching staff; and 3) the existence of a competitive team. The over-representation of blacks and Hispanics among amateur and professional boxers may be explained largely by the availability of facilities, competition, and trainers in inner-city boxing gyms. Boxers tend to be recruited by friends or relatives who are already in boxing. Promising beginners do not have to pay for lessons because they usually serve as sparring partners for professionals and may "earn their keep" by appearing on amateur boxing cards or in preliminary contests on professional cards (Weinberg & Arond, 1952; Hare, 1974). Whites, few of whom grow up in inner-city areas near a gym, have far less access to boxing opportunities.

The sports opportunity structure appears to be much more efficient at explaining the facts in Table 8–1 than the general occupational structure. Blacks are greatly over-represented in top level basketball, football, track and field, and baseball. *The best facilities, coaching, and competition in these sports are found in school programs.* Costs for participation in these sports are almost totally borne by the schools, so lack of finances is not a barrier to a low-income student. Schools spend substantial amounts to provide proper facilities, and coaches are almost always well qualified. High-school competition in these sports is intense enough to stretch the talents of even the best players.

Contrast the "school" sports with tennis, swimming, or golf. The best coaches are affiliated with private clubs. Parents of would-be competitors have to pay a substantial tuition for lessons. Travel costs also contribute to the cost of participation. High schools may field teams in these sports, but the real competition is in contests arranged by the private clubs. School competition is "just for fun" to serious club competitors. Schools may have tennis facilities and a pool, but the best courts and the best pools are probably in private clubs. Schools compete during a limited season, but athletes in these sports must compete all year round in club competition if they are to reach their full potential.

Financial barriers to black participation in these sports are easy to see when the average black family income, about $19,500, is compared to that of white families, about $34,000 (Information Please, 1991). Social barriers are not as easy to discern, but the fact that the majority of blacks believe they have experienced discrimination (Wattenberg, 1991, p. 68) indicates that such barriers do exist. Even successful black major-league professional athletes are likely to report having experienced some forms of discrimination (Johnson, 1991).

I was a member of the board of directors of a small swimming club during the middle 1980s. One action the board took was to delete a bylaw that, in effect, had excluded minorities from the club. The bylaw had already fallen into disuse, but it had barred blacks for a number of years. Very public cases such as the Shoal Creek Country Club incident illustrate the fact that many elite country clubs still practice racial exclusion policies.

Another barrier is geography. Some years ago John Rooney (1974) demonstrated fascinating geographical patterns in the "production" of athletes in several sports (see also Curtis & Birch, 1987). Rooney only touched on urban-suburban-rural variations, but the location of facilities clearly affects participation, as in the case of boxing. Access to sports facilities by children in the city of Oakland was clearly influenced by what region of Oakland the children lived in (Medrich et al., 1982, pp. 190–191). Black children were concentrated in baseball, football, and basketball; white suburban children had access to a much wider variety of sports because they could afford lessons and facilities were available in the neighborhood (Figure 8–1).

If aspiring black athletes have limited access to "country club" sports, they have excellent access to quality coaching and competition in the "school" sports. Playground basketball is an excellent training ground for basketball skills. Many blacks, but few whites, have access to year-round playground basketball against quality competition. Basketball requires a variety of precise skills as well as athletic talent. Much like tennis, no one can expect to develop into a superior player without exposure to this year-round training ground. Young black males have access to Little League or publicly sponsored baseball opportunities. (Softball for girls appears to be much less accessible in publicly sponsored programs.) As players reach junior high school they begin to play on school-sponsored teams at school facilities with professionally qualified coaches provided by the school. Track and football also become available in junior high school or early in high school.

In contrast to sports like tennis, golf, or even bowling, these school sports are

FIGURE 8–1 Sports like golf, swimming, gymnastics, and tennis have been available in private clubs, but not in schools. Consequently, few black athletes have had the opportunity to participate in these sports.

(Courtesy University of the Pacific)

easily accessible to aspiring participants. Facilities, equipment, travel, and coaching are all provided as part of the school program at little or no expense to the athlete. The best coaching is found in the schools. The best, and perhaps the only, competition is in school leagues. Young people are required to attend school, so there is little or no problem with geographical accessibility.

School sports, then, are easily accessible to young black athletes, while club sports are not. One reason why black athletes excel so much in these sports is the best black talent is concentrated in football, baseball, basketball, and track; the white talent is dispersed over a much wider variety of sports (Phillips, 1976, p. 50).

Some variations cannot be explained by the sports opportunity structure. Table 8–2 lists track-and-field events. In the United States most events are dominated either by black or white athletes. Track and field is "a sport" at American schools, but it is really a variety of sports. Each event is a school sport, and each event provides roughly equivalent professional opportunities to top performers. The racial patterns apply both to men and women. These patterns have remained stable for more than a quarter century. Only the triple jump, 400-meter intermediate hurdles, and the 400-meter dash have changed from "mixed" to black domination. The 800-meter run has changed from white to black domination.

The absence of top black competitors from distance events may be explained by ecological factors—inner-city neighborhoods are not good areas for ten-mile training runs. The pole vault may be unavailable to many black athletes. The absence of excellent black shot putters and discus throwers cannot be easily explained. Neither can the spectacular absence of good white sprinters. White American sprinters *should* be about as good as white European sprinters, a few of whom appear among the world's best sprinters every year, but they are not. The talent is out there, but why is it not being attracted to the starting blocks?

The topic of racial variations in sports participation has been clouded by ideological statements on the one hand (see Davis, 1990) or by simple-minded natural ability ideas on the other. Whatever the distribution of natural talent between blacks and whites for certain track-and-field events, it cannot explain the near total absence

TABLE 8–2 Black-White Track and Field Performance Differences

Strong Black Domination	Mixed	Strong White Domination
100 and 200 meters	High jump	1,500 meters, mile run
400 meters	800 meters	3,000 meter steeplechase
High hurdles		5,000 and 10,000 meters
Intermediate hurdles		Marathon
Long jump		Shot put
Triple jump		Discus
		Pole vault
		Javelin
		Hammer throw

of whites from the sprints or of blacks from the throws. Some social, economic, or environmental factors are operating to produce these variations. Some future sport sociologist will perform a service by uncovering what these factors are.

Race and Playing Position

The integration of major league baseball through the 1950s and '60s was rightly seen by observers as a glittering example of progress in racial justice. With no real government pressure major-league baseball had moved from complete exclusion of blacks in the 1940s, to token integration in the early '50s, to numerical over-representation in the 1960s. This put baseball, along with professional basketball and football leagues that had made similar progress, among the leading institutions in the United States in black participation. Perhaps only the military, especially the Army, had comparable black representation. Schools, churches, government, and business organizations remained relatively segregated.

An article by Aaron Rosenblatt (1967) demonstrated that the big advances in racial integration did not mean that racial discrimination had been eliminated. Rosenblatt showed that the collective batting average of black baseball players in the major leagues was about 20 points higher than white averages. He showed that this higher performance was produced by an absence of weak-hitting black players. Good black hitters, even average black hitters, were not excluded from opportunities, but weak black hitters appeared to have been excluded in favor of weak-hitting white players (Rosenblatt, 1967, pp. 52–53). That is, Rosenblatt discovered evidence of racial discrimination against black players, but only those of *marginal ability*.

Presumably baseball officials could not afford to exclude a good black player, as another club would probably hire him and he could help beat the team that failed to hire him. Weak players were another story. Marginal players picked up by an opposing team would not play much and, if they did play, they would pose no threat. Consequently there was no competitive "cost" to be paid for excluding a marginal black player in favor of a similarly marginal white player.

Rosenblatt (1967) also reported a tendency for black players to play outfield rather than infield positions. Black pitchers were conspicuously rare compared to black outfielders (p. 52). Rosenblatt did not develop all the possible reasons for the absence of black pitchers. He did suggest that there might be some pressure against black-white confrontations. This idea was probably wrong. White and black players in professional football and basketball were routinely confronting each other with little or no problem, and the few black pitchers in baseball experienced no special problems with the "brush back" pitches that all pitchers occasionally throw.

A few years after Rosenblatt's article appeared John Loy and Joseph McElvogue (1970) expanded on Rosenblatt's ideas and extended the analysis to football. Others examined the case of basketball (Yetman & Eitzen, 1971; Eitzen & Tessendorf, 1978).

Loy and McElvogue introduced a *theory* to explain the facts of racial variations in different sports. A look at football and baseball alignments revealed that white players tended to be concentrated in spatially central positions; blacks tended to be more concentrated in peripheral positions like outfielder, wide receiver, or cornerback. Loy and McElvogue drew on Oscar Grusky's (1963) observation that players in central positions were likely to have responsibility for communication with other players and coordinating the actions of teammates. That is, for leadership. Hubert Blalock (1962, 1967) had also observed that racial discrimination in the workplace tended to be most pronounced in jobs that required social interaction with peers and control over peers (Loy & McElvogue, 1970, pp. 6–7). That is, central positions required leadership, and discrimination was stronger against black candidates for central positions (Figure 8–2).

Centrality Theory

What has come to be known as *centrality theory* focuses not on spatial centrality itself but on the leadership responsibilities that seem to go along with playing "in the middle." Leadership entails:

1. Communication with teammates.
2. Coordination, or control of teammates.

A third aspect of centrality was suggested by Blalock:

> To the extent that it is difficult to prevent the minority from acquiring the necessary skills for high performance the lower will be the degree of discrimination. (Blalock, 1967, p. 99)

One "necessary skill" for central positions is judgment or decision making. Central positions require leadership, but are also the "so-called brains positions" (Loy & McElvogue, 1970, p. 18). Given this "game knowledge" requirement we can add a third aspect of centrality:

3. Sound tactical judgment—game knowledge.

Loy and McElvogue considered all infield positions in baseball to be central (recall that "central" is synonymous with "leadership") while outfielders were noncentral. Later analysis (Phillips, 1983) recognized that the positions of catcher, shortstop, and second base are more central than first base or third base, which in turn are more central than the outfielders. Catchers, especially, run the team, "handling" pitchers and giving signs to teammates regarding defensive tactics. Shortstops and second basemen must communicate with each other to defend against bunts, steals, and hit-and-run plays. They also must "call" for who takes fly balls to the infield and

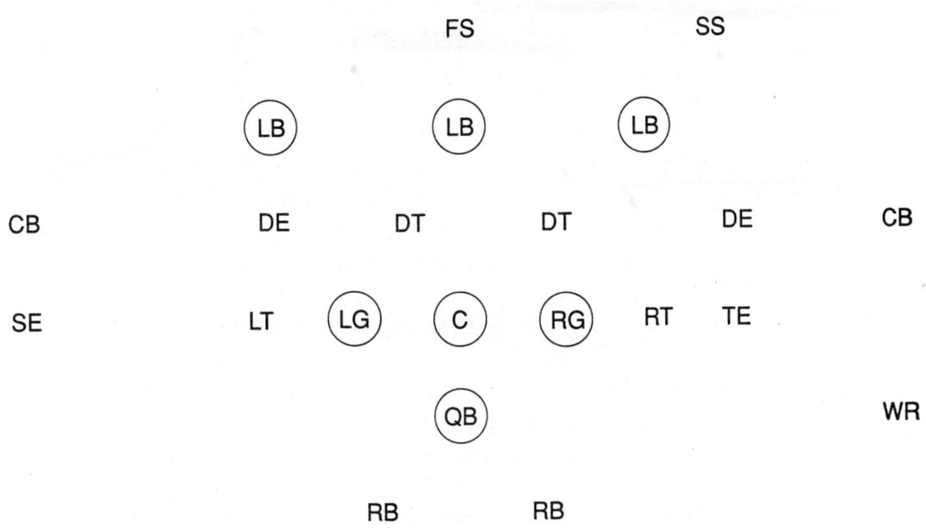

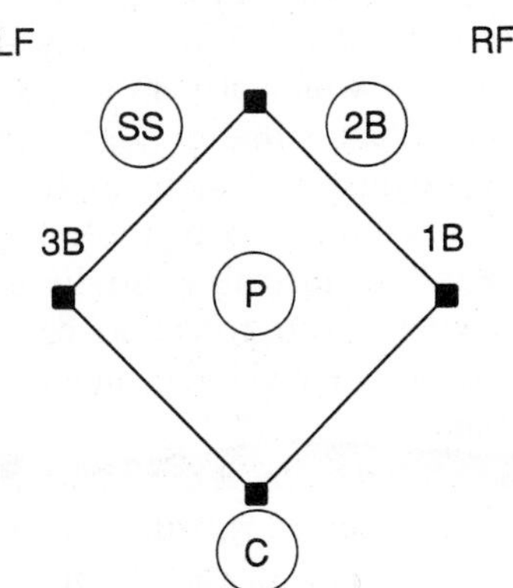

FIGURE 8–2 Central Positions in Football and Baseball*

*After Loy and McElvogue (1970). Central positions are circled.

correctly decide whether or not to "cut off" throws from the outfield to home. First and third basemen have fewer of these kinds of responsibilities, and outfielders have least of all.

Loy and McElvogue considered quarterback, center, and guard the most central positions in offensive football. The leadership role of the quarterback is obvious. Centers on most teams call blocking assignments so they are clearly leaders. Guards, as well as tackles, must operate as a unit by reacting *as a team* (i.e., correctly) to defensive tactics. Wide receivers, running backs, and tight ends are less a part of this unit, so these positions are less central. On defense the linebackers were seen as the most central positions (see Figure 8–2). Linebackers must communicate changing defensive tactics to linemen and read the offense once a play begins. That is, much like offensive linemen, linebackers are expected to communicate with teammates and correctly read and react to the actions of the offense. Defensive linemen and backs were considered noncentral.

The most central position in modern basketball is point guard. Since the defense can pressure one guard, both guards must be prepared to lead—to recognize defensive tactics and call the most appropriate offense to attack it. Aside from the point guard, basketball positions change continually with no fixed leadership responsibilities. All good basketball players should be able to spot opposing offensive and defensive tactics, but the guards have the most need for this ability. Thus, the guards in basketball are more central than the positions of forward or center.

Centrality explained the major league facts rather well. Table 8–3, which outlines black/white representation in major league football, basketball, and baseball in 1970, shows that blacks were somewhat over-represented in baseball. Not counting pitchers, who were a special position, or Latin Americans, who are properly considered a separate race-ethnic category, blacks accounted for about 24 percent of all major-league players, compared to about 12 percent black representation in the general population of the United States. Only about 6 or 7 percent of pitchers were black. Nearly half of the white players played at the central positions of catcher, shortstop, and second base, while only a handful of blacks played there. Fully 72 percent of the black players played outfield, compared to 29 percent of white players. NCAA basketball teams tended to play black players more at forward and center (these positions are indistinguishable in a lot of offensive schemes) and less at the central position of guard. The center in basketball does not control his or her teammates like guards do. Indeed the center in a passing offense is not even spatially central most of the time.

Only about 25 percent of black professional football players were at the central positions of quarterback, center, guard, and tackle, while 63 percent of their white teammates were. The positions of center and quarterback were conspicuous for the absence of blacks. Only 6 percent of the black defensive players played at the central position of linebacker, compared to 38 percent of the white players. Blacks were concentrated at the least central football positions of wide receiver, running back, and defensive back.

Centrality theory was to receive some challenges. Latin American players who were not white and who had limited fluency in English were, nonetheless, well represented at the central positions of shortstop and second base (Phillips, 1977, pp. 96–97). Why did baseball not exclude Latin Americans from the central, leadership positions as they did blacks? A second significant problem with centrality theory

TABLE 8–3 Black-White Distribution across Central and Noncentral Positions: Major League Football, Basketball, and Baseball

Professional Football 1968*					
Offense			Defense		
Position	White	Black	Position	White	Black
Center	12%	0%	Linebacker	38%	6%
Quarterback	11	2	Defensive End	19	16
Guard	22	5	Defensive Tackle	19	16
Tackle	18	18	Defensive Back	24	62
Tight End	9	9			
Wide Receiver	16	26	Total	100% (192)	100% (94)
Running Back	11	41			
Total	99% (220)	101% (66)			

*Adapted from Loy and McElvogue (1970, pp. 12–13).

NCAA Basketball 1970†		
Position	White	Black
Guard	44%	34%
Center	20	15
Forward	36	52
Total	100% (189)	101% (842)

†Calculated from Berghorn, Yetman, and Hanna (1988, p. 117).

Major League Baseball 1969‡		
Position	White	Black
Catcher	22%	1%
Shortstop	13	3
2d Base	12	6
3d Base	13	4
1st Base	11	13
Outfield	29	72
Total	100% (210)	99% (67)

‡Calculated by the author. See Phillips (1983).

involved whether some noncentral positions might require leadership. Did Loy and McElvogue err in their designation of central and noncentral positions? Probably not for baseball and basketball, but there may be a problem for football. The free

EXHIBIT 8–1 The Right Way and the Wrong Way to Construct Percentage Tables

Data relating to racial representation at different positions in sports frequently appear in sport sociology textbooks and journal articles, as in Table 8–4.

TABLE 8–4 Black, White, and Latin American Representation at Different Baseball Positions—1988 Season*

Position	White	Black	Latin Americans	Totals
Catcher	85% (55)	5% (3)	11% (7)	101% (65)
Shortstop	42 (18)	19 (8)	40 (17)	101 (43)
2d Base	57 (29)	18 (9)	26 (13)	101 (51)
3d Base	75 (35)	19 (9)	6 (3)	100 (47)
1st Base	68 (34)	26 (13)	6 (3)	100 (50)
Outfield	41 (63)	49 (75)	10 (15)	100 (153)

*Data gathered by the author.

The table provides some interesting information. Most catchers are white. Two-fifths of the shortstops are Latin Americans, and one half of the outfielders are black. But are we really interested in how *playing positions differ* by race or are we interested in how *races differ* by playing position?

To discover how races differ from one another (we refer to Latin Americans as a "race" here even though we know they are not) we must run the percentages in the other direction (Zeisel, 1968, Ch. 3).

TABLE 8–5 Black, White, and Latin American Representation at Different Baseball Positions—1988 Season

Position	White	Black	Latin Americans
Catcher	24% (55)	3% (3)	12% (7)
Shortstop	8 (18)	7 (8)	29 (17)
2d Base	12 (29)	8 (9)	22 (13)
3d Base	15 (35)	8 (9)	5 (3)
1st Base	15 (34)	11 (13)	5 (3)
Outfield	27 (63)	64 (75)	26 (15)
Totals	101% (234)	101% (117)	99% (58)

The new table is based on the same data as Table 8–4, but it provides much more useful information for sociological analysis. Now we can compare blacks to whites and Latin Americans instead of first basemen to outfielders and shortstops. Table 8–5 tells us how race affects the position players are likely to play. Table 8–4 appears to tell us how position played affects the race of players!

safety in football, a position largely occupied by blacks, probably should have been treated as central by Loy and McElvogue. The free safety must call pass-coverage changes in response to offensive maneuvers such as "man in motion" plays. The free safety, like the linebackers, must read the offense before he reacts. That is, the free safety has plenty of leadership responsibility and must possess tactical knowledge as well.

The lumping of the free safety with other defensive backfield positions probably exaggerated the extent to which blacks appeared to be excluded from central, leadership positions on defense. One wonders if sport sociologists assumed the free safety was noncentral *because* many blacks played this position. If so, this is an example of tautology (see Chapter 7). Central positions are in effect defined as positions with few black occupants. Then it is discovered that there are few black occupants of central positions. Exhibit 8–1 presents another problem associated with the literature on centrality. Researchers occasionally lose sight of cause and effect when they construct percentage tables as shown in Tables 8–4 and 8–5.

Whatever the challenges, centrality theory has helped explain racial variations in other sports. In English soccer, black players are over-represented at the forward positions. For example, 51 percent of all black players are forwards, compared to 27 percent of whites; only 1 percent of black players play goalkeeper, compared to 10 percent of whites. Goalkeeper is clearly the most central position in soccer. The goalkeeper has to direct the defensive players as they organize against fast-break attacks. Blacks also tend to play outside fullback and outside midfield rather than in the center. Center fullbacks and center halfbacks have more leadership responsibilities than outside players (Maguire, 1988; Melnick, 1988). Blacks are also under-represented at the central position of setter in women's intercollegiate volleyball (Eitzen & Furst, 1988).

The centrality theory even relates to the absence of blacks from the ranks of coaches in professional and college sports. Coaches are leaders. Coaches must have a variety of skills, including thorough tactical knowledge. Rosenblatt (1967) noted the almost complete absence of blacks from coaching and managerial positions in professional baseball (p. 52), an absence that persists today (see also Yetman & Eitzen, 1972; Leonard, Ostrosky, & Huchendorf, 1990; Loy, Curtis, & Sage, 1978). Even though blacks have for years constituted about 20–25 percent of all major league players (not counting pitchers or Latin Americans), as of 1992 only two of the 26 major-league managers, Gaston of Toronto and McRae of Kansas City, were black.

The pattern in other sports is similar. As of 1992 only two of 28 NFL head coaches were black. Blacks constitute fully 58 percent of all NFL players. The National Basketball Association has by far the best record among major sports for hiring black coaches, yet the number is surprisingly low considering the overwhelming black majority among NBA players. As of the fall of the 1991–92 season only six of 28 NBA coaches were black. The record of NCAA institutions in developing black leadership in football and basketball programs has been abysmal. Only a handful of the hundreds of NCAA institutions (not counting historically black colleges) have black head coaches, even though a high percentage of the players (the pool from which coaches are selected in future years) are black. Among 298 Division I basketball schools there are only 45 black head coaches. Among 106 Division IA football schools there are *no* black head coaches ("College Football," 1992).

Alternatives to Centrality Theory

A theory in science should be retained until it is disproven, or until a better theory becomes available. "Better" means: 1) a more complete explanation of the facts or 2) a simpler explanation of the facts. Curtis and Loy (1978, pp. 303–309) provide a review of several alternative theories. The following section elaborates on the Curtis-Loy discussion.

Physical Ability

Chapter 7 of this book considered physical ability theories of black-white athletic performance and concluded that no such theory had been demonstrated. No one knows which, if any, black-white physical differences can explain why the overwhelming majority of the fastest sprinters in the United States are black. Whatever the reason *why* it is so, many more blacks than whites possess the speed required of would-be outfielders in baseball and of defensive backs, wide receivers, and running backs in football. Track fans recognize the names of many NFL stars—Gault, Brown, Walker, Green, Okoye—who were also world-class sprinters. Can speed explain the absence of blacks from central positions?

In baseball not much. Blacks in major league baseball have historically been well represented at first baseman. This position requires little speed or agility. The positions of shortstop and second baseman do require speed and agility, yet blacks were absent from these positions in past years (see Table 8–3). While catchers and third basemen are not expected to be especially fast runners, there is no rule that excludes fast runners from these positions. Not all outfielders have to have outstanding speed. Many teams can field one slow-running outfielder (if he can hit) with little defensive loss.

Speed can explain the high percentage of blacks occupying the "wide" positions on offense and defense in professional football (see Table 8–3 for 1968 and Table 8–6 for 1988), but it does not explain several other variations. Speed is a special asset for quarterbacks, yet few blacks play quarterback. Linebackers must cover speedy offensive backs, yet white players have historically predominated at this position. Among offensive linemen, guards must have the best speed because they often must pull and lead running plays. But black linemen are found more often at the "slower" tackle position. Blacks often play the "big, fast" positions of fullback and tight end, but they have been far less well represented at the similarly big, fast position of linebacker.

A comparison of the years 1968 and 1988 (Tables 8–3 and 8–6 as well as Tables 8–4 and 8–5 in Exhibit 8–1) creates problems for any "natural ability" explanations

TABLE 8–6 Racial Distribution across Football Positions, 1988*

Offense			Defense		
Position	White	Black	Position	White	Black
Center	15%	2%	Linebacker	45%	33%
Quarterback	23	1	Defensive End	18	16
Guard	18	4	Defensive Tackle	22	5
Tackle	20	6	Defensive Back	15	46
Tight End	14	11			
Wide Receiver	5	37	Total	100% (174)	100% (368)
Running Back	5	39			
Total	100% (317)	100% (314)			

*From Lapchick (1989).

of variations in racial representation in playing positions. If blacks lacked the "necessities" to play shortstop, second base, point guard, or linebacker in 1968, how can they play these positions so successfully today?

Stereotyping by Coaches

The stereotyping hypothesis contends that coaches have stereotypes or images of the "character" of white and black athletes and images of the ideal character of players at certain positions (Brower, 1972; Williams & Youssef, 1975). The image coaches have of the character required of quarterbacks or catchers is thought to be consistent with the coaches' stereotype of white players, while the image of ideal defensive backs or outfielders is thought to be consistent with coaches' stereotype of black players.

Jonathan Brower (1972) interviewed several NFL coaches and scouts. He found that views of the "black" positions like running back or defensive backs emphasized terms like "instinctive," "gifted," and "athletic ability"; "white" positions such as quarterback, linebacker, or offensive linemen were seen as requiring "brains," "a technical approach," or "leadership ability." Blacks, seen as lacking these qualities, were excluded by coaches from these positions.

The racial stereotyping theory is in most respects the same as centrality theory. Something in the minds of coaches and scouts creates resistance to black occupancy of positions that require leadership and game knowledge. But is stereotyping the mechanism that excludes black players from central positions?

The stereotyping hypothesis presents two problems. First, the evidence in the two studies of racial stereotypes among coaches is limited to questionnaire or interview responses by fewer than 50 individuals! No one has demonstrated a strong consensus among a large, national sample of coaches with respect to racial stereotypes—or position stereotypes for that matter. Second, there are reasons to doubt the argument that racial stereotypes, an attitude, motivate racial discrimination. Irwin

Deutscher (1973) argued convincingly that attitudes do not cause behavior. If anything, it is behavior that causes attitudes (Aronson, 1991, Ch. 5). If attitudes do not cause behavior, stereotypes do not cause discrimination.

Outcome Control

Harry Edwards (1973) argued that racial variations in position occupancy in football and baseball were produced not only by the leadership responsibility associated with central positions, but by the *outcome control* wielded by occupants of central positions. Edwards' discussion of what "outcome control" means leaves the reader confused (pp. 209–210), but there is no doubt that if the occupants of central positions—catchers, pitchers, quarterbacks, linebackers, centers—make errors, the fate of the entire team is affected no matter how well other team members play. Edwards overlooked some positions occupied by blacks in which outcome control was extremely important. Defensive backs in football must make the right converges against offensive pass patterns. Punt and kickoff receivers must execute their job perfectly. Players batting third, fourth, and fifth in baseball are expected to do more than just hit the ball hard. They must be able to sacrifice (via bunt or fly) and execute the hit-and-run play if their team is to score runs. Blacks are not under-represented in any of these key positions.

Self-Selection

Could it be that the idea that racial variations in position result not from discrimination as centrality claims, but from free choice by young players? Barry McPherson (1975), seeing the dominance of centrality theory, sought to introduce some new thinking by suggesting that racial differences in *socialization* experiences might explain the variations in playing position. Specifically, McPherson thought role modeling, imitation of someone one admires, could produce the differences. Perhaps young black aspirants sought to imitate famous black players in their sport.

McPherson argued that since the first black players in major league baseball played at first base and in the outfield, it was no surprise that more recent athletes favored the same positions. Early black football professionals played defensive back and running back, and so did the black football professionals of the 1970s (McPherson, 1975, p. 965). McPherson's role-modeling explanation served to offer new alternatives to centrality theory, but the role-modeling explanation was wrong.

About half of the first black players in the major leagues played *central* positions—Roy Campanella and Elston Howard were catchers; Jackie Robinson played second base; Don Newcomb, Joe Black, and Satchel Paige were pitchers. That is, McPherson's assertion that blacks had played only first base and outfield was wrong. Catcher Roy Campanella, second baseman Jackie Robinson, and pitcher Satchel Paige ultimately were elected to the Baseball Hall of Fame—pretty good role models! Yet few black players play these positions even today. As of 1992 only about 4 percent of the major-league pitchers were black, and there were *no* full-time black catchers (again, recall that Latin Americans, many of whom are black, are not counted in this case).

A second reason for the rejection of the role-modeling hypothesis is that blacks have often occupied central positions early in their careers. D. Stanley Eitzen and David Sanford (1975) traced the careers of 387 professional football players. These players were concentrated in the "black" positions at the professional level, but many of them had played at central positions in high school and college. It would seem that they would be more able to play their favorite position in amateur high-school and college football than the professional level, where financial considerations must outweigh personal preferences. So much for the argument that black athletes "choose" noncentral positions to be like famous role models.

Cost

Marshall Medoff (1977, 1986, 1987) argues that the racial distribution across positions in baseball has been produced by variations in the cost of learning different positions, not discriminatory assignment by coaches. Medoff has argued that centrality cannot explain recent increases in the number of blacks in central positions, but the economic explanation can (1987, p. 279). Medoff argues that black economic conditions have improved in recent decades and more blacks have the financial resources to pay the higher cost of learning to pitch, catch, or play shortstop.

This explanation would make sense if black participation in sports like volleyball, swimming, or tennis were at issue, but it is very questionable in the case of baseball.

Norman Yetman (1987) took Medoff to task on the empirical ground that black income probably has not increased. I rejected the whole hypothesis on three grounds. First, aspiring baseball players do not "choose" the position they play as Medoff's theory contends. Team needs determine who plays where (this is relevant to the role-modeling hypothesis also). Baseball players frequently change positions during their careers in response to team needs. For example, Jackie Robinson played first base, second base, third base, and outfield at different times in his career. He played shortstop when he was in the old Negro Leagues. Which position did he "choose" to play?

Second, development costs are borne by baseball teams, not by the players themselves. Thus, the idea of different development costs for different positions becomes irrelevant. All a young ballplayer needs is a glove. The worse (cheaper) the glove the better the player will learn to catch. Other equipment is provided by teams even at the Little League level. Of course, school and professional baseball organizations provide coaching, facilities, and equipment at no cost to players.

Finally, the cost of player development is driven much more by offensive skills (hitting) than by defense (Phillips, 1988). A number of excellent defensive players never make it to the major leagues, but few first-rate hitters are kept in the minors. Weak defensive players may be placed at first base, in an outfield position, or, in the American League, at designated hitter. If it is hitting rather than fielding that drives development costs, then Medoff's contention that "blacks would tend to specialize in those positions that have less . . . development costs" (1987, p. 287) is irrelevant as players in all defensive positions must learn to hit.

Race and Opportunity to Play

Centrality theory had a profound impact on the sociology of sport, but the observation that racial discrimination fell on blacks of *marginal ability* also led to a lot of subsequent research. Rosenblatt (1967) argued that higher black (and Latin American) batting averages meant that management hired good black players but not bad black players. Bad white players were hired instead.

Imagine a university that has one entrance standard for group X and another for group Y. Suppose members of group X must have a high-school GPA of 3.0 to be admitted, while members of group Y only need a GPA of 2.5. Because there are almost no weak group X students, they may be expected to earn a higher average college GPA than group Y. If the entrance standard were equalized, a number of group X students with poor high-school grades would be admitted. These weaker students would lower the collective college GPA of the X group. It is likely that a few Y students with high-school GPAs of 2.5 or 2.6 would not be admitted because they would be replaced by a few X students with a 2.6 or higher average. The decrease in the number of weak students would elevate the collective Y GPA.

It appears that major league baseball had a higher entrance standard for blacks than whites. Year after year blacks as a group outperformed their white teammates, achieving a collective batting average about 15–20 points higher than white players (Rosenblatt, 1967; Phillips, 1983).

Table 8–7 shows batting and slugging averages for white, black, and Latin American players in the 1969 and 1988 seasons. Batting average is the most popular measure of a player's offensive performance. It is calculated by dividing total hits by at bats and multiplying by 1000 to eliminate the decimal (hits/at bats × 1000). Slugging average uses *total bases* as the denominator in place of hits. A single is one base, a double is two bases, and so forth. Slugging average is considered a better measure of offensive productivity than batting average because it takes *power* hitting into account. Carl Yaztremski of the Boston Red Sox had a mediocre batting average of 255 in 1969, but his superior slugging average of 507 made him one of the most-feared hitters in the American League. Cecil Fielder of Detroit is a present-day example of a dangerous power hitter with a deceptively low batting average.

In 1969, black and Latin American batting averages were about 20 points higher than the white average, mirroring Rosenblatt's earlier findings. Rosenblatt's analysis can be fruitfully extended in two ways (Phillips, 1983). First, slugging averages can be calculated to provide comparisons with this more appropriate measure of offensive productivity. Slugging average comparisons for 1969 show black players (SA = 431) out-hitting whites (SA = 380). Latin American players who had a high collective batting average (BA = 271, equal to that of blacks) had a low slugging average (SA = 325), indicating that Latin American batters were good singles hitters but not power hitters.

TABLE 8–7 Hitting Statistics: White, Black, and Latin American Major League Baseball Players: 1969 and 1988*

	All Players: 1969		
	White (N = 210)	Black (N = 67)	Latin American (N = 49)
Batting Average	252	271	271
Slugging Average	380	431	375
	Outfielders Only: 1969		
	White (N = 60)	Black (N = 48)	Latin American (N = 16)
Batting Average	260	275	292
Slugging Average	407	441	413
	All Players: 1988		
	White (N = 234)	Black (N = 117)	Latin American (N = 58)
Batting Average	258	263	258
Slugging Average	387	396	368
	Outfielders Only: 1988		
	White (N = 63)	Black (N = 75)	Latin American (N = 15)
Batting Average	262	265	264
Slugging Average	409	402	404

*From Phillips and Boelter (1990).

Second, some effort to control for racial differences in positions played is necessary. It happens that baseball managers are willing to sacrifice good hitting for good defense by players in the central positions of shortstop, second base, and catcher. First and third basemen and outfielders are expected to be good hitters. Offensive productivity takes precedence over defense in these positions. Because blacks were, and are, largely absent from central positions, a comparison of blacks and whites was also a comparison of outfielders and first basemen to catchers and infielders. Whites could be expected to have relatively poor hitting statistics because so many more whites played at the "weak hitting" central positions. Latin Americans were, and are today, also much more represented at the central positions than blacks.

The second part of Table 8–7 examines outfielders only. Here the effects of racial differences in position played are minimized since everybody plays outfield. Black outfielders still out-hit white outfielders in 1969, 275 to 260 in batting average and 441 to 407 in slugging average. The few Latin American outfielders were excellent hitters (BA = 292) but less effective than blacks at slugging average, 413 vs. 441.

Table 8–8 shows clearly that the higher black batting and slugging averages were produced by the exclusion of marginal black hitters. Only 9 percent of the 67 black

TABLE 8-8 White and Black Slugging Average Distributions, 1969*

	All Players							
	<300	300–349	350–399	400–449	450–499	500+	Total	(Base N)
White	21	24	25	16	8	6	100	(210)
Black	9	19	21	18	16	16	99	(67)
	Outfielders Only							
	<300	300–349	350–399	400–449	450–499	500+	Total	(Base N)
White	12	23	23	22	12	8	100	(60)
Black	8	17	19	19	21	17	101	(48)

*From Phillips and Boelter (1990).

players in 1969 had slugging averages below 300, while fully 21 percent of the white players did. Was this discrepancy produced by differences in positions played? Partly. The outfielders only section shows 8 percent of black outfielders and only 12 percent of white outfielders hitting below 300, but it is still clear that a much higher proportion of weak-hitting white players were provided the opportunity to play major league baseball. This table illustrates what Norman Yetman and Stanley Eitzen (1972, p. 20) called "unequal opportunity for equal ability."

Note that the proportion of black players is higher at the top-hitting levels and tails off at the lower levels, while white hitters are much more likely to be among the weaker hitters. In a "no discrimination" situation the black and white distributions would be approximately the same. Assuming that potential discriminators could not afford to overlook good black hitters, because other teams would hire them and they would come back and help beat the discriminating team (a pretty safe assumption), it is changes among weak hitters that will equalize the two distributions. A number of weak-hitting white players would be replaced by several not-quite-so-weak black hitters to create an equitable situation.

Using raw numbers from Table 8-8 allows us to show this another way. In 1969 no fewer than 34 of the 67 black major leaguers had slugging averages above 400. Only 63 of the 210 whites hit that well. If we combine the 34 blacks and 63 whites, some 97 ballplayers were "good hitters" (SA better than 400); 34/97, or 35 percent, of these good hitters were black. There were 44 whites with slugging averages under 300 in 1969; only six blacks (!) had slugging averages that low. While blacks constituted 35 percent of the good hitters in 1969 they provided only 12 percent (6/50) of the bad hitters. Weak-hitting blacks simply were not getting a fair chance to play.

Other observers showed that blacks tended to be well represented among starters but were relatively rare among bench players in basketball and football in the late 1960s and early 1970s. Yetman and Eitzen (1972) showed that marginal black basketball players were being excluded in favor of marginal white players. Black basketball players were more likely to start and less likely to be substitutes than their white teammates. Black players were more likely than whites to be among the scoring leaders on their teams and less likely to be among those with the lower scoring averages (see also Johnson & Marple, 1973). In other words, there was room for blacks who could contribute to team success but not for those who were weaker players. Weaker blacks were replaced by weak whites.

Marginality is not as easy to demonstrate in football. The individual performance of a running back is dependent on the performance of his teammates, not only blocking opposing players but forcing the opposition to concentrate on other offensive threats. Minutes played might be seen as a measure of a player's contribution to team effort, but this may be affected by tactical considerations. A team that runs a lot will be on the field a lot; a passing team will not play as many offensive minutes. Players may be substituted in running or passing situations. Recognizing the ambiguity of measures of individual contribution to team success in football (recall that for basketball and especially for baseball these measures are *not* ambiguous), I report Gerald Scully's (1973) findings about marginality in professional football with some reservation. Scully found that black offensive backs had a better yards-per-carry average than white backs. Black backs and receivers scored more often than their white counterparts. They also had more carries and more pass receptions than whites. Given the pattern of excluding marginal black players in other sports it is not unreasonable to suspect that the better black performances result from a dearth of weak black players, who, if they played, would pull the average black performance down to parity with white players in the same positions.

Progress: The End of Discrimination in Sport?

The statistics indicating black-white differences in performance, coupled with the absence of any credible alternative explanations, has led some sport sociologists to treat black-white performance differences as direct indicators of racial discrimination. If racial discrimination is to be viewed as differential treatment of persons who are alike on all relevant factors but different in race, and if measures of the performance of athletes can be separated from the influence of relevant factors (e.g., getting along with others, telling good jokes, level of motivation) that might be correlated with race and performance (i.e., that might provide alternatives to discrimination as the explanation of racial differences), then the performance differentials may be seen as direct measures of racial discrimination (see Pascal & Rapping, 1970, pp. 1–2). That is, the black-white gap in batting performance or black-white variations in playing position may be seen as racial discrimination itself. I am taking a position similar to that of stimulus-response psychologists here. Race may be seen as the stimulus (S) and performance differentials the response (R). Many would prefer to look for discrimination in the "black box" between the S and the R, but what counts is the consequence itself—performance differences.

Has there been a reduction in discrimination? Have the measures of discrimination discussed changed toward equity? Insofar as performance differences may be seen as a demonstration of racial discrimination, the disappearance or reduction of these differences must be seen as a demonstration of the reduction or elimination of discrimination.

Marginality

Hubert Blalock's discussion of discrimination against blacks in professional sports proposed 13 conditions that should affect the level of racial discrimination. Two are related to the notion of marginality:

> The greater the importance of high individual performance to the productivity of the work group, the lower the degree of minority discrimination by employers.
>
> The greater the competition among employers for persons with high performance levels, the lower the degree of minority discrimination by employers. (Blalock, 1967, p. 98)

Marginal players do not provide "high individual performance" and consequently there is little competition for their services. But we know that some clubs in baseball, notably the Dodgers, Giants, and Pirates, sought out black and/or Latin American talent early on (Klein, 1989, p. 98) and "marginal" players could prove rather important given a limited roster (24 in major league baseball) and a long season. A comparable competition in professional football was provided by the old All American Football Conference, most notably, the Cleveland Browns, who absorbed black talent that was excluded from the NFL. When the two leagues merged, NFL teams were faced with competitive pressure to hire the best talent, even if that talent was black, or face a competitive disadvantage (Young, 1963, p. 146). The eagerness with which present day NFL teams seek out "plan B free agents" from unprotected lists suggests that "marginal" players today may be rather important members of their teams, even though they are less important than starters.

Whether or not competitive pressure provided an explanation, discrimination against marginal black players has virtually disappeared in professional baseball and basketball. Since it was difficult to demonstrate in football in the first place, I will not attempt an argument about change in marginal discrimination in that sport.

Yetman and Eitzen observed in 1984 that discrimination against marginal blacks in professional basketball had largely disappeared, although it had been evident during earlier decades:

> In professional basketball, where they have come to dominate the game, blacks were slightly over represented in starting roles until 1970 when equal numbers of blacks were starters and non-starters. Following Rosenblatt's approach in comparing white and black batting averages, we compared the scoring averages

> of black and white basketball players for the five seasons (1957–58, 1961–62, 1965–66, 1969–70, 1974–75) of our analysis. Although scoring averages were identical for both races in 1957–58, blacks outscored whites in remaining years by an average of 5.2, 3.3, 2.9, and 1.5 points, respectively. Although a slight gap remains between scoring averages of whites and blacks, the magnitude of these differences has declined as the percentage of black players in the league has increased. (Yetman & Eitzen, 1984, p. 339)

Forrest Berghorn, Norman Yetman, and William Hanna (1988) found a similar trend in collegiate basketball. In 1966, blacks constituted 17.4 percent of the top-three scorers and only 4.8 percent of the number eight, nine, and ten scorers on NCAA Division I, II, and III teams. By 1985, blacks were represented less in the top-three scoring positions on teams, 11.9 percent, and more among the bottom-three scorers, 7.9 percent. The situation is far from "no discrimination," in which the proportion of blacks would be approximately the same at all scoring ranks, but it is clear that "as the participation level of blacks has increased, the inequality in scoring position has steadily decreased" (Berghorn, Yetman, & Hanna, 1988, p. 114. See also their Table 7 on page 115). This, of course, reflects a reduction in this form of discrimination—instead of hiring (perhaps a proper term, at least for nationally ranked college teams) only the best black players, coaches are now recruiting more and more of the weaker black players who would have been passed over in favor of white players in the past.

It is baseball where the phenomenon of marginality was first demonstrated, and it is baseball where the change is the most explicit. The phenomenon of marginality disappeared in 1988. The 1988 portion of Table 8–7 shows that blacks had a slightly higher combined slugging average than whites and Latin Americans (blacks = .396, whites = .387, Latin Americans = .368), but when position was controlled (i.e., when only outfielders were considered, as there are an insufficient number of blacks at any other single position), the performance (black = .402, white = .409, Latin American = .404) of players proved to be virtually equal. Black-white performance differentials have been diminishing for several years (Phillips, 1983), so it is likely that blacks of marginal ability really do receive a fair opportunity to play together.

It would be wise to retain certain reservations. This phenomenon may still occur in the minor leagues. It probably still exists at the position of pitcher as it has been observed in the past. Nonetheless, the statistic that has been used to demonstrate discrimination now demonstrates nondiscrimination.

Centrality

The phenomenon of centrality still persists in baseball, but it has changed. The positions of second baseman and shortstop were "integrated" during the early 1970s and 1980s, respectively. Today there is a healthy black (and Latin American) representation at these two central positions. This increase in the number of black middle infielders clearly constitutes progress. Unfortunately, the position of catcher still appears to be almost closed to black aspirants. Only three of 65 catchers in the 1988 season were black, and none were starters (Phillips, 1991).

Professional football, like baseball, has seen some clear progress, but some positions appear to retain barriers against black participation. A recent study of major college football programs indicates the same situation still exists (Jones, Leonard, Schmidt, Smith, & Talone, 1987). Loy and McElvogue (1970) provided summary tables of black and white representation in central and noncentral positions on offensive and defensive teams in the National Football League. The positions of quarterback, center, and guard on offense, and linebacker on defense, were considered central.

Recall that centrality refers not to spatial centrality in a team lineup but to the functional requirement for leadership, interaction, and judgment (coordination of the efforts of teammates) that characterize these positions. A comparison of 1968 to 1988 reveals a curious pattern. There has been substantial progress on defensive teams. In 1968 only 6 percent of black players were in central positions. Two decades later this number had risen to 33 percent. Table 8–9 provides Q coefficients (a measure of correlation) to summarize the degree of centrality (black under-representation in central positions) in 1968 and 1988. The coefficient for defensive players dropped dramatically from .81 to .25—clear progress.

Offensive positions tell a different story. Here there has been a small *increase* in the Q coefficient—.86 to .89 since 1968. This is produced by increasing white occupancy of central positions, not by any decreasing black representation. Nevertheless, this apparent increase in black-white differences in playing central positions on offense can at best be interpreted as no progress. However, the sharp increase in the number of black players since 1968 has affected black representation in central positions. Although only a small fraction of all black offensive players play center or guard (see Table 8–6), some 9 percent of all centers and 20 percent of all guards are black. That is, while black offensive players still tend to play at noncentral positions, some central positions have a healthy black representation.

John Schneider and D. Stanley Eitzen (1989) argue that even the increase in the proportion of blacks playing linebacker on defense should not be seen as progress. They argue that the modern 3–4 defensive alignment (three down linemen and four linebackers) creates a more noncentral role for the two outside linebackers. They observe that blacks are more often outside linebackers and whites are more often inside linebackers (Schneider & Eitzen, 1989, pp. 326–327). I believe they are wrong. Outside linebackers should be seen as central. Indeed, the nearly all black position of free safety (vs. strong safety) should also be considered central.

One linebacker (of four) calls defensive assignments, almost invariably relaying a signal from a defensive coach. Aside from this play-calling function linebackers do not perform the leadership/interaction role in the sense that centers and quarterbacks do. Linebackers are required to perform the decision-making function of central positions. The tactical training required of linebackers calls to mind a proposition about discrimination that appeared in Blalock but was not explicitly employed by Loy and McElvogue in their discussion of centrality:

FIGURE 8–3 The "centrality" phenomenon has largely disappeared in intercollegiate and professional basketball, but it has remained evident in baseball and football.

(Courtesy University of the Pacific)

> To the extent that it is difficult to prevent the minority from acquiring the necessary skills for high performance, the lower will be the degree of discrimination. (Blalock, 1967, p. 99)

Loy and McElvogue clearly implied the importance of tactical decision making (a necessary skill for high performance in central positions) as a characteristic of central positions:

> [T]here appears to be a myth among coaches that Negro players lack judgment and decision-making ability. This myth results in black athletes being excluded from positions requiring dependent or coordinative tasks as such activities generally require greater judgment. . . . In short, the central positions in major

league baseball and football are typically the most responsible or so-called "brains positions." (Loy & McElvogue, 1970, p. 18)

Inside and outside linebackers, along with free safetys, are clearly "brains" positions. Players at both positions must first read the offense (the offense, of course, tries to deceive the defense, making a read difficult) and then react according to a set of rules to assure that all potential receivers are covered. Outside linebackers, just as inside linebackers, may exercise some control over down linemen in potential blitz situations by calling off a planned blitz or signaling which rushing lane the linebacker will take. The free safety on most teams calls pass coverage as he reads the intentions of the offense. If we apply a "brains" or tactical-judgment criterion to the idea of centrality, the positions of outside linebacker and free safety (the control criterion also applies to linebackers) should be considered central. Counting free safety as central would bring black and white NFL defensive players close to parity on the centrality issue.

Professional basketball has long been free of the centrality form of discrimination. Eitzen and Yetman (1977) found no tendency to exclude blacks from the central position of guard. Blacks in college basketball were proportionately under-represented at the position of guard in 1970 (34 percent of the black players were guards and 44 percent of the whites were), but by 1975 the same percentage (43 percent) of blacks as whites played guard, and by 1985 more blacks than whites played guard (46 percent vs. 42 percent).

Sources of Change

The special case of basketball, in which black and white aspirants have equal access to central positions, has led Berghorn, Yetman, and Hanna (1988) to begin exploring the reasons for the dropping of barriers. While barriers have not been eliminated in other sports, they have been lowered. It might be profitable to shift our efforts from demonstrating the existence of discrimination and developing theories to explain it (centrality, self-selection, innate ability) to the development of explanations for observed *changes* in discrimination.

There are three good examples of this trend toward using changes in discrimination patterns to test theories of discrimination. If a given factor is a cause of discrimination, then changes in patterns of discrimination should be preceded by changes in the cause or causes.

Marshall Medoff's "economic hypothesis" simply contends that players with limited economic resources (i.e., poor kids) will "tend to specialize in those positions that have relatively less expensive skill and development costs" (Medoff, 1987, p. 278). Medoff argues that the increase in the number of blacks in the central positions (which are relatively expensive to learn) has been produced by long-term improvements in black income and school integration. Norman Yetman has argued that no such improvements have taken place (Yetman, 1987). An earlier section of this chapter showed that Medoff's theory is probably wrong, but it provides a good example of the utility of using change to help test the veracity of theories.

Changes in black participation can disprove theories that postulate enduring black-white differences as the cause of differences in participation. Innate racial differences cannot explain an absence of black shortstops or point guards at one time and an abundance of them a few decades later.

Perhaps the most promising theoretical approach produced by recent changes is suggested by Berghorn, Yetman, and Hanna (1988). These authors use the "skewed sex ratios" idea of Kanter (1977) and apply it to skewed racial ratios. Berghorn and colleagues argue that increases in black representation in basketball make it exceedingly difficult to continue old "stacking" practices. There were just too many blacks in the NBA to allow stacking on the basis of race. I made a similar argument about the rise in the number of black shortstops. With a lot of black second basemen, whose physical prerequisites and training are very similar to that of shortstop, it became difficult for baseball organizations to exclude black players from the position of shortstop (Phillips, 1991). One could make a similar argument about football given the increasingly large number of black players on defense (see Table 8–9).

The ongoing changes provide more than an opportunity for sociologists to test theories. Whatever the dynamics behind them, changes are taking place. Many barriers are eroding, even though some remain firmly in place (especially in coaching and management—see Lapchick, 1989). Something is *causing* these changes. Sport

TABLE 8–9 NFL Football Centrality by Race: 1968 and 1988*

	Offense			
	1968		1988	
Position	White	Black	White	Black
Central (QB, C, G)	45%	6%	56%	7%
Non-Central (All Others)	55	94	44	93
Totals	100 (220)	100 (66)	100 (317)	100 (314)
	Q = .86		Q = .89	
	Defense			
	1968		1988	
Position	White	Black	White	Black
Central (LB)	38%	6%	45%	33%
Non-Central (All Others)	63	94	55	67
Totals	101 (192)	100 (94)	100 (174)	100 (368)
	Q = .81		Q = .25	

*1968 data from Loy and McElvogue, 1970, pp. 12–13; 1988 data from Lapchick, 1989, p. 4.

sociology has had an important part in the exposing of discrimination in sport. Perhaps by exposing the causes of change, we can have some effect on its elimination.

Summary

One of the first facts addressed by sport sociologists was racial variations in sports participation. While it appears that many more blacks than whites are involved in competitive sports, the fact is that whites are about equally involved. Blacks appear to be more prominent than they really are because they are concentrated in five highly visible sports—football, baseball, basketball, track and field, and boxing.

Edwards (1973) has argued that blacks are in these sports because they see sports as a professional opportunity. Seeing other avenues closed, they pursue sports with a professional attitude. This explanation has been criticized on the ground that blacks do not do well in the (potentially) highly lucrative sports of tennis and golf. Track and field is *not* a professional opportunity for any but a handful of world-class athletes, yet blacks participate in this sport in large numbers. Finally, black women are over-represented in the same sports black men are (not counting boxing), yet there are few professional opportunities for women in these sports.

An alternative explanation emphasizes the *sports opportunity structure* rather than the general American occupational opportunity structure. This view sees blacks participating in those sports in which facilities, coaching, and competition are easily accessible. This means sports available in school settings. Black participants are rare in sports like tennis and swimming. These sports, while available in school settings, present a financial barrier (they are expensive) and a social barrier. The best coaching, facilities, and competition in these sports are found in club settings where social access by blacks is limited.

A second kind of racial variation in participation involves position played in sports in which large numbers of blacks and whites participate. Blacks have been under-represented in *central* positions in baseball, football, and basketball. Central positions are positions requiring leadership and judgment. The tendency for blacks to be excluded from central positions appears to be diminishing—it is still very pronounced in baseball (almost no black catchers) and football (few black centers or quarterbacks), but it has disappeared in basketball. Blacks are still badly under-represented in professional coaching and management jobs, and especially in college athletic departments.

Racial discrimination has most affected blacks of *marginal ability*. Blacks have historically been well represented among starters in all sports but relatively rare on the bench. This suggests that blacks had to be better than whites if they were to be hired. This type of discrimination appears to have diminished sharply in basketball, baseball, and probably football as well.

One task for future sport sociologists will be to explain how and why discrimination has decreased between the 1970s and the 1990s.

Notes

1. This section and the next closely follow the discussion of the same subject in Phillips (1976, pp. 46–50).

2. Many of the present arguments and data are from Phillips and Boelter (1990).

References

Aronson, E. (1991). *The Social Animal*, 6th ed. New York: Freeman.

Berghorn, F. J., Yetman, N. R., and Hanna, W. E. (1988). Racial participation and integration in men's and women's inter-collegiate basketball: Continuity and change, 1958–1985. *Sociology of Sport Journal, 5,* 107–124.

Blalock, H. M. (1962). Occupational discrimination: some theoretical propositions. *Social Problems, 9,* 240–247.

Blalock, H. M. (1967). *Toward a Theory of Minority Group Relations.* New York: Wiley.

Bledsoe, T. (1973). Black dominance in sports: Strictly from hunger. *The Progressive, 37*(June), 16–19.

Brower, J. J. (1972). *The Racial Basis of the Division of Labor among Players in the National Football League as a Function of Stereotypes.* Paper presented at the annual meeting of the Pacific Sociological Association, Portland, OR.

Brown, R. C. (1969, April). *The Black Athlete in Perspective.* Paper presented at the 26th annual convention of the National College Physical Education Association, Pittsburgh.

Cashmore, E. (1982). *Black Sportsmen.* London: Routledge & Kegan Paul.

Coleman, J. S. (1961). *The Adolescent Society.* New York: Free Press.

Coakley, J. J. (1990). *Sport in Society: Issues and Controversies.* St. Louis: Times Mirror/Mosby.

College football lacks black coaches. (1992). *San Francisco Chronicle* (February 22), Section D, 5.

Curtis, J. E., and Birch, J. S. (1987). Size of community of origin and recruitment to professional and Olympic hockey in North America. *Sociology of Sport Journal, 4,* 229–244.

Curtis, J. E., and Loy, J. W. (1978). Race/ethnicity and relative centrality of playing positions in team sports. *Exercise and Sport Sciences Review, 6,* 285–313.

Davis, J. P. (1966). The Negro in American sports. In J. P. Davis, Ed. *The American Negro Reference Book.* Englewood Cliffs, NJ: Prentice Hall.

Davis, L. R. (1990). The articulation of difference: white preoccupation with the question of racially linked genetic differences among athletes. *Sociology of Sport Journal, 7,* 179–187.

Deutscher, I. (1973). *What We Say/What We Do.* Glenview, IL: Scott Foresman.

Edwards, H. (1973). *Sociology of Sport.* Homewood, IL: Dorsey.

Eitzen, D. S., and Furst, D. (1988, November). *Racial Bias in Women's Collegiate Sports.* Paper presented at the meeting of the North American Society for the Sociology of Sport, Cincinnati, OH.

Eitzen, D. S., and Sanford, D. C. (1975). The segregation of blacks by playing positions in football: Accident or design? *Social Science Quarterly, 55,* 948–959.

Eitzen, D. S., and Tessendorf, I. (1978). Racial segregation by position in sports: The special case of basketball. *Review of Sport and Leisure, 3,* 109–138.

Eitzen, D. S., and Yetman, N. R. (1977). Immune from racism? Blacks still suffer from discrimination in sports. *Civil Rights Digest, 9* (Winter), 3–13.

Grusky, O. (1963). The effects of formal structure on managerial recruitment: A study of baseball organization. *Sociometry, 26,* 345–353.

Hare, N. (1974). A study of the black fighter. In G. A. Sage, Ed. *Sports in American Society,* 2nd ed. Reading, MA: Addison-Wesley, pp. 369–379.

Information Please Almanac (1991). Boston: Houghton Mifflin, pp. 812–813.

Jones, G., Leonard, W. M., Schmitt, R. L., Smith, D. R., & Talone, W. (1987). Racial Discrimination in College Football. *Social Science Quarterly, 68,* 70–83.

Johnson, N., and Marple, D. (1973). Racial discrimination in professional basketball. *Sociological Focus, 6,* 6–18.

Johnson, W. O. (1991). A matter of black and white. *Sports Illustrated, 75* (August 5), 44–47.

Kanter, R. M. (1977). Some effects of proportions on group life: skewed sex ratios and responses to token women. *American Journal of Sociology, 82,* 965–990.

Klein, A. M. (1989). Baseball and underdevelopment: the political economy of sport in the Dominican Republic. *Sociology of Sport Journal, 6,* 95–112.

Lapchick, R. (1989). Blacks in the NBA and NFL. *CSSS Digest, 1*(2), 1, 4–5.

Leonard, W. M., Ostrosky, T., and Huchendorf, S. (1990). Centrality of position and managerial recruitment: The case of major league baseball. *Sociology of Sport Journal, 2,* 294–301.

Loy, J. W., and McElvogue, J. F. (1970). Racial segregation in American sport. *International Review of Sport Sociology, 5,* 1–23.

Loy, J. W., Curtis, J. E., and Sage, J. N. (1978). Relative centrality of playing position and leadership recruitment in team sports. *Exercise and Sport Sciences Review, 6,* 257–284.

McPherson, B. D. (1975). The segregation by playing position hypothesis in sport: An alternative explanation. *Social Science Quarterly, 55,* 960–966.

Maguire, J. A. (1988). Race and position assignment in English soccer: A preliminary analysis of ethnicity and sport in Britain. *Sociology of Sport Journal, 5,* 257–269.

Medoff, M. H. (1977). Positional segregation and professional baseball. *International Review of Sport Sociology, 12* (1), 49–56.

Medoff, M. H. (1986). Positional segregation and the economic hypothesis. *Sociology of Sport Journal, 3,* 297–304.

Medoff, M. H. (1987). A reply to Yetman: Toward an understanding of the economic hypothesis. *Sociology of Sport Journal, 4,* 278–279.

Medrich, E. A., Roizen, J., Rubin, V., and Buckley, S. (1982). *The Serious Business of Growing Up.* Berkeley: University of California.

Melnick, M. (1988). Racial segregation by playing position in the English football league: Some preliminary observations. *Journal of Sport and Social Issues, 12* (2), 122–130.

Pascal, A. H., and Rapping, L. A. (1970). *Racial Discrimination in Organized Baseball.* Santa Monica, CA: Rand.

Phillips, J. C. (1976). Toward an explanation of racial variations in top-level sports participation. *International Review of Sport Sociology, 11* (3), 39–53.

Phillips, J. C. (1977). Some methodological problems in sport sociology literature. *International Review of Sport Sociology, 12* (1), 93–99.

Phillips, J. C. (1983). Race and career opportunities in major league baseball: 1960–1980. *Journal of Sport and Social Issues, 7* (2), 1–17.

Phillips, J. C. (1988). A further comment on the "economic hypothesis" of positional segregation in baseball. *Sociology of Sport Journal, 5,* 63–65.

Phillips, J. C. (1991). The integration of central positions in baseball: The black shortstop. *Sociology of Sport Journal, 8,* 161–167.

Phillips, J. C., and Boelter, J. (1990, April). *The End of Racial Discrimination in Sport?* Paper presented at the meeting of the Pacific Sociological Association, Spokane, WA.

Rooney, J. (1974). *A Geography of American Sport.* Reading, MA: Addison-Wesley.

Rosenblatt, A. (1967). Negroes in baseball: The failure of success. *Transaction, 4* (September), 51–53.

Schneider, J. J., and Eitzen, D. S. (1989). The perpetuation of racial segregation by playing position in professional football. In D. S. Eitzen, Ed. *Sport in Contemporary Society.* New York: St. Martin's, Ch. 31.

Scully, G. W. (1973). Economic discrimination in professional sports. *Law and Contemporary Problems, 39,* 67–84.

Scully, G. W. (1989). *The Business of Major League Baseball.* Chicago: University of Chicago.

Wattenberg, B. J. (1985). *The Good News Is the Bad News Is Wrong.* New York: Touchstone.

Wattenberg, B. J. (1991). *The First Universal Nation.* New York: The Free Press.

Weinberg, S. K., and Arond, H. (1952). The occupational culture of the boxer. *American Journal of Sociology, 52,* 460–469.

Williams, R. L., and Youssef, Z. I. (1975). Division of labor in college football along racial lines. *International Journal of Sport Psychology, 6* (1), 3–13.

Yetman, N. R. (1987). Positional segregation and the economic hypothesis: A critique. *Sociology of Sport Journal, 4,* 274–277.

Yetman, N. R., and Eitzen, D. S. (1971). Black athletes and intercollegiate basketball teams: An empirical test of discrimination. In N. R. Yetman and C. H. Steele, Eds. *Majority and Minority.* Boston: Allyn and Bacon, pp. 509–517.

Yetman, N. R., and Eitzen, D. S. (1972). Black Americans in sports: Unequal opportunity for equal ability. *Civil Rights Digest, 5* (August), 20–34.

Yetman, N. R., and Eitzen, D. S. (1984). Racial dynamics in American sport: Continuity and change. In D. S. Eitzen, Ed. *Sport in Contemporary Society.* New York: St. Martin's, pp. 324–345.

Young, A. S. (1963). *Negro Firsts in Sports.* Chicago: Johnson.

Zeisel, H. (1968). *Say It with Figures.* New York: Harper & Row.

Chapter 9

Women in Sport: A Revolution in Progress

In June of 1969 Jane Swagerty graduated from high school and looked forward to college. Jane also hoped to continue her swimming career on a college team. Jane had won the Bronze Medal in the 100m backstroke in the 1968 Olympic Games. After the games, the individuals who had finished first and second retired, so Jane was arguably the best 100m backstroker in the world.

To train for the Olympic Games Jane had moved about 80 miles from home to live in Santa Clara, California, and train with the Santa Clara Swim Club. She was able to attend high school in Santa Clara while doing the hard training required of a world-class athlete. After the Olympics she returned home to finish school.

Although Jane was a good student, no college offered her a scholarship. She even had to search for a college that had a women's team! She was faced with the decision whether to give up college to continue international-class swimming or give up top-class swimming to pursue her education. She chose the latter, and attended a small college in Oregon. The school had a swim team, so she could at least compete, although not on an elite level. Jane did not compete in the 1972 Olympics. She quit the sport after a few years, mainly because of lack of challenge and lack of support (see Exhibit 9–1).

Megan Dunn graduated from high school in 1991. She was no Olympic medalist, but she was an outstanding swimmer. Megan received inquiries from several top college swimming programs. She could have accepted scholarship offers from four or so different schools, all with expert coaches, state-of-the-art facilities, and first-class competition. She finds swimming rewarding thanks to the coaching, the facilities that give her an opportunity to improve, and the fun of competing in league, regional, and national-level meets.

EXHIBIT 9–1 The Post-Olympic Career of a Bronze Medalist

Jane Swagerty, 1968 Olympic Bronze Medalist at the 100-meter backstroke, shares her experience of returning from the triumph of winning an Olympic medal. In 1969 the American educational system did not provide any high caliber swimming programs for women; thus, Jane had to choose between postponing her education to continue her world class swimming career or giving up her swimming to pursue her education. Many colleges had excellent men's programs in 1969, but not one had a scholarship for a woman, even if she was an Olympic medalist.

It's the Olympic Games. All of the world stops to watch for two weeks. The athletes have trained for this moment in history and are here to test themselves against each other. Heroes are made before our eyes and we all watch as champions go up on the victory stand to receive their medals. Also realized is the fact that all Olympians, be they medal winners or not, are only a small percentage of the world's athletes. They are the cream of the crop—the elite.

Then suddenly the moments are memories. The athletes have to pack their belongings and souvenirs from other athletes—pins, clothing, anything that will remind them of the life-lasting memories.

Looking back on when I stood up on the awards stand to receive my medal, I can remember everything as if it was yesterday. For me, standing on the awards stand was a culmination of years of hard work, dedication, and determination. I was so proud of the fact that I had actually succeeded in a lifelong goal. I really did it! The self-satisfaction was overwhelming—at that moment I felt that I could do anything if I put my mind to it.

The problem following the Olympics happens to many Olympians. What do I do now? I remember saying this to myself the day after I had won my medal. It was a question that was very scary to me. What did I have to go back to when I returned to school? There were no girls' swim teams in high school. It wasn't even a consideration, even though there were many good swimmers where I lived. There were no college scholarships for female swimmers that were available to me. I continued to swim with a local swim club in Stockton, California, where I lived. Five months after returning from the Olympics, my brother was killed in a bicycle accident. This changed my life considerably. I wanted to stay home with my family the next school year, which was my Freshman year in college. I attended a junior college which had a very good swim program. I swam on the junior college team for fun. I didn't train very hard, just hard enough to win races. My future in swimming was looking very hazy. How was I to continue swimming for another four years until the next Olympics? I couldn't continue to swim in a high-caliber program and continue my education at the same time.

I had heard of a women's swim team up in Ashland, Oregon, where my older brother was attending college. I decided to transfer there to take advantage of the swim team opportunity and to be away from home, but not too far away. I swam only for fun. I didn't train very hard, only hard enough to win. I couldn't see myself swimming for another three years, especially when a high-caliber program involved going back to Santa Clara, California, and trying to fit a college education in at the same time. It was time now to consider the possibilities of retiring. I felt at this time in my life I wasn't

EXHIBIT 9–1 *Continued*

mentally prepared to continue to train hard for the 1972 Olympics, given the circumstances. My coach had stated to me that he really didn't think I had reached my potential as a swimmer, but I wasn't able to make the commitment to the sport anymore. I had reached my goal of going to the Olympics and I was satisfied with that. I do wonder sometimes how I could have performed at the 1972 Olympics. But, under the circumstances, I was never able to find out.

The transition back into the mainstream of society is difficult—one that I deal with every day. It wasn't the norm to be a female athlete—especially in high school when a guy would be intimidated by someone who was athletically better in some way. I tried to fit in with everyone else, which I think I did a good job of. The consequences were that I pushed my success aside and forgot about who I really was.

I realize now that the Olympics are a part of me, something that will always be there. What I must do is push forward constantly and remember that the drive inside me is always there and it can be drawn on for strength.

This chapter addresses the question of why women like Jane Swagerty were denied the opportunity to participate in school and college sports, and why women like Megan Dunn, two decades later, have come to enjoy opportunities nearly equal to those available to their male classmates.

Veblen on Sport and Gender

The first two chapters of Thorstein Veblen's 19th-century classic *The Theory of the Leisure Class* (1953) provides a framework for an understanding of the traditional cultural resistance to female participation in competitive sports. Veblen's basic argument was that the wealthy in American society contributed little to the useful economic productivity, and it was this absence of useful productivity that made the wealthy respectable! The very utility of the average worker's productivity made his or her work not respectable. For this reason a pretty, but useless, flower garden on the front lawn would be classier than a vegetable garden; a liberal-arts college would be more prestigious than an engineering school; and a more expensive wine would be considered better than a cheaper wine of comparable quality, precisely because it was more expensive.

Veblen noted that the distinction between "honorific" activities, which confer respect or distinction on the actor, and plain work has existed since the earliest days of human civilization or, in Veblen's colorful language, "the lower stages of barbarism" (p. 33). Activities involving government, religion, war, and sports confer honor in virtually all societies (Veblen, 1953, p. 21). In the earliest hunter-gatherer societies these activities were reserved for men. Several reasons have been proposed for this.

The biological facts of pregnancy and nursing undoubtedly limited primitive women's mobility, while the band suffered little from occasional absences by some men. Thus, male participation in war and hunting activities made sense for the well being of the group. There are surely more reasons than biological fitness but, whatever they are, it is clear that activities that could bring public esteem were almost universally reserved for men.

One dissident voice is occasionally cited in sociology texts. In *Sex and Temperament in Three Primitive Societies* Margaret Mead (1935) claimed to have discovered three societies in eastern New Guinea in which sex roles differed widely. Of greatest interest were the Tchambuli. In this small society women did most of the work and ran the village affairs, while men spent most of their time indoors gossiping and painting their faces. Experts on Melanesian cultures, also familiar with the peoples studied by Mead, have argued that Mead saw what she wanted to see during her brief visits with the three primitive societies (Hoebel, 1958, p. 391).

Keen readers of Mead have recognized the gossip and face painting by Tchambuli men as the activities of head-hunting raiders who had been enjoined by the Australian government from actual fighting. So they did what was left—planning, bragging, and engaging in religious propitiation about now-forbidden warfare. That is, Mead's face painting and gossip amounted to the archetypal male functions of war and religion!

It is not surprising that the activities of war, hunting, government, religion, and sports were all treated as honorific. While these are clearly separate spheres today, they were not distinct in early hunting-gathering cultures. The tactics and weapons used in hunting—ambush or surprise attack with spears and arrows—worked well in warfare too. Both the hunt and military raids on other bands required proper religious or magical preparations by those qualified to perform them. Both hunting expeditions and military sorties required leadership (government). The proper distribution of the game killed or goods seized required leadership. Sports, such as they were, allowed individuals to demonstrate the skills and character required of a good hunter or fighter.

According to Veblen, the predatory nature of hunting and fighting came to color the whole masculine role, while women were left to more mundane, but much more productive, activities.

> In such a predatory group of hunters it comes to be the able-bodied men's office to fight and hunt. The women do what other work there is to do—other members who are unfit for man's work being for this purpose classed with the women. But the men's hunting and fighting are both of the same general character. Both are of a predatory nature; the warrior and the hunter alike reap where they have not strewn. Their aggressive assertion of force and sagacity differs obviously from the women's assiduous and uneventful shaping of materials; it is not to be accounted productive labor, but rather an acquisition of substance by seizure. Such being the barbarian man's work, in its best development and widest divergence from women's work, any effort that does not involve an assertion of prowess comes to be unworthy of the man. . . . So tenaciously and with such

> nicety is this theoretical distinction between exploit and drudgery adhered to that in many hunting tribes the man must not bring home the game which he has killed, but must send his woman to perform that baser office. (Veblen, 1953, pp. 28–29)

The near universality of hunting being reserved as an activity for men is demonstrated by G. P. Murdock's (1935) review of tasks "appropriate" for women and men in 224 preindustrial societies. Likewise, female warriors are virtually unknown in premodern societies except in mythology (Goldberg, 1973). Women predominate in the "in house" chores like cooking, gathering fuel or food, or hauling loads.

Veblen argued that while routine work was considered unworthy of the best men, their excellence in challenging activities like hunting or fighting came to define manhood. The trophies gained from successful forays demonstrate men's worth. At least part of the role of modern sporting achievement in the achievement of male status was suggested by Veblen:

> When the community passes from peaceable savagery to a predatory phase of life, the conditions of emulation change. The opportunity and the incentive to emulation increase greatly in scope and urgency. The activity of the men more and more takes on the character of exploit; and an invidious comparison of one hunter or warrior with another grows continually easier and more habitual. Tangible evidences of prowess—trophies—find a place in men's habits of thought as an essential feature of the paraphernalia of life. Booty, trophies of the chase or of the raid, come to be prized as evidence of preeminent force. Aggression becomes the accredited form of action, and booty serves as *prima facie* evidence of successful aggression. (Veblen, 1953, p. 30. Italics in original.)

Likewise, the modern (until the last few decades) role of women in sport is suggested by Veblen's description of primitive origin of class distinctions based on wealth. Women of a rival group might be seized for the "trophy" value, but they also provided material wealth to the successful raider. The contemporary college song girl/yell leader comes to mind in the following quotation:

> The ownership of women begins in the lower barbarian stages of culture, apparently with the seizure of female captives. The original reason for the seizure and appropriation of women seems to have been their usefulness as trophies. The practice of seizing women from the enemy as trophies gave rise to a form of ownership-marriage, resulting in a household with a male head. This was followed by an extension of slavery to other captives and inferiors, besides women, and by an extension of ownership-marriage to other women than those seized from the enemy. The outcome of emulation under the circumstances of a predatory life, therefore, has been on the one hand a form of marriage resting on coercion, and on the other hand the custom of ownership. The two institutions

> are not distinguishable in the initial phase of their development; both arise from the desire of the successful men to put their prowess in evidence by exhibiting some durable result of their exploits. Both also minister to that propensity for mastery which pervades all predatory communities. From the ownership of women the concept of ownership extends itself to include the products of their industry, and so there arises the ownership of things as well as of persons. (Veblen, 1953, p. 34)

Veblen went on to argue that social development has changed the primitive situation in which wealth came to be conferred upon the most honorable of men, i.e., the best hunters and warriors. Modern societies confer honor on the wealthiest of men. The wealthy today may or may not be the most noble among us. Veblen thought real nobility consisted in productive work, not flashy wealth. I have digressed a bit to introduce a topic discussed in Chapter 10.

Theory of the Leisure Class was written in 1899. At that time, the most prominent sports were played by the wealthy, especially in colleges. True, professional bicycling, boxing, and baseball were popular, and poor boys could play on church-sponsored teams, but high-school and college sports, especially football, enjoyed a lot of public attention. These school sports belonged to the well-to-do, the leisure class. Leisure class manhood was seen as the modern manifestation of the primitive head men—the most skilled and cunning of aggressors. Sport was seen as a modern manifestation of the predatory temperament that characterized the most successful of barbarians.

> Chicanery, falsehood, browbeating, hold a well-secured place in the method of procedure of any athletic contest and in games generally. The habitual employment of an umpire, and the minute technical regulations governing the limits and details of permissible fraud and strategic advantage, sufficiently attest the fact that fraudulent practices and attempts to overreach one's opponents are not adventitious features of the game. In the nature of the case habituation to sports should conduce to a fuller development of the aptitude for fraud; and the prevalence in the community of that predatory temperament which inclines men to sports connotes a prevalence of sharp practice and callous disregard of the interests of others, individually and collectively. (Veblen, 1953, p. 181)

Sport, of course, was almost exclusively a male activity, and the competitive spirit was in Veblen's time thought to be exclusively the province of men. Veblen's brilliantly ironic analysis had 19th-century industrial societies led by a wealthy, but nonproductive leisure class who were respectable precisely because they were wealthy but nonproductive. Sport, as well as, sportsmanship, was not a high development of admirable modern character traits, but a vestige of the primitive predaceous spirit that helped savages to succeed. This savage spirit—self-centered, cunning, rapacious—served the business class well.

Real virtue could be found not in the wealthy business classes, but in the humble homemaker or industrial worker whose steady work produced the useful products that constitute real wealth.

Veblen's theory is of special interest here because it points to the universal denial of honorific activities to women and to the role of women as trophies for successful men. Nineteenth-century scholars liked to think of (then) modern, Western society as the successful culmination of thousands of years of cultural evolution. Veblen argued that modern society, in fact, was no better than savage societies and that many of the key features of savage and barbarian cultures also characterized modern, civilized societies. Among these was the denial to women of the opportunity to achieve at honorific activities along with the denial of honor to women's activities.

Sport, of course, is an honorific activity. Competitors gain respect by competing against and overcoming an opponent. Sporting opportunities have historically been denied to women. This persists even today. Women's sports are not taken as seriously as men's, with the possible exception of artistic sports like figure skating and gymnastics. Margaret Duncan (1990) has shown that even the public acclaim devoted to these sports may be based more on sex appeal than competitive values. This illustrates the denial of honor to women even when they achieve at honorific competitive activities. Duncan (p. 35) provides a telling *Sports Illustrated* photograph of the 1984 Romanian women's gymnastics team receiving their medals. The photograph shows neither the medals nor the gymnasts' smiling faces; it provides a rear view of their legs and bottoms as they bend over to receive their medals. Photographs depict male winners much less in terms of sexual qualities and much more in terms of their achievements and their character.

This suggests the second and, perhaps, main place of women in sports—as trophies. Desmond Morris, in his entertaining book *The Soccer Tribe* (1981), asserts that successful soccer players "earn" the most attractive women for wives just as primitive hunters do. One college football magazine has a regular photo feature on yell leaders and song girls (never overdressed) called "Honey Watching." Most football teams, right down to the Pop Warner (youth) level have yell leaders, and dance teams. To provide maximum freedom of motion for yell leading and dance movements, these girls wear very brief costumes. Or are they female trophies, the symbolic sexual property of their teams?

Assessment

Veblen's theory should not be taken literally. He enjoyed jabbing at the upper classes of his day, equating their conduct with that of savages and barbarians. On the other hand, he and many critics of his day believed that the wealthy, who contributed little to the real social well being of their society, enjoyed extremely generous material and nonmaterial rewards while the ordinary worker, who *did* contribute to societal well being, received neither wealth nor honor.

Veblen was a cultural evolutionist. Like many 19th-century theorists he thought societies evolved from lower to higher forms as did biological life forms. Cultural evolutionism went wrong in assuming that evolution necessarily went from "worse" (lower) to "better" (higher) forms. There is nothing in Charles Darwin's thinking to suggest that a modern, highly adapted life form, say a salmon, is "better" than a primitive, less highly adapted form like a shark (to stay with fish). Veblen did not make this mistake, but he did fall victim to a second error. Evolution implies the tracing of the history of a single culture from its ancient origin to the present. This was impossible because of the lack of archeological evidence about ancient social life. Lacking evidence about their own past, cultural evolutionists sought clues to the ancient past of, perhaps, British culture in *modern* stone-age societies. Does it make sense to seek out the origins of British culture by studying Australian aborigines or North American Eskimos?

Whatever its weaknesses, there are a lot of strengths in Veblen's argument. For our purposes it does not matter whether the denial of individual honor to women is inherited from our cultural past or the product of present conditions. What matters is that this denial is not new, and it is virtually universal. Both men and women tend to discount the achievement of women (Goldberg, 1968; Pauludi & Bauer, 1983) and, as any salary survey will reveal, we undervalue jobs traditionally done by women. Virtually every other society, whatever the economic or political system, does much the same.

Is the notion of woman as trophy or property inherited from the past? We cannot say for sure about the prehistoric past, but British society has viewed women as the property of father or husband throughout its history (Queen, Habenstein, & Adams, 1961). Modern vestiges of this abound. The traditional marital vow for the bride is "love, honor, and obey." Traditionally, the bride abandons her family name and takes her husband's name. Even the contemporary term "trophy wife," the taking of a young, attractive wife by a wealthy divorced businessman, seems to support Veblen's argument that women may still be viewed at least somewhat as property, perhaps as trophies of successful competition.

Sources of Resistance to Competition for Women

Victorian View of "Women's Spheres"

English-speaking nations inherit a secular and religious tradition that denies honorific activity to women, even to wealthy women. Any respect a woman might gain would be based on the status of her father or husband. A rather contemptuous view of women in the middle 18th century is reflected in a letter written by Lord Chesterfield to his son:

> Women then are only children of a larger growth; they have an entertaining tattle and sometimes wit, but for solid reasoning and good-sense, I never knew in my life of one that had it, or who reasoned or acted consequentially for four-and-twenty hours together. Some little passion or humor always breaks in upon their best resolutions. Their beauty neglected or controverted, their age increased or their supposed understandings depreciated instantly kindles their little passions, and overturns any system of consequential conduct that in their most reasonable moments they might have been capable of forming. A man of sense only trifles

> with them, as he does with a sprightly, forward child; but he neither consults them about nor trusts them with serious matters, though he often makes them believe that he does both, which is the thing in the world that they are proud of. (quoted in Queen, Habenstein, & Adams, 1961, p. 252)

Whether it was driven by a belief about the innate simplicity of women or, as some believe, a social need for a domestic service, the notion that the "woman's sphere" extended to care of husband, home, and children, and no farther, was widely accepted. This was to limit efforts to provide education to women in the United States, even upper-class women. Education for women was justified in terms of enhancement of the woman's sphere, not expanding it. New schools for women in the middle 19th century gained acceptance by emphasizing training in religion and domestic arts. Reform-minded educators would sneak in more standard liberal-arts topics and even calisthenics under the smoke screen of health and character development (Kendall, 1973).

This 19th-century notion of a proper woman's place is found in more recent views about woman's sport. American secondary schools in the 1920s and '30s had become coeducational, but sports competition was separate and unequal in the overwhelming majority of school systems. The objection to competitive girls' sports was based on a perceived threat to their "reproductive functions" and, perhaps more importantly, a perceived threat to their feminine, wifely character.

> Competitive athletics foster a kind of brusqueness and keenness which is not agreeable to the male of the species when carried into the home. It does not contribute to a woman's preparation for better, happier, living. (Miles, 1936, p. 104)

The "brusqueness and keenness" were clearly the main concern of critics of competitive sports for girls. Miles (1936) favored recreational sports for all girls, so he could not have been too concerned with threats to their reproductive systems. Rather, the concern was the psychic stress of serious competition vs. recreational "play days" (see Forsythe, 1939, Ch. 14). This stress brings out determination, tenacity, and goal orientation—i.e., brusqueness and keenness—among the competitors. Educators feared that these qualities might interfere with girls' future happiness (or, perhaps, the happiness of their husbands) as homemakers (Figure 9–1).

Possible physical harm to women was also a genuine concern. Females were seen as delicate. Stressful physical activity was seen as harmful to body as well as character (Lenskyj, 1984). The chief physical concern was damage to the reproductive function, but emotional damage was a concern as well. The benefits of regular exercise were, until the 1960s or so, very much a topic of debate in medical circles, so fear for the health of female athletes was understandable (Lancaster, 1978).

Significantly, this concern for possible physical and emotional damage was not extended to working-class women. Wives of farmers had long assisted in arduous tasks such as plowing, loading of wagons, and harvesting of grains. All this in addition

FIGURE 9–1 The posture and attire of these turn-of-the-century tennis players suggest that serious competition was not appropriate in women's sports of that day.

(Holt-Atherton Department of Special Collections; University of the Pacific Libraries)

to their normal tasks of hauling water, churning butter (a strenuous exercise, especially when the butter thickens), cleaning house, and producing food, clothing, and candles for household consumption (Riley, 1980). Likewise, household maids and women factory workers faced arduous 12-hour days, followed by their own housework. Nobody felt compelled to protect these women from undue stress.

Perhaps the most spectacular instance of this 19th-century class-linked view of women is the 1893 case of Lizzie Borden of Fall River, Massachusetts. As the story goes,

> Lizzie Borden took an ax
> And gave her mother forty wacks
> And when she saw what she had done
> She gave her father forty-one.

Actually, Lizzie's father received only 10 wacks and her mother fewer, but the result was a double murder. The evidence of Lizzie's guilt was strong. Lizzie was observed burning bloodstained clothes. A detached ax head, also stained, was found. Lizzie was known to have hated her stepmother. She stood to inherit hundreds of thousands of dollars as soon as she became an orphan.

Evidence or no evidence, in the eyes of the jurors she could not have done it. She was a well bred, well-to-do New England woman. She taught Sunday School. Such women simply weren't capable—too gentle, too weak, too delicate—of an ax murder. The all-male jury did not even weigh the evidence at her trial. They immediately voted to acquit her; they chatted for an hour to avoid appearing to have neglected to deliberate (Jacob, 1978).

Many in Fall River suspected the Borden's Irish maid Bridget Sullivan, who, like Lizzie, was in the house at the time of the killings. Irish, Catholic and poor, Bridget was thought capable of such a deed, even though there was no evidence to suggest she was the murderer. Two images of "woman" existed in Fall River. One was the docile, loving, devout, fragile middle- and upper-class New Englander. The other was more lusty, tough, and not too moral. This image, reserved for the poor, especially the poor immigrant, made Bridget suspect (Jacob, 1978). This kind of woman might have taken well to sports competition, but they never had the opportunity.

Young women attending school either were from middle- or higher-class families, or aspired to be, so their physical activity was limited to walking and mild gymnastics to promote health and good posture—no sports allowed (see also Lindsay, 1970).

Marianna Trekell (1975) argued that the gradual acceptance of women in sports paralleled the demise of the Victorian attitude toward women spurred by such "liberation" events as woman's suffrage, the freedoms of the 1920s "flapper era," the participation of women in industry during World War II, and the gradual opening of education and professional opportunities to women in the 1950s and 1960s. This acceptance probably helped Canadian women more than their American counterparts. American women during that era had access to club sports like swimming and tennis, but most "school" sports (e.g., basketball, track and field) were available on a play day or recreational level only. In Canada a much wider variety of sports was available, both on a club basis within the community and throughout the school system. Both clubs and educational institutions fielded trained competitive sports teams (Jerome, 1991, personal communication).

Wendy Jerome, a professor of sports psychology at Laurentian University in Ontario, relates her experience as a young Canadian coach, newly arrived in Oregon in the early 1960s. Asked to teach a high-school girls team how to play basketball, she took the approach she took in Canada and taught the game. After weeks of drill and training her team entered a "Girls Athletic Association Play Day." Recreational play days were the only school sports opportunities for girls at the time. Her team utterly crushed the competition in the play day tournament. It turned out that "recreational sports for all," the supposed philosophy of girls' play days, did not include teaching girls how to play the game properly. Jerome's well-drilled team found no real competition. Coach and players were made to feel unwanted at the social events associated with the tournament. Quality, even that of a "just for fun" team that happened to be well coached, was not appreciated (see Exhibit 9–2).

EXHIBIT 9–2 Recollections of a Coach

Wendy Jerome was probably the first woman in North America to coach men at the university level. Her experiences as a Canadian coaching in Oregon during the 1960s, and later coaching in Canada, illustrate many of the issues raised in this chapter. Dr. Jerome's coaching success also suggests that women can achieve competitive success and personal fulfillment from coaching, even at the highest level.

Going to school in the United States was a culture shock for me. There were many differences between the two English-speaking North American countries. Girls did not participate in sports; they held "Play Days." No women trained. Competitiveness was frowned upon. Professional educators not only actively involved themselves in preventing the two sexes from participating together but also set up a system of disinformation that discouraged girls from any activity that required running over 100 yards, throwing a heavy object, running and jumping, or that might have any body contact. According to even the latest textbooks, women were too fragile, they would become masculinized, and on and on and on went the horror stories. I almost fainted when I found out that at university, the men's and women's physical education programs did not even share the same building. Separate departments, separate buildings, and frequently, separate courses was the standard case . . . particularly in the activities. When I attempted to bring a men's class into the women's gym so we could have some mixed doubles, I thought the place would explode. I couldn't believe that an enlightened nation, a world leader, could be so backward. With my attitude, they must have thought I had two heads or something.

Although I tended to be somewhat shy, I did not hesitate to verbalize my opinion about this archaic attitude toward sport at every opportunity. I tried to be positive about it, but I am sure that a lot of people got tired of listening to me and were glad to see me go.

An incident that stands out in my mind was a professional physical educator's conference, the Northwest AAHPER group. I attended a panel discussion that was held on women's sport. I sat in the audience and found myself being roundly chastised by the panelists, women physical educators from Oregon, who were very much against competitive activities for girls. I always got great pleasure out of the fact that a few years later these same women who publicly criticized me, were forced, because of a growing interest among female students, to hire women coaches. Shortly after that change, the professional physical education program because co-educational.

Returning home, I was asked to coach with one of the city track clubs sponsored by the Kinsmen. It was a year of trial and error for me, but we did have some success and I was asked to coach the Edmonton team that was being sent to Winnipeg for the first indoor meet. A number of my athletes were named to the team, and I thought it would be a great experience. So I said yes and did go. However, there were a lot of hard feelings on the part of a rival male coach who felt that he should have been chosen. It took a little of the pleasure away. The kids did reasonably well. At the provincial meet that spring, a number of the athletes did extremely well. One young man set a long jump record that held for many years.

After another year, I found myself back in Eugene where I was teaching at a local high school. I organized a girls' basketball team that competed in a Play Day. We won every game and had no points scored against us; for this, we were berated by the

EXHIBIT 9–2 *Continued*

organizers and isolated by the rest of the people there. How was I to know nobody practiced or trained for those things? I also coached girls in track and field for another Play Day, following which I was approached by some of the parents in the area to start a girls' track club. I was delighted to have both the opportunity and the support. We started with girls from the high school, but we quickly found others that were interested in training.

The University sponsored All-Comer meets and was beginning to hold the odd race or jump for girls. I would take our girls to those events and watch for other girls who might like to join us. It was at one of these meets that I first saw Margaret Johnson run. She was a skinny, little black girl who took three lanes to run a short sprint. She was all over the place. But she was fast.

I asked her if she would like to join our club, which trained a short distance out of town. She was interested, but said she would have to ask her mother. She also wanted to know if her best friend could also join. As it turned out, I drove Margaret home that evening and spoke to her mother. She agreed, as long as I could pick the kids up and bring them home.

It wasn't long before I knew I had something. Most of the girls I coached did well in their events. . . . They had skill and a little coaching; most of their opponents did not. Thus, it wasn't that I was a great coach. But Margaret was different. When she was 13 (1964), I had stated in the Eugene paper that this girl would make the 1968 Olympic team. She was phenomenal.

Within a few months, the girls' races at the All-Comer meets were absolutely no challenge for her. I began running her in the 15–16 year old boys' races. When she began winning, the boys stopped racing. I was asked not to do that any more.

One incident from that time period stands out in my mind. Jim Puckett, a former Oregon sprinter, was teaching on the opposite side of town from me and had begun to coach girls as well. He coached a pretty, little blond girl named Janice Hughes. She was good. Sometimes in their early races, Janice would beat Margaret; but as Margaret's techniques and confidence grew, Janice could not touch her. The Eugene Register-Guard would report the results of the races as "Janice Hughes 2nd." Somewhere down at the bottom of the article in the fine print reserved for a listing of the results, Margaret's name would appear. That hurt Margaret a lot.

Finally, through a bit of pull from my husband, I had an opportunity to speak to the sport reporter responsible for track-and-field events. I let him know how I felt. To apologize, he did a wonderful article on her, which contained my Olympic prophesy, and thereafter gave a less biased view of the results.

A couple of years later, my husband and I returned to Canada. I applied for and received a job teaching physical education in a large high school on the outskirts of Vancouver. The school board was very excited about my arrival and were much more interested in my appointment as the school track coach than they were in my teaching physical education. I was also asked to take the position of head coach of the New Westminster Track-and-Field Club, . . . an established club with good community backing. I loved it; even though, at first, it wasn't easy. The club had a number of talented young male athletes, but few women. As a coach at the high school, I soon convinced a lot of the girls to be involved with both teams.

Continued

EXHIBIT 9–2 *Continued*

My first year coaching with the school, the team moved from 32nd to 3rd place in the standings. Were we proud! We also won the provincial title in girls' cross country three years in a row. The boys on the track team were also good. In the three years I was there, they set a number of provincial and Canadian records in the 100-, 200-, and 400-meter races as well as the steeplechase. Two attended colleges in the United States on scholarships.

I enjoyed the coaching in New Westminster. The kids were a lot of fun and generally worked hard. We had no discipline problems to negatively affect the group. Team spirit was good. We tried to promote team spirit by having a get together of some type once a month. No dates; no drinking. We did let parents come to the Christmas party and join in games. We had one party where everyone had to bring a musical instrument, and we created a team song. They played and sang, and I taped it. It's wasn't too good; but I still have the tape.

While I was coaching in the Lower Mainland, we participated in a number of large national meets. During one, athletes that I had coached in Edmonton and Oregon came to compete. The New Westminster kids and I planned a get together so they could all meet each other socially and compare notes on the "coach." We went to the Pacific National Exhibition, first, then back to my house for pizza. They really had a good time getting to know the people behind the names they had heard about.

After three years, it was back to Oregon for a doctorate, and back to coaching Margaret. I had no time to coach a club; so, she worked alone to prepare herself for the Olympics. I would warm up with her, demonstrate what I wanted, and then do a lot of yelling to keep her moving. Sometimes her husband would be there, and he would be the rabbit to pull her along.

It was hard for Margaret. She cleaned up at her school meets, but I tried to keep her running against people who would push her to her limit. At 15, she ran against the Asian champion and almost beat her. I ran her against the Canadian champion. Against men at the All-Comer meets. The only thing she didn't run against was a horse—probably because I didn't know anyone who owned one around Eugene.

The summer before the Mexican Olympics, things were coming around. She tied the world record for the 100 meters but was having a bad time with her 200-meter race. She hated the 200. *Track and Field News* had called her the worst combination sprinter in the world.

So we worked. We took the race apart and then tried to put it back together again. She was to forget about winning and times, and she was to work on the race and what she was supposed to do in each segment. We ran her against men on the Oregon track team who offered to be rabbits to pull her under 24 seconds. No dice. So, she went to the 1968 nationals as one of the top ranked 100-meter runners in the world and as a nobody in the 200-meter race.

I was unable to go to the nationals, so we kept in touch by phone. She ran the 200-meter heat in 23.8 seconds, and the final in 23.5. By the end of the summer, she ran 23.2; by the Olympics, 22.8.

We went to the Olympic Trials, where as a practically unknown teenager, she was trying to beat Tyus and Farrell for a place on the team. One thing in our favor was the fact that the 200 came before the 100. I know she could make the team in the 100; but I wanted to assure that spot by a good showing in the 200. So, we prepared, physically

EXHIBIT 9–2 *Continued*

and psychologically. She won the heat easily. In the semifinals, she had to face Farrell. She came off the curve ahead, but she started looking for Farrell and lost the lead. We discussed the game plan again between the races, . . . emphasizing what to do off the curve.

The final race was in the evening. I managed to keep Margaret away from outside pressures, and we watched the tarantulas come out of the hills in Walnut and into the practice area. That really kept our mind off the race for a while. Before she ran, we focused on the task at hand. I must have prayed, but I don't remember. When the gun went off, I stood transfixed at the beginning of the straight. Her start was good, the curve was good, and she came off the curve alongside Tyus and Farrell. I thought I would die. And then, she seemed to pull ahead, pumping her arms the way she had been trained to, focused completely on the finish line. She crossed first. I almost burst. *Sports Illustrated* indicated in their next edition that I had won the "standing-jump-up-and-down-a-lot" competition that day. Do you know, I can't even remember what happened in the 100. Obviously, she finished in the top three, because she also represented the United States in that race. But for me, the trials had been successful after the 200.

Margaret went on to Mexico suffering from pneumonia and was almost sent home. However, they allowed her to stay. She made all three sprint finals, winning a gold medal in the relay. I know she was terribly disappointed, but I was so proud of what she had accomplished. She could have competed in Munich four years later, but she was married and quit running right after the Mexico Olympics as a result of pressure from her husband.

My relationship . . . with the males on the track teams I coached was an interesting one. Because I enjoyed what I was doing and liked them as people, we got along well and had a lot of fun. Also, track was a new and exciting thing to me; I was still learning so I was not rigid in my approach. . . . I was willing to listen to them and try out their ideas. Also, I never talked down to the athletes; we were in this together. We had established rules they were expected to follow, but they had a say in what those rules might be. The boys were treated as young men, and expected to act as such. There were certain social niceties, such as holding doors, carrying heavy things, and so forth, that they did for me and for which I expressed appreciation. I took time to listen to problems and give academic advice to all the athletes I coached. My home was always open to them, and many took advantage of my hospitality when things were difficult for them at home. I treated them like my own children, expecting certain behaviors both in my home, in school, and on the track. They never disappointed me. Almost all completed university. Over 90 percent went on to coach. A large percentage continued to compete at the national and master's levels.

A fault of many female coaches who coach males is that they feel they have to control the situation and the male athletes. I believe you have to have control over situations, but even in Canada, male egos are somewhat fragile. A female coach cannot trample the masculinity of a male athlete and expect to succeed. I respected the different social roles; I respected the egos of my athletes. For me, it worked.

I think that the attitude we developed (the athletes and I) was mutual respect and love. As an example of the latter, let me tell you about a track and field coaches

Continued

EXHIBIT 9–2 *Continued*

conference we sponsored. I gave a presentation on psychology. In the question period following the presentation, we discussed the topic of the relationship between coach and athlete. I expressed concern with the number of sexual relationships existing between male coaches and female athletes. I felt that the coach was taking advantage of the athlete in these situations and that the behavior was unethical. Many female athletes still felt uncomfortable at high levels of competition in sports, such as track, and sought evidence that their femininity had not been compromised. A sexual liaison that developed from this need for reinforcement was inappropriate and potentially harmful to the athlete. They asked whether the same situation also occurred with female coaches and male athletes. Obviously, because this type of environment is not a common one, I felt that while such relationships may occur, I did not believe that it would be as frequent (based on percentages) as it was with males. My response hit a nerve.

Three years after beginning my coaching at Laurentian University, I was nominated to coach the Canadian track-and-field team at the World Student Games in Moscow. I was very excited when I was awarded the position. It wasn't until 14 years later that I realized that I was the first woman named to be a head coach of a Canadian track team. It was an interesting experience. The team had one of the most successful international records ever obtained by a Canadian track team.

The following year, I was named to coach the Ontario team to the Junior Olympics meet that was held in Canada. Ontario and British Columbia met head-to-head over the years, sharing the honors of winning the meet. I handled the track events; others handled the jumping and field events.

All the time I grew up, I was never aware that I was not allowed to play any sport or pursue any career. I followed my interests as far as they would take me. I worked hard to be the best I could be at any given time. Perhaps I was naïve. I was the first woman to do a couple of things related to the sports I was involved with. I have actively pursued change when I felt it inhibited opportunities for kids of either sex.

How could I see things improving? Less competition at early ages. Save it until the midteens. More opportunities to play at sports in a recreational sense. Today, everything is organized. You can seldom access equipment or facilities, unless you are on a team of some kind. Using schools and community centers as sites for school sports teams. Improving coaches through required training. Improved control of coaches by leagues and sport governing bodies. The ethical and moral standards of coaches are not under the control of anyone at this time, and a great number of problems occur because of this. Some way must be found to apply sanctions to those whose behavior is inappropriate (e.g., sexual overtures, physical abuse, encouraging cheating, abetting substance abuse). Many argue that we can't do much to coaches, because we can't afford to lose any. . . . We are short of people willing to take time to coach kids and we can't afford not to coach them.

I think women's sport has come a long way. I would like to see more women encouraged to coach. This could be done by providing assistance with child-care. I would like to see the stories of some of our female athletes told through the medium of film . . . to provide motivational role models for girls. I am concerned with drug use among female athletes, as with males.

Sport and Female Empowerment

Some have argued that the Victorian view of women had a sinister side. Criminologists have entertained a theory that rape functions as a *"conscious process of intimidation"* (Brownmiller, 1975, p. 15) by which men keep women in their place. Brownmiller contends that this form of domination exists in all societies. Of interest here is Brownmiller's contention that male resistance to female participation in sports stems from a male desire to keep women from developing the sort of character traits that would help them resist intimidation and to fight an attacker. That is, to keep them in their place.

> There are important lessons to be learned from sports competition, among them that winning is the result of hard, sustained and serious training, cool, clever strategy that includes the use of tricks and bluffs, and a positive mind-set that puts all reflex systems on "go." This knowledge, and the chance to put it in practice, is precisely what women have been conditioned to abjure. (Brownmiller, 1975, p. 402)

Brownmiller did not present this idea as the product of the serious reasoning required in theory construction, but some have taken it seriously. Some evidence suggests that societies with more sexual inequality are more prone to having a higher incidence of rape. However, careful studies of indices of sexual inequality and rape rates in different cities and states in the United States indicate that gender inequality is not correlated with rates of rape. Therefore, the empirical evidence does not support the contention that gender inequality is enforced by rape (Gibbons, 1987, pp. 277–280).

There is an obvious theoretical flaw in this line of reasoning, whatever the correlation between inequality and rape in different societies. The Brownmiller theory is *teleological*. A teleological theory is one that claims events happen because of goal-oriented, purposeful behavior. You train hard in order to get in shape in the future. You study today to get a good grade tomorrow. Tomorrow's goal motivates today's behavior (see Park, 1969, pp. 88–93).

Brownmiller clearly argues that men use rape for a future purpose—intimidation of all women. But "men" as a collectivity are not capable of any goal-oriented behavior without a *mechanism* for setting goals and motivating individual agents to act in ways that will help achieve the goals (see Buckley, 1967, pp. 52–58). Without a clear statement about the nature of the mechanism (a secret board of directors? an office of intimidation?) arguments like "Men use rape to intimidate women and ensure gender inequality" are about as scientifically useful as "Giraffes grew long necks in order to reach the leaves high up in trees, and ensure a special advantage to giraffes."

In the absence of evidence demonstrating the existence of an effective control mechanism, the Brownmiller thesis must be considered false. There is no reason to believe that either rape or male resistance to sports for women have been part of an organized male conspiracy aimed at preventing women from acquiring the means to resist intimidation.

As a rule the best place to seek the causes of a social phenomenon is the phenomenon itself. Neither Brownmiller nor Veblen do this, preferring "grand theories" that focus on whole societies. The most plausible explanation of resistance to female sports participation may well be found in the more humble setting of the American school athletic departments of the 1950s and '60s.

Educational Policies Against Women's Sports

If women in the United States during the 1950s and '60s were more and more free to pursue occupational and recreational activities outside the home, why was there no parallel growth in women's sports participation, outside the country-club sports of swimming and tennis? American women were hardly oppressed (compared to previous generations) during the 1960s. Women were marrying later, remaining in the work force longer, entering previously men's occupations in large numbers, achieving more years of education and eschewing many traditional constraints (Wattenberg, 1985, Ch. 27). The answer may be in deliberate school policies.

Put yourself in the shoes of a male high-school athletic director in 1971. Chances are you do not have the funding, staff, and facilities you think you should have to run your (boys only) athletic program. It should be obvious to you that girls are not interested in sports. After all, few of them play. Those who do have a play-day program designed by women for women. Would you want to take gym time, personnel, and money from already overreached boys' programs to provide competitive opportunities for girls, who are not interested anyway? *Adding to girls' programs meant subtracting from boys' programs.* The typical athletic director might or might not have entertained ideas about what sort of sports program was "right" for girls, but he had a vested interest in preserving the program he had developed. Any suggestion to transfer resources to a girl's program was liable to be rejected out of hand.

This explanation is not as grand as those focusing on cultural views of femininity in American society or male oppression of females, nor does it seem to be as sophisticated. However, it seems to fit the facts better. Women in the 1960s violated all sorts of Victorian constraints. The hippie movement, political radicalism, and miniskirts of the 1960s hardly suggest that women in the United States lacked the freedom to participate in sports! Aside from a handful of sports, mainly swimming, diving, and tennis, sports in the United States were available in schools to boys only. It makes sense to look to the schools for the source of barriers to girls' participation.

Title IX

We may disagree about the sources of resistance to the opening of sports opportunities to women, but there is no question about how those barriers were overcome. In June of 1972, a law was passed by the United States Congress. Title IX of the package of educational amendments spelled out in plain language what schools would do in the future with respect to women's sports.

> No person . . . shall on the basis of sex, be excluded from participation in, be denied the benefits of, or be subjected to discrimination under any education program or activity receiving Federal assistance. ("U.S. Code," 1990)

The law went on to make a few exceptions for the church-related schools that discriminated on the basis of religious doctrine or military schools that discriminated on the basis of some reasonable military doctrine but, for the remaining majority of schools and colleges, the law required equal access to all programs. Failure to provide for equal treatment could result in a loss of Federal funding and a civil suit by the aggrieved student.

Playing Opportunity

Sports, of course, were probably the most sex-segregated programs in schools and colleges. A series of court decisions made clear the fact that equal access meant equal access. This included facilities, prime practice time, financial support, and support for JV programs (Figure 9–2). The results of this law were sudden and spectacular. In 1971 about 7 percent of all high-school athletes were girls. This translates to approximately 300,000 participants. A decade later 35 percent of all high-school athletes were girls. The number had jumped to nearly two million! In 1971 there were virtually no college athletic scholarships for women. A decade later there were over 10,000 (Murphy, 1988, p. 276)!

Title IX rapidly opened up the sports opportunity structure for women. Whereas schools had maintained separate and unequal programs, Title IX required equal opportunity for both sexes. While the law produced dramatic progress toward equality, there is still a long way to go. Progress has more often than not been accomplished via law suits or threats of litigation. This was true in the early Title IX years (Felshin, 1974) and is true today (Grant, 1989).

Is the pressure of potential litigation really necessary to assure continued progress for women's sports? An episode in the history of Title IX may be instructive. In 1984 the U.S. Supreme Court interpreted the scope of Title IX to include only those particular programs in schools and colleges that receive *direct* Federal assistance. Before this decision, all programs of institutions were covered if any part of the institution received Federal assistance. The 1988 Federal Civil Rights Restoration Act, enacted over a presidential veto, clarified the meaning of Title IX to include all programs of schools and colleges—not just those receiving direct Federal assistance. The 1984–88 period saw a reduction in the number of athletic scholarships available to women (Acosta & Carpenter, 1990)! This suggests that without the force of law, the quality of women's athletic programs would be in jeopardy. Progress in women's sports still requires "taking" from the men's share of school resources, so men may be expected to resist progress for women.

Christine Grant (1989, p. 46) cites a lawsuit on which Washington State University was required to increase funding (scholarships, travel, coaching) for women's athletes until the percentage of females among athletes approximated the percentage of females in the student body. Grant argues that these funds could easily be taken from

FIGURE 9–2 Title IX opened up a variety of sports opportunities to women in American schools. Contrary to the prediction of some, women were quick to take advantage of those opportunities.

(Courtesy Patty Gash)

bloated (for men only) football budgets (p. 47). If the principles in the decision become accepted as a legal precedent, it could have a profound impact on school and college sports' programs.

Coaching and Administration

One obvious problem area with respect to equal opportunity is coaching and administration. Vivian Acosta and Linda Jean Carpenter (1985, 1988) have followed changes in the number of women in coaching and administration in American colleges. Table 9–1 shows changes in the percentage of women's teams coached by women since 1978, the year Title IX first required colleges to fully implement equal opportunity for women. The percentage of teams coached by women has *declined* since 1978. If anything, one would expect an increase in the percentage of female coaches as more and more women gained experience in competitive sports, but the

TABLE 9–1 Percentage of Women Coaching NCAA Women's Teams, 1978–1990*

	Percent Women	Number of Female Coaches	Number of Male Coaches
1978	58.2	2,449	1,759
1980	54.2	2,636	2,227
1982	52.4	2,693	2,177
1984	53.8	2,862	2,458
1986	50.3	2,805	2,772
1988	48.3	2,780	2,977
1990	47.3	2,706	3,012

*From Acosta and Carpenter (1990, p. 6).

reverse has been true. The same pattern has been found in high-school coaching (Hasbrook, 1988).

Has the rapid expansion of women's sports created a shortage of qualified female coaches? No. Table 9–1 shows that the *number* as well as the percentage of female coaches has declined since 1984, while the number of male coaches has increased during the period.

This tendency to hire male coaches rather than females in an era when the supply of qualified women is increasing suggests that female coaches are not receiving fair treatment. This, of course, violates the nondiscrimination provisions of Title IX. Joy Desensi and Linda Koehler (1989, p. 56) cite evidence of salary discrimination in the sport-management industry (which presumably includes coaching) along with evidence of a pattern of discrimination against women in coaching. Acosta and Carpenter (1990) found that a sizeable proportion of female coaches believed they had been unfairly treated.

What are the sources of this apparent discrimination? There are *structural factors* that limit the access. Knoppers (1989) cites three. First, a lack of opportunities to advance into administration makes coaching less attractive to women than to men, who might anticipate a career leading to a future administrative post. Acosta and Carpenter (1990) show that only a third of the administrative jobs in women's programs are held by women! Second, women lack power—access to resources and information. Women coaches, with limited budgets, cannot bring new assistants on board or acquire the financial resources that many big time men's programs can. An "old boys' network" appears to put women at a disadvantage in using the influence of previous coaches to help land a job. Third, the very fact that few women are in coaching and administration prevents them from resisting unfair treatment. In an organization with many women, a would-be discriminator would have to contemplate a potential backlash if he or she were to treat a woman unfairly. When few women are involved in an organization, the potential for the backlash is reduced.

Social psychological factors also appear to affect the likelihood that a female coach will be hired. Male administrators appear to believe that women are unqualified even when they are well qualified. Male administrators also appear to be more likely than female administrators to believe women to be unable or unwilling to accept the burden of travel and long hours associated with coaching (Acosta & Carpenter, 1990; Hasbrook, 1988).

Table 9–2 lists ideas for increasing the number of women in coaching and sports administration. These suggestions, provided by male and female coaches (Acosta & Carpenter, 1990), seem to be "on target." They speak to increasing access to old boys' networks through internship programs and organizational activity. The "draw" of coaching to qualified women is addressed in terms of salary. Access to administration might be gained through training in marketing and fund raising. These suggestions appear to provide a good agenda for reducing discrimination against women in athletics.

Female Athletics: Problems

Chapter 5 of this book concluded that sports participation had few if any effects on the personality or social skills of athletes. The only clear effects were to have fun and to see some improvement in school performance. A recent survey of school-age female students and their parents (Wilson Sporting Goods, 1988) revealed that most girls are involved in sports on at least a recreational level, and few experience

TABLE 9–2 Some Suggested Ways to Increase Female Representation among Athletic Administrators*

Intern and graduate assistant programs—women need the opportunity to gain experience in different aspects of athletics.
Encourage females to be active in athletic *associations* (and provide funding to get to meetings).
Educate young women about how to *use the system* better.
Networking skills need to be better developed—network within your own school.
Recruit women, provide *training* opportunities.
Raise salaries.
More camps, institutes, and workshops to get coaching experience.
Increase amount of *grass-root* employment available to women.
Find men who are willing to act as mentors for women.
Increase training on contract negotiation, marketing, fund raising, etc.
Make profession *compatible with the time demands of family* responsibilities for both sexes.
Use *large and unbiased search committees.*
Be positive, stop scaring off prospective coaches with stories of discrimination.
Offer *equal pay scale.*
Treat both men and women with *professional respect.*
Actively encourage athletes to enter profession.
Sensitize college administration to the need for fairness.
Provide *more publicity* on women's programs.
Use *affirmative action* and related legislation better.
Keep trying, don't give up.

*Adapted from Acosta and Carpenter (1990).

any problems. Indeed, most report positive benefits ranging from enjoyment to friendship to added prestige. Exhibit 9–3 even offers an example of women in weightlifting sometimes exceeding the accomplishments of men in a similar weight class.

There are problems, though. A recent study of 93 national-caliber female distance runners (Clark, Nelson, & Evans, 1988) indicates that a substantial percentage of these runners have relied on strict dieting to lose weight, to be "perfectly thin" for running. This dieting is clearly unnecessary for serious distance runners, who may literally "run their asses off" while eating a normal, healthy, high-carbohydrate diet. About one-third of these runners exhibited some form of problem in their eating behaviors (p. 130). A similar situation with problem dieting was discovered in a survey of college women athletes in a variety of sports (Rosen, McKeon, & Hough, 1986).

One diet-related problem that affects overly thin women athletes is amenorrhea. According to Clark, Nelson, and Evans (1988, p. 134) amenorrhea is not a benign effect of distance running. Many more (72 percent vs. 36 percent) of the amenorrheic runners had experienced a stress fracture and, when a stress fracture occurred, amenorrheic runners were substantially more likely to experience multiple fractures rather than a single fracture (Clark, Nelson, & Evans, 1988, p. 134). Amenorrhea is also linked to osteoporosis in young runners.

This suggests that coaches, parents, and friends of female athletes, and the athletes themselves, need to be well informed about proper nutrition and must consider nutrition a part of the training program. Rigid dieting and potentially related binging-purging behavior have no place in athletic training. That they are commonplace among experienced female athletes constitutes a problem. Insofar as younger athletes are learning these behaviors from older teammates it is a social problem.

A second problem is less specific, but nonetheless real. A student of mine, an "All American" candidate, believes that even the finest women's sports programs are not taken as seriously as men's programs are. Her feeling is justified.

This chapter has documented the trend toward hiring male coaches for women's teams, even while the supply of qualified female coaches increases. The tendency for media coverage to sexualize women's sports events has also been documented. Grant (1989, p. 48) has shown that in 1988 women accounted for only 9 percent of the faculty representatives in the NCAA, 28 percent of the NCAA council memberships, and 33 percent of the standing NCAA committees. Women represent a mere 16 percent of the directors of women's college athletic programs. With a few notable exceptions, female representation on governing bodies of Olympic sports is even worse. These numbers do not suggest respect for women—and neither does the rather shabby treatment women journalists have received at the hands of some professional sports organizations (Bloch, 1990).

Whatever the problems, the overall picture is one of progress. The progress is driven by legal standards that require equal opportunity and by individuals and organizations devoted to creating fair opportunities for women in sports. The U.S. Olympic governing bodies in rowing, swimming, and volleyball have 50 percent women, or nearly that, on their governing councils. The U.S. Rowing Association has adopted a policy requiring 50 percent female representation on its national board

EXHIBIT 9–3 A Sport in Which Women Can Outperform Men?

John McBride, strength and conditioning coach for UOP athletic teams, is conducting research on male and female powerlifters. Women may have a slight mechanical advantage in one lift—the dead lift—when the sumo style is used. McBride's interest in powerlifters was piqued by his observation of perhaps the only clear example of a standard sports event in which the best women sometimes excel over men in the same weight class.

FIGURE 9–3 The deadlift, at least in lighter weight classes in drug-free competition, is one sport in which female competitors may be able to compete on a par with males.

(Courtesy Janelle Day)

It is generally accepted that women cannot compete directly against men in sports involving speed, strength, and power. There have been instances in at least one unlikely sport where noteworthy exceptions have been recorded. In the sport of powerlifting, there have been two cases in the 1980s where the best woman was better than the best man.

In 1983, the best deadlift for the year by a female in the 52kg class (114 lbs.), as recorded by the American Drug Free Powerlifting Association (ADFPA), was 190.5kg. The best deadlift for the year by a male in the same class was 177.4kg. In this particular case, the female outperformed the male by 13.1kg, or lifted 7.38 percent more than the male. In 1985 at the ADFPA Men's Nationals, the best deadlift posted in the 52kg class

EXHIBIT 9–3 *Continued*

was 174.6kg. The same year at the ADFPA Women's Nationals, the best deadlift was 182.5kg. In this instance, the female outlifted the male by 7.9kg or 4.52 percent more.

These data should not be taken to imply that women should compete directly against men. The performance differences in the open (not necessarily drug-free) deadlift show women to have about 70 percent the strength of men. As one goes up in weight classes or compares the other powerlifts, the difference becomes even more distinct.

On the other hand, the strong performance by women in the lighter weight categories in drug-free powerlifting indicates that females are capable of achieving much more than previously thought, and that they should not be limited by preconceived ideas of their capabilities or limitations.

and among its regional representatives (Bloch, 1990). It would appear that this movement continues to move us toward further equality even against resistance.

Summary

Thorsten Veblen and others have offered theories of how and why women have been excluded from honorific activities like sport. Such exclusion, although more pronounced in premodern societies, still exists today. Some argue that it is a "strategy" to keep women in a subordinate position. Others contend it is a cultural carryover from Victorian times. Perhaps the resistance is simply a result of competition between men's and women's programs for scarce resources.

When a federal law, Title IX, was passed in 1972, it revolutionized women's sport in the United States. The law produced a tremendous expansion of sports opportunities for women in American schools, and it appears to be preventing a reduction of such opportunities in recent years. However, Title IX has not prevented occupational discrimination against women in coaching and athletic administration.

Although early observers expressed fear that sports participation would harm women, no harm is evident, except for some unhealthy dieting among some athletes.

References

Acosta, R. V., and Carpenter, L. J. (1985). Women in athletics: A status report. *JOPERD, 56* (August), 30–34.

Acosta, R. V., and Carpenter, L. J. (1990). Women in intercollegiate sport: 1977–1990. (Available from the authors Department of Physical Education, Brooklyn College, Brooklyn, New York).

Bloch, G. B. (1990). A sporting chance. *Health, 22* (February), 30–31, 84.

Brownmiller, S. (1975). *Against Our Will: Men, Women and Rape.* New York: Simon and Shuster.

Buckley, W. (1967). *Sociology and Modern Systems Theory.* Englewood Cliffs, NJ: Prentice Hall.

Clark, N., Nelson, M., and Evans, W. (1988). Nutrition Education for Elite Female Runners. *The Physician and Sports Medicine, 16* (February), 124–134.

Desensi, J. T., and Koehler, L. S. (1989). Sport and Fitness Management: Opportunities for Women. *JOPERD, 60* (March), 55–57.

Duncan, M. C. (1990). Sports photographs and sexual difference: Images of women and men in the 1984 and 1988 Olympic Games. *Sociology of Sport Journal, 1,* 22–43.

Felshin, J. (1974). The social view. In E. W. Gerber, J. Felshin, P. Berlin, and W. Wyrick, Eds. *The American Woman in Sport.* Reading, MA: Addison-Wesley, pp. 179–282.

Forsythe, C. E. (1939). *The Administration of High School Athletics.* New York: Prentice Hall.

Gibbons, D. C. (1987). *Society Crime and Criminal Behavior.* Englewood Cliffs, NJ: Prentice Hall.

Goldberg, P. (1968). Are women prejudiced against women? *Trans-Action, 5* (April), 28–30.

Goldberg, S. (1973). *The Inevitability of Patriarchy.* New York: Morrow.

Grant, C. H. B. (1989). Recapturing the Vision. *JOPERD, 60* (March), 44–48.

Hasbrook, C. A. (1988). Female coaches—Why the declining numbers and percentages? *JOPERD, 59* (August), 59–63.

Hoebel, E. A. (1958). *Man in the Primitive World,* 2nd ed. New York: McGraw-Hill.

Jacob, K. A. (1978). She couldn't have done it, even if she did: Why Lizzie Borden went free. *American Heritage, 29* (February), 42–53.

Kendall, E. (1973). Beyond mother's knee: Female education before 1900. *American Heritage, 24* (June), 12–16, 73–78.

Knoppers, A. (1989). Coaching: An equal opportunity occupation? *JOPERD, 60* (March), 36–43.

Lancaster, P. (1978). Inhale! . . . Exhale! *American Heritage, 29* (October), 4–13.

Lenskyj, H. (1984). "A kind of precipitate waddle:" early opposition to women running. In N. Theberge and P. Donnelly, Eds. *Sport and the Sociological Imagination.* Fort Worth: Texas Christian University, pp. 153–161.

Lindsay, R. L. (1970). Women's place in nineteenth century Canadian sport. *CAHPER Journal, 37,* 25–28.

Looney, D. S. (1991). You should have it so good. *Sports Illustrated, 75* (October 14), 90–101.

Mead, M. (1935). *Sex and Temperament in Three Primitive Societies.* New York: Dell.

Miles, C. M. (1936). *Play and Recreation for Children and Adults* (Physical Education and Recreation Bulletin, Book 6). Albany: State University of New York.

Morris, D. (1981). *The Soccer Tribe.* London: Jonathan Cape.

Murdock, G. P. (1935). Comparative data on division of labor by sex. *Social Forces, 15,* 551–553.

Murphy, P. J. (1988). Sport and gender. In W. M. Leonard, *A Sociological Perspective of Sport.* New York: Macmillan, Chapter 8, pp. 289–333.

Paludi, M. A., and Bauer, W. D. (1983). Goldberg revisited: What's in an author's name? *Sex Roles, 9,* 387–390.

Park, P. (1969). *Sociology Tomorrow.* New York: Pegasus.

Paton, G. A. (1975). The historical background and present status of Canadian physical education. In E. F. Zeigler, Ed. *A History of Physical Education and Sport in the United States and Canada.* Champaign, IL: Stipes, pp. 432–449.

Queen, S. A., Habenstein, R. W., and Adams, J. B. (1961). *The Family in Various Cultures.* Chicago: J. B. Lippincott.

Riley, G. (1980). "Not gainfully employed." Women on the Iowa frontier, 1833–1870. *Pacific Historical Review, 49,* 237–264.

Rosen, L. W., McKeon, D. B., and Hough, D. O. (1986). Pathogenic weight-control behavior in female athletes. *The Physician and Sports Medicine, 16* (January), 79–86.

Trekell, M. (1975). The effect of some cultural changes upon the sport and physical education activities of American women, 1860–1960. In E. F. Zeigler, Ed. *A History of Physical Education and Sport in the United States and Canada.* Champaign, IL: Stipes, pp. 155–166.

U.S. Code Annotated. (1990). Volume 20, Chapter 38 §1681. St. Paul: West.

Veblen, T. (1953). *The Theory of the Leisure Class.* New York: Mentor. (Originally published in 1899.)

Wattenberg, B. J. (1985). *The Good News Is the Bad News Is Wrong,* rev. ed. New York: Touchstone.

Wilson Sporting Goods Co. (1988). *The Wilson Report: Moms, Dads, Daughters and Sports.* River-Grove, IL: Wilson Sporting Goods Co.

Chapter 10

The Business of Sport

The Foundation of Major League Baseball

Early-day professional baseball was a rather tumultuous affair. Gambling and attendant fixing of games were a part of baseball. Team quality varied widely, with top-class professional teams frequently competing against poorly organized, far less talented opposition. Liquor and gambling led to a "saloon" atmosphere at many games. With limited league organization players frequently moved from team to team. Players involved in misconduct (mainly the fixing of games) could find a new team to play for with little trouble. Eastern teams would often neglect to take promised Western tours late in the season, leaving teams in Cincinnati, Chicago, and St. Louis with no home-gate receipts on the abandoned dates.

Seeing these problems as an impediment to the success of baseball as a business, Chicago White Stockings president William Hulbert sought to organize a meeting to place baseball on a more rational, businesslike footing in 1875. In a letter to Harry Wright of Boston, then the premier baseball club in America, Hulbert proposed a new league of professional baseball clubs. The new league would enforce stringent eligibility rules for clubs and offer a better brand of baseball by restricting membership to the strongest clubs both in terms of finances and playing quality.

Hulbert's motives went far beyond the desire to provide quality baseball to the public. Being president of a Western club, he was tired of being stiffed by weak Eastern clubs that would neglect to fulfill agreements to travel West for games, and of losing bankrupt clubs midway through the season—again a loss of home playing dates. Hulbert suggested that the new league be limited to eight teams, each playing ten games against the other seven teams, providing 35 home games for each team. He pointed out to Wright that the admission of two additional candidates would produce a ten team league, each probably playing eight games against the other nine teams, 36 home games for each team. This would mean Chicago could substitute a game against a weak drawing opponent "that would draw $150.00—for a game with the Bostons that would draw $1,500.00" (Hulbert, 1875, February 1 letter to Harry Wright, Chicago Historical Society). By limiting the league to the strongest clubs, each club could expect stability and a solid gate income for each home game. Again appealing to the bottom line, Hulbert added "I am sure you don't want to leave any chances of playing in Chicago and St. Louis—if more than 8 clubs are crowded in you *will* lose at least one game in each city without any corresponding decrease in expenses!" (Hulbert, 1875, letter to Harry Wright).

About one year after Hulbert's letter to Harry Wright, Hulbert arranged a meeting of leaders of eight of the strongest baseball clubs. A new National League of Base Ball Clubs was created at this meeting. The new league made a number of changes. Perhaps the most important was the term baseball clubs for "base ball players." Hulbert saw the player-managed organizations of the day (most were amateur or professional clubs run by players themselves) as incapable of the self-discipline required of a long-term business venture. Several league rules were drafted to cut out these shaky organizations. Each club was required to represent a city of 75,000 or more. Annual dues were raised from a traditional $10 to $100. Player eligibility rules were adopted. Clubs were required to provide sufficient security for games and to send results of home games promptly to the league secretary. The league was empowered to expel any club that disbanded, violated a league rule, or broke a contract with a player (Reidenbaugh, 1976). Each club was promised an exclusive franchise—one club to a city.

Thanks in part to Hulbert's leadership, league rules were enforced. When Philadelphia and New York failed to make their final Western road trips in the first year of the league's operation they were, to their surprise, expelled. Rule or no rule, such failures had not resulted in punishment in previous years (Reidenbaugh, 1976, p. 30). Louisville withdrew from the league in 1878 when, after leading the league with 15 games remaining in the season, they failed to win any of their remaining games! A team investigation revealed a sordid (but, by standards of the day, not at all uncommon) game-fixing conspiracy involving three key Louisville players and several gamblers (see Cusick, 1974, Ch. 6). The Cincinnati club was expelled in 1878 for failure to pay its dues and again in 1880 for selling beer at its games and for playing Sunday games—both forbidden in the hope of making baseball a respectable game, suitable for attendance by women and children. In spite of the loss of four of its eight original members, the National League was able to attract new clubs and maintain financial stability.

The new league was challenged twice by rival leagues. The Cincinnati club, expelled in 1880, led the formation of the American Association of Base Ball Clubs. The American Association clubs lowered the admission price to $.25, half that of National League clubs, and allowed Sunday games and the sale of beer.

These practices undoubtedly served to replace some of the income lost because of the lower admission rate. The American Association thrived during the 1880s but by 1891 it fell apart, with four clubs joining the National League and four clubs folding (Rader, 1983, pp. 116–117).

One source of the demise of the American Association was the ascension of a new rival league, the Player's League. Restricting player salaries was not a goal of the original league members, but a secret "gentleman's agreement" in 1879 created a rule that reserved players to one league club for life. This rule, later made a standard player contract clause, effectively limited a player's choice to playing for the salary his team offered, or not playing in the Major Leagues. Because players had virtually no alternative job opportunities that paid as well as baseball, they had to take what team owners offered.

This rule allowed clubs to control salary expenses and make a regular profit, an important factor in the survival of the league, but, predictably, it was not popular among players. After attempting to force a more generous salary policy from league owners, the Brotherhood of Professional Baseball Players formed a rival league in 1891. This league has been depicted as a genuine player-owned enterprise (Hoch, 1972, p. 42), but it really was a cooperative between players and investors with both to share in the profits. This of course would eliminate the salary limitations like those imposed by the established leagues. The players league was able to attract most of the best players and outdrew rival National League teams. However, a spirited trade war left the new league unable to attract the financial backing to support a second year of operations (Rader, 1983, pp. 117–119). National League salaries improved somewhat thanks to special inducements to attract players back from the Players League, but the player reserve system became established. This system would remain in place depressing player salaries until 1976, when it was largely eliminated via an agreement between the Major League Players Association and the two major leagues.

From Player Reservation Rule to Free Agent Agreements

Economist James Scoville (1974) showed that the player reservation rule, which was adopted by all professional sports leagues as they emerged, clearly depressed player salaries. Table 10–1 illustrates sharp salary increases that have followed the institution of even limited competition for players during "wars" between new major leagues and established leagues. He also reported that the 1966 adoption of a common draft by the American Football League and the National Football League, limiting competition for new players, led to a reduction in new player salaries by one-third to one-half (Scoville, 1974, p. 200). Small wonder that the emergent players associations in all sports have sought as a first priority to allow some form of free agentry to allow market forces to set salaries, rather than have salaries dictated by team general managers.

Today all major professional sports leagues have some sort of player/management arrangement that allows players to offer their services to the highest bidder after a number of years in the league. Baseball has the most explicit agreement of all the major sports and the most interesting history as well.

The baseball reservation rule remained in place for nearly 80 years following the 1891 season, punctuated only by occasional holdouts by players who were dissatisfied

TABLE 10–1 The Effect of Competition on Player Salaries

	Salary Increase	
Average NBA salaries during ABA-NBA "War" 1967–1971*	1967–68: $25,000	1970–71: $40,000 (+ 60%)
Average NHL salaries during NHL-WHA "War" 1970–1973*	1970–71: $24,000	1972–73: $40,000 (+ 60%)
Major League Baseball salaries after limited free agentry was imposed†	1976: $51,500 1977: $76,066	1978: $99,876 (+ 94%)

*From Scoville (1974, pp. 198–200).
†From Scully (1989, p. 152).

with their salaries, and rare lawsuits that were quickly settled or that lost in court. The baseball player reservation rule was substantially strengthened by a 1922 U.S. Supreme Court decision that effectively removed professional baseball from the authority of Federal antitrust law. The Baltimore franchise of the defunct Federal League, a short-lived rival league, had sued the major leagues for buying some Federal League clubs, causing the league to collapse. The Court ruled that major league baseball did not engage in interstate commerce (even though both leagues operated in several different states!), so it did not come under the sway of the Sherman Antitrust Act (Rivkin, 1974).

The first serious challenge to the player reservation practice was brought by Curt Flood, an outfielder for the St. Louis Cardinals. Flood had been traded to Philadelphia in 1969 and sued to prevent the trade. The position of Major League Baseball was that Flood had signed a contract and should honor it. Flood's position—and the position of the Major League Players Association who financed the case—was that the reserve rule unfairly depressed his salary, limited his freedom to select nonseason residence and business opportunities, and limited his baseball opportunities. In the end, the Supreme Court recognized the players' position but found in favor of the owners on the basis of the existing 1922 court decision (Scully, 1989, p. 31).

The obvious approach for the players was to seek through tough bargaining what they could not acquire with lawsuits. In 1966 the Major League Players Association hired Marvin Miller, a respected labor negotiator, to serve as director. Miller focused on issues of minimum player salaries, pension contributions, and grievance procedures, but free agentry was always the main long-term goal.

The ultimate power of a union lies in its ability to stage a successful strike (see Table 10–2). A union that lacks the member loyalty or economic resources to sustain a strike has very little real power in negotiations. A union that can mount a successful strike possesses the essence of power—control of a resource the opposing side wants or needs, in this case the services of players (see Berkowitz, 1986, p. 215). Given the credible threat of a costly strike, profit-maximizing owners must be willing to make concessions, as long as the concessions are less costly in the long run than the potential costs of a strike.

TABLE 10–2 Recent Player Strikes*

League	Date	"Winner"	Issues†
NFL	July–August 1970	Players	Preseason pay, pension contributions.
Major League Baseball	April 1972	Players	Pension contributions.
NFL	July–September 1972	Players	Free agentry; broadcast revenue sharing.
Major League Baseball	June–August 1981	Unclear	Free agentry (interclub compensation system).
NFL	September 1987	Owners?	Liberalized free agentry; pension fund.
NHL	April 1992	Players	Liberalized free agentry; unity of players' association.

*Sources: Dwoykin, 1985; Scoville, 1974; Scully, 1989; Eitzen and Sage, 1989.
†In almost every strike the strength of the players associations was an important underlying issue.

An obvious first step for baseball (and football) management was to test the mettle of the players' unions. After all, these unions had a history of breaking up rather than staying together when confronting management. The first confrontation in baseball occurred in the beginning of the 1972 season. A 1970 NFL player strike met with considerable success when only 21 of 1,300 players reported to preseason camp (Scoville, 1974, p. 275). But would baseball players show the same solidarity? Just as the season began the players struck, canceling games through April 13. The owners then agreed to player demands for increased medical and pension contributions by owners. More importantly, the players association demonstrated its ability to stand together during a strike.

In 1976 the baseball salary structure was jolted by an arbitrator's decision that players could become free agents by playing out an "option year" at a small salary decrease after their contract expired. Twenty-four free agents went on the market that year. According to Leigh Montville (1990, p. 102), the average player salary in 1976 was about $52,000, but the average free agent secured a salary over $200,000!

The owners quickly sought to negotiate some restrictions on free agentry. The players association agreed to limit free agentry rights to players. During the six-year period, salary arbitration was available to players who felt they deserved a salary increase. The owners also sought to impose a compensation rule requiring clubs that signed free agents to compensate the other club with a journeyman player from their roster.

The players would have none of this, as it served to discourage competition among clubs in the signing of free agents. This led to a second collision in 1981. The players struck for 58 days, right in the middle of the season, forcing the owners to give up the compensation rule (Scully, 1989, pp. 35–39).

The owners responded to the new threat of runaway salaries that open competition for free agents might bring by developing an old fashioned "gentleman's agreement" to restrain offers. An arbitrator found that this collusion restrained salary growth during the middle 1980s. This issue, still not fully resolved, amounted to a clear violation of the agreement the owners had made with the players in 1981 (see Smith, 1991).

There can be little doubt that any collusion by owners has dissolved in recent years. In late 1991 first baseman Wally Joyner, a .290 to .300 hitter with a home-run production of about 20 per year, signed a one-year contract with Kansas City for $4.2 million! Bobby Bonilla, a hitter of Joyner's caliber, moved from Pittsburgh to the New York Mets for nearly $6 million a year for five years.

Tom Candiotti, an above-average-but-far-from-great pitcher, recently agreed to a contract with the Los Angeles Dodgers worth nearly $3.9 million annually. Chicago Cubs pitcher Mike Morgan recently signed a four year agreement calling for about $3.1 million annually. Morgan's lifetime win-loss record is well under .500. Average player salaries increased by 20 percent in 1990 and by 43 percent in 1991 (see Figure 10–1)!

The immense salaries being offered to free agents suggest two conclusions. First, on the safe assumption that owners do not pay players more than they are worth,

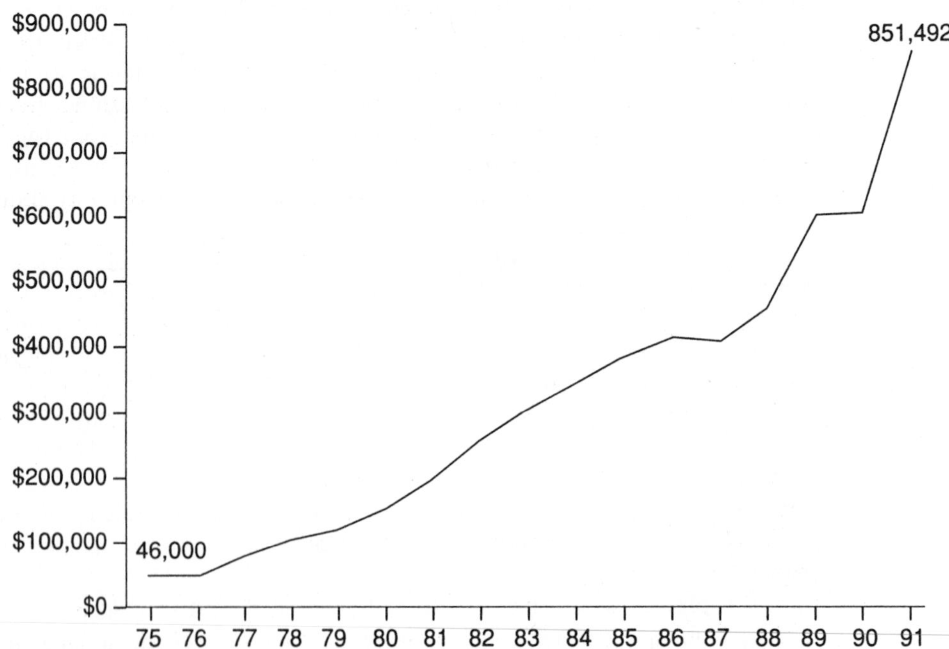

FIGURE 10–1 Average Salary of a Major League Baseball Player, 1975–1991

Sources: Scully, 1989; "Average baseball salary," 1991.

players have long been underpaid. In Marxist terms owners have exploited the players, paying them salaries far below their real worth. The owners have appropriated for themselves the surplus value produced by the players. In most un-Marxist terms this situation has been remedied by the institution of a relatively free market for player services[1] (see Scully, 1989, Ch. 8). Scully (1989) found that most major-league baseball clubs have been profitable, especially when the value of tax advantages, appreciation of franchise values, and value to allied businesses of owners (helping beer sales, low fees for broadcasting rights) are considered.

Free agentry has clearly served to increase player share of gross club revenues (Scully, 1989, p. 144). The National Basketball Association owners and players have negotiated a sort of profit-sharing agreement by establishing a "salary cap" for each club amounting to 53 percent of gross league revenues (Eitzen & Sage, 1989, p. 213). As league revenues increase so will the salary cap—shades of the 1891 players league! The National Football League Players Association has long sought a baseball-like free-agent policy. Given the high revenues of NFL franchises and relatively low player salaries, they have a legitimate gripe. At one point the NFL Players Association demanded 55 percent of television revenues on the ground that people tune in to watch the players, not the owners. With their "defeat" in the 1987 strike, the Players Association has officially gone out of existence. This presumably invalidates the authority of any standing labor agreement between owners and players, exposing the NFL to antitrust lawsuits. The draft system and free-agent rights appear to be likely targets of future suits. The present NFL policy allows clubs to protect 35 of its 45 player roster, with the remaining 10 becoming free agents. This has been good for the plan-B free agents, but the other 35 players on each roster lack the freedom they seem to deserve under antitrust law.

The second conclusion about player salaries involves the influence of television. What would happen if TV revenues were to *decrease* in future years? Baseball's agreements with CBS and ESPN expire in 1993. Both networks say they have lost money on these contracts, so they may be reluctant even to match the existing deals. Both the NBA and the NFL rely heavily on network-television revenues. A small decline in television revenues could lead to renewed conflict between players and owners because the present salary structure is so heavily subsidized by these revenues.

Revenues and Costs

Like any business, professional sports organizations are out to make money. This means realizing more revenue than costs. Professional sports leagues are different than most businesses in that they enjoy certain advantages that can make an apparent loss become a profit.

The Paradox of Franchise Values

Professional sports franchises actually involve nothing more than the right to participate in league competition with an exclusive area of operation.

Presumably the value of these franchises is determined by the potential profitability of operating a team. An investment in a franchise would be irrational unless it promised to earn substantial profits. After all, the same money could be invested in bonds, real estate, or blue-chip stocks for a low-risk profit of 8 or 9 percent over the long run. Even a bank savings account might be expected to earn 6 percent or so in the long run.

Oddly enough, owners of franchises do not report consistently strong profits. As Gerald Scully put it, "Whining about the lack of profit from owning a baseball club has been a sacred tradition among owners from time immemorial" (1989, p. 210). Baseball clubs have long reported costs exceeding revenues by 10 to 20 percent. Neither football nor basketball nor hockey owners have reported high profits.

Why then has the value of sports franchises appreciated so much? The answer lies in special advantages enjoyed by owners of sports franchises.

Tax Advantages Purchase of a sports franchise entails two main assets. First, it gives the right to operate as a member of a particular sports league. Second, the franchise owner receives the contracts of a *team of players*. These players are a depreciating asset—a fraction of their value is lost each year. Suppose the owner (actually the "owner" is most often a corporation or partnership, not a person) can demonstrate that 35 percent of the purchase cost was for players. Suppose also that the franchise sold for $100 million. The $35 million allocated to player contracts may be depreciated over the "useful life" of the average player. If straight-line depreciation were employed over a five-year useful life, depreciation cost would be $7 million per year. Even if the club were to earn a $7 million profit, it would owe no taxes (Scully, 1989, pp. 130–133)! No businesses other than sports franchises can depreciate the value of their employees. The value of professional sports player contracts is substantial, so this special treatment constitutes a generous tax subsidy.

Scully (1989) mentions two additional tax advantages. First, the value of franchise appreciation is not taxed each year. Rather, this is taxed when the franchise is sold. This amounts to a deferred tax liability. In fairness, capital-gains taxation must be deferred because the amount of gain is unknown until the franchise is placed on the market for sale. Nonetheless, this delay in paying for appreciation in the worth of franchises amounts to a tax break (see Table 10–3).

The second advantage has to do with player development costs. Scully (1989, p. 132) explains that sports organizations treat these costs as a current expense on their tax forms. Another way to treat development expenses would be as an investment, the size of which would determine player value—at a level far below current levels. Should a team sell a player, it would be liable for the difference between the modest development cost (basically the cost of running scouting, minor-leagues, and training camps divided by the number of players who are placed on the major-league roster in an average year) and the usually high income a sale brings.

TABLE 10–3 Sample Franchise Appreciation

Football	
Denver Broncos	*Dallas Cowboys*
1980 $35 million	1960 $600,000
1984 $70 million	1984 $80 million
	1989 $140 million
Baseball	
Texas Rangers	*New York Mets*
1986 $40 million	1960 $1.8 million
1988 $138 million	1978 $16 million
	1980 $21.1 million
	1986 $100 million
Average Major League Franchise	
1960s $6.5 million	
1970s $10.4 million	
1980s $40–100 million	
National League–New Expansion Franchises	
1990s $95 million	

*Sources: Scully, 1989, p. 148; Eitzen and Sage, 1989, p. 207.

Under the present system there is no tax liability for a sale. It should be noted that the liberalization of free agentry has dramatically reduced player trades and sales. Teams simply acquire their needs via the free-agent market.

Value to Affiliated Businesses The large majority of sports franchises are owned by corporations or partnerships that can use the team to improve the associated business enterprises. A broadcasting company (e.g., TBS-Atlanta, owned jointly with a baseball club) may negotiate a low-cost broadcasting contract. A property owner may sell his or her sports team the right to use his or her property for offices or a training center. The owner of a privately held sports arena (e.g., Madison Square Garden or Maple Leaf Gardens) may rent the facility to a jointly owned sports team (New York Knicks or Toronto Maple Leafs). Brewers (Annheuser-Busch, Molson, Carling) may "buy" exclusive advertising rights for locally televised games of jointly owned teams at favorable rates. That is, professional sports teams may be used to enhance the profitability of jointly owned enterprises (see Scully, 1989; Eitzen & Sage, 1989).

The paper losses experienced by many sports franchises may be used to offset profits in other enterprises, providing a tax advantage to jointly owned businesses. Scully describes two ways this may be done. First, an owner may borrow money from a jointly owned corporation to finance a sports enterprise. The sports enterprise will show loan payments as a business expense, depressing profits or perhaps creating a paper loss. A second, less important, way to create losses is simply to grant oneself large bonuses or valuable perquisites at the expense of club profits. In fact, there is no expense, as it is the right hand paying the left (see Scully, 1989, Ch. 7).

Public Subsidies Because professional sports leagues operate as a business cartel the supply of competing clubs is somewhat smaller than the demand for franchises. Several cities would like to attract an NFL or an NBA franchise. Many cities would like to have a major-league baseball franchise. A recent *Newsweek* article (Kaplan, 1991) reports that six American cities are competing for two National League baseball expansion franchises. Vancouver, British Columbia, would also be a potential National League market. San Jose and Santa Clara, California, are competing for the (apparently) soon-to-relocate San Francisco Giants. San Jose is building a modern $133 million facility for the new San Jose Sharks hockey franchise. Oakland, with city schools unable to adequately provide high-school sports, offered $50 million in inducements to get the Raiders to return to Oakland.

The leadership of many cities sees major professional sports franchises as important assets to the city economy. Sports events attract dollars to city restaurants and hotels. Convention business may be improved by the availability of major sports events. A few jobs, but only a few, are created by sports events. On the other hand, many of the dollars spent on sports would be spent on some other form of entertainment if a sports team were not available. An average major-league baseball club spends about $40 million annually, about the same as three healthy sized high schools. The high schools undoubtedly employ a lot more local people than a baseball club, and more of the salaries stay in the community. One ought to be skeptical of the financial benefits provided by big time sports franchises (see McPherson, Curtis, & Loy, 1989, pp. 129–130).

The main subsidy cities provide is favorable rent on city-owned facilities. Cities may also offer special tax breaks to encourage sports franchises to relocate. The San Francisco Giants have stated their intention to move from Candlestick Park, a miserable place for baseball because of a cold summer wind, unless a more suitable stadium could be built. The city of San Francisco offered to construct a new stadium nearer to downtown (but just as cold in the summer) but, when the issue was put on the ballot, it was twice defeated.

This opened the door to other cities. Denver expressed some interest, but it appears that either Santa Clara or San Jose, about an hour's drive south of the present stadium, with *much* nicer summer evenings, will compete for the privilege of erecting a multimillion dollar stadium complex for the Giants. San Jose has offered to issue municipal bonds to finance building on city-owned land at a cost of $185 million. The Giants have agreed to provide $30 million toward this project. The city can anticipate spending another $40 million on improvements to nearby roads. The $15 million annual cost for the municipal bonds will be raised by an increase in city utility taxes, which will equal about $20 per year for each resident of the city (Dietz, 1992).

Given the general prosperity of this region—it is also known as Silicon Valley—one wonders how much citizens of either of these communities will benefit from a major-league ball club. Some sociologists might ask who will benefit from the new franchise and who will shoulder the costs? Is it in the best interest of the average taxpayer to pay an extra tax to subsidize the relocation of the Giants? Voters in both communities will have the opportunity to decide this in future referendums.

Team Revenue

Sports franchises earn revenue from two main sources: broadcasting rights and gate receipts. Concessions and parking may add a substantial amount of income but many franchises receive only a fraction of the money, splitting profits with the cities that own the stadiums. Licensing is a final income source. Whoever sells hats, shirts, pajamas, and other souvenirs with team logos on them must pay a royalty fee to the owner of the trademark, the professional franchise.

The bulk of team costs is player salaries. Baseball and hockey incur considerable player-development costs because of their minor-league development systems. The NBA and NFL are fortunate to have colleges providing player-development services. The new World League of Professional Football may turn out to serve a player-development role, although its main function appears to be market development (see Maguire, 1990).

Scully (1989) provides average costs and revenues for major-league clubs over several years. Table 10–4 provides a "snapshot" of the income and outgo of an average major-league baseball club in 1983. Not counting the special benefits to sports franchises, the average team lost money. The future profitability of any club will be driven by player salaries and broadcasting revenues. A potential new source of broadcasting revenue is pay-per-view (PPV) television. Homesick fans who live out of a team's TV market may "buy a ticket" to watch their favorite team on pay-TV. Professional wrestling (not really a sport) and boxing have been successful with this medium, so baseball, hockey, football, and basketball may go the same route (Stump, 1991). This would enable displaced fans to "attend" games of their favorite team via pay-TV rather than by driving to the stadium and purchasing a ticket.

Like all other sources of income, the value of PPV television will be contingent on team popularity. Scully (1989) has shown that team revenue is determined by market size (which pay-per-view TV might expand) and winning percentage (p. 122). Any single team can maximize revenue by achieving an outstanding winning percentage, but overall league revenues are contingent on many clubs having respectable win-loss records. The playoff system in the NBA and the NHL reflects a desire to keep as many clubs as possible "in the running" for as long as possible. Teams with losing records routinely make the playoffs in these leagues. By including a maximum number of teams in the playoffs, leagues can increase fan interest in regular-season contests as well as benefit from revenues in a greater number of playoff games.

The future of big time professional sports appears to be secure. One has to believe

TABLE 10–4 Average Major League Baseball Revenues and Costs for 1983*

Revenues	20,064,000
Game Receipts	10,370,000
Broadcast Fees	6,267,000
Concessions and Other	3,426,000
Costs	22,625,000
Team	10,665,000
Player Salaries	8,256,000
Player Development	2,180,000
Team Replacement	2,334,000
Stadium Operations	2,668,000
Sales	1,724,000
General and Administrative	2,449,000
Spring Training	414,000
Miscellaneous	192,000
Profit (Loss), Baseball Operations	(2,562,000)
Other Income (Expense)	(624,000)
Interest Income	199,000
Interest Expense	(776,000)
Other	(47,000)
Profit (Loss) before Taxes	(3,186,000)

*From G. W. Scully, *The Business of Major League Baseball*, p. 118. © 1989 The University of Chicago.

that sophisticated owners will neither pay salaries that will produce a business loss nor allow a weak franchise to go bankrupt, as this would reduce the income of all franchises.

Unsuccessful major-league sports efforts such as the United States Football League, the American Professional Soccer League, and Major League Volleyball (which drew the best women players) have been characterized by lack of credibility that they showed the "best" level of competition. Second-class competition, whatever its intrinsic merit, does not attract spectator interest when major-league competition is accessible on television. The Bay Area Blackhawks soccer team experienced a considerable jump in attendance after they defeated Chivas, a top Mexican professional team, and the National Team of Honduras. Unfortunately, rival teams in the American Professional Soccer League have not established a similar claim to credibility, so the Blackhawks and the league are struggling to maintain solvency. If more clubs can demonstrate their quality against internationally recognized teams, the league will probably succeed. If not, it will probably fail.

Smaller sports leagues may be assisted by corporate sponsorships in the future. Corporations presently sponsor a number of sports events, most notably tennis and golf tournaments. They also sponsor some teams in auto racing, speedboat racing, and bicycle racing, but European corporations are much more active in sponsorship of their teams than American corporations are. Perhaps in the future such "minor" sports as volleyball (Beach Volleyball already is well sponsored), track and field, and soccer (in the United States and Canada) will gain solid sponsorship and a small niche in the sports market.

Some Allied Industries

Gambling

A nationwide audience follows the sports of baseball, football, basketball, and hockey. Most of us have heightened our interest in these games by betting with a friend on the outcome at one time or another. Some derive their chief enjoyment of sports through wagering. That is, there is a substantial demand for wagering opportunities, and this demand stimulates supply.

Sports bookmaking is big business in the United States. James Frey (1985, p. 196) reports that race and sports bookmakers handled an estimated $24 *billion* in bets in 1983, with a revenue of $2.5 billion or so. Much of the race betting is lawful but, outside Nevada and New Jersey (Atlantic City), sports bookmaking is illegal.

Major-league sports generally oppose any legalization of gambling on their events. In 1984 the Canadian Government established a betting scheme in which betters could wager on the outcome of several major-league baseball games, with the government paying out roughly half of the handle to winners and retaining half for game expenses and profit (a sort of "painless tax"). Major league baseball opposed this baseball pool on the grounds that association with gambling would despoil baseball's wholesome image. The major leagues also feared that gambling might threaten the integrity of the sport. Canadian provinces also opposed the scheme, not because of the integrity of baseball, but because the federal pool would compete with already established provincial lotteries, diverting money from the lotteries to the federal baseball pool (Frey, 1985, pp. 201–202).

Objections to the legalization of sports gambling appear to fall into two classes, moral and financial. Many people do not like the idea of legally sanctioning a vice like gambling. Part of the reason major sports organizations object is the justified fear that gambling would taint the image of professional sports. Image is an important financial asset to sports teams and leagues. A public suspicion that games might be "fixed" by crooked gambling interests could result in lowered gate receipts and a reduced TV audience (Frey, 1985, p. 210). Curiously, gambling interests, even legal gambling interests, may oppose legalization of sports gambling (as did the Canadian provinces) to prevent a loss of their share of the gambling market. For example, lawful off-track betting parlors could be expected to lose business to a newly legalized sports bookmaking enterprise.

The argument that legal gambling might somehow threaten the integrity of sports appears to be wrong. Over 95 percent of the sports betting in the United States, about $24 billion worth, is handled by illegal bookmakers (Frey, 1985, p. 196). Legalization of sports gambling could be expected to draw money away from these underworld bookies toward aboveboard, legally regulated bookies. It seems naive to believe that gamblers placing bets with legal bookmakers would be likely to try to fix games, while those already betting with illegal, possibly mob-controlled bookmakers would not. Insofar as gambling threatens the integrity of sports, sports are already thoroughly threatened. Legalization of sports gambling could only be expected to reduce this threat (Smith, 1990).

Legal and illegal sports bookies serve as brokers of bets on highly visible sports events. To bet on the outcome of a professional football game a person must stop by the bookie's office. The office may be a bar, a magazine store, a gas station, or some other front business. Good customers can place their bets by telephone, in effect taking a loan from the bookmaker. To place a $100 wager the bettor hands the bookie $110 or so. The extra $10 is a commission paid to the bookmaker for his or her services. This commission is only paid on losses. Winners get their $110 back, plus $100 in winnings.

The successful bookmaker must have several business skills. The bookmaker makes a 5 percent commission on all bets handled *if* an equal amount is bet on each team. To encourage equal wagering the bookie creates a *line* that requires bettors to predict not only the winning team but the point differential as well. Thus, "Chicago over Minnesota by 9" means a Chicago backer wins only if Chicago wins by 9 points or more. If not enough people bet on Minnesota and Chicago wins by 9 or more points, the bookie loses money. It is important that the line attract an equal amount of wagering on the two teams. A successful bookie has the knowledge to do this.

A successful bookmaker may occasionally "take a bath" by accepting too many bets on the losing side of a game or, more correctly, a number of games, thereby having to pay out more money to winners than he or she collected from losers. This temporary cash-flow problem cannot as a rule be quickly covered by a legitimate bank loan. Herein lies one of the reasons bookmakers are likely to be linked with organized crime. The best, and perhaps the only, source of short-term, no-questions-asked loan is the local loan shark. Loan sharking is a standard organized crime business that makes loans to "friends" at exorbitant (20 percent per week) interest, but this may seem a good deal to a bookie with temporary cash-flow problems. Bookmakers may also occasionally require debt-collection services, which loan sharks can provide.

A second tie-in with organized crime is protection from authorities. Bookmaking operations, like any service business, must be accessible to the public if they are to make money. This means remaining at one location with one telephone number for a long time. If a would-be bettor can find a bookmaker, so can an arresting officer. No illegal bookmaking operation can succeed without somehow avoiding police interference. Law-enforcement officials may choose to overlook a harmless, honest bookie in that no one is being hurt, otherwise law-abiding citizens are involved in placing bets, and the police have more important priorities than to prosecute a bookmaker who may well be acquitted even if the case against the bookie is strong. They may also refrain from interfering thanks to payoffs or favors to political leaders.

These payoffs may be provided by an organized crime figure. Few bookmakers are so successful that they can afford to pay off mayors and city council members, but an organized crime figure may assure protection of small-time bookies in return for a share of the profits. Organized crime may also protect the territory of a bookmaker from encroachment by rival bookies, although most small bookmakers have such a personalized clientele that such protection is unnecessary (see Wincanton Gambling and Corruption, 1967).

This natural tie-in with organized crime and government corruption provides the strongest argument for the legalization of gambling as well as some other vices (Barnes & Teeters, 1959). While most established sports organizations oppose legalization, the Major Indoor Soccer League has expressed the view that legalized betting would heighten interest in the game with little threat of "fixing" games, especially compared to the threat from illegal gamblers (Frey, 1985, p. 211).

Newspapers and Magazines

Sports fans can find a more than ample supply of sports information in their local paper. Newspapers have learned that coverage of popular sports attracts readers. Increases in circulation allow increases in advertising revenue, which make the newspaper profitable. The first sports journalism in North America emerged during the 1830s, emulating an English trend toward special sports journals on horse racing and boxing. Soon, large newspapers began publishing commentary on and descriptions of important horse races and boxing matches (Betts, 1953). The post-Civil War era, especially the 1890s, saw the establishment of a host of sports magazines devoted to a single sport, such as hiking, hunting, bowling, golf, and cycling. Regular newspaper sports pages first appeared in the New York *Sun* and the New York *World* in the 1880s. The *World,* under publisher Joseph Pulitzer, was the first paper to establish a special sports desk to cover boxing, racing, baseball, football, and other sporting events. Sports pages soon were adopted by most major newspapers in order to compete for readership (Betts, 1953).

Several writers have commented on the content of newspaper sports pages. Several biases are obvious.

Major sports are emphasized. Football, basketball, baseball, hockey, golf, and tennis receive ample coverage, while other sports tend to be left out (Gelinas & Theberge, 1986; Lever & Wheeler, 1984). Absence of coverage may diminish the appeal of some sports, especially on the local level. Coverage of a triathlon, for example, might be expected to increase participation and spectatorship.

There is some disagreement over whether lack of interest leads to lack of coverage or lack of coverage leads to lack of interest. Reader interest can clearly stimulate coverage. Gamblers demand information on horse racing and betting lines on college and professional games. Newspapers provide it, even though there is no mass interest in horse racing and most fans are more interested in game outcomes than betting lines. Public-relations flacks recognize that coverage can stimulate fan interest, especially for irregular events like golf and tennis tournaments or boxing matches. Hence, the papers and sports organizations maintain a mutually beneficial relationship. Teams provide access to reporters so they can write stories that stimulate circulation for the paper. These stories also generate spectator interest in the team.

It will be interesting to see the effect of the trend toward "one paper towns" on sports reporting. In a city with two or more competing papers sports coverage will be driven at least in part by competition for subscribers, but what will happen in a major city with only one newspaper? One suspects that the amount of sports coverage might be reduced, and the power of the sports editor might be increased insofar as he or she can choose which events to cover and what to ignore. This power will be limited by professional standards (maintaining a high-quality sports page), by community demand (some disgruntled readers may stop getting newspapers altogether), and by competition from regional or national papers and television reporting.

Women's events are deemphasized. A number of sport sociologists have observed that coverage of women's sports is very limited (Gelinas & Theberge, 1986; Bryant, 1980; Lenskyj, 1988). The coverage that is given often stereotypes female athletes. This is especially true in sports magazines. Hilliard (1984) found a bias toward emphasizing the femininity of female athletes, while writing about masculine character traits, like aggressiveness and tenacity, of male athletes. Systematic examinations have shown that popular magazine photographs and stories emphasize the sexuality or sexual attractiveness of female athletes, while emphasizing dominance and action in male athletes (Duncan, 1990; Lumpkin & Williams, 1991).

Margaret Carlisle Duncan (1990, p. 40) describes this as a *"political strategy"* designed to deny power to women (see also Sabo & Runfola, 1980). This notion that the trivialization of women's sport represents some sort of conspiracy by news editors is probably wrong. Reporting bias is best explained by a concern for sales (Lumpkin & Williams, 1991; Coakley, 1990, pp. 291–292; Smith, 1976) along with limitations on the time and knowledge of sports reporters and available space in sports pages. Coverage of anything "new" requires changes in established routines for gathering news. It will take strong pressures to change comfortable routines that have served reporters well in the past (Theberge & Cronk, 1986). *The Sportswoman* magazine constituted one effort to provide serious coverage of women's sports. The effort failed in 1977 when the magazine went broke for lack of subscribers (Coakley, 1990, p. 290). This suggests that the behavior of newspaper sports pages and sports magazines is guided by reader demand, not by an effort by journalists to oppose women's sports.

Criticism is muted With a few notable exceptions (Howard Cosell being the most notable), sports journalists in print or broadcast media emphasize the entertainment aspect of sport and avoid controversial issues. Political or business reporting is not considered good unless it analyzes several sides of issues. No competent political reporter would merely rewrite campaign material provided by candidates. Rather, the reporter would look for problems and contradictions in the politician's career. Even a minor sexual indiscretion or the utterance of a bad joke might generate a flurry of news stories and opinion columns.

Sports controversy on the other hand appears to be limited. Who should start as quarterback? Should this or that manager be dismissed? Sports reporters usually do not seek out serious stories about such underlying issues as academic irregularities or racial bias in sports.

Few mainstream newspapers had anything to say about the exclusion of black players from major league baseball in the post-World War II era, even though racial discrimination was clearly illegal in New York and Boston, home of five major league clubs (Tygiel, 1983). Harry Edwards (1973, p. 250) relates how he received a large volume of hate mail and numerous death threats in response to his criticism of racial discrimination in sports. Several sports writers who wrote stories sympathetic to Edwards' views received similar treatment. Readers of sports pages do not seem to be comfortable with serious controversy about sports.

Although the traditional "cheerleading" orientation toward sports writing appears to have been supplemented with more serious reporting in recent years (Smith, 1976), sports reporting in print and broadcast media may still be described as bland insofar as the treatment given really important aspects of sport. This may be attributable to pressures and privileges dispensed by sports organizations to assure favorable press coverage. Smith (1976) argues that advertisers may not want their products to be associated with controversial or unpleasant material. Sports organizations may gain favorable coverage by providing news releases for reporters or by using friendship, privileges (special access to information), threats (denial of access), and favors such as direct payments, gifts, or an occasional lavish party for friends in the press (Smith, 1976).

In fairness to sports writers, pressure and privilege have often influenced news writing on the most significant of issues. Robert Conquest (1986, Ch. 17) has chronicled the Soviet Union's government-induced famine in the Ukraine from 1929 to 1932. Although some *15 million* Ukrainians were starving to death, many Western journalists found no evidence of this and reported accordingly. The reason that they found no evidence is they did not open their eyes. Rather, they relied on government-supplied information (press releases) and well-staged "inspection tours." In return for closing their eyes to what has to be the most monstrous crime in modern history, these journalists were given access to interviews with high-ranking officials and to other news. Of course, journalists who did seek out the truth were promptly expelled from the country. Neither did the Western press expose the monstrous prison camp system in the Soviet Union until the Soviets themselves abetted this in Nikita Khrushchev's de-Stalinization campaign of the 1960s. Many Vietnam War reporters relied on military press releases rather than seeing events for themselves, perhaps contributing to the American self-delusion about the progress of that war.

Any criticism of the quality of sports writing must be tempered by the recognition that many of the finest writers of the century were sports writers. John Tunis, Paul Gallico, John Kiernan, and Grantland Rice showed that sports writing can be important as literature even if it is not terribly good at uncovering social problems.

Television

Television stations are in the business of selling advertising. To sell advertising they must attract viewers. To attract viewers they must provide programming that will entice a fair share of the viewing public. Sports events, especially on Saturdays and Sundays, are a powerful attraction. A popular sports event also gives a network the opportunity to plug other network shows, hopefully increasing the audience of those programs too. Consequently, television networks and local television broadcasters are willing to pay large fees for the right to broadcast popular sports events (see Table 10–5).

How large? In 1989 CBS radio signed an agreement to pay major league baseball $50 million for national broadcast rights. This money, distributed across 26 major-league teams, amounts to about $500,000 per team each year. Shortly thereafter, CBS television signed a $1.06 *billion* four-year agreement to televise regular season and playoff games. This brings in approximately $10 million per team each year of the agreement. During the first two years of this agreement CBS lost over $160 million, although the company may have recouped some of those losses in the value of promotions for prime-time programs ("World Series a Hit . . .," 1991). The NFL and the NBA command similarly lucrative fees from the major networks. The National Hockey League has a relatively small $8 million agreement with SportsChannel, but most hockey clubs have lucrative local-TV contracts.

A look at products advertised on televised sports events reveals a lot about the audience that watches them. Beer is the leading product extolled in advertisement on nationally televised sports. Automobile companies also advertise, and shaving products are also frequently seen. The target of these advertisements is the young male audience. Other types of audiences are targeted on other types of programs. Keep track of the kinds of commercials airing on Saturday morning, on the daily evening news, and during prime-time and late-night programs for a day or two. You will see how sharply advertisers target different kinds of audiences that watch different

TABLE 10–5 Some Recent Network Broadcasting Agreements*

League	Total Fee	Duration	Annual Fee
Major League Baseball	$1.06 billion	4 years	$265 million
National Football League	$400 million	4 years	$100 million
	$3.65 billion	4 years	$901 million
National Basketball League	$600 million	4 years	$150 million
National Hockey League	$8 million	1 year	$8 million
NCAA (Championship Tournaments, mainly men's basketball)	$1 billion	7 years	$14.3 million
College Football Association	$300 million	5 years	$60 million

*Compiled from several news sources.

kinds of programming. Who makes up these audiences is carefully monitored by polls conducted by TV rating companies.

Advertisers are willing to spend a lot of money to gain access to national sports audiences. According to *Broadcast*, a radio-TV trade magazine, a 30-second spot in a 1991 World Series game sold for $100,000–150,000, down from about $275,000 in 1988. The cost of a 30-second spot during the 1992 Superbowl was $800,000.

The main impact of television, and before that radio, on major-league sports is a significant increase in club revenues. For example, at the time CBS signed its $1 billion agreement with major league baseball, average expenditures per club amounted to about $40 million (Scully, 1989, p. 127). The new agreement provided approximately $10 million per club each year, *25 percent of the total expenditures of an average club.* Local broadcasting rights negotiated by the individual clubs also bring in an important share of club revenue, with clubs in bigger markets such as New York and Los Angeles enjoying a revenue advantage over clubs in smaller markets such as Calgary and Milwaukee (see Horowitz, 1974, p. 295).

Some observers fear that organizations in bigger media markets will be able to offer higher salaries on the free agent market, allowing them to attract more outstanding players and giving them a competitive advantage. To the extent that this scenario is true, it reflects a situation that has existed since the days before television. Teams in bigger markets have always had a revenue advantage over teams in smaller markets. Certain team dynasties, most notably the New York Yankees of the 1920s and the 1950s, appear to demonstrate the connection between revenue and ability to field a winning team. But such dynasties as the Cleveland Browns (1950s) and Green Bay Packers (1960s) of the National Football League or the Edmonton Oilers of the National Hockey League (1980s) demonstrate the ability of franchises in smaller markets to compete. Scully (1989, pp. 94–95) found no tendency for teams from larger cities to have higher winning records in professional baseball.

Roger Noll (1974, pp. 416–417) has suggested several ways professional leagues can minimize the threat of rich franchises dominating poorer ones. Clubs might divide income more evenly. Thus, clubs with lucrative local broadcasting contracts might share some of their wealth with less fortunate clubs. Home clubs might share 25 percent of home-broadcast and gate revenues with visiting clubs, and another 25 percent with the league, to be distributed among distressed franchises. Another option would involve expanding the number of teams, placing more teams in the most lucrative markets, thus reducing the market available to the more wealthy franchises.

New York, with a metropolitan population of about 18 million, supports two NFL franchises while Denver, population about 2 million, supports one. Perhaps two additional franchises could be placed in the New York market, reducing the disparity in earning potential between the New York teams and the Denver team. This would also increase football viewing opportunities available to New York fans.

On the other hand, Denver had a better record than either New York team in 1991, and New Yorkers have plenty of good ways to spend their entertainment dollars without two or three new NFL teams. It appears that lots of good (modestly paid) athletes are more important to a winning franchise in any sport than a few highly paid superstars, and that good management succeeds where big money does not. It would seem prudent to postpone trying to solve the problem of domination by rich professional sports franchises until they really do begin to dominate. The limited revenue sharing already in place in professional leagues, along with shares of network television contracts, appears to be working well enough insofar as competitive balance is concerned.

A Final Word

A final word about sport as a business is appropriate. Suppose we accept a generous estimate that the amount of money generated by the sports industry (teams, TV, sporting goods, schools, etc.) is about $60 billion (Figler & Whitaker, 1991, p. 127). How important is this money to the economy of the United States? The total gross national product (estimated value of all goods and services purchased) in the United States in 1989 was $5.2 trillion. This means about 1.15 percent of the American economy is somehow related to sports, or $240 for each man, woman, and child (assuming a U.S. population of 250 million). What would happen if all sports and sports-related spending were to vanish next year? A hypothetical family of four would have an extra $960 to spend. Some of this would probably go into savings, some to purchase clothing (but not sports shoes or baseball caps or the like), and some to entertainment (other than sports). Taxes might be lowered as there would be no spending on PE classes, gyms, or playgrounds. Freed from coaching or attending sports practices and events, family members would probably take up new hobbies, perhaps gardening or home repair. *The money not spent on sports would be spent somewhere.*

If sports disappeared the economy would hardly notice. Sports dollars, virtually all of it discretionary spending (as opposed to such nondiscretionary expenses as rent, food, and medical care), would simply be spent elsewhere. The economy would not shrink. Wealth would be redistributed from sports-related businesses toward other businesses. From a macroeconomic point of view there would be a small loss in value to the economy because the money would be spent on second choices rather than on the first choice—sports. On the other hand, a lot of attractive second choices would be available. From a dollars-and-cents point of view sports just is not vital to the economy.

In another sense sports is vital. I asked you to imagine a situation in which sports vanished. I must admit that I cannot imagine this myself. We may disagree about the proper role of competition for kids or the amount of public money that should be spent for big time sports. We may debate whether women are allowed fair access to sports opportunities or whether sport hinders academic progress in schools and colleges. But we probably agree that there can be no disappearance of sports. There would still be open fields to run on, objects to carry, kick, or throw, and friends to challenge. As a part of our culture, sport helps define us as a people. In this sense, sport is certainly important—and certainly worthy of our concern and serious study.

Note

1. To avoid any misapprehension let me say that the labor market in most industries is *not* free, especially from the viewpoint of the workers who must keep homes and pay bills every month. Free-market economics cannot be expected to establish "just" wages in an unfree marketplace, so government regulation is appropriate. The baseball market was governed by baseball owners for their benefit. Now the players have a strong voice in that governance.

References

Average baseball salary rises 42.5 percent to $851,492. (1991). *San Francisco Chronicle* (December 5), B4.

Barnes, H. E., and Teeters, N. K. (1959). *New Horizons in Criminology,* 3rd ed. Englewood Cliffs, NJ: Prentice Hall.

Berokwitz, L. (1986). *A Survey of Social Psychology,* 3rd ed. New York: Holt, Rinehart, & Winston.

Betts, J. R. (1953). Sporting journalism in nineteenth-century America. *American Quarterly, 5,* 39–56.

Bryant, J. (1980). A two-year selective investigation of the female in sport as reported in the paper media. *ARENA Review, 4*(2), 32–44.

Coakley, J. J. (1990). *Sport in Society: Issues and Controversies,* 4th ed. St. Louis: Times Mirror/Mosby.

Commissioner worried about escalating salaries. (1991). *Stockton Record* (December 10), C5.

Conquest, R. (1986). *The Harvest of Sorrow.* New York: Oxford.

Cusick, D. C. (1974). *Gentlemen of the Press: The Life and Times of Walter Newman Haldeman.* Unpublished masters thesis, Department of History, University of Louisville.

Dietz, D. (1992). Giants, San Jose strike deal. *San Francisco Chronicle* (January 16), 16.

Duncan, M. C. (1990). Sports photographs and sexual difference: Images of women and men in the 1984 Olympic Games. *Sociology of Sport Journal, 7,* 22–43.

Dwoykin, J. B. (1985). Balancing the rights of professional athletes and team owners: The proper role of government. In A. T. Johnson and J. T. Frey, Eds. *Government and Sport: The Public Policy Issues.* Totowa, NJ: Rowman and Allanheld, pp. 21–40.

Edwards, H. (1973). *Sociology of Sport.* Homewood, IL: Dorsey.

Eitzen, D. S., and Sage, G. W. (1989). *Sociology of North American Sport,* 4th ed. Dubuque, IA: William C. Brown.

Figler, S. K., and Whitaker, G. (1991). *Sport and Play in American Life,* 2nd ed. Dubuque, IA: William C. Brown.

Frey, J. H. (1985). Gambling, sport and public policy. In A. T. Johnson and J. H. Frey, Eds. *Government and Sport: The Public Policy Issues* Totowa, NJ: Rowman and Allanheld, pp. 189–218.

Gelinas, M., and Theberge N. (1986). A content analysis of the coverage of physical activity in two Canadian newspapers. *International Review for the Sociology of Sport, 21,* 141–149.

Hilliard, D. (1984). Media images of male and female professional athletes: An interpretative analysis of magazine articles. *Sociology of Sport Journal, 1,* 251–262.

Hoch, P. (1972). *Rip Off the Big Game.* Garden City, NY: Anchor.

Horowitz, I. (1974). Sports broadcasting. In R. G.

Noll, Ed. *Government and the Sports Business.* Washington, DC: Brookings, pp. 275–323.

Johnson, A. T., and Frey, J. H. (1985). Gambling, sport, and public policy. In A. T. Johnson and J. H. Frey, eds. *Government and Sport: The Public Policy Issues.* Totowa, NJ: Rowman and Allanheld, pp. 189–218.

Kaplan, D. A. (1991). Buy me into the ball game. *Newsweek, 117* (April 15), 56–57.

Lenskyj, H. (1988). *Women, Sport and Physical Activity. Research and Bibliography.* Ottawa: Ministry of State, Fitness and Amateur Sports.

Lever, J., and Wheeler, S. (1984). The *Chicago Tribune* sports page, 1900–1975. *Sociology of Sport Journal, 1,* 299–313.

Lumpkin, A., and Williams, L. D. (1991). An analysis of *Sports Illustrated* feature articles, 1954–1987. *Sociology of Sport Journal, 8,* 16–32.

McPherson, B. D., Curtis, J. E., and Loy, J. W. (1989). *The Social Significance of Sport.* Champaign, IL: Human Kinetics.

Maguire, J. (1990). More than a sporting touchdown: The making of American football in England, 1982–1990. *Sociology of Sport Journal, 7,* 213–237.

Montville, L. (1990). The first to be free. *Sports Illustrated, 72* (April 16), 98–114.

Noll, R. G. (1974). Alternatives in sports policy. In R. G. Noll, Ed. *Government and the Sports Business.* Washington, DC: Brookings, pp. 411–428.

Rader, B. G. (1983). *American Sports: From the Age of Folk Games to the Age of Spectators.* Englewood Cliffs, NJ: Prentice Hall.

Reidenbaugh, L. (1976). 100 Years of National League Baseball. *Sporting News* (June 5), 27–30, 38.

Rivkin, S. R. (1974). Sports leagues and antitrust laws. In R. G. Noll, Ed. *Government in the Sports Business.* Washington, DC: Brookings, pp. 387–410.

Sabo, D. F., and Runfola, R. (1980). *Jock-Sports and Male Identity.* Englewood Cliffs, NJ: Prentice Hall.

Scoville, J. G. (1974). Labor Relations in Sports. In R. G. Noll, Ed. *Government in the Sports Business.* Washington, DC: Brookings, pp. 185–220.

Scully, G. W. (1989). *The Business of Major League Baseball.* Chicago: University of Chicago.

Smith, C. (1991). Too much money is never enough. *New York Times* (May 22), B11.

Smith, G. A. (1990). Pools, parlays, and point spreads: A sociological consideration of the legalization of sports gambling. *Sociology of Sport Journal, 7,* 271–286.

Smith, G. T. (1976). A study of a sports journalist. *International Review of Sports Sociology, 4* (3), 5–25.

Stump, M. (1991). Pro leagues readying to enter PPV waters. *Broadcasting* (May 13), *120,* 54–55.

Taft, D. R., and England, R. W. (1964). *Criminology,* 4th ed. New York: Macmillan.

Theberge, N., and Cronk, A. (1986). Work routines in newspaper sports departments and coverage of women's sports. *Sociology of Sport Journal, 3,* 195–203.

Tygiel, J. (1983). *Baseball's Great Experiment.* New York: Oxford.

Wincanton Gambling and Corruption (1967). In *Task Force Report: Organized Crime,* Appendix B. *President's Commission on Law Enforcement and Administration of Justice,* pp. 64–74.

World Series a hit, but CBS still in the hole. (1991). *Broadcasting, 121* (October 28), 23–24.

Index